Organization Theory
and Public Management

JONATHAN R. TOMPKINS
University of Montana

THOMSON
™
WADSWORTH

Australia • Canada • Mexico • Singapore • Spain
United Kingdom • United States

THOMSON
WADSWORTH

Publisher: Clark Baxter
Executive Editor: David Tatom
Senior Development Editor: Stacey Sims
Assistant Editor: Rebecca Green
Editorial Assistant: Reena Thomas
Technology Project Manager: Michelle Vardeman
Marketing Manager: Janise Fry
Marketing Assistant: Tara Pierson
Advertising Project Manager: Kelley McAllister
Signing Representative: Warren Abraham

Project Manager, Editorial Production:
Catherine Morris
Art Director: Maria Epes
Print/Media Buyer: Rebecca Cross
Permissions Editor: Stephanie Lee
Production Service: Johnstone Associates
Cover Designer: Jeanette Barber
Cover Image: C. Lee/PhotoLink, Getty Images
Compositor: Pre-Press Company, Inc.
Text and Cover Printer: Malloy Incorporated

For more information about our products, contact us at:

Thomson Learning Academic Resource Center
1-800-423-0563

For permission to use material from this text or product, submit a request online at **http://www.thomsonrights.com**.

Any additional questions about permissions can be submitted by email to **thomsonrights@thomson.com**.

Thomson Wadsworth
10 Davis Drive
Belmont, CA 94002-3098
USA

Asia
Thomson Learning
5 Shenton Way #01-01
UIC Building
Singapore 068808

Australia/New Zealand
Thomson Learning
102 Dodds Street
Southbank, Victoria 3006
Australia

Canada
Nelson
1120 Birchmount Road
Toronto, Ontario M1K 5G4
Canada

Europe/Middle East/Africa
Thomson Learning
High Holborn House
50/51 Bedford Row
London WC1R 4LR
United Kingdom

Latin America
Thomson Learning
Seneca, 53
Colonia Polanco
11560 Mexico D.F.
Mexico

Spain/Portugal
Paraninfo
Calle Magallanes, 25
28015 Madrid, Spain

Library of Congress Control Number: 2004106130

ISBN 0-534-17468-X

 This book is printed on acid-free recycled paper.

⌘

Contents

⌘

Preface

The literature relating to complex organizations is so rich and diverse that determining how to present the material is a challenge in itself. This book divides the literature into major schools of thought and examines each in turn. It takes a historical approach in which each school is examined in the chronological order in which it emerged and gained prominence. This is not to suggest, however, that organization theory has evolved over time in a linear fashion. Far from it. Some schools of thought have built on earlier ones, some have rejected earlier theories and offered alternative paradigms, and still others have struck off in entirely new directions. Despite these twists and turns, the chronological approach has several advantages. It enables the reader to place each school in a specific historical context, trace the development of core organization and management concepts over time, and gain a comprehensive understanding of organization theory as a whole.

This book is written with present and future public managers in mind. Knowledge of organization theory can be an enormous asset to managers at all levels as they struggle to define program objectives, overcome constraints, and accomplish their mandated purposes. Armed with theoretical and conceptual knowledge, they can better identify the factors that affect organizational performance, determine how these factors interrelate, and decide how best to resolve problems and attain goals. Knowledge of organization theory can also create new ways of viewing organizational challenges and open up new avenues for pursuing change. In short, organization theory, supported by intuition and common sense, can be a powerful guide to action. For this reason the chapters that follow do more than examine particular schools of thought. They also explore the implications of each school for management practice and organizational performance.

Beneath the current dissatisfaction with government performance lies partially conflicting expectations and values. Taxpayers expect elected officials to hold the line on agency budgets (economy) and they expect public managers to get the biggest bang for the buck (efficiency). Consumers of government services expect their needs to be satisfied (program effectiveness) and other stakeholders expect their interests to be taken into account when policies are made and implemented (responsiveness). Elected officials, and the public at large, expect public servants to carry out their duties in a legal, ethical, and responsible manner (accountability). Everyone who comes in contact with government expects to be treated fairly (equity and due process). And government employees expect to be sufficiently empowered that their actions can make a meaningful difference in the quality of peoples' lives (public service). These partially conflicting values provide important clues about how to define superior government performance. A high-performing agency is one that achieves its mission and carries out its mandates efficiently, effectively, and responsibly, and with due regard for responsiveness, equity, economy, and the ethic of public service. Reformers on the left and right may argue about the relative priority of these values and how they are best realized, but they tend to agree that how well government performs is a matter of vital concern to all of us.

A basic premise of this book is that organization theory has much to say to public managers about how to strengthen government performance. This does not mean, however, that the book is grounded in *managerialism*—an ideology that holds managers to be uniquely qualified by the nature of their training to make fundamental decisions for their organizations and for society as a whole. Nor does it advocate a particular reform ideology, such as the New Public Management creed that holds that techniques commonly used in the private sector—including specification of clear objectives, performance measurement, rewards contingent upon performance, and greater use of market mechanisms—are the key to improved government performance. In drawing out the implications of theory for practice, this book relies instead on the following assumptions:

1. There is no generic model of management that applies equally well to public and private sector organizations.

    All complex organizations face similar problems relating to planning, organizing, budgeting and staffing, but decisions about *which* management tools or practices to use and *how* to use them depend upon the unique purposes and contexts that distinguish the public from the private sector.

2. "Good management," while important, does not guarantee superior government performance; nor is it a panacea for the nation's economic and social ills.

By blaming the nation's social and economic ills on "bad management," managerialism diverts attention away from other determinants of government performance, including flawed policies, inadequate budgets, and demoralized staffs. However, if effective management is not a sufficient condition of superior government performance, it is nevertheless a necessary one. Because government agencies perform functions that affect the quality of life of every member of society, how well they are managed is critically important.

3. Economy and efficiency are not the sole criteria by which government performance should be judged.

Government in a democratic state is the means by which the polity achieves its collective purposes. For this reason its performance must be judged by criteria other than economy and efficiency alone, including the value, quality, and effectiveness of its products and services, the legal and ethical responsibility of its actions, the fair and equitable treatment of those with whom it comes in contact, and its responsiveness to the needs and interests of relevant stakeholders, including the public servants who work within them.

4. The exercise of managerial power is not the sole province of managers.

The management profession was founded on the premise that efficiency requires the separation of thinking from doing and that managers alone are uniquely qualified to make key decisions. In reality, agency staff members are capable of considerable individual and group self-management, that is, the exercise of responsible decision-making power within the scope of their knowledge and expertise.

These caveats are set forth for a reason. It is important to avoid preconceived biases so that we can approach each school of thought on its own terms and draw out its implications for public management as objectively as possible. To assist us in this task, Chapter 1 introduces organization theory as a field of study, Chapter 2 establishes the unique context of public management, and Chapter 3 presents three analytical frameworks for assessing the theories of organization reviewed in the chapters that follow.

Special thanks are due to those who assisted me in writing this book. Foremost among them are my wife Debra, who helped me improve the readability of the final manuscript, and Judy Johnstone, for her very careful editing. I also wish to thank those who reviewed the manuscript and provided me with invaluable suggestions. Among them are Juanita Firestone, Department of Sociology, University of Texas at San Antonio; Carol Waters, Department of Social Sciences, Texas A&M International University; Martha Dede, Graduate Center for Public Policy and Administration, California State University, Long Beach; Bradley Wright, Department of Political Science, University of North Carolina at Charlotte; Alan Eisner, Department of Management, Lubin School of Business, Pace University; and John Harris, Department of Business Administration, University of Wisconsin—Green Bay.

⌘

FOR DEBRA

1

⌘

An Introduction to Organization Theory

A **complex organization** is an organization so large and structurally differentiated that it cannot be managed effectively by a single individual. Corporations, government agencies, hospitals, nonprofits, and most voluntary associations fall into this category. The importance of complex organizations to society cannot be overstated. They are the primary instruments through which modern societies achieve their social, political, and economic objectives. Business enterprises, for example, provide consumer goods and services that contribute in important ways to the material well-being of society. Similarly, government agencies provide public services and collective goods that shape the overall quality of life. All of this is possible because complex organizations can bring together and coordinate the human, financial, and physical resources needed to achieve the monumental tasks demanded of them. Without complex organizations modern societies could not explore outer space, undertake large-scale construction projects, research and develop labor-saving technologies, hold their enemies at bay, or ameliorate the effects of poverty and disease. The needs of modern societies and the problems they face require the type of large-scale efforts that only government agencies and other complex organizations can provide.

Organization theory is the study of how and why complex organizations behave as they do. Specifically, it is the study of formal structures, internal processes, external constraints, and the ways organizations affect and are affected by their members. Understanding today's complex organizations is essential to the practicing manager because knowledge is the key to effective action. Theoretical knowledge places managers in a better position to understand how organizational realities both facilitate and constrain their efforts. It also helps them understand the complex interrelationships among organizational variables. This in turn helps managers to diagnose problems and decide upon appropriate courses of action. In short, there is much to be gained from the study of organization theory.

This book takes a performance-oriented approach to the study of organization theory. Its primary aim is to assist in making useful connections among organization theory, management practice, and organizational performance. Achieving this goal is constrained by the fact that the field of organization theory is broad in scope and without clear boundaries. It comprises a seemingly endless body of scholarly works from a diverse range of academic disciplines. The focus of any particular theorist may range from the lone individual performing a narrowly defined task to the organization as a whole seeking to survive in a hostile environment. As a result, mastering organization theory can be a daunting, even overwhelming, objective for students of management. The challenge for this book is to introduce organization theory in a way that is easily digestible and ultimately useful to current and future managers. It begins and ends with a deceptively simple question: How can organization theory enhance managerial effectiveness and organizational performance? As will soon become apparent, the question is more easily asked than answered.

ORGANIZATION THEORY
AS A FIELD OF STUDY

Organization theory is neither a single theory nor a unified body of knowledge. Rather, it is a diverse, multidisciplinary field of study. Scholars from many disciplines have contributed to the field, examining organizations from various perspectives, focusing their analysis at different levels, and seeking answers to different questions. Although this field has a wealth of useful information to offer, its breadth and diversity prevent it from being readily digested and mastered. Confronted with literally thousands of works, students of management may well experience a moment of panic as they contemplate how to master organization theory and the lessons it has to offer. For effective learning to occur, the diversity and complexity of the field must somehow be reduced to readily digestible portions. This is typically accomplished by grouping works with similar theoretical assumptions or research objectives and studying each body of literature in turn.

One such strategy entails dividing the field of organization theory into three broad subfields. The first, also called **organization theory**, embraces a macro perspective—focusing on the organization itself as the basic unit of analysis and seeking to explain how and why organizations behave as they do.[1] Works in this subfield typically investigate structural arrangements (e.g., levels of hierarchy, lines of authority, and degrees of departmentalization) and how they are affected by goals, strategies, size, technologies, and environmental constraints. They often examine the effects of structural arrangements on organizational participants as well. Foremost among those embracing a macro perspective are sociologists. It was Robert Merton and his students at Columbia University in the late 1940s, for example, who first outlined the boundaries of a field of study dealing with organizations.[2] This macro perspective will be evident in Weber's theory of bureaucracy (Chapter 4), administrative management theory (Chapter 6), structural-functional theory (Chapter 10), and open systems theory (Chapter 11).

A second subfield, generally called **organizational behavior**, takes a micro perspective—focusing on individuals and groups as the basic units of analysis and seeking to understand their behaviors and interrelationships. Works in this subfield typically investigate the attitudes, motivations, and performance levels of organizational members. A primary purpose of research in this subfield is to help managers understand how to align individual and organizational interests so that everyone is served by the attainment of organizational objectives. Foremost among those contributing to research in this subfield are social psychologists and management specialists. This micro perspective is reflected in human relations theory (Chapter 8), natural systems theory (Chapter 9), and human resources theory (Chapters 12 and 13).

Finally, it is possible to identify a third subfield that cuts across the preceding two. The term **management theory** refers to those works in the larger field of organizational analysis that focus specifically on management processes and practices. Such works are often prescriptive in tone and applied in nature, analyzing organizations in terms of ways to improve management practice and organizational performance. Examples include Frederick Taylor's *Principles of Scientific Management* and Douglas McGregor's *The Human Side of Enterprise*.

Although some scholars prefer to think of organization theory, organizational behavior, and management theory as separate fields of study, as a matter of convention the term **organization theory** is widely used to refer collectively to all three sets of literatures. Given the purpose of this book— to explore the linkages between management practice and organizational performance—it is important for analysis to focus on all three dimensions of organizational life: structure, behavior, and practice.

Because these subfields are themselves rather broad and therefore difficult to master, another strategy is to divide the field of organization theory into distinct schools of thought, regardless of the subfield to which they relate, and to study them more or less in the order of their historical emergence. This chronological approach has several advantages. First, it allows us to anchor our understanding of each school of thought by placing it within a specific context. For example, Frederick Taylor's advocacy of close supervision is more understandable in the context of the early twentieth-century factory system than it would be in the context of the government agency of today. Second, the chronological approach allows us to see the evolutionary character of organization theory

Exhibit 1.1 Major Schools of Thought

School of thought	Central focus	Historical era	Representative theorists
The theory of bureaucracy (Chapter 4)	Identifying the structural characteristics that facilitate administrative efficiency.	1890s–1910s	Max Weber
Scientific management theory (Chapter 5)	Using scientific study and rational planning to enable fast and efficient task performance.	1890s–1920s	Frederick Taylor Frank Gilbreth Henry Gantt
Administrative management theory (Chapter 6)	Identifying the administrative principles that allow organizations to accomplish complex tasks.	1910s–1930s	Henri Fayol James Mooney Luther Gulick
Pre-human relations theory (Chapter 7)	Enhancing morale and securing cooperation by depersonalizing the authority relationship.	1920s	Mary Parker Follett
Human relations theory (Chapter 8)	Adjusting workers to the workplace and securing their cooperation using various behavioral methods.	1930s–1940s	Elton Mayo Fritz Roethlisberger
Natural systems theory (Chapter 9)	Maintaining cooperative systems by offering inducements and exercising moral leadership.	1930s–1940s	Chester Barnard
Structural-functional theory (Chapter 10)	Identifying the functional and dysfunctional consequences of bureaucracy.	1940s–1950s	Robert Merton Philip Selznick Alvin Gouldner Peter Blau

continued

as it has developed over time, albeit in a nonlinear fashion. Ideas found to be inadequate or incomplete often give rise to new ideas about how to organize and manage. Finally, examining one school of thought at a time allows us to tackle the field of organization theory in more readily digestible packages.

MAJOR SCHOOLS OF THOUGHT

Beginning with Chapter 4, each chapter will introduce a specific school of thought and assess its significance for management practice. These schools, identified in Exhibit 1.1, are simply constructs that help us assimilate the wealth of knowledge about organizations. Although the labels assigned to them are somewhat arbitrary, they are among the labels used most often to define the boundaries of this broad and diverse field of study.

Exhibit 1.1 continued

School of thought	Central focus	Historical era	Representative theorists
Open systems theory (Chapter 11)	Keeping the organizational system viable through internal maintenance and external adjustment.	1950s–1970s	Katz and Kahn James D. Thompson Joan Woodward Emery and Trist Burns and Stalker Lawrence and Lorsch
Human resources theory (Chapters 12, 13)	Enhancing motivation and productivity by satisfying the full range of human needs.	1940s–1960s	Kurt Lewin Rensis Likert Abraham Maslow Chris Argyris Douglas McGregor Frederick Herzberg
Quality management theory (Chapter 14)	Institutionalizing a cultural commitment to continuous improvement and customer satisfaction.	1950s–1980s	Armand Feigenbaum W. Edwards Deming Joseph Juran Kaoru Ishikawa
Organizational culture and leadership theory (Chapter 15)	Creating a culture committed to high performance through visionary leadership and symbolic management.	1980s–1990s	Edgar Schein William Ouichi Pascale and Athos Tom Peters

Exploring these schools of thought is important to practicing managers because each offers an explicit or implicit theory of organizational effectiveness. More specifically, each provides a unique lens through which to view and understand organizational dynamics, a distinct set of concepts and methods for improving performance, and a specific set of values for linking organizational means to organizational ends. A few representative examples serve to underscore the relevance of these schools of thought to what public managers do:

- **Scientific management theory** emerged in the early 1900s as industrial engineers such as Frederick Taylor sought to put every aspect of task performance and industrial production on a rational and efficient basis. It holds that organizational performance is enhanced by systematizing work operations, standardizing tasks, and providing economic incentives to induce superior performance. Efficiency and productivity are the primary values.

- **Administrative management theory** grew out of the efforts of theorists in the United States and abroad in the 1920s and 1930s to identify fundamental, perhaps even universal, principles for structuring and managing complex organizations. It holds that organizational performance is enhanced by establishing an administrative structure characterized by clear lines of authority from top to bottom, a distinct division of labor among departments, and delegation of power and authority to administrators commensurate with their responsibilities. Structural and administrative rationality are the primary values.

- **Human relations theory** emerged in the late 1920s as Harvard psychologists sought to interpret the results of experiments conducted at a Western Electric plant in terms of human feelings and perceptions. It holds that organizational performance is enhanced by treating workers with respect, replacing close supervision with a more relaxed and sympathetic form of supervision, encouraging workers to vent their feelings, and developing cohesive work teams. Personal adjustment, cooperative behavior, and social cohesion are the primary values.

- **Human resources theory** evolved out of human relations theory as behavioral scientists in the 1950s and 1960s began to delve more deeply into the relationship between satisfying human needs and attaining organizational objectives. It holds that organizational performance is enhanced by developing each worker's unique talents, creating and sustaining an environment of openness and trust, removing constraints on personal autonomy and individual discretion, enriching work, and providing opportunities for everyone to participate in decision making. Human development and intrinsic satisfaction are the primary values.

- **Systems theory** arose in several disciplines in the early 1900s as scientists came to realize that the many variables relating to a particular phenomenon must be understood holistically—that is, as a system rather than as a set of simple cause-and-effect relationships. From the perspective of systems theory, the successful organization is one that achieves both internal integration and external adaptation; it is one that maintains an optimal fit between its mission and strategies, its internal systems and structures, and the forces in its external environment that create both opportunities and threats.

- **Quality management theory** took root in Japan in the second half of the twentieth century as American management consultants urged the Japanese to compete on the basis of product quality and customer satisfaction. It holds that organizational performance is enhanced by designing products and services to meet or exceed customer expectations and by empowering workers to find and eliminate all factors that undermine product or service quality. Primary values include product or service quality, continual improvement, collective problem solving, and customer satisfaction.

- **Organizational culture and leadership theory.** This body of theory, at least as it relates to management, developed in the 1980s and 1990s as scholars searched for an explanation for the growing success of Japanese business firms. It holds that organizational performance is enhanced by articulating a clear vision of success and the values that underlie that vision, symbolizing values and vision in every action management takes, encouraging members to adopt these values and vision as their own, and creating a strong organizational culture in which shared values and vision tie members together in common cause. Intrinsic satisfaction, social cohesion, and commitment to organizational purposes are the primary values.

It should be apparent from the above examples that organization theory provides answers to the kinds of questions public managers face daily, including how to coordinate and control work activities, how to motivate employees to work toward organizational objectives, and how to define and improve organizational effectiveness. But it should be equally clear that these answers, taken together, do not comprise a single, comprehensive, agreed-upon theory of organizational behavior or performance. As noted earlier, diverse and divergent schools of thought have emerged over time precisely because the field of organization theory is multidisciplinary. Theorists have asked different questions for different reasons and focused their analysis on different variables and levels. Some have set out to explain or **describe** how things work based on systematic research, while others have been content to **prescribe** how things *should* work based on secondary data and their personal ideologies. In addition, some theorists have built upon or reacted to previous schools of thought, while others have launched out in entirely new directions.

All of this helps explain why it is unrealistic to expect there to be a single, comprehensive theory of organization. And yet it is a comprehensive understanding of organizational structure and behavior that we hope to achieve. Although no single school enables us to comprehend all aspects of organizational life, each provides a unique perspective and supplies an important piece of the puzzle. Each helps us understand or explain certain aspects of organizational structure and behavior so that we can begin to put together our own theory of organizations and how best to manage them.

Developing our own theory is important because theory has the power to inform practice. As Kurt Lewin once said, "There is nothing so practical as a good theory."[3] If it is true that management decisions are driven either explicitly or implicitly by an underlying theory of management, then it is critically important for each manager's personal theory to be a good one, one that is broadly informed by theoretical and conceptual knowledge as well as experience. The manager who operates on the basis of only one or two theoretical perspectives necessarily limits his or her effectiveness as a manager. By studying organization theory, present and future public managers can learn to comprehend the flux of organizational life in a more holistic fashion and assess organizational problems from multiple perspectives. An important part of this learning process is putting together a "conceptual tool kit" comprising theories and concepts borrowed from each school of thought. This tool kit can then be drawn upon as needed to explain various facets of organizational life and to determine how best to resolve problems and attain goals.

Although managers and their staffs cannot control every aspect of organizational life, they can learn how to adjust key variables, or adjust to them, in ways that improve agency functioning. The chapters that follow are designed to tease out the implications of organization theory for management practice so that present and future managers can perform their assigned roles more effectively.

NOTES

1. L. L. Cummings, "Toward Organizational Behavior," *Academy of Management Review 3* (January 1978), 91.

2. W. Richard Scott, *Organizations: Rational, Natural, and Open Systems* (Englewood Cliffs, NJ: Prentice Hall, 1992), 9.

3. Alfred J. Marrow, *The Practical Theorist: The Life and Work of Kurt Lewin* (New York: Teachers College Press, Columbia University, 1977), 128.

2

⌘

The Distinctive Context
of Public Management

Chapter 1 argued that the study of organization theory can help us understand organizational dynamics, learn to diagnose and resolve problems, and provide effective leadership in pursuit of organizational objectives. But there is a difficulty. Insights derived from organization theory are not equally applicable to all organizations or to all situations. Indeed, because most of the theoretical literature was written with private businesses in mind, it is possible to argue that organization theory holds little or no relevance for public agencies at all. In truth organization theory does hold a great deal of relevance for public agencies, but it is not to be found in a generic one-size-fits-all package. The relevance of theory must be teased out for each agency individually. The task of the present chapter is to isolate the distinctive features of the context in which public management takes place, as well as the distinctive differences among public agencies, so that the relevance of theory for individual agencies can be determined.

CONTEXTUAL CHARACTERISTICS
OF PUBLIC MANAGEMENT

The belief that government agencies can and should be run like a business is deeply ingrained in our political culture. As early as 1868 a resolution adopted by the National Manufacturers' Association stated that it was "indispensable that public affairs be conducted on business principles."[1] Nineteen years later a young professor of history and political economy named Woodrow Wilson called for a "practical science of administration" dedicated to making the business of government "less unbusinesslike."[2] In 1926 Leonard D. White, author of the first textbook in this new field of study, defined public administration as "the business side of government."[3] And somewhat more recently J. Peter Grace, chairman of President Reagan's Private Sector Survey on Cost Control, claimed that the government could save tens of billions of dollars by adopting the "commonsense business management practices that every company must use, from the corner drug store on up to General Motors, if it is to succeed."[4] Its popularity notwithstanding, the belief that government can and should be run like a business rests on the questionable assumption that public and private management are fundamentally alike and that management techniques used in the private sector are readily transferrable to the public sector.

Fortunately, we need not enter into the debate over whether public and private organizations are fundamentally alike or different. As Hal Rainey has written, this debate has tended to oversimplify both similarities and differences.[5] Instead, we must explore the unique features of the context in which public management takes place so that we can better assess the applicability of theoretical concepts to government agencies and the difficulties that may be encountered in attempting to transfer "business techniques" from the private to the public sector.

The central question with which this book is concerned is how to enhance government performance. This question places the spotlight squarely on those aspects of public management that are unique and those features of the organizational context that uniquely constrain public managers in carrying out their mandated purposes. Although management may entail the same basic functions in public and private organizations, **how** these functions are carried out can vary greatly between the two sectors. Similarly, techniques of business management may be transferred to the public sector but **how** they are implemented and used, as well as the probabilities of their success in enhancing agency performance, can also vary a great deal. Thus, although public and private hospitals or public and private utilities may perform the same functions and face similar problems, most public agencies are distinctly different from private businesses because they exist to execute the law. By virtue of their special trust, public managers are responsible for promoting values that go beyond efficiency, economy, and effectiveness, including responsiveness, equity, and public service. Because of their unique normative environment, public managers must operate through actions which are "as fair as possible, and as uniform as possible, and which can be taken publicly and publicly explained."[6] And because of the central importance of accountability in a democratic state, public managers are subject to constraints not experienced by their private sector counterparts. Their decisions must be made within the limits of delegated authority, internal regulations, and the provisions of constitutional and statutory law.

The schools of thought examined in the chapters that follow offer ideas about how to structure organizations, design work processes, coordinate work activities, motivate employees, and set goals and plan for their attainment. If these ideas are to serve as guides to management practice they must be relevant for and adapted to the distinctive political, legal, and institutional context in which public management takes place. The sections that follow identify specific contextual characteristics that must be taken into account when applying theory to practice.

Fragmented Authority

To protect citizens from an overbearing government James Madison designed a constitutional system that dispersed power and fragmented authority. The designers of state constitutions followed Madison's lead. At both levels power is dispersed among three branches of government, each possessing its own scope of authority and yet subject to extensive checks on its powers. Whereas most business firms are self-contained, autonomous organizations, public agencies are not. Most are units within the executive branch which is, in turn, just one part of the larger authority system that we call government. As such they are subject to the control of the chief executive and the checks that the legislative and judicial branches of government can lawfully impose. Far from being self-contained and autonomous, they are charged with achieving purposes set by others, with the resources provided by others, and in accordance with procedures imposed by others. In short, they are enmeshed in a governing system that is not intended to operate in a quick and efficient manner. Indeed, a system in which authority is fragmented and inefficiency is expected makes little sense outside of the context of democratic governance.

The primary consequence of fragmented authority for agency management is readily apparent: Public managers do not have the same freedom as their private sector counterparts to set goals, alter their missions, or adjust their methods. For example, although public agencies can engage in strategic management, generally they cannot do so with the same degree of freedom enjoyed by private firms. The portability of strategic management from the private to the public sector is limited by the fact that an agency's mission—the business that it engages in, its fundamental purposes, and the basic goals it exists to achieve—is determined externally by the legislature.[7] Although considerable discretion is exercised in interpreting the agency's mandates, all such deliberations must take place within parameters set by law. Agencies are not completely free, for example, to define their own missions, choose their own structures, designate their own favorite "customers," create their own rules, or define their own standards of success.[8] Public agencies can and do engage successfully in strategic management, but they do so in a context in which basic goals have already been fixed and in which choices about how to carry out their missions are constrained by law.

Fragmented authority also means that public managers must often consult broadly with officials outside of their agencies before taking action, and they must be prepared for the possibility that their actions or intended actions may be overruled or preempted at any time by the decisions of legislative, judicial, or executive officials pursuing their own political agendas and protecting their own institutional prerogatives. Although the constitutional separation of powers helps limit the abuse and misuse of power, it also contributes to a process of managerial decision making that is difficult, complex, and time consuming.

An Open, Accessible, and Responsive Decision Process

If public agencies are not self-contained, autonomous entities, neither are public managers free to deliberate among themselves behind closed doors and announce their decisions when they are through. Whereas business firms can establish goals and make policies in a relatively closed fashion, public agencies do so through a process that is remarkably open to public scrutiny, accessible to interested parties, and responsive to the needs and concerns of specific individuals and groups. Openness, accessibility, and responsiveness are integral parts of what makes a democratic regime democratic. Everyone reserves the right to watch, participate, and exert influence, and agency officials are expected to listen and respond in appropriate ways. Many of these rights and expectations are codified in law. Open meetings laws, for example, require agency deliberations to be open and accessible to the public. Freedom of information laws require agency actions and records to be open to public scrutiny. Administrative procedure acts require public notice of proposed changes in administrative rules, comment periods, and public hearings before new rules can be put in force. And citizen advisory boards are often established by law and attached to agencies to ensure that input is received and accountability maintained.

Having to make decisions in an open, accessible, and responsive manner holds important implications for agency management. First, it means that agency executives have less freedom to determine the outcomes of decision processes than their private sector counterparts. The final mission statement, management plan, policy objective, or administrative regulation is rarely decided upon by agency executives acting alone and in accordance with their experience, expertise, and personal preferences. Instead it is typically a product of the many compromises needed to find an acceptable middle ground among various competing values and interests. Due to the influence exerted by external parties, executives often perform less as decision makers and more as negotiators and facilitators, agreeing to things they might not otherwise agree to in order to secure a workable compromise. In addition, the need to be responsive to external authorities reduces their control over agency performance. A study of state agencies in Ohio, for example, found that efforts to build agency capacity and improve performance often came to naught because of pressures brought to bear by their political overseers.[9]

Second, the many procedural requirements by which openness, accessibility, and responsiveness are guaranteed add to the length and complexity of the decision-making process. Because of the time it takes to complete impact studies, schedule comment periods, hold hearings, carry on negotiations, and complete rewrites, it is not unusual for the approval of a new regulation or management plan to take several months, if not years. Working in an environment in which important decisions are made slowly, with many starts and stops, tends to foster frustrations, sap energies, and rob officials of a sense of sustained forward momentum.

Third, close scrutiny by the media, interest groups, and elected officials tends to make public managers more cautious and less willing to take risks. Knowing that decisions will be second-guessed, rules challenged, and new initiatives viewed with suspicion, public managers try to anticipate how others will react to proposed changes and avoid taking actions that may provoke intense criticism. Such calculations can lead them to adopt rule changes or plans that they believe are politically acceptable but which they would not otherwise have made if the choice had been theirs alone. Similarly, the strong emphasis on accountability and the attendant fear of being called on the carpet by an oversight body may cause them to avoid doing anything new or innovative. Donald Warwick found this to be the case in the U.S. State Department: "If fear is not the dominant motivational appeal, it usually lurks in the background. The bureaucrat quickly learns that he may be subject to attack from many fronts: head-hunting columnists, headline-hunting congressmen, irate constituency groups, opportunistic White House assistants, rivals in other agencies, a fickle agency director, or consumers' groups."[10] Working in an environment where rewards for risk-taking are few and the hazards many "creates a strong pull toward the tried and true." Although the State Department may represent an extreme case, the level of public scrutiny and oversight experienced by public managers no doubt injects an element of caution into managerial decision making and raises the risks involved in undertaking efforts to improve agency performance.

As the foregoing analysis indicates, public agencies cannot be run in the same way as a business because decision making must be open, accessible, and responsive. This requirement of democratic governance adds to the length and complexity of agency decision making, reduces the ability of public managers to determine the outcomes of their decision processes, and tends to make them more cautious and risk-averse, thereby undermining their ability or willingness to pursue innovations aimed at improving agency performance.

Ambiguous, Intangible, and Partly Unattainable Goals

The mandated goals of public agencies are frequently ambiguous in meaning and intangible in nature. In some instances goal ambiguity is due to the difficulty inherent in defining legislative intent concretely and precisely, either because legislators lack the necessary expertise or because they cannot reach an acceptable agreement. When Congress passed The Civil Rights Act of 1964, for example, it prohibited discrimination without even attempting to define it; supporters understood that no legislation would be forthcoming if it had to await agreement on the meaning of the term. In other instances goal ambiguity is due to the abstract, intangible nature of what agencies are asked to accomplish. Whereas the goals of business firms can be defined in relatively concrete terms, such as growth, sales, and profits, agencies are charged with accomplishing much

---

Ambiguous, Intangible, and Often Conflicting Goals

". . . national forests are established and shall be administered for outdoor recreation, range, timber, watershed, and wildlife and fish purposes."

The Multiple Use and Sustained Yield Act of 1960

At first glance the mandated purposes of the U.S. Forest Service seem perfectly clear. The law identifies six "multiple uses" and instructs the Forest Service to utilize the resources of the forests "in that combination that will best meet the needs of the American people." But many difficult questions remain: Which of these multiple uses has highest priority? What should forest managers do when timber harvesting degrades watersheds and blue-ribbon fishing streams? What should forest managers do when a tree-thinning project promises to improve the habitat for elk while degrading it for lynx? Is managing the national forests as complex ecosystems even possible? As these troubling questions suggest, goals and mandates that seem so clear on paper become something else entirely when it comes to implementing them.

---

more nebulous goals, such as reducing poverty, rehabilitating criminal offenders, and protecting air and water quality. Poverty, crime, and pollution are intractable problems whose causes are not always known or, if known, largely outside of the agency's control. How to go about attaining these goals, and whether they can be attained at all, remain open questions.

That agencies often face ambiguous and intangible goals holds important management implications. First, it places agency executives in the middle of contesting parties seeking to define what the goals and tasks of the agency are or should be. Because reasonable people can disagree on such matters, public managers often experience intense pressure from external and internal stakeholders and political overseers seeking to influence how the agency's core task is defined and carried out. This adds greatly to the complexities and uncertainties executives experience as they work to attain mission-related objectives.

Second, where goals are ambiguous and intangible in nature it is especially difficult for managers to establish performance standards and measure results. In many instances agency outputs are unobservable and unmeasurable. This limits the applicability of such management tools as strategic planning, management by objectives, and performance measurement. These tools assume that goals are relatively clear, concrete, and attainable, that success in attaining them can be measured and, consequently, that agencies and their staffs can be held accountable for producing the desired results. But where goals are vague and abstract it is very difficult to observe work performance, measure outputs, and set appropriate performance standards. For example, classroom learning is not readily observable or measurable. Standardized test scores can demonstrate that learning has occurred but cannot reveal how much of the increase is due to the efforts of the teacher.[11]

Where clear goals cannot be specified, firm performance standards cannot be set, and outputs cannot be readily observed or measured, there is a strong tendency for political overseers and agency managers to exercise accountability by circumscribing the behavior of agency officials with rules and procedures and refusing to delegate discretionary authority downwards. Compliance with rules and procedures then substitutes for attainment of results as an indicator of accountable behavior and successful performance. As Donald Warwick noted in his study of the U.S. State Department, "Goal ambiguity and the absence of firm performance criteria favor the development of rules and fixed operating procedures. Rules and standards have the advantage of being means-oriented, if not ends-oriented, guides to success. The official may not be sure of what he has produced or how well he has produced it, but he can be sure that he did it in the right way."[12] This helps explain why public agencies often seem more process-oriented than goal-oriented. It has much to do with the ambiguous, intangible, and partly unattainable nature of their goals, goals that are typically very different in kind than those of their private sector counterparts.

Procedural Constraints

Private managers are free to advance the interests of their firms as they see fit, as long as their actions are not specifically prohibited by law. Public managers, by contrast, are free to act only within the scope of their lawfully delegated authority and in accordance with externally imposed systems of rules and procedures. Consequently, public managers encounter many more constraints and enjoy much less freedom of choice than their private sector counterparts. This limits their ability to pursue organizational objectives in a purposeful and deliberate fashion. Having identified appropriate courses of action, public managers find it much more difficult to put their decisions into effect.

The use of rules and procedures to constrain managerial discretion reflects the emphasis placed on accountability in a democratic state. Because public officials exercise the coercive powers of the state and spend tax dollars, democratic norms require that they be held accountable for their actions. As noted earlier, where accountability cannot be achieved by setting clear goals and monitoring results, the apparent alternative is to replace managerial discretion with rules. Historically, legislative bodies have relied upon centralized control systems to prevent fraud, waste, and misuse of authority, and to ensure fairness in hiring employees, distributing benefits, and awarding contracts. Merit-based personnel systems were instituted to safeguard the merit principle against the intrusions of patronage and to protect employees from arbitrary, capricious, or discriminatory treatment; line-item budgets and standardized accounting procedures to ensure that funds are expended for their authorized purposes and in a fiscally responsible manner; and purchasing and bidding systems to ensure that supplies and equipment are obtained at the best available price and that contracts are awarded in a fair and unbiased manner. Not only do these systems specify the rules and procedures that managers must follow but they are also enforced by central personnel, budget, and purchasing offices that demand strict compliance.

Procedural rules and reporting requirements tend to reduce the timeliness of hiring decisions, discourage supervisors from taking justified disciplinary actions, limit their ability to reward their best workers, prohibit them from moving funds from one budget category to another in response to changing needs, create lengthy delays in obtaining required supplies and equipment and, in general, deny managers the flexibility they need to advance the objectives of their agencies. As these examples suggest, the problem with centralized control systems is that "constraining people from doing anything wrong often simultaneously constrains them from doing anything right."[13] This was a major theme in Vice President Gore's 1993 National Performance Review, which described "structures of overcontrol and micromanagement" in the federal government that leave "good people trapped in bad systems."[14] Although much red tape can be eliminated, operating in a democratic system of governance means that public managers are and will continue to be subject to a degree of accountability that is far more detailed and pervasive than that in the private sector. In many cases the public manager longs to say "Yes, let's do it!" but the rules and procedures say "No, not so fast." In a work environment such as this it is easy to become constraint-oriented rather than outcome-oriented.

Political Constraints

Perhaps the most fundamental difference between private and public management is that the latter takes place in a highly politicized environment in which agency decisions are shaped to a substantial degree by external pressures and political considerations. There are three reasons for this. First, the distributive, redistributive, and regulatory policies of government affect the well-being of every member of society. Because agency decisions produce benefits for some and impose costs on others, affected individuals and groups will seek to influence the exercise of administrative discretion. Second, the norms of democratic governance dictate that all affected parties must have opportunities to influence agency decisions either directly or through their elected representatives. This means that those outside the boundaries of the agency cannot be ignored or shut out of the administrative process. Finally, the constitutional separation of powers obliges public managers to serve two external masters, the chief executive and the legislature, each claiming to represent the will of the people and each seeking to establish political control over agency decisions. Elected executives work through their appointees to make sure that agency decisions are consistent with their political agendas, individual legislators pressure agency officials to respond to the needs of their constituents, appropriations committees attach provisions to budget bills detailing how funds are to be spent, and legislatures amend the law to prevent, or at least constrain, the agency from doing what the legislators dislike. As a result, agency goals are set and implemented in the context of cross-cutting political pressures. Decision making is slower and more disjointed than in the private sector, bearing few of the characteristics of rational planning and policy making described in the generic management literature.

Politics affects public management in specific ways. First, it causes middle- and upper-level managers to be externally directed, focusing their time and effort on their boundary-spanning responsibilities. These responsibilities include identifying stakeholder concerns, responding to critics, mediating between contending interests, negotiating agreements, and building political coalitions to support their management plans and policy objectives. Carrying out the mission of an agency in an intensely political environment is not easy. The mission of the U.S. Forest Service, for example, is to maximize stewardship of the nation's natural resources by sustaining healthy and productive ecosystems. Although this may seem straightforward enough, in practice it is accomplished only by balancing the contending views and interests of loggers, miners, hikers, horseback riders, skiers, and users of motorized vehicles. In the course of developing management plans and agency regulations much of the manager's time is spent in soliciting comments, holding hearings, working out compromises, and negotiating agreements. In addition, managers must often build coalitions of supporters to help them obtain the budgetary resources, political clout, and operating autonomy needed to achieve their policy objectives. All of this not only makes the decision-making process highly complex and time consuming but it also requires managers to possess strong negotiating, conflict resolution, and coalition-building skills.

Because they are obliged to respond to a wide range of external demands, public managers find it particularly difficult to manage their time and focus on goal attainment. A study by Porter and Van Maanen found, for example, that middle managers in government were much more likely than middle managers in industry to cite the needs and demands of those outside of their organizations as an important variable affecting how they spent their time.[15] The government managers reported spending more time interacting with people, either on the phone or in face-to-face meetings, and less time on operational planning and task accomplishment. They also reported feeling "rushed," with "not enough time to get things done you want to do." One consequence of working under the crush of communications from external parties and feeling obligated to respond to their needs and demands is that it distracts managers from their internal responsibilities, including defining the agency's core task, communicating a clear sense of purpose, and sustaining staff morale and forward momentum.

A second way that politics influences public management is by injecting political criteria into the choice-making process. The generic management model, with its emphasis on long-term planning, cost-benefit analysis, and rationalistic criteria such as efficiency and cost-effectiveness, has limited applicability in a highly politicized environment. For example, decisions by agencies to close veterans' hospitals, military bases, or rural post offices are often reversed due to intense public outcry despite having been made on the basis of their cost-effectiveness and only after careful study of the available alternatives. It is not unusual for citizens to demand the services that veterans' hospitals, military bases, and rural post offices provide even if they must be provided at a loss.

In short, public management is as much about fashioning compromises among competing political interests as it is about the rational attainment of organizational objectives. Because they operate in a highly political environment, public managers cannot make decisions based solely on analysis of costs and benefits, rational means–ends calculations, or efficiency and effectiveness criteria. Nor are they free to interpret the agency's mission, set priorities, formulate objectives, and plan for their attainment solely on the basis of their professional training and expertise. Rational intentions and mission-oriented plans often play only a limited role in determining agency actions and policy outcomes because of the large number of parties that want to be involved and the amount of political influence they can bring to bear.

THE LIMITS OF GENERIC MANAGEMENT MODELS

Many of those who argue that government agencies can and should be run in a more "businesslike" fashion also believe in the possibility of developing a generic model of management, one that specifies practices and techniques that are applicable in all organizational settings. One such model underlies the recent managing-for-results reform movement, including the efforts of the National Performance Review (NPR) team in 1993 to "reinvent" the federal government. At the kick-off meeting with Vice President Gore the NPR staff received wallet-sized laminated cards asserting that excellence is achieved by creating a clear sense of mission, delegating authority and responsibility, replacing regulations with incentives, developing budget-based outcomes, and measuring success by customer satisfaction.[16] This set of generic prescriptions begs a critical question: Do department heads, agency directors, and bureau chiefs have the same freedom of movement, scope of authority, and probabilities for success as their private sector counterparts in setting goals, monitoring performance, and achieving results? If the analysis presented earlier in this chapter is correct, they do not.

Asking government agencies to operate in a more "businesslike" fashion is perfectly appropriate, as long as it is clearly understood that general management principles and practices might need to be modified to fit the unique context of public management and that the probabilities for their success in enhancing organizational performance may not be as high as in the private sector because there are values at stake other than effective attainment of mission-related goals. These conclusions are central to the purposes of this book. They emphasize that the principles and practices associated with each school of organization theory must be assessed in terms of their relevance to public organizations in general and to each agency in particular.

Exhibit 2.1 summarizes why it is difficult to apply generic management models in governmental settings. Elements typically found in generic models are identified on the left and some of the limits on their applicability to public agencies are summarized on the right.

Exhibit 2.1 Limits on the Use of Generic Management Models in Government

Elements of a generic model	Limits on their applicability in public agencies
Establish clear goals and clear sense of mission.	Basic goals are externally determined by the legislature.
	Legislative bodies rarely define goals in clear and concrete terms.
	An open and accessible decision process allows external parties to influence how goals will be defined and achieved.
	Agencies are often assigned multiple, conflicting goals, making it difficult to establish a shared sense of mission.
Delegate authority and responsibility for achieving goals.	Legislative bodies are reluctant to grant full autonomy because it reduces their ability to hold agencies responsive to their wishes.
	Elected executives are reluctant to grant full autonomy for the same reason.
	Top managers are reluctant to delegate authority and responsibility downward because they know they will be held accountable for the "mistakes" of their subordinates.
	The vague and abstract nature of goals encourages external overseers and agency managers to rely on procedural rules to ensure accountability, further reducing possibilities for empowerment.
Identify desired outputs and outcomes and measure results.	Where goals are ambiguous and intangible, and where outputs and outcomes are unobservable, it is extremely difficult to identify appropriate performance indicators and measure results.
Hold employees accountable for results by linking rewards to performance.	Linking rewards to performance is impossible where appropriate performance indicators cannot be identified.
	Linking rewards to performance is inappropriate where failure to produce desired results is due to inadequate resources or factors beyond the agency's control.
	Public managers often lack the authority and resources needed to reward superior performance.
	Agencies are responsible for secondary goals, including fairness, openness, and responsiveness, which constrain the attainment of mission-related objectives.

DIFFERENCES BETWEEN
AND AMONG PUBLIC AGENCIES

Not only do public and private organizations differ, but public organizations differ among themselves. Government bureaucracy is not a single, monolithic entity that can be described in terms of a single, fixed set of characteristics. Individual agencies can and do vary greatly in terms of the environments they face, the technologies they rely upon, the kinds of workers they employ, and the nature of their outputs and outcomes. These variations hold important implications for ways in which individual agencies are organized and managed. Consequently, the differences between and among agencies must also be considered when assessing the relevance of organization theory for public agencies. The sections that follow highlight a few of the most important sources of variation.

Differences in Political Environments

As noted earlier, public managers often have limited effective control over the decisions they make in the course of strategic planning, goal setting, and rule making. How much effective control they possess tends to vary with the political environments they face.[17] Regulatory agencies, for example, typically impose costs on particular industries and therefore experience a high degree of conflict. They are deeply dependent on the regulated industry for information and on powerful support groups to help them carry out their missions. Effective control over key agency decisions is often low in such situations, especially where the coalition of supporters traditionally favoring regulation has weakened. Other agencies, such as the U.S. Social Security Administration, distribute benefits to influential client groups with program costs widely dispersed. An agency of this kind tends to experience higher effective control because a dominant interest favors its goals and no organized group opposes it, although even here the client group may try to influence how the agency carries out its task. Still other agencies, such as the U.S. Forest Service, must contend with several rival interests seeking to influence the agency's goals and plans. Although this reduces autonomy and the timeliness of decisions, public managers may still enjoy a considerable degree of effective control if the rival interests are equally balanced in terms of power and influence. In such instances interest group pressures often set the outer boundaries of decision making while leaving managers relatively free to define the agency's mission and determine the best way to carry it out in accordance with legislative intent and professional norms.

An intensely political and hostile environment imposes limits on what public managers can do and what results they can hope to achieve. With their choices constrained by powerful stakeholders they are not as free as managers facing more placid environments to define their task, create a shared sense of mission, and pursue strategic objectives in a direct and efficient manner. Consequently, some of the schools of thought examined in the chapters that follow (scientific management and administrative management theory, for example) may have limited relevance for managers facing environments of this kind.

Differences in Technology

The relevance of a particular school of thought may also depend on the core technology used. The ways agencies are organized and managed, and whether they perform in regular and predictable ways, depend in part on their technical means of production. Technology in this instance refers broadly to the system of tools and techniques used by an organization to carry out its tasks. In 1967 sociologist James D. Thompson created a scheme for classifying organizations according to their core technology.[18] A **long-linked technology** involves relatively routine tasks performed in succession. The mass-production assembly line provides an example. As each worker completes a distinct task, the assembly line passes the product to the next worker. With this type of technology it is relatively easy to select tools, construct appropriate work-flow arrangements, plan for the completion of work objectives, and direct the actions of workers through the use of standardized operating procedures. This type of technology is found in the public sector where paperwork must be processed or routine matters investigated, such as handling applications for permits or licenses, auditing tax forms, or collecting evidence at a crime scene.

A **mediating technology** links people together in order to satisfy their respective needs. A state employment security office provides an example. It creates a link between those seeking jobs and those seeking to fill jobs. This type of work technology is less routine because it brings multiple clients together who are widely distributed in time and space. Consequently, it requires standardized methods that go beyond simple operating procedures.

Finally, an **intensive technology** involves altering a product or person in a way that cannot be standardized because the workers' actions must be based on constant evaluation and feedback. A public hospital provides an example of this type of technology. Different medical treatments and diagnostic devices are used depending on the symptoms presented and various adjustments are made depending on how the patient responds to treatment. Determining which tools to use and how to use them cannot be fully standardized because each case is unique and considerable judgment is required. In addition, coordination of work must be achieved more by personal agreements backed up by professional standards than by centralized control and the exercise of formal authority.

Although Thompson's classification scheme goes only a small way toward differentiating among public organizations, it does help establish how technology influences the setting of objectives, the management of people, and the structure of work. It helps to explain why some agencies perform in a regular and predictable manner and others do not. As with political environments, the relevance of a particular school of thought for a specific agency may depend on that agency's core technology.

Differences in Employee Characteristics

Employee characteristics may also affect the relevance of particular schools of thought. The efficacy of alternative theories about directing, supervising, and motivating employees may depend, for example, on what the workers value, the amount of training and education they have received, and the amount of intellectual capital their jobs require. Well-educated employees tend to place a higher value on individual autonomy and personal growth than do less well-educated employees.[19] Consequently, those schools of organization theory that emphasize narrow division of labor, routinization of work, and economic incentives are likely to have limited relevance for agencies with highly educated workforces.

Similarly, a high proportion of government employees hold knowledge-intensive jobs.[20] These jobs involve the creation of knowledge or the creation of "smart products" through the application of "trained intelligence." Employees holding these jobs are not interchangeable labor commodities whose job performance depends on their manual dexterity or accumulated experience. Rather, the quality of their work depends on their intellectual capacity and the human capital they invest in their work. Special efforts are required to attract, develop, and retain workers of this kind. In addition, many of these workers are professionally trained. Because they believe their behavior is governed by externally defined codes of conduct, professionally trained employees are less inclined to abide by the preferences of managers or respond to traditional organizational incentives. Creating a shared sense of mission is especially difficult in agencies employing different types of professionals, each trying to define the task of the agency in terms of their own external reference points. Once again, those schools of organization theory that emphasize the routinization of work, the exercise of formal authority, and the use of economic incentives are likely to have limited relevance for agencies that rely extensively on professionally trained workers and knowledge-intensive jobs.

Differences in Outputs and Outcomes

The relevance of a particular school of thought may also depend on whether the agency's outputs (immediate work products) and outcomes (ultimate results) are concrete and observable. James Q. Wilson has developed a four-fold classification scheme to capture these differences. In a **production** agency the goals are clear and the outputs and outcomes readily observable. Consequently, it is relatively easy to design a compliance system that achieves desired results in a predictable manner. Much as suggested in the generic management literature, clear objectives and work standards are set, outputs and outcomes are measured, and workers are held accountable for results. In these respects production agencies can be "run like a business," although they still must contend with the many procedural and political constraints that characterize the public sector. Examples include the U.S. Postal Service with respect to delivering the mail and the U.S. Social Security Administration with respect to generating social security checks.

A **procedural** agency is one in which the outputs or work activities are observable but the outcomes are not. For example, the staff of a mental hospital can be observed providing various forms of treatment but the results in terms of restored mental health are not immediately apparent. Similarly, health and safety inspectors can be observed enforcing rules relating to use of hazardous chemicals, but whether enforcement actually protects the health of workers cannot be determined with confidence. In the absence of observable outcomes agency managers tend to rely on procedural rules to limit discretion and reduce "mistakes." When controversy erupts, managers can assure clients or political overseers that the rules were followed faithfully. Consequently, this type of agency tends to be means- rather than results-oriented. How the job is performed is more important than whether the desired outcomes are achieved. Where outcomes are unobservable it is very difficult for agency managers to adopt the managing-for-results prescriptions found in the generic management literature.

A **craft** agency is one in which outcomes but not outputs can be observed. Managers may not know what a fire fighter or a criminal investigator is doing in the field, but they can determine the results as measured by fires extinguished and criminal cases closed. Such agencies can be more goal-oriented than procedural agencies. Because they can evaluate outcomes there is less need to micro-manage workers by constraining their decisions with endless rules. Consequently, craft agencies tend to be more decentralized than procedural agencies.

A **coping** agency is one in which neither outputs nor outcomes are readily observable. Although school administrators can observe a schoolteacher giving lessons, in practice they rarely do so. As a result, neither the outputs (lessons) nor the outcomes (learning) are easily observed. Under these circumstances managers may have no clear idea about how to improve agency performance and may become very complaint-oriented as a result. Unable to verify the facts of the situation, the manager may choose to side with a complaining client over a dedicated staff member, appeasing the client at the expense of internal morale. Managers of these agencies must cope with a difficult situation. In keeping with the public school example, they must try to hire the best applicant without knowing what the best applicant looks like and they must develop, evaluate, and retain good teachers without valid measures for distinguishing good teachers from bad. Procedures are typically put in place to control workers and the most observable activities are measured, but without much hope that they will guarantee high performance.

Managers are often said to be responsible for establishing clear goals and performance standards, measuring outputs and outcomes, and holding employees accountable for results. Wilson's analysis suggests that their ability to do so depends on whether agency outputs and outcomes are readily observable. Consequently, those schools of organization theory that assume a high degree of formal rationality in connecting means and ends are likely to have less relevance where this criterion cannot be satisfied.

SUMMARY

Many of the contextual elements described in this chapter are clearly constraints. Constraints, as defined by James D. Thompson, are structural and procedural conditions to which an organization and its management must adapt.[21] The constraints faced by public managers—limited authority, ambiguous goals, externally imposed rules, inadequate resources, and political demands—cause many managers to adopt a psychology of failure. As Steven Cohen has observed, these managers "lower their expectations, abandon any sense of vision, and ridicule those who retain ambitious goals."[22] Having deliberately chosen to be caretakers rather than leaders, these managers focus on avoiding controversy and doing only what is necessary to keep their agencies functioning. Although this might seem like a rational response to a difficult situation, the tasks public agencies perform are too essential to the well-being of society to allow a psychology of failure to persist. Public agencies *can* be managed effectively, as the many awards given for excellence in government clearly demonstrate.[23] The key to effective management, according to Cohen, "is an active and aggressive effort to overcome constraints and obstacles."[24] Effective managers are those who can maneuver skillfully among the many political demands and administrative constraints to create an environment in which they can achieve desired results.

Although active and sustained leadership is important to effective management, so too is conceptual and theoretical knowledge. Having established the distinctive context in which public management takes place, we are now able to assess what organization theory can teach us about overcoming constraints and organizing and managing effectively.

NOTES

1. William E. Nelson, *The Roots of American Bureaucracy, 1830–1900* (Cambridge: Harvard University Press, 1982), 120.

2. Woodrow Wilson, "The Study of Administration," *Political Science Quarterly 2* (June 1887), 201.

3. Leonard D. White, *Introduction to the Study of Public Administration* (New York: Macmillan, 1939), preface to first edition.

4. J. Peter Grace, *Burning Money: The Waste of Your Tax Dollars* (New York: Macmillan Publishing, 1984), 5.

5. Hal G. Rainey, *Understanding and Managing Public Organizations* (San Francisco: Jossey-Bass, 1991), 21.

6. Paul H. Appleby, *Big Democracy* (New York: Knopf, 1945), 6.

7. Arie Halachmi, "Strategic Planning and Management? Not Necessarily," in J. Steven Ott, Albert C. Hyde, and Jay M. Shafritz (eds.) *Public Management: The Essential Readings* (Chicago: Nelson-Hall Publishers, 1991): 241–54.

8. Ronald C. Moe and Robert S. Gilmour, "Rediscovering Principles of Public Administration: The Neglected Foundation of Public Law," *Public Administration Review 55* (March/April 1995), 138.

9. Barton Wechsler and Robert W. Backoff, "The Dynamics of Strategy in Public Organizations," *Journal of the American Planning Association 53* (Winter 1987): 34–43.

10. Donald P. Warwick, *A Theory of Public Bureaucracy* (Cambridge: Harvard University Press, 1975), 102.

11. James Q. Wilson, *Bureaucracy: What Governments Do and Why They Do It* (New York: Basic Books, 1989), 168.

12. Warwick, *A Theory of Public Bureaucracy,* 85.

13. Robert D. Behn, "The Big Questions of Public Management," *Public Administration Review 55* (July/August, 1995), 321.

14. Al Gore, *From Red Tape to Results: Creating a Government that Works Better and*

Costs Less (New York: Times Books/ Random House, 1993), 2.

15. Lyman W. Porter and John Van Maanen, "Task Accomplishment and Management of Time," in James L. Perry and Kenneth L. Kraemer (eds.), *Public Management: Public and Private Perspectives* (Palo Alto: Mayfield Publishing, 1983): 212–24.

16. Ronald C. Moe, "The 'Reinventing Government' Exercise: Misinterpreting the Problem, Misjudging the Consequences," *Public Administration Review 54* (March/April 1994), 111.

17. See James Q. Wilson, *Bureaucracy,* especially chapter 5.

18. James D. Thompson, *Organizations in Action* (New York: McGraw-Hill, 1967), 15–18.

19. Daniel Yankelovich, *New Rules: Searching for Self-Fulfillment in a World*

Turned Upside Down (New York: Random House, 1981).

20. Eugene B. McGregor, *Strategic Management of Human Knowledge, Skills, and Abilities* (San Francisco: Jossey-Bass, 1991), 33.

21. Thompson, *Organizations in Action.*

22. Steven Cohen, *The Effective Public Manager: Achieving Success in Government* (San Francisco: Jossey-Bass, 1988), 5.

23. Agency awards are given by The Council for Excellence in Government and Harvard University's John F. Kennedy School of Government, and by the International Personnel Management Association; awards to outstanding practitioners are given by The American Society for Public Administration and The National Academy of Public Administration.

24. Cohen, *The Effective Public Manager,* 13.

3

⌘

Management Practice and Organizational Performance

Because government agencies exist to serve the public interest, it is essential that they perform in a superior manner. It is not good enough for firefighters to arrive at a fire in twenty minutes if they are fully capable of arriving in twelve. Lives and property hang in the balance. Similarly, it is not good enough for public hospitals to reduce postsurgery infection rates from 25 to 15 percent. Too many patients will continue to die. And it is not sufficient for drivers' license bureaus to process renewals efficiently. They should also be conveniently located, offer comfortable waiting rooms, and treat customers with civility and respect.

As taxpayers, citizens have a right to expect "the biggest bang for the buck," but beyond considerations of cost-effectiveness lie other important concerns, such as responsiveness, fairness, and quality of service. The interests of all citizens are served when government agencies use resources prudently, operate efficiently, and address society's problems effectively. In the current environment of declining confidence in public institutions, it is especially important for agencies to perform well. As governments lose their credibility with the public, they lose their ability to attract and retain the best available talents. Ultimately, they lose their capacity to govern. These considerations—the important role governments play in shaping the quality of life, the serious and complex problems facing society, and the perception (right or wrong) that governments at all levels are not doing enough to address these problems—underscore the importance of doing everything possible to enhance the performance of government agencies.

Many factors constrain the performance of agencies other than poor management. These include ill-conceived public policies, inadequate resources, and social and economic conditions over which agencies have little control. Although better management offers no panacea for overcoming these constraints, it can make a positive difference. Generally speaking, the more effective managers are in performing their tasks the more successful agencies are in achieving their objectives.[1] Charged with making authoritative decisions about agency objectives and the allocation of resources, managers are the ones primarily responsible for ensuring that plans are well-made, human talents fully developed and utilized, and mandated results achieved.

A key aim of this book is to explore what organization theory can tell us about managing public organizations more effectively. This chapter introduces three conceptual frameworks that are used in the chapters that follow to assess the contributions of each major school of thought. Together they provide stable points of reference for comparing the contributions of one school to another. Attention is focused on these frameworks because they correspond to three foundational questions facing public managers committed to exercising leadership in pursuit of organizational excellence:

1. What defines an effective organization and what values and methods will bring it into being?
2. How can the organization's many work activities be coordinated and controlled so that organizational objectives are in fact accomplished?
3. What can managers do, if anything, to encourage high levels of motivation and performance on the part of employees?

To assist us in answering these foundational questions, the first conceptual framework identifies four models of organizational effectiveness, the second presents six mechanisms for coordinating and controlling work activities, and the third outlines four strategies for motivating employees.

FOUR MODELS OF ORGANIZATIONAL EFFECTIVENESS

Although organizational effectiveness is a central theme in the field of organization theory, there is no agreement about what it means. The only point of agreement is that it does not refer to a single attribute of organizations or a specific criterion for assessing performance.[2] Effectiveness means something different depending on who is doing the judging, the level of analysis, and whether the focus is inputs, outputs, or processes. Consequently, effectiveness has little meaning outside of the specific criteria used to assess it. To address this problem Robert E. Quinn and John Rohrbaugh developed a conceptual scheme that identifies and groups the criteria analysts most often have in mind

Exhibit 3.1 The Competing Values Framework: Four Models of Organizational Effectiveness

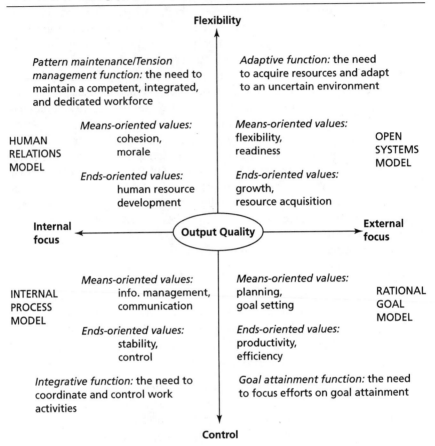

Flexibility

Pattern maintenance/Tension management function: the need to maintain a competent, integrated, and dedicated workforce

Adaptive function: the need to acquire resources and adapt to an uncertain environment

HUMAN RELATIONS MODEL

Means-oriented values: cohesion, morale

Ends-oriented values: human resource development

Means-oriented values: flexibility, readiness

Ends-oriented values: growth, resource acquisition

OPEN SYSTEMS MODEL

Internal focus ← **Output Quality** → **External focus**

INTERNAL PROCESS MODEL

Means-oriented values: info. management, communication

Ends-oriented values: stability, control

Means-oriented values: planning, goal setting

Ends-oriented values: productivity, efficiency

RATIONAL GOAL MODEL

Integrative function: the need to coordinate and control work activities

Goal attainment function: the need to focus efforts on goal attainment

Control

SOURCE: Adapted with permission from Figures 3 and 4, Robert O. Quinn and John Rohrbaugh, "A Spatial Model of Effectiveness Criteria: Towards a Competing Values Approach to Organizational Analysis," *Management Science* 29 (March 1983): 363–373. Copyright 1983, The Institute of Management Sciences, now the Institute for Operations Research and the Management Sciences (INFORMS), 901 Elkridge Landing Road, Suite 400, Linthicum, Maryland 21090-2909 USA.

when assessing organizational effectiveness.[3] Quinn and Rohrbaugh labeled their conceptual scheme the *competing values framework.*

Quinn and Rohrbaugh asked a panel of individuals with research interests in the area of organizational analysis to produce a list of discrete, organization-level criteria relating to effectiveness and then to assess the degree of conceptual similarity between every possible pairing of these criteria. Multidimensional scaling techniques were used to identify the basic dimensions defining how analysts conceive of organizational effectiveness. Three such dimensions emerged from their analysis. The first dimension, **focus**, is indicated by the horizontal line in Exhibit 3.1. The value criteria to the left of center reflect an internal concern for the well-being, development, and efficiency of employees (e.g., morale), whereas those to the right of center reflect an external concern for the well-being and development of the organization itself (e.g., growth). The second dimension, **structure,** is represented by the vertical line in Exhibit 3.1. Those values above the center point reflect a concern for flexibility and change, whereas those below the center point reflect a concern for stability and control. The last dimension, **time horizons,** distinguishes between an emphasis on means (e.g., planning and goal setting) and on final outcomes (e.g., productivity).

When these three dimensions are juxtaposed as shown in Exhibit 3.1 they reveal four competing models of organizational effectiveness. The **human relations model** focuses internally on the people who comprise the organization, emphasizes the need for structural flexibility, and stresses social cohesion, morale, and training as means for achieving a competent and integrated workforce. This model offers a theory of organizational effectiveness that we will find reflected in human relations theory (Chapter 9) and human resources theory (Chapters 12 and 13). The **open systems model** emphasizes the external needs of the organization and stresses structural flexibility and readiness as a means for adapting to an uncertain environment and securing the resources necessary for survival. This model's theory of organizational effectiveness is reflected in structural functional theory (Chapter 10) and open systems theory (Chapter 11). The **rational goal model** emphasizes planning and goal setting to achieve organizational goals in an efficient and productive manner. Its theory of organizational effectiveness may be seen in scientific management theory (Chapter 5) and administrative management theory (Chapter 6). Finally, the **internal process model** stresses information management and communications as means for coordinating and controlling work activities so that tasks are carried out in a disciplined and predictable manner. Its theory of organizational effectiveness is apparent in both scientific management theory (Chapter 5) and Weber's theory of bureaucracy (Chapter 4). As will be seen in later chapters, each school of thought tends to embrace one or two of these models of effectiveness, whereas none embraces all of them.

Quinn and Rohrbaugh also noted a basic similarity between these four models and the institutional prerequisites of any system of action.[4] According to sociologist Talcott Parsons, organizations are subject to "functional imperatives" that must be satisfied if they are to achieve their goals and maintain themselves as viable social systems.[5] To satisfy these imperatives all organizations must acquire resources and adjust to forces in their external environments (**adaptive function**), develop plans for attaining goals and direct their members in accomplishing them (**goal attainment function**), integrate and coordinate the work activities of individuals and organizational units in ways that are mutually supportive (**integrative function**), ensure the continued commitment of members to the organization and its goals (**pattern maintenance function**), and iron out the tensions that inevitably arise as organizations fail to satisfy all of their members' needs (**tension management function**). As indicated in Exhibit 3.1, each model of organizational effectiveness contributes to the satisfaction of one or two of these functional imperatives, but none contributes to the satisfaction of all five. The clear implication is that no social system seeking to remain viable can rely on a single model of organizational effectiveness. These models must be pursued in combination, and in an integrated, holistic manner, as circumstances warrant.

The competing values framework provides a highly useful way of thinking about organizational effectiveness and management's role in facilitating it. First, it emphasizes that organizational effectiveness is multidimensional in nature. It can be assessed in terms of any of several distinct criteria. Whether an organization is judged effective depends on who is doing the judging and which criteria are used. Second, it integrates key effectiveness criteria into a single conceptual scheme, one which indicates the relevance of each to organizational success. Finally, it emphasizes that these effectiveness criteria represent sets of partially competing values. The sets that are diagonal from each other in Exhibit 3.1 tend to be polar opposites. Flexibility, for example, is difficult to achieve except at the expense of control, and productivity is difficult to achieve except at the expense of cohesiveness. Every manager, according to Quinn, confronts a basic paradox: "We want our organizations to be adaptable and flexible, but we also want them to be stable and controlled. We want growth, resource acquisition, and external support, but we also want tight information management and formal communication. We want an emphasis on the value of human resources, but we also want an emphasis on planning and goal setting."[6]

Although the tensions between these values are an inherent part of institutional life, Quinn emphasizes that the values themselves are not mutually exclusive. Organizations can be simultaneously cohesive and productive, stable and flexible. And managers can learn to pursue contradictory values, Quinn suggests, by developing the capacity to use different frames of reference as circumstances change:

> The people who come to be masters of management do not see their work environment only in structured, analytic ways. Instead, they also have the capacity to see it as a complex, dynamic system that is constantly evolving. In order to interact effectively with it, they employ a variety of different perspectives or frames. As one set of conditions arises, they focus on certain cues that lead them to apply a very analytic and structured approach. As these cues fade, they focus on new cues of emerging importance and apply another frame, perhaps this time an intuitive and flexible one. At another time they may emphasize the overall task, and at still another they may focus on the welfare of a single individual.
>
> Because of these shifts, masters of management may appear to act in paradoxical ways. They engage the contradictions of organization life by using paradoxical frames.[7]

Each of the major schools of thought in the field of organization theory offers a distinct frame of reference. To ensure internal consistency, each tends to ignore certain effectiveness criteria and the value contradictions they represent.[8] Each tends to embrace a particular model of effectiveness, thereby offering only a partial view of how effectiveness is achieved. Only by isolating each school's contribution to our understanding of organizational effectiveness can a holistic perspective begin to emerge, a perspective that simultaneously addresses stability and change, flexibility and control, and individual and organizational needs. Exhibit 3.1 is used in the chapters that follow to assist with this analysis. How to interpret and apply this framework may not yet be entirely clear, but it will become so as the remaining chapters unfold.

SIX MECHANISMS FOR COORDINATING AND CONTROLLING WORK ACTIVITIES

A second fundamental question confronting public managers is how to coordinate and control work activities so that agency goals are in fact accomplished. Complex organizations can accomplish tasks that one or a few individuals acting alone cannot. They do so by dividing the work that needs to be accomplished into discrete tasks, each of which contributes in its unique way to the attainment of organizational goals. This is called **task specialization.** They also do so by grouping related activities together and assigning each group to an appropriate office or department within the larger organizational structure. This is called **departmentalization.** Unfortunately, although task specialization and departmentalization allow complex organizations to accomplish great things, they also increase problems of coordination and control. The more work activities are divided and departmentalized the more likely it becomes that organizational members will work at cross purposes, fail to accomplish their assigned tasks as instructed, make decisions that are inconsistent with organizational goals, or exercise administrative discretion in ways that are politically embarrassing to those higher in the chain of command. Consequently, all organizations find it necessary to coordinate and control the disparate work activities created through the division of labor.

Coordination means that activities, both within and across departments, work in harmony with one another to promote organizational objectives. Coordination tends to break down in practice for a variety of reasons. Individuals may work at cross purposes because they have received contradictory instructions or are unaware that plans, policies, or circumstances have changed. Similarly, their efforts may fail to mesh with the efforts of other organizational members because they don't truly understand "the big picture" of how everyone's tasks are interrelated and interdependent. Or, workers may come to identify with the values and interests of their respective departments so strongly that they act to advance those values and interests at the expense of those of other departments or the organization as a whole. Ensuring that these kinds of breakdowns do not occur is one of management's primary responsibilities.

Control, by contrast, means ensuring that assigned tasks are performed, policies followed, and objectives achieved as intended. Although the term has negative connotations, control need not entail a complete loss of individual freedom. In its institutional meaning it refers to a variety of tools for monitoring performance, collecting information, and taking corrective action to close the gap between actual and desired levels of performance. When the performance of individuals and work units match expectations, then work activities

Exhibit 3.2 Six Mechanisms for Coordinating and Controlling Work Activities

Mutual adjustment	Workers consult with each other informally about what needs to be accomplished and how. Responsibility for coordination and control rests with those who do the work.
Direct supervision	A supervisor is assigned to take responsibility for a group of workers and a managerial hierarchy is established to integrate the efforts of all work groups. The supervisor issues personal instructions and monitors individual performance.
Standardization of work processes	Work is programmed in advance of its execution by developing rules and standard operating procedures specifying how everyone is to perform assigned tasks. Coordination is built into the work process itself and control is achieved by strictly limiting each worker's discretion.
Standardization of work outputs	Work outputs are programmed in advance by providing each work group with product specifications or performance goals and allowing members considerable latitude in determining how to achieve them. Control is exercised by collecting output data, requiring corrective action when needed, and rewarding and sanctioning workers based on results achieved.
Standardization of worker skills	Workers are employed who possess the knowledge and skills needed to make appropriate decisions. Educational institutions and professional associations are relied upon to provide standardized training. Professionally trained workers are largely self-coordinating and self-controlling.
Standardization of values	Organizational leaders communicate and act upon a clear vision of what the organization exists to do, where it should be headed, and what values should guide it. Coordination and control is facilitated by commitment of organizational members to shared, internalized values and ideals.

SOURCE: Based in large part on Henry Mintzberg, *Structure in Fives* (Prentice-Hall, 1993), pp. 3–7.

are said to be "under control." Of course, it is possible for there to be too much control. Detailed rules and regulations, stifling red tape, and complex reporting requirements can easily inhibit creativity, discourage risk taking, kill motivation, and reduce work efficiency. Different work situations call for different kinds and degrees of control. It is part of management's task to find that kind and degree of control that is best suited to each work situation.

According to management scholar Henry Mintzberg, complex organizations generally rely on one or more of the mechanisms of coordination and control shown in Exhibit 3.2.[9] Although these mechanisms represent conceptually distinct categories, in practice they are typically used in overlapping combinations. The first of these mechanisms is **mutual adjustment.** Coordination is achieved by workers consulting with each other informally about what needs to be accomplished and how it will be done. Control rests with those who do the work. It takes the form of self-direction and self-management, with members of the work group reaching agreement about performance goals and how to close the gap between actual and desired performance levels. Mutual adjustment tends to work well for small organizations where members working side by side can readily discuss matters informally and work out ways to integrate their actions and accommodate their respective needs. It is also utilized by self-directed work teams within large organizations, although in this instance other mechanisms are required to coordinate the efforts of teams operating in different units and at different levels of the organization.

A second mechanism, generally adopted when informal consultation is no longer feasible, is **direct supervision.** Coordination is achieved by assigning a supervisor to take responsibility for a group of workers and establishing a managerial hierarchy to integrate the efforts of all work groups within the organization. Supervisors issue formal rules and personal instructions to group members in a manner they believe will produce the desired results. Conflicts between units are referred upward to the supervisor, who is responsible for all of the parties to the dispute. Under direct supervision, responsibility for control as well as coordination passes from the members of the work group to the supervisor. Control is exercised by requiring workers to obtain approval before taking certain kinds of actions, enforcing workplace rules, monitoring individual performance, and issuing instructions for corrective action.

Although widely used, direct supervision has clear limits as a mechanism of coordination and control. First, its success is highly dependent on the ability of supervisors to determine which rules and instructions will produce coordinated action and desired results. Second, where change is rapid, uncertainty high, and information limited, systems based on personal supervision quickly become overloaded as supervisors turn to higher authorities for assistance with nonroutine situations. Lastly, interpersonal conflicts often break out as supervisors seek to assert and maintain their authority over members of the work group. For these reasons most organizations find that they cannot rely on direct supervision alone and supplement it with some form of standardization, that is, standardization of work processes, outputs, skills, or values.

A third mechanism is **standardization of work processes.** Here work is programmed in advance of its execution by developing rules and standard operating procedures specifying how everyone involved in a work process is to perform tasks. Coordination is built into the work process itself and control is achieved by strictly limiting each worker's discretion so that mistakes are kept to a minimum and workers do not flounder about trying to determine how best to perform their assigned tasks. Work standardization is a more impersonal mechanism of coordination and control than direct supervision. Because workers are directed by standardized rules and procedures, there is generally less interpersonal conflict between workers and supervisors. However, work standardization tends to be effective only where conditions are stable and the work is simple, routine, and predictable. This is because uncertainty and complexity greatly undermine management's ability to prescribe in advance the best way to perform a task in all or most situations. In addition, work standardization is not well-suited to highly complex tasks where creativity and judgment are essential to task accomplishment.

A fourth mechanism is **standardization of work outputs.** Here the desired results, rather than the work itself, is programmed in advance. Each work group is provided with product specifications or performance goals and its members are then given considerable latitude in determining how to achieve them. Outside the realm of manufacturing, where product specifications are set by engineers, coordination is achieved through a process of planning and goal setting. Performance goals are established for each unit by management and when they are achieved in combination with the goals of all other units they result in the coordinated attainment of organizational objectives. Because goal setting helps coordinate interdependent tasks while allowing individual workers a high degree of discretion, it is well suited to complex, nonroutine work that requires considerable judgment. Supervisors exercise control by requiring that output data are collected and reported, by rewarding those who meet their goals, and by pressing those who do not to make necessary adjustments. In today's vernacular this mechanism is referred to as managing for results.

A fifth mechanism is **standardization of worker skills.** When neither the work nor its outputs can be standardized, as is often the case in public agencies, organizations can at least make sure that those who must exercise discretion in performing their tasks possess the knowledge and skills needed to make appropriate decisions. This mechanism achieves indirectly what the others seek to achieve directly. It relies on educational institutions and professional associations to provide workers with a standardized body of knowledge and skills. Professionally trained workers are largely self-controlling and self-coordinating. They work together in coordinated fashion because they know what needs to be done, how to do it, and what role each member of the work group must play in accomplishing it. Control is largely internal. Professionally trained workers fulfill their duties in a responsible manner because they have internalized the standards of their profession. From management's perspective, however, this mechanism is less than ideal. Professionally trained workers are typically less responsive to internal authorities than to external standards. They tend to believe in the importance of their work and their duty to their clients, beliefs which sometimes cause them to resist organizational directives.

The final mechanism of coordination and control is **standardization of values.** Although the five structural mechanisms described above are proven means of achieving coordination and control, a shared sense of mission and the values for accomplishing it are also powerful unifying forces. *Shared sense of mission* refers to a common understanding of what an organization exists to do, where it should be headed, and what values should guide it. All organizations are governed by shared cultural norms, but in some organizations leaders actively seek to shape them. This is accomplished by communicating and acting upon a clear vision of organizational success and the values that they believe contribute to success, values such as collegiality, egalitarianism, or quality service. Leaders hope that their vision and values will be internalized by the organization's members, causing them to work together to achieve their common ideals without the need for direct supervision. Coordination is facilitated because values, or shared meanings, provide common reference points that allow staff members to align their activities with one another in pursuit of a common purpose. Control is also facilitated. The great advantage of shared values is that it provides agency heads with a measure of confidence that staff members will act in specific situations as they would want them to act.

It bears repeating that organizations rely on different mixes of these six mechanisms depending on the nature of their work tasks, the skill levels of their workers, the situations they face, and the predispositions of their leaders. As Mintzberg put it,

> At the very least, a certain amount of direct supervision and mutual adjustment is always required, no matter what the reliance on standardization. Contemporary organizations simply cannot exist without leadership and informal communication, even if only to override the rigidities of standardization. In the most automated (that is, fully standardized) factory, machines break down, employees fail to show up for work, schedules must be changed at the last minute. Supervisors must intervene, and workers must be free to deal with unexpected problems.[10]

Not all organization theorists have appreciated this point. The schools of thought reviewed in later chapters tend to emphasize one or more of the six mechanisms of coordination and control while ignoring others. For this reason Exhibit 3.2 provides a valuable conceptual tool for determining the particular focus of each school of thought and ascertaining the relevance of particular methods of coordination and control for specific agencies.

FOUR STRATEGIES FOR
MOTIVATING EMPLOYEES

Employee motivation is another key factor affecting how well organizations perform. **Motivation** is an internal force that leads employees to comply with organizational directives and carry out their responsibilities in an acceptable if not superior manner. It also leads some employees to demonstrate special qualities such as enthusiasm, creativity, and a high regard for excellence. Motivation begins with each individual's needs and desires and the relative importance attached to them. According to most contemporary theories of motivation, the wish to satisfy deeply felt needs and desires creates a tension within people, driving them to find ways to satisfy the needs and desires so that the tension might be reduced. For example, employees who strongly value the respect of colleagues may be motivated to perform all duties conscientiously and to assist others in performing their work assignments. If colleagues respond with appreciation and respect, these employees are likely to continue the behaviors. Conversely, if the need for respect is not satisfied, the employees may engage in other, less constructive behaviors.

Personal motives include the need to belong to something larger than the self, contribute to activities that are consistent with one's values, be recognized by others who are held in respect, avoid pain or punishment, experience personal growth, and obtain more pay so that material needs and desires can be satisfied. No two individuals have the same motives because motives arise out of each person's cumulative life experiences and the values derived from them. For this reason managers wishing to intervene constructively in the motivational process must find ways to link the behaviors required by the organization with the motives commonly held by employees. According to social psychologists Daniel Katz and Robert L. Kahn, organizations require three kinds of behaviors from individuals to ensure effective organizational functioning.[11] First, organizations require people to join and remain with the organization. A long-term commitment from employees not only contributes to organizational functioning but also helps reduce costs associated with absenteeism and turnover. Second, organizations need employees to perform their work roles dependably and to meet or exceed established performance standards. Finally, organizations require behaviors that go well beyond dependable role performance. These behaviors include dedication, cooperation, creativity, innovation, and a demonstrated willingness to do the little things that contribute so much to protecting and promoting organizational interests.

A variety of motivational strategies is required to elicit these behaviors. For example, strategies that are successful in encouraging employees to join and remain with the organization may do little to encourage dependable role performance. Similarly, strategies that are successful in encouraging dependable role performance may do little to elicit creativity, innovation, or a commitment to excellence. Exhibit 3.3 summarizes four motivational strategies identified by Katz and Kahn.[12] Each relies on different methods of motivation and each elicits different kinds of behaviors. Although the theories discussed in later chapters tend to advocate one or two of these strategies, in practice different combinations of these strategies are required at different times and with different groups of employees. Decisions regarding which strategies to use and when to use them vary according to the agency's strategic objectives, the nature of the jobs in question, the employee needs and expectations, and the availability of various kinds of rewards.

The **legal compliance strategy** involves securing obedience and reliable behavior from employees through the exercise of formal authority. Obedience and reliability are achieved by issuing formal directives and workplace rules and enforcing them through the use of sanctions. Employees are motivated to comply with rules and directives either because they accept their legitimacy or because they wish to avoid the sanctions that managers can legally impose. As a motivational strategy, legal compliance relies heavily on directing and controlling human behavior. It recognizes that all organizations must secure at least some minimum level of reliability from employees in the performance of their work roles. After all, organizational effectiveness is threatened when employees do not come to work on time, do not cooperate

Exhibit 3.3 Four Motivational Strategies

Legal Compliance

Using rules, formal directives, and sanctions to direct and control employee behavior. Employees may come to work, comply with rules, and satisfy minimum role requirements, either because they accept the legitimacy of organizational authority or fear being sanctioned.

Instrumental Rewards

Using rewards to induce desired behaviors.

Rewards for Performance

Distributing pay, promotions, and recognition based on individual performance. Employees may meet or exceed role expectations because they value the material and psychological satisfactions that money, advancement, and recognition can provide.

Considerate Leadership

Adopting a leadership style based on being attentive to employees and considerate of their needs. This strategy may improve morale. It might also induce those who value the respect, support, and approval of persons in authority to meet or exceed their role requirements.

Group Acceptance

Creating a work environment that allows employees to socialize, form group bonds, and enjoy the approval of their peers. This strategy may induce those who value affiliation and peer approval to meet or exceed role requirements, assuming that group norms are consistent with organizational objectives.

Job Identification

Offering work that is interesting, challenging, and responsible. Employees may come to work, meet or exceed role requirements, and possibly exhibit greater creativity and innovativeness. They may do so because they identify with the jobs and find their work intrinsically rewarding.

Goal Congruence

Hiring employees whose goals and values are congruent with the organization's and/or socializing employees so that they internalize organizational goals and values. Employees may come to work, remain with the organization, meet or exceed role requirements, and exhibit greater creativity, innovativeness, and institutional loyalty. They may do so because they identify with the organization's mission and values and because contributing to them reinforces their own self concept.

SOURCE: Based in large part on Daniel Katz and Robert L. Kahn, *The Social Psychology of Organizations* (New York: Wiley, 1966), pp. 336–68.

---

with supervisors and coworkers, and do not perform work tasks dependably. Katz and Kahn are quick to point out, however, that although this strategy encourages routine compliance with role requirements it is unlikely to energize employees to perform above standard or exhibit innovation, creativity, or loyalty. Indeed, if used alone, this strategy will only ensure that workers do the bare minimum required to avoid sanctions.

The **instrumental rewards strategy** relies upon tangible and intangible rewards to induce employees to meet or exceed established performance standards. This strategy assumes that employees who perform in a superior manner do so because the rewards are instrumental in realizing personal objectives or fulfilling personal needs. In addition to the system rewards that all employees receive, Katz and Kahn identify three other kinds of instrumental rewards. **Performance rewards** include pay increases, promotions, and recognition. The manager's task is to ensure that appropriate rewards are available, are within the reach of hard-working employees, and are distributed on the basis of demonstrated results. According to Katz and Kahn, performance rewards can improve the quantity and quality of work performance but are unlikely to spark innovation, creativity, loyalty, or commitment. The rewards associated with **considerate leadership** come in the form of respect, support, and approval from persons in authority. Employees who value these rewards may enjoy higher levels of job satisfaction, according to Katz and Kahn, but not necessarily higher levels of productivity. Finally, the rewards associated with **group acceptance** include the satisfaction derived from affiliating with other employees in formal and informal work groups, including a sense of belonging and the approval of peers. Psychologists have identified the need to affiliate with other people as one of the most basic of human needs. It includes the need to develop friendships, give and receive affection, and belong to something larger than the self. Katz and Kahn suggest that employees whose affiliation needs are satisfied through group membership may come to work and perform their roles dependably, but only if the norms of the group support organizational objectives. Whether they will demonstrate superior performance, or creative and innovative behaviors, is much less certain.

The **job identification strategy** focuses on the intrinsic rewards received by those who delight in their work. It entails designing jobs so that they are interesting, challenging, and responsible. By expressing their skills and abilities in accomplishing challenging tasks, employees derive the intrinsic rewards of self-respect and pride of accomplishment. Employees also satisfy their basic need to feel competent and self-determining in relation to their environment. The manager's task is to design jobs with enough variety, complexity, and autonomy that they are intrinsically rewarding to those who perform them. According to Katz and Kahn, although employees may be motivated in this way to perform their jobs in a superior manner, and may also demonstrate creativity and innovation, they won't necessarily be motivated to remain with the organization or to protect and promote its interests.

The **goal congruence strategy** seeks congruence between the values and goals of employees and those of the organization. When values and goals are congruent, employees derive intrinsic satisfaction from knowing that they are engaged in work that is personally meaningful. Working to fulfill cherished beliefs also reinforces employees' self-concepts by confirming that they are the kind of person they wish to be. The internalization of organizational values can result from either a natural matching process or deliberate socialization by the employer. In the first instance congruence occurs when an individual self-selects an organization because of an anticipated identity of values. Persons committed to preserving the environment, for example, may gravitate toward agencies engaged in environmental protection. Congruence may also result from efforts by the employer to socialize employees in organizational goals and values. The underlying purpose is to foster an emotional attachment to the organization so that employees revel in its accomplishments and suffer with its failures. According to Katz and Kahn, this strategy may motivate employees to come to work, remain with the organization, exceed role requirements, and exhibit special qualities such as innovation, creativity, and a willingness to protect organizational interests.

Because needs and expectations vary greatly among individuals, and because jobs and the availability of rewards often vary greatly within an organization, managers cannot afford to rely on any one motivational strategy. It should also be kept in mind that the strategies identified above refer to general patterns rather than detailed and exclusive prescriptions for motivating employees. In practice, managers must employ them in ways and combinations tailored to the specific circumstances they face. As Katz and Kahn note, an organization is not like a single individual. Hence there is no single problem of motivation for the entire organization and no single answer regarding how best to motivate employees.[13] The strategies identified in Exhibit 3.3 simply provide a point of departure for comparing the theories of organization explored in the chapters that follow and for isolating the motivational strategy that each tends to emphasize.

SUMMARY

Because government agencies are the primary vehicles by which the public interest is realized, it is essential that they perform in a superior manner. Although many factors affect organizational performance, the quality of management is among the most important. Generally speaking, the more effective managers are in carrying out their responsibilities the more successful agencies are in achieving their goals and objectives. The chapters that follow explore the linkages between organization theory, management practice, and organizational performance.

The conceptual frameworks introduced in this chapter will assist us in this exploration. Together they will help us determine what each school of thought has to say about three key aspects of management: the partly conflicting roles managers must play if they are to help their organizations attain their goals and maintain themselves as viable social systems, the means by which to coordinate and control work activities, and the strategies by which to encourage employee motivation. In addition, these analytical frameworks provide conceptual categories that may be used by practicing managers to apply their knowledge of organization theory to concrete situations. In practice these conceptual categories can help managers assess the problems they encounter and how to respond to them.

NOTES

1. Research supports this generalization. See, for example, Jeff Gill and Kenneth J. Meier, "Ralph's Pretty-Good Grocery versus Ralph's Super Market: Separating Excellent Agencies from the Good Ones," *Public Administration Review 61* (January/February 2001), 9–17.

2. John P. Campbell, "On the Nature of Organizational Effectiveness," in Paul S. Goodman and Johannes M. Pennings (eds.), *New Perspectives on Organizational Effectiveness* (San Francisco: Jossey-Bass, 1977), 13–57; Richard M. Steers, "Problems in the Measurement of Organizational Effectiveness," *Administrative Science Quarterly 20* (December 1975), 546–58.

3. Robert E. Quinn and John Rohrbaugh, "A Competing Values Approach to Organizational Effectiveness, *Public Productivity Review 5* (June 1981): 122–40.

4. Robert E. Quinn and John Rohrbaugh, "A Spatial Model of Effectiveness Criteria: Toward a Competing Values Approach to Organizational Analysis," *Management Science 29* (March 1983), 363–77.

5. Chandler Morse, "The Functional Imperatives," in Max Black (ed.), *The Social Theories of Talcott Parsons: A Critical Examination* (Englewood Cliffs, NJ: Prentice-Hall, 1961), 100–152; Talcott Parsons, "General Theory in Sociology," in Robert K. Merton, Leonard Brown, and Leonard

S. Cottrell, Jr. (eds.), *Sociology Today: Problems and Prospects* (New York: Basic Books, 1959), 3–38; Talcott Parsons and Neil J. Smelser, *Economy and Society: A Study in the Integration of Economic and Social Theory* (Glencoe, IL: The Free Press, 1956), 16–20.

6. Robert E. Quinn, *Beyond Rational Management: Mastering the Paradoxes and Competing Demands of High Performance* (San Francisco: Jossey-Bass, 1988), 49.

7. Quinn, *Beyond Rational Management,* 3–4.

8. Andrew H. Van de Ven, book review of *In Search of Excellence: Lessons from America's Best-Run Companies, Administrative Science Quarterly 28* (December 1983), 621–24.

9. The first five methods are identified by Henry Mintzberg, *Structure in Fives: Designing Effective Organizations* (Englewood Cliffs, NJ: Prentice-Hall, 1983).

10. Mintzberg, *Structure in Fives,* 7–8.

11. Daniel Katz and Robert L. Kahn, *The Social Psychology of Organizations* (New York: John Wiley & Sons, 1966), 337–38.

12. The description of these strategies is drawn primarily from Daniel Katz and Robert L. Kahn, *The Social Psychology of Organizations,* 336–68.

13. Katz and Kahn, *The Social Psychology of Organizations,* 336.

4

⌘

Max Weber's
Theory of Bureaucracy

The first systematic study of modern bureaucracy was undertaken by the German sociologist Max Weber in the early 1900s. Although reference is often made to his "theory of bureaucracy," Weber didn't actually propose a theory of organization as such. His analysis was primarily descriptive and its purpose was limited to defining the essential characteristics of the modern bureaucratic form of administration. Nonetheless, it is possible to derive an implicit theory of organizational effectiveness from his work. This implicit theory holds that administrative rationality is achieved by dividing work into specialized administrative functions, assigning each function to a specific office, placing clear limits on each office's scope of authority, arranging all offices in a hierarchy of authority, organizing officials on a career basis, and requiring them to carry out directives with strict discipline and in accordance with clearly delineated rules.

This chapter examines the characteristics of Weber's ideal-type model of bureaucracy and assesses the usefulness of this model for understanding and managing today's complex organizations. It closes with a discussion of the relevance of Weber's analysis for public management and government performance. In reading this chapter it is important to keep in mind that Weber studied bureaucracy from a broadly historical and comparative perspective. His work has much to say about bureaucracy as an administrative form but very little to say about how actual bureaucracies differ or the conditions under which some perform better than others.

Max Weber 1864–1920

Max Weber was born in Erfurt, Germany in 1864. He studied law, economics, and philosophy at the University of Heidelberg and later at the University of Berlin. After completing requirements for a doctoral degree, Weber accepted a position as professor of economics at the University of Freiberg in 1894 and a similar position at the University of Heidelberg in 1896. His career as a university professor lasted only five years. A self-driven, hardworking person, Weber experienced a debilitating mental breakdown in 1898 and remained a semi-invalid for the next four years. In 1903 he began writing and researching again and a private inheritance soon gave him the financial independence he needed to work as a private scholar for the rest of his life. It was in the months immediately following his illness that Weber published his most famous and controversial work, a series of essays entitled *The Protestant Ethic and the Spirit of Capitalism.* In these essays he argued that capitalism resulted not only from a material desire for wealth but also from religious beliefs that encouraged individuals to save and reinvest their earnings. In defending his thesis, Weber turned to the comparative study of religious, political, and economic institutions. The major part of his sociological work, which dealt with the rationalization of economic and political life, was never completed. In 1919 he accepted a teaching position at the University of Munich where he died a few months later of pneumonia at the age of 56. His *Theory of Social and Economic Organization,* Part I of which was translated into English in 1947, was published after his death.

WEBER'S THEORY OF SOCIAL CHANGE

Weber sought to understand the social, political, and economic institutions of the present by contrasting them with the institutions of the past. In doing so he identified a trend, particularly evident in Western societies, which he referred to as the **process of rationalization.** Where once people relied on spiritual authorities, such as the priestesses at Delphi, to reveal truth and offer guidance, increasingly people came to rely on systems of law, the results of scientific experimentation, and their own powers of reason as guides. Institutions became increasingly rational in the sense that they were deliberately and systematically structured to achieve specific purposes. Relationships between ends and means became a matter of careful calculation.

In *The Protestant Ethic and the Spirit of Capitalism,* for example, Weber describes how the business corporation, the commodity and stock exchange, the system of public credit based on government subsidies, and the factory system for the production of goods were deliberately developed to facilitate the attainment of monetary profit.[1] Unlike Karl Marx, who believed such developments are determined primarily by the economic interests of a particular social class, Weber believed that they are shaped by the distinct ideas and beliefs, as well as the material interests, of various status groups in society. The rise of capitalism, for example, was driven in part by the willingness of Protestants to work hard and reinvest their earnings as a way of demonstrating their state of grace. Their protestant beliefs gave meaning to their economic behaviors and accelerated the development of capitalism.

Analysis of the rationalization process inevitably led Weber to the study of bureaucracy. He believed that, just as capitalism represents the highest stage of rational development in economic systems, bureaucracy represents the highest stage of rational development in administrative systems. In the political realm, for example, the advent of bureaucracy reflected a growing cultural commitment to replacing personal, arbitrary, and amateurish forms of government administration with impersonal, systematic, and professionalized forms. Weber viewed bureaucracy as being more rational than the administrative forms that preceded it because it exercised control on the basis of technical expertise and in accordance with carefully defined rules.

POLITICAL AUTHORITY
AND ADMINISTRATION

Weber's approach to sociology is apparent in his analysis of political authority. Unlike other scholars of his time, Weber did not hesitate to acknowledge that power underlies most social relationships. Political rulers, for example, exercise power to assure their continued dominance over the ruled. Coercion is often used to guarantee compliance. Similarly, administrators exercise power over their subordinates to assure the latter's compliance with organizational directives. But although rulers and administrators can govern through the use of force, the exercise of power is most effective when the authority of those exercising power is regarded as legitimate by the people who are expected to obey.

As Weber saw it, governments represent "moral orders"—sets of authoritative rules and institutional arrangements—that impose certain obligations on their members, including the obligation to obey. The appearance of a civil servant at the office at a fixed time each day, Weber argued, cannot be explained by habit or self-interest alone. This routine social act results in part from a belief in the legitimacy of the prevailing moral order and the duty to obey those in authority. The civil servant is careful to fulfill official obligations not only because disobedience carries adverse consequences but also because failure to do so is "abhorrent to the sense of duty, which, to a greater or lesser extent, is an absolute value to him."[2] Understanding this, rulers and administrators take deliberate steps to encourage acceptance of their right to command, thereby reinforcing the duty to obey.

Three Types of Legitimate Authority

Where their authority is accepted as legitimate, rulers and administrators need not rely as heavily on coercion, either in relation to the citizenry or the members of administrative offices. But what is the basis of this perceived legitimacy? Weber identified three conceptually pure types of authority: charismatic, traditional, and legal-rational. All rulers, according to Weber, base their claims of legitimacy on one or more of these pure types.

Charismatic authority is based on the extraordinary personal qualities and deeds of the leader. Followers accept the legitimacy of the leader's authority because of acts of heroism, extraordinary religious sanctity, exemplary character, supernatural powers, or demagogic appeals. Acceptance is often reinforced by the followers' devotion to the cause or mission that the leader espouses. Historical examples might include Jesus of Nazareth, Martin Luther King, and Mahatma Ghandi. Because respect is accorded to a particular person rather than to the person's office, charismatic authority tends to survive only as long as the people maintain their faith in the leader's magical powers, spirituality, or heroism. It thus provides a relatively unstable basis on which to govern unless it is combined with other types of authority.

Traditional authority is based on longstanding traditions that define who has the right to govern. This right is usually based on the principle of hereditary succession. Followers accept the legitimacy of the leader's authority because they believe in the sanctity of doing things the way they have always been done. The ruler is obeyed because members of his or her family or class have always been followed. Obedience is owed to the individual who occupies the traditionally sanctioned position of authority as a matter of personal loyalty. Although power is often exercised in a highly personal and arbitrary manner, traditional regimes tend to persist as long as the rulers continue to respect prevailing norms and customs. Examples of traditional rulers might include Egyptian pharaohs, Arabian patriarchs, African chieftains, and Asian and European feudal lords.

Legal-rational authority is based on a system of laws or rules and the right of those elevated to authority under those rules to exercise power. The legitimacy of this type of authority rests on a belief in reason as a means of ordering social relationships. The prevailing legal order is legitimate to the extent that its members accept it as a reasonable system of governance. In contrast to charismatic and traditional authority, legal-rational authority is much more impersonal. Obedience is owed primarily to the impersonal system of governance itself. Specific individuals are owed obedience only when acting within the scope of their delegated authority and when carrying out their legally defined duties. Examples of legal-rational rulers include presidents, prime ministers, constitutional monarchs, and administrators who have been delegated authority to perform specific duties. Legal-rational authority is the basis of governance in most modern religious and economic institutions as well.

Three Corresponding Types of Administration

Weber concluded that the particular type of administrative system adopted by rulers to ensure that their policies and commands are carried out is determined largely by the basis on which their authority rests. As illustrated in the following, rulers relying on tradition to legitimate their governing authority generally adopt patriarchal, patrimonial, or feudal forms of administration. By contrast, rulers relying on legal-rational authority generally adopt the bureaucratic form.

Type of governing authority	*Type of administrative system*
a. charismatic	a. charismatic
b. traditional	b. patrichal, patrimonial, or feudal
c. legal–rational	c. bureaucratic

Administration involves the exercise of power by an administrative staff over rank-and-file employees or organizational members. It is through this staff that "the execution of the supreme authority's general policy and specific commands" is achieved.[3] As with the exercise of political power over the citizenry, the successful exercise of administrative power also depends on perceptions of legitimacy. For example, if charisma is the basis of governing authority, it is likely to be the basis of administrative authority as well. In short, Weber not only identified three pure types of legitimate authority but also three corresponding pure types of administration.

Charismatic administrations tend to be loosely organized and unstable. "Disciples" are chosen by the leader based on their own charisma and personal devotion. They do not comprise a true administrative organization because they do not have fixed duties to perform in accordance with specific rules or customs. Rather, disciples assist the charismatic leader in accomplishing his or her mission in whatever ways seem appropriate. Their ability to command obedience from others depends in large part on their own charismatic qualities and the degree of regard or favor extended to them by the leader.

According to Weber, **traditional** administrative systems may be patriarchal, patrimonial, or feudal in nature. **Patriarchal administration** represents the pure type of traditional authority. It exists where the head of a household, a patriarch, rules over an extended family and its servants. Administrators are family members, servants, slaves, or personal favorites who are charged with satisfying the household's food, clothing, and protection needs. Because the ruler's authority does not extend beyond the household, there is no administrative staff other than the household staff.

Patrimonial administration is a form of patriarchal administration that arises when the patriarch attempts to govern subjects outside of his extended family. As the size of the kingdom increases, the patriarch establishes a more decentralized administrative system to meet the needs of the royal household, collect taxes, and ensure the continued obedience of his subjects. Under patrimonialism there is no consistent division of labor among officials. The patriarch views political administration as his personal affair and delegates authority to administrative officials as needed to accomplish specific tasks. As personal retainers, each official's privileges may be granted and withdrawn at any time according to the whims of the ruler. The latter may treat officials arbitrarily, and officials in turn may treat subjects arbitrarily, unless prevailing customs dictate otherwise. No formal body of rules exists to protect either administrators or subjects from arbitrary and capricious treatment. The clearest examples of patrimonial administrative systems existed in ancient Egypt under the pharaohs.

Feudal administration also arises where a patriarch seeks to govern subjects outside of his extended family. The primary difference is that administrative officials are geographically dispersed political allies rather than personal retainers tied to the royal household. The purely personal relationship between ruler and administrator is replaced by a contractual relationship in which a knight or baron promises loyalty to the feudal lord or king in exchange for a grant of property. In much of Europe, for example, feudal lords were allowed to derive private income from their landed estates and maintain political jurisdiction over them as long as they provided military assistance to the monarch when it was required. The body of feudal lords did not comprise a hierarchy of officials with clearly defined administrative duties. They served more to ensure the ruler's continued political control over a particular territory. In practice, this decentralized, contract-based system of administration usually existed alongside the patrimonial administration of the royal household. The modern nation-state in the West evolved out of this combination of patrimonialism and feudalism.

The type of administrative apparatus corresponding with legal-rational authority Weber labeled **bureaucratic.** It is best understood in contrast to the earlier administrative forms. The position of the administrator, as well as his or her relations with the ruler, the ruled, and other officials, are strictly defined by impersonal rules. These rules delineate in a rational way the hierarchy of authority, the rights and duties of every official, the methods of recruitment and promotion, and the means by which administrative duties are carried out. The bureaucrat is neither a personal retainer nor a political ally but a technically trained career administrator who enjoys considerable job security.

Although bureaucratic forms of administration have existed in the past, it is only with the modern state that bureaucracy has reached its most fully developed form. Unlike traditional forms of administration, which were organized somewhat haphazardly to ensure the ruler's continued domination, the bureaucratic form is systematically organized to achieve specific purposes such as justice, economic prosperity, or social well-being. The bureaucratic form thus represents the culmination of the process of rationalization. Over time it has gradually penetrated all social institutions. Armies, churches, and universities have lost many of their traditional aspects and are now administered largely by impersonal rules.

THE ADMINISTRATOR'S ROLE IN GOVERNMENT

Weber believed that every state is originally founded on force.[4] Rulers subsequently establish administrative agencies to ensure the state's continued existence and the successful implementation of their policies. Once the administrative apparatus is in place, the authority of rulers over the ruled becomes a matter of "organized domination." In the modern democratic state, according to Weber, the respective duties of politicians and administrators are quite distinct. The proper role of politicians, in Weber's view, is to define and pursue specific policy goals. Assuming that they wish to exercise true leadership on the public's behalf, Weber believed they must pursue their political causes with passion, a feeling of responsibility, and a sense of proportion.[5] By contrast, Weber believed that the proper role of career administrators is to implement the policies of elected officials dutifully, without passion, and without regard to political considerations:

> According to his proper vocation, the genuine official . . . will not engage in politics. Rather, he should engage in impartial "administration." . . . The honor of the civil servant is vested in his ability to execute conscientiously the order of the superior authorities, exactly as if the order agreed with his own conviction. This holds even if the order appears wrong to him and if, despite the civil servant's remonstrances, the authority insists on the order. Without this moral discipline and self-denial, in the highest sense the whole apparatus would fall to pieces.[6]

Weber's distinction between politics and administration is similar to the one Woodrow Wilson made in 1887 except that Wilson was more optimistic than Weber about the willingness of bureaucrats to serve as guardians of the public interest.[7] Weber described the power of the fully developed bureaucracy as "overtowering." He viewed bureaucrats as a distinct status group and warned that they will use their expertise and access to privileged information to maximize their autonomy, thereby increasing their ability to resist the will of their political superiors. In his view the fundamental problem for politicians, and ultimately for democracy, is how to exercise enough political control over civil servants to ensure that they remain disciplined, obedient, and impartial in carrying out their administrative duties.

These two themes—the proper role of administrators in a democratic society and the importance of keeping their power in check—are explored extensively in the public administration literature. The scope of this chapter is limited to the implications of Weber's analysis for management practice and organizational performance. The central concern is not the political control exercised by politicians over bureaucrats as much as the administrative control exercised by senior administrators over their staffs.

WEBER'S IDEAL-TYPE BUREAUCRACY

In the course of his sociological studies Weber constructed a series of "ideal types" to capture the essential, defining characteristics of social phenomena. Examples include the three types of legitimate authority and the corresponding types of administration identified earlier. Weber purposefully constructed these conceptually pure ideal types as methodological tools. He believed existing phenomena can be understood best by analyzing the extent to which they conform or fail to conform to the characteristics of each pure type. Government in sixteenth-century England, for example, might be understood as reflecting various elements of the patrimonial, feudal, and legal-rational types of authority. The usefulness of this conceptual scheme, Weber acknowledged, "can only be judged by its results in promoting systematic analysis."[8]

Weber concluded from his comparative analysis that the bureaucratic form of administration is the most rational—that is, the one most deliberately constructed based on ends-means calculations. He theorized that bureaucracy's superiority is a product of specific structural characteristics. These characteristics, derived from his analysis of modern institutions, comprise his ideal-type bureaucracy. Before introducing Weber's ideal-type bureaucracy, it is important to note that the term can be misleading. It has led some scholars to conclude that Weber found bureaucracy to be ideal in the sense of perfect. This is far from the case. In developing his ideal-type model Weber sought to capture the *idea* of bureaucracy without implying that it represented a perfected form of administration.

Nowhere in Weber's work do we find a clear statement of the elements comprising his ideal-type bureaucracy. However, a general discussion of them is found in two places: Parts 1 and 3 of his master work, *Wirtschaft und Gesellschaft*.[9] Exhibit 4.1 identifies the key structural elements of bureaucracy as abstracted from these two sections.

As Exhibit 4.1 suggests, Weber's ideal-type model defines bureaucracy as a set of structural elements for controlling and coordinating work activities so that administrative duties are performed in a reasonable and calculated manner. In addition to these structural elements the day-to-day process of administration is also infused with **a spirit of formal impersonality** that ensures predictable results and fair and impartial treatment of clients. Weber did not mean, as some have suggested, that bureaucracy requires civil servants to be cold and distant in their relations with clients or each other. He only meant that bureaucracy requires them to perform their duties in a manner free of personal favoritism or bias.

Weber believed that the "fully developed bureaucracy" is the most technically efficient of the many historical forms of administration. Indeed, he viewed it as "completely indispensable" for meeting the needs of modern society. In his words,

> Experience tends universally to show that the purely bureaucratic type of administrative organization—that is, the monocratic form of bureaucracy—is, from a purely technical point of view, capable of attaining the highest degree of efficiency and is in this sense formally the most rational known means of carrying out imperative control over human beings. It is superior to any other form in precision, in stability, in the stringency of its discipline, and in its reliability. It thus makes possible a particularly high degree of calculability of results for the heads of the organization and for those acting in relation to it.[10]

Exhibit 4.1 Weber's Ideal-Type Bureaucracy

Fixed official duties	The work of bureaus is systematically divided so that officials have clearly defined duties and are delegated authority to make decisions within their own sphere of competence.
Hierarchy of authority	Positions are arranged hierarchically according to their level of authority; each lower office is under the control and supervision of a higher one; subordinates are accountable to their superiors through a clear chain of command.
Systems of rules	Behavioral rules limit the scope of authority and constrain the official's personal conduct; technical rules define how work is to be performed and decisions made.
Technical expertise	Officials are selected and promoted based on their competence to perform specific, specialized duties.
Career service	Bureaucracies comprise officials who have chosen public service as a career, who receive a salary for their services, and whose offices are not their personal property.
Written documentation	Officials maintain written records of all rules, decisions, and administrative actions.

Before assessing the implications of Weber's theory for public management it is necessary to consider how each of bureaucracy's structural elements contributes to the attainment of organizational goals. This is the functional side of bureaucracy. Generally speaking, each of these elements are functional to the extent that they help the organization achieve one or more of the four functional imperatives identified in Chapter 3. The following analysis examines each structural element in turn.

Fixed Official Duties

Under charismatic and traditional forms of administration, tasks were assigned to disciples or personal retainers on an ad hoc basis. Administrators performed different tasks at different times according to the particular needs or whims of the ruler. Their titles and responsibilities changed frequently and the scope of their authority was seldom clearly defined. From Weber's perspective this represented a highly irrational way of conducting official business. Under the bureaucratic form, by contrast, the overall administrative task is systematically divided into fixed, largely permanent areas of official jurisdiction. This promotes administrative rationality in several ways. First, operational continuity results because all necessary functions are continuously performed by permanent offices. As individuals at the highest levels of authority come and go, a corps of well-trained career officials remains to carry out the work of government. Second, the resulting specialization of function encourages individual competence. Officials become very good at their work as they train for and develop expertise in specific areas of administration. Third, the bureaucratic form increases accountability. Officials are less likely to abuse their authority or shirk their duties when their responsibilities are fixed and clearly spelled out. Finally, this form enhances predictability. The division of labor is planned so that each official contributes in a unique way to accomplishing the organization's overall task. Because each official has prescribed functions to perform in prescribed ways, those in authority can issue directives with the full expectation that they will be carried out as intended.

Hierarchy of Authority

Each office in the bureaucratic organization is arranged hierarchically according to its assigned level of authority. The result is a firmly ordered system of superior and subordinate relationships in which each lower office is supervised by a higher one and decisions made at higher levels are passed downward for lower officials to implement. Although status differences also exist in charismatic and traditional administrations, what makes bureaucracy unique is the clearly delineated chain of command that allows those at the top systematically to coordinate and control the activities of those working below them.

Coordination refers to the organization's ability to integrate the efforts of all of its members so that its overall task is accomplished. According to Weber, bureaucracy's hierarchically ordered chain of command provides a highly rational means of achieving coordinated effort. Each official takes responsibility for subordinates, issuing instructions to them and monitoring their actions. Similarly, every official is accountable to a higher official for his or her own actions. Coordinated effort is also facilitated by the flow of communications up and down the chain of command. Control refers to the ability of those in higher positions to ensure that the work of subordinates is accomplished in prescribed ways. Control, like coordination, is achieved through a chain of superior-subordinate relationships in which superiors have a right to issue directives and subordinates have a duty to obey.

Systems of Rules

Bureaucracy, according to Weber, is characterized by systems of rules which are "more or less stable" and "more or less exhaustive."[11] These rules are of two kinds: behavioral and technical. Behavioral rules are found in a bureau's policies and workplace conduct codes. They function as instruments of control by prohibiting behaviors defined by rule makers as contrary to organizational norms or to a well-ordered and disciplined workplace. Examples include rules prohibiting tardiness, theft, and acts of insubordination. According to Weber, officials comply with behavioral rules both because they accept their legitimacy and because they fear the sanctions attached to their use. Other behavioral rules promote accountability by requiring officials to perform their duties in an ethical and responsible manner. Examples include financial accounting rules and rules governing conflicts of interest.

Technical rules, by contrast, prescribe how officials are to perform their required tasks. They may take the form of administrative rules derived from statute law or internal operating procedures as typically found in policies-and-procedures manuals. Their essential purpose is to specify how officials are to respond in various situations and under various conditions. They thus function as instruments of control by greatly narrowing each official's range of discretion. By communicating in considerable detail what is to be done and how, they leave very little room for decisions that higher authorities might deem unwarranted. Rules also increase predictability by ensuring that every task is performed in a uniform manner, regardless of the number of persons engaged in it.

Similarly, technical rules provide a second means of coordination. Each person's work can be coordinated with the work of others, not only through direct supervision and informal consultation but also through standardized procedures that build disciplined performance into the work process itself. Firefighters, for example, cannot afford to stop each time they arrive at a fire to figure out who will attach the hose to the hydrant and who will go up the ladder. Nor can they afford to wait for a supervisor to make a determination. These matters must be coordinated in advance through the use of technical rules.[12]

Technical rules also promote operational efficiency by reducing decision situations to a matter of identifying and applying the appropriate rule. Over time agencies develop standard operating procedures so that similar cases can be handled in a similar fashion. This allows officials to turn their attention to handling nonroutine cases. According to Weber, even where an official's work is highly complex, legal and professional standards exist to guide them in handling specific cases.

Finally, the application of abstract rules to particular cases promotes impartiality toward employees and clients. According to Weber, the technical superiority of bureaucracy is due in no small measure to the manner in which individuals are treated. Under patrimonial and feudal systems, decisions involving clients or other officials were personal in character. Each situation was handled as a unique case and decisions were made on the basis of personal considerations. A new official might be appointed on the basis of nepotism, a subordinate might be promoted or disciplined because of a supervisor's personal biases, or a client might receive special treatment by evoking an official's pity or sympathy. Weber understood that officials who develop strong feelings about particular subordinates or clients are likely to let those feelings influence their official decisions, often without their being aware of it. The great virtue of bureaucracy, according to Weber, is that decisions are made in a detached, impersonal manner in accordance with pre-established rules. In Weber's words, bureaucracy "develops the more perfectly the more the bureaucracy is 'dehumanized,' the more completely it succeeds in eliminating from official business love, hatred, and all purely personal, irrational, and emotional elements which escape calculation."[13]

Technical Expertise

According to Weber, "Bureaucratic administration means fundamentally the exercise of control on the basis of knowledge. This is the feature of it which makes it specifically rational."[14] Whereas patrimonial and feudal officials were amateurs in administrative matters, modern bureaucrats are selected and promoted based on their technical expertise. This increases the competence of the administrative staff and improves their work efficiency. It also means that administrative tasks are performed with greater impartiality. In Weber's words, "The more complicated and specialized modern culture becomes, the more its external supporting apparatus demands the personally detached and strictly 'objective' *expert*, in lieu of the master of older social structures, who was moved by personal sympathy and favor, by grace and gratitude."[15]

Career Service

Feudal lords, priests, and personal retainers performed their official duties as secondary occupations, received rents or fees from their offices, and remained at least partly dependent on their superiors for their livelihoods. Modern bureaucrats, by contrast, are career professionals who receive salaries for their work and enjoy considerable job security. A career civil service contributes to the technical superiority of bureaucracy in three ways. First, a fixed salary and a relatively high degree of job security encourages organizational commitment. Not dependent on their superiors for their livelihoods, bureaucrats can devote themselves to their professional obligations. Their loyalty is to the civil service as a whole rather than the person highest in authority.

Second, officials who prepare for professional careers can perform their duties with greater competence than the officials in patrimonial and feudal systems who performed their duties as secondary occupations. Modern officials choose government service as a vocation, train for it, and are appointed based on their training. Finally, separating the office from the officeholder increases the bureaucrat's impartiality. According to Weber, this separation reinforces the idea that civil servants are temporary custodians of the public trust who carry out official duties during working hours and who are not to exploit the office for personal gain. It also reinforces the idea that civil servants are not to demonstrate personal or political favoritism toward anyone.

Written Documentation

Recording administrative decisions in writing helps ensure operational continuity. As elected officials and administrators come and go, new decisions continue to be guided by decisions made in the past. Written documentation also facilitates accountability. Higher authorities can use these records to evaluate agency performance and hold subordinates accountable for their actions. Conversely, bureaucrats charged with improprieties can use them to show that they followed the rules and carried out their duties responsibly. Written documentation thus provides protection for subordinates as well as supervisors.

WAS WEBER WRONG ABOUT BUREAUCRACY'S TECHNICAL SUPERIORITY?

Today we tend to think of bureaucracies as slow, inefficient, and uncaring, bogged down by too many layers of authority, too many rules, and too much red tape. This contemporary understanding is difficult to reconcile with Weber's description of bureaucracy as the embodiment of rationality. Consequently, it is tempting to conclude that Weber was simply wrong about bureaucracy's technical superiority. Such a conclusion is unwarranted, however, because Weber's analysis is broadly historical and comparative in scope. He did not suggest, for example, that each and every bureaucratic organization will perform at an optimal level. He asserted only that bureaucracy is superior "to *any other form* in precision, in stability, in the stringency of its discipline, and in its reliability [emphasis added]."[16] Weber intended his ideal-type bureaucracy to be understood as a conceptually pure form of administration, which, from a historical and comparative perspective, is relatively efficient and effective in carrying out commands and implementing policies. If bureaucracy as a system is relatively precise, stable, disciplined, and reliable, the same is not necessarily true for every organization within it. A given organization may possess many of the defining structural features of bureaucracy and yet be highly inefficient and unreliable in practice.

Weber understood that outside the conceptual realm complex organizations are subject to many imperfections. Some of these imperfections arise from the "irrational" element—emotions, personalities, individual needs, and politics—that he deliberately excluded from his ideal-type model for methodological reasons. Others arise from the bureaucratic structure itself (see Chapter 10). In either case, these imperfections do not undermine Weber's basic conclusion that the structural characteristics of bureaucracy reflect a higher degree of rationality and allow for a higher degree of technical efficiency than earlier administrative forms.

LIMITATIONS ON THE USEFULNESS OF WEBER'S MODEL

Weber's contribution to organization theory is unquestionably brilliant. His ideal-type bureaucracy has provided the point of departure for countless empirical studies. Even today the structural dimensions Weber identified—task specialization, centralization, and formalization—remain the principal dimensions along which we think about and study organizational design. Nonetheless, there are clear limitations on the usefulness of Weber's model for improving or sustaining organizational performance.

The model's usefulness is limited for three reasons: it fails to provide a holistic or comprehensive theory of organization; it views organizational performance as the product of a fixed set of structural attributes; and it is time-bound, capturing the process of rationalization as reflected in the institutions of the early 1900s but failing to imagine its continuing evolution.

Limitations of a Structural Model

Weber's purpose was to isolate the structural elements explaining the technical superiority of the modern, bureaucratic form of administration. As noted earlier, he deliberately left out of consideration the "irrational" elements affecting the performance of bureaucratic institutions, including politics, personalities, and human emotions. Consequently, Weber's model emphasizes the structural variables required to understand and explain organizational dynamics while ignoring other important variables relating to human behavior, technology, and process. Although Weber's model served his purposes well, those who are charged with improving or sustaining organizational performance require a more comprehensive theory of organization, one that encompasses not only more variables but also the interrelationships among them.

Few theorists have attempted to develop a comprehensive theory of organization. Thus, to note that Weber was not fully comprehensive is not to criticize his work or discount the importance of his contributions to organization theory. It is simply to acknowledge the limited usefulness of his model for persons seeking more than a structural understanding of complex organizations.

Limitations of Defining Bureaucracy
as a Fixed Set of Attributes

Weber's ideal type captures the essence of the bureaucratic form of administration in terms of a fixed set of attributes (e.g., narrow division of labor, offices arranged in a hierarchy of authority, systems of rules). The "fully developed bureaucracy" is described by Weber as being highly specialized, centralized, and formalized. This suggests that organizations are either bureaucratic or they are not, depending on whether they possess these fixed attributes. In practice, however, we know that bureaucratic organizations vary greatly. Some, for example, are highly specialized but not highly routinized; others are highly centralized but not highly formalized. Thus it is difficult to determine whether an organization belongs to the class of bureaucratic institutions as defined by Weber. Researchers have gotten around this problem by simply recasting Weber's fixed attributes as empirical dimensions and proceeding to measure the extent to which selected organizations are, for example, specialized, centralized, and formalized.[17]

The situation is different, however, when Weber's model is used as a guide to practice. Because Weber defines the bureaucratic form of administration as being technically superior to all other forms, there is a strong suggestion that if an organization is not highly centralized, specialized, and formalized it cannot be administratively rational. Weber's analysis comes very close to stating a "one best way" theory of organizational effectiveness. Nothing in Weber's analysis acknowledges that the optimal degree of centralization, specialization, or formalization is necessarily contingent upon such factors as environmental uncertainty, task complexity, or employee characteristics.

Although equating higher levels of centralization, specialization, and formalization with administrative rationality may make sense from a broadly comparative and historical perspective, it makes much less sense from a concrete managerial perspective. The research findings reported in Chapter 10, for example, indicate that organizational performance is often undermined when bureaucracy's structural attributes are taken to an extreme. In practice, performance is often undermined by authority structures that are *too* highly centralized (procedural delays, red tape, institutional rigidity), official duties that are *too* narrowly defined (inter-unit conflict, line-staff conflict, bureaucratic runaround), work processes that are *too* highly regimented and depersonalized (stifled initiative, goal displacement), discretionary authority that is *too* greatly limited (overconformity, institutional rigidity), and systems of rules that are *too* exhaustive and all-encompassing (goal displacement, institutional rigidity, suboptimal role performance). In short, not only does Weber's ideal-type fail to provide useful guidance regarding the degree of bureaucratization that is optimal for a specific organization but it can also mislead us by implying that more specialization, centralization, and formalization is better than less.

By extension, Weber's analysis implies that any deviation from the ideal type inevitably reduces administrative rationality. Taken too literally, this assumption can lead managers into the trap of **Weberian orthodoxy.** This is the doctrinaire belief that the administratively efficient organization must be highly centralized, reflect a clear chain of command from top to bottom, place a heavy emphasis on accountability and control, and achieve a high degree of work routinization. The danger inherent in this belief is that it can discourage managers from even considering administrative reforms not sanctioned by Weber's model. For many managers, the orthodox model is the only operating model to which they have been exposed. Confronted with the need to restructure their agencies they automatically turn to the orthodox model for guidance. Because reforms that depart from this model are not considered worthy of discussion, Weberian orthodoxy acts as a brake on innovation and change.

Donald Warwick provides a telling example in his study of the U.S. State Department. When Deputy Under Secretary William Crockett attempted to create a flatter, more decentralized structure by eliminating three levels of middle management, he was met with considerable resistance. The prevailing belief was that such reforms simply would not work because they were inconsistent with orthodox managerial principles, principles heavily influenced by Weber's description of bureaucracy. Warwick concludes that social scientists have, on the whole, "treated Weber's conceptualization of bureaucracy as a sacred legacy to be interpreted but never radically changed. As a result, our theoretical understanding of public organizations, and therefore of the full range of organizations, remains seriously limited."[18]

To avoid Weberian orthodoxy managers must resist viewing bureaucracy as a single, fixed organizational form. The structural elements in Weber's ideal type are best viewed as variables to be adjusted according to the internal and external requirements of each organization. Public agencies need not be tall, rigid, and tightly disciplined to be effective. The key question confronting managers is not whether to adopt a bureaucratic form of administration but what degree of bureaucratization is most appropriate for their particular agency.

Limitations of a Time-Bound
Conception of Bureaucracy

Because Weber wrote from the perspective of his own time and place, he may have been unduly influenced by his admiration for the Prussian military and civil services. Political scientist Dwight Waldo observed, for example, that there is a very close resemblance between the characteristics of the Prussian army and Weber's ideal-typical criteria for the bureaucratic form of organization.[19] The problem with this, according to Waldo, is that a model of bureaucracy constructed with early twentieth-century military and civil bureaucracies in mind may have very little relevance today. The process of rationalization did not come to a halt in the early 1900s, nor did society cease to change. As Waldo put it, the theorist of democratic organization must credit Weber for a good picture of his day "but he must refuse to believe this is the prettiest of all pictures; he must not simply look backward to see what types of societies have been but must look forward into a future of new and now-unknown types of societies."[20]

It seems Weber failed to appreciate the extent to which bureaucracy would continue to evolve as part of the process of rationalization that he described so well. What seemed highly rational to Weber in the early 1900s, such as strict obedience to authority and limited discretion, cannot be viewed as the embodiment of rationality today. Too many circumstances have changed. Government's tasks have become more complex, jobs have become more knowledge-intensive, workers have become better educated, and the larger culture has become more egalitarian. Most jobs can no longer be reduced to a fixed set of operating procedures, and most employees will not tolerate a highly authoritarian work environment. Although complex organizations remain bureaucratic in character, much as Weber described them, today's public managers need not rely as much on formal structure to coordinate work activities or on the legal compliance strategy to elicit desired behaviors from employees. Less intrusive methods of control and alternative motivational strategies are now available.

If Weber's model is not entirely relevant for purposes of improving and sustaining the performance of today's organizations, neither is it entirely irrelevant. To one extent or another complex organizations still rely on hierarchically arranged offices and systems of rules to coordinate and control work activities. Nonetheless, it has become fashionable in some circles to define bureaucracy as a failed and obsolete form of administration. Many contemporary critics of government, for example, prefer to define bureaucracy in terms of its dysfunctions. These critics view bureaucracy not as offices arranged in a hierarchy of authority with work processes performed according to fixed rules, but as a form of administration that is slow, inefficient, and incapable of innovation. In *Reinventing Government,* for example, Osborne and Gaebler describe bureaucracy as an obsolete and failed form of administration and call for the development of an alternative administrative form.[21]

Given bureaucracy's continued evolution it is premature to conclude that bureaucracy is an obsolete and failed administrative form. Elliot Jacques has argued, for example, that the hierarchical kind of organization we call bureaucracy is the only form that can enable an organization to employ large numbers of people while maintaining unambiguous accountability for the work they do. The properly structured hierarchy, according to Jacques, "can release energy and creativity, rationalize productivity, and actually improve morale."[22] In his view the search for an alternative kind of organization is wrong-headed because hierarchy itself is not to blame for our organizational problems. Instead, managers are largely to blame for not employing the principle of hierarchy properly. According to Jacques, "The problem is not to find an alternative to a system that once worked well but no longer does; the problem is to make it work efficiently for the first time in its 3000-year history."[23] Managers, Jacques concludes, must "stop casting about fruitlessly for organizational Holy Grails and settle down to the hard work of putting our managerial hierarchies in order."[24]

WEBER'S THEORY OF BUREAUCRACY
IN PERSPECTIVE

Organizations may be viewed from multiple perspectives—structural, behavioral, political, and cultural. Each perspective contributes in its own unique way to a holistic, comprehensive understanding of complex organizations. Weber's structural perspective has been and continues to be very useful in this respect. It not only helps us understand how structure can be used for purposes of coordination and control but it also continues to serve as a widely recognized point of departure for investigating problems of organizational design and behavior.

It must be remembered that Weber did not set out to develop a comprehensive theory of organizational effectiveness. If his analysis has little to say about how actual bureaucracies differ or the conditions under which some perform better than others, this does not lessen the importance of his contributions or the relevance of his ideal-type model. Weber's model continues to have particular relevance for production agencies, those agencies where work is routine in nature and outputs are observable and measurable.

RELEVANCE FOR PUBLIC MANAGEMENT

The remainder of this chapter explores the relevance of Weber's theory of bureaucracy for public management and organizational performance. This exploration is guided by the three conceptual frameworks introduced in Chapter 3.

Models of Organizational Effectiveness

As indicated in Exhibit 4.2, Weber's analysis of bureaucracy emphasizes the values associated with the **internal process model.** This model asks managers to serve as monitors and coordinators to ensure that work activities are carried out as intended and in a stable and predictable manner. At the heart of Weber's analysis lies a concern for the integrative function and the means by which work activities are coordinated and controlled. According to Weber, the structural elements of bureaucracy provide the quintessential means by which the integrative function is accomplished. Supervision of one office by another allows work activities to be monitored and corrected as needed. Written records contribute to both operational continuity and accountability. Finally, rules and operating procedures help ensure that each task is performed in a way that contributes to the organization's overall objectives. This underscores the relevance of Weber's theory for management practice. Bureaucracy's structural elements provide one set of means by which managers can help fulfill the organization's integrative function.

To a lesser extent Weber's analysis focuses on the **rational goal model** and the values of efficiency, productivity, and goal attainment. This model asks managers to serve as directors and producers to ensure that desired results are achieved. Weber's theory identifies structural means for accomplishing the goal attainment function. Fixed official duties, as defined in statute law and reflected in formal job descriptions, direct the attention of bureaucrats to their mandated responsibilities. The hierarchically ordered chain of command enables managers to plan and direct the work of subordinates and encourage them to achieve high levels of productivity. Finally, systems of rules specify exactly how tasks are to be performed. According to Weber, it is this routinization of work that explains the high degree of predictability of results associated with bureaucracy.

Generally speaking, all organizations must arrange themselves internally to achieve desired results and they must seek stability to the extent that it is possible in a turbulent environment. And yet the implications of Weber's theory for management practice are troubling in two respects. First, the manager who focuses on the integrative function may do so at the expense of the adaptive function. Rules and other systems of control inevitably create rigidities that can undermine an organization's ability to adapt successfully to changing circumstances. Methods designed to make organizations operate like well-oiled machines have limited applicability for agencies that function in turbulent and highly politicized environments. In such environments it is very difficult to standardize work and formalize rules and still maintain the capacity to adapt successfully to changing conditions.

Second, the manager who focuses on the goal attainment function may do so at the expense of the pattern maintenance/tension management functions

**Exhibit 4.2 The Competing Values Framework:
Four Models of Organizational Effectiveness**

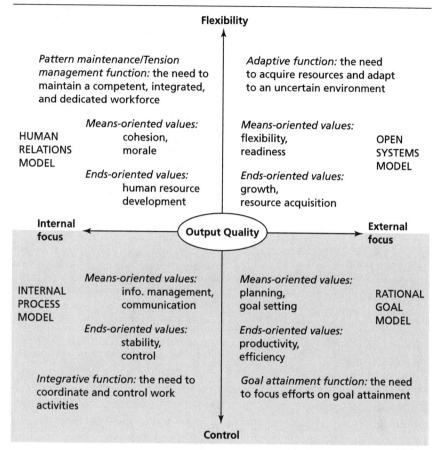

*Pattern maintenance/Tension
management function:* the need to
maintain a competent, integrated,
and dedicated workforce

Adaptive function: the need
to acquire resources and adapt
to an uncertain environment

HUMAN
RELATIONS
MODEL

Means-oriented values:
cohesion,
morale

Means-oriented values:
flexibility,
readiness

OPEN
SYSTEMS
MODEL

Ends-oriented values:
human resource
development

Ends-oriented values:
growth,
resource acquisition

Internal focus ← **Output Quality** → **External focus**

INTERNAL
PROCESS
MODEL

Means-oriented values:
info. management,
communication

Means-oriented values:
planning,
goal setting

RATIONAL
GOAL
MODEL

Ends-oriented values:
stability,
control

Ends-oriented values:
productivity,
efficiency

Integrative function: the need to
coordinate and control work
activities

Goal attainment function: the need
to focus efforts on goal attainment

Flexibility (top) — **Control** (bottom)

SOURCE: Adapted with permission from Figures 3 and 4, Robert O. Quinn and John Rohrbaugh, "A Spatial Model of Effectiveness Criteria: Towards a Competing Values Approach to Organizational Analysis," *Management Science* 29 (March 1983): 363–373. Copyright 1983, The Institute of Management Sciences, now the Institute for Operations Research and the Management Sciences (INFORMS), 901 Elkridge Landing Road, Suite 400, Linthicum, Maryland 21090-2909 USA.

and the associated values of morale and social cohesion. This is entirely possible where managers rely heavily on their formal authority to ensure disciplined obedience and where civil servants are allowed to exercise very little discretion. Weber acknowledged that civil servants are likely to feel trapped in the bureaucratic apparatus but he apparently found this to be a necessary cost of securing disciplined task performance. Weber's analysis notwithstanding, there is more than one way to accomplish the integrative and goal attainment functions. The suggestion that bureaucracy's structural elements provide an effective means for accomplishing these functions is open to question. Bureaucracy provides one means of integrating internal processes and focusing

Exhibit 4.3 Six Mechanisms for Coordinating and Controlling Work Activities

Mutual adjustment	Workers consult with each other informally about what needs to be accomplished and how. Responsibility for coordination and control rests with those who do the work.
Direct supervision	A supervisor is assigned to take responsibility for a group of workers and a managerial hierarchy is established to integrate the efforts of all work groups. The supervisor issues personal instructions and monitors individual performance.
Standardization of work processes	Work is programmed in advance of its execution by developing rules and standard operating procedures specifying how everyone is to perform assigned tasks. Coordination is built into the work process itself and control is achieved by strictly limiting each worker's discretion.
Standardization of work outputs	Work outputs are programmed in advance by providing each work group with product specifications or performance goals and allowing members considerable latitude in determining how to achieve them. Control is exercised by collecting output data, requiring corrective action when needed, and rewarding and sanctioning workers based on results achieved.
Standardization of worker skills	Workers are employed who possess the knowledge and skills needed to make appropriate decisions. Educational institutions and professional associations are relied upon to provide standardized training. Professionally trained workers are largely self-coordinating and self-controlling.
Standardization of values	Organizational leaders communicate and act upon a clear vision of what the organization exists to do, where it should be headed, and what values should guide it. Coordination and control is facilitated by commitment of organizational members to shared, internalized values and ideals.

SOURCE: Based in large part on Henry Mintzberg, *Structure in Fives* (Prentice-Hall, 1993), pp. 3–7.

attention on goal attainment, but one which, if relied upon injudiciously, may prove highly counterproductive. This concern is discussed more fully in the sections that follow.

Mechanisms for Coordinating and Controlling Work Activities

As shown in Exhibit 4.3, Weber's descriptive analysis focuses attention on direct supervision, standardization of work processes, and standardization of worker skills as methods for coordinating and controlling work activities. The arrangement of offices in a hierarchy of authority facilitates **direct supervision.** Each official is expected to comply with the formal directives of the superior officer and to carry them out in a highly disciplined manner. Routine work activities are coordinated and controlled through the **standardization of work processes.** Rules and procedures for handling routine cases are specified by those at the top of the organizational hierarchy. Workers are expected to follow the mandated rules and procedures to the letter. Coordination is built into the work process itself and control is exercised by strictly limiting each worker's discretion so that mistakes are kept to a minimum, workers do not flounder about trying to determine how best to perform their assigned tasks, and each decision is made with complete impartiality.

Direct supervision and standardization of work processes are most applicable in *production* agencies. As noted in Chapter 2, production agencies are characterized by routine work processes, observable outputs and outcomes, and stable environments. Examples include document-processing agencies, such as those charged with reviewing tax returns or applications for licenses, permits, or public assistance. But the use of these structural mechanisms for purposes of coordination and control poses certain problems for agencies including production agencies. One problem inherent in the use of work standardization is that it imposes rigidities on the organization, which, although it promotes predictability of task performance in stable environments, tends to undermine the organization's ability to adapt successfully to a changing environment. In addition, where work tasks require considerable independent judgment and discretion, as is often the case in public agencies, the manner in which tasks are to be performed cannot be programmed in advance. Work standardization tends to work well as a mechanism of coordination and control only when the work is relatively routine and requires little independent judgment.

Another problem inherent in the use of structural control mechanisms is their cost in human terms. Although Weber viewed direct supervision and standardization of work as defining characteristics of modern administration, he understood that these mechanisms could prove counterproductive even in agencies where the work is routine and the environment stable. He described organizations as operating much like a machine, with every part systematically coordinated and controlled. In his words, "The fully developed bureaucratic mechanism compares with other organizations exactly as does the machine with the non-mechanical modes of production."[25] But, although mechanical efficiency may be beneficial from the organization's perspective, Weber acknowledged that it is achieved partly at the bureaucrat's expense. Subject to strict discipline and oppressive routines, officials are reduced to cogs in the larger mechanical apparatus:

> The individual bureaucrat cannot squirm out of the apparatus in which he is harnessed. In contrast to the honorific or avocational "notable," the professional bureaucrat is chained to his activity by his entire material and ideal existence. In the great majority of cases, he is only a single cog in an ever-moving mechanism which prescribes to him an essentially fixed route of march. The official is entrusted with specialized tasks and normally the mechanism cannot be put into motion or arrested by him, but only from the very top.[26]

Weber's use of the machine metaphor underscores the ideal-type bureaucracy's obsession with control. Bureaucracy is deliberately designed to eliminate as much uncertainty as possible and to keep variations in human behavior to a minimum. The bureaucratic machine thus tends to treat bureaucrats as means rather than as ends in themselves, and by restricting each individual's discretion it also tends to rob work of its meaning. As a consequence, motivation and job satisfaction are undermined and conflict is created between supervisors and subordinates. Much of management's time must be devoted to managing the conflicts created by the bureaucratic structure and ameliorating the effects of strict discipline and oppressive routines.

Weber's analysis also draws attention to **standardization of worker skills** as a supplement to direct supervision and work standardization. Weber was among the first to note the distinction between authority based on an official's position in the formal hierarchy and authority based on an official's personal expertise. He acknowledged that as government officials are trained for career service they develop professional norms and skills that enable them to exercise discretion in goal-oriented ways without as much need for direct supervision or work standardization. As the nature of government work has become more complex, knowledge-intensive, and nonroutine, and as the environments in which agencies operate have become more turbulent, the need for government officials to exercise discretion and independent judgment has become much greater. For such agencies, regardless of how measurable their outputs and outcomes may be, standardization of skills has become increasingly relevant as a mechanism for ensuring coordination and control.

This does not mean that hierarchy and rules are no longer important. Organ and Greene found, for example, that while explicit statements of policies and procedures increased role conflict among scientists and engineers, they also increased task clarity and identification with the organization.[27] Structural control mechanisms remain an important management tool, but one with clear limits. Problems tend to arise when organizations insist upon *strict* hierarchical controls and *extensive* routinization. A point is eventually reached beyond which the gains in administrative efficiency are outweighed by the costs associated with organizational rigidity, reduced motivation, and wasted human potential. A highly centralized system characterized by "strict discipline and oppressive routines" is just one of many possible structural arrangements and most likely not the optimal arrangement for most public agencies today.

Motivational Strategies

As indicated in Exhibit 4.4, Weber's theory of bureaucracy emphasizes the **legal compliance strategy.** This strategy involves using formal directives, rules, and sanctions to motivate compliance. Weber viewed bureaucracy as a system of control, a system that increases "the probability that certain specific commands (or all commands) from a given source will be obeyed by a given group of persons."[28] According to Weber, compliance is strongest where it is reinforced by the belief that the institutional order is legitimate and binding. Where this belief exists, officials understand that they are obeying not only their superiors but also an impersonal legal order that they view as legitimate.

Weber's interest in administrative rationality led him to embrace the legal compliance strategy as a means of minimizing variability in human behavior. However, managers seeking to achieve other values—including internal cohe-

Exhibit 4.4 Four Motivational Strategies

Legal Compliance

Using rules, formal directives, and sanctions to direct and control employee behavior. Employees may come to work, comply with rules, and satisfy minimum role requirements, either because they accept the legitimacy of organizational authority or fear being sanctioned.

Instrumental Rewards

Using rewards to induce desired behaviors.

Rewards for Performance

Distributing pay, promotions, and recognition based on individual performance. Employees may meet or exceed role expectations because they value the material and psychological satisfactions that money, advancement, and recognition can provide.

Considerate Leadership

Adopting a leadership style based on being attentive to employees and considerate of their needs. This strategy may improve morale. It might also induce those who value the respect, support, and approval of persons in authority to meet or exceed their role requirements.

Group Acceptance

Creating a work environment that allows employees to socialize, form group bonds, and enjoy the approval of their peers. This strategy may induce those who value affiliation and peer approval to meet or exceed role requirements, assuming that group norms are consistent with organizational objectives.

Job Identification

Offering work that is interesting, challenging, and responsible. Employees may come to work, meet or exceed role requirements, and possibly exhibit greater creativity and innovativeness. They may do so because they identify with the jobs and find their work intrinsically rewarding.

Goal Congruence

Hiring employees whose goals and values are congruent with the organization's and/or socializing employees so that they internalize organizational goals and values. Employees may come to work, remain with the organization, meet or exceed role requirements, and exhibit greater creativity, innovativeness, and institutional loyalty. They may do so because they identify with the organization's mission and values and because contributing to them reinforces their own self concept.

SOURCE: Based in large part on Daniel Katz and Robert L. Kahn, *The Social Psychology of Organizations* (New York: Wiley, 1966), pp. 336–68.

---

sion, productivity, and adaptability—will quickly discover its limitations. The legal compliance strategy may motivate workers to satisfy minimum role requirements but, in the absence of other motivators, it is unlikely to induce workers to perform in a superior manner or demonstrate innovative or adaptive behaviors. In fact, if it is not implemented with infinite care, this strategy can undermine trust, generate resentment, and discourage innovative behaviors. Thus, whereas formal authority is the basis of all legitimate bureaucratic action, its use as a motivational strategy has limitations that Weber may not have fully appreciated.

Because public agencies rely on formal authority to ensure accountability, the key decision confronting managers is not *whether* to adopt the legal compliance strategy but *how* to implement it effectively in combination with other strategies. The difficulty inherent in its use is that it can easily degenerate into autocracy. Concerned with "losing control," supervisors may adopt a command-and-control approach in which they issue commands, exercise close supervision, and enforce rules strictly, while offering no other justification than "I am the boss." Under this approach supervisors insist on obedience not because of their professional expertise or personal qualities but because of the position they hold in the formal chain of command. Over time they lose sight of the fact that there is more than one way to implement the legal compliance strategy. For example, it can be implemented through impersonal rules that prescribe how work is to be performed or through general policy statements that leave considerable discretion to each worker. Similarly, managers can insist upon blind obedience to rules or they can secure consent by explaining the rationale behind them and allowing broad participation in their development. The dysfunctional consequences of taking a rule-driven, punishment-centered approach to management are examined in Chapter 10.

SUMMARY

Weber's implicit theory of organizational effectiveness focuses primarily on administrative rationality. It holds that administrative rationality is achieved by dividing work into specialized administrative functions, assigning each function to a specific office, placing clear limits on each office's scope of authority, arranging all offices in a hierarchy of authority, organizing officials on a career basis, and requiring them to carry out directives with strict discipline and in accordance with clearly delineated rules. Among the most important implications of Weber's analysis for public management and organizational performance are the following:

- **Organizations as rational instruments.** The unfolding process of rationalization described by Weber suggests that government agencies are more than "organized forms of domination." They are also deliberately designed instruments for achieving important societal purposes. Public managers are responsible for adjusting the agency's structure as needed to ensure that it continues to achieve its mandated purposes.

- **Determining the appropriate degree of bureaucratization.** Managers are best served by viewing bureaucracy as a set of structural variables rather than a fixed set of attributes. Public agencies do not need to be tall, highly centralized, and rule-bound to be effective. Managers are responsible for determining the degree of bureaucratization that makes most sense for their agencies in light of their unique missions, environments, and circumstances.

- **A bias toward stability and predictability.** As indicated in Exhibit 4.2, Weber's analysis is biased in favor of organizational stability and predictability of results. Managers who attend disproportionately to these values risk sacrificing the values associated with the human relations and open systems models of effectiveness, including social cohesion, morale, and organizational adaptability.

■ **Structure as a basis for coordination and control.** Weber's ideal-type model reveals how organizational structure can be used to coordinate and control work activities. However, structural controls such as direct supervision and standardized rules and procedures are not equally suited to every situation. Used judiciously, they may be appropriate in production agencies where work is routine and environments stable but less so in other kinds of agencies.

■ **Formal authority as a basis for motivating employees.** The formal authority inherent in supervisory positions provides a basis for "motivating" employees to comply with organizational rules and directives. However, several of the schools of thought discussed in later chapters emphasize the dangers involved in relying too heavily on formal authority to secure compliance. The latter may be obtained at the expense of upward feedback, positive attitudes, and dedication to the job.

In the final analysis Weber's "theory of bureaucracy" remains descriptive in nature. It can help managers think through the relationships between structural variables and organizational performance but it cannot help them determine the degree of bureaucratization that is optimal for their individual agencies. Nonetheless, thinking about bureaucracy in terms of structural variables encourages managers to look for those points on each of several structural dimensions that will allow their agencies to function more efficiently and effectively. It also reminds them that there is no one set of structural arrangements for optimizing organizational performance. Their task is to adjust structural variables continually as internal and external conditions change. In doing so, they must avoid Weberian orthodoxy, the mistaken belief that organizations must be tall, highly centralized, and rule-bound to reap the benefits of increased rationalization. Weberian orthodoxy only serves to constrain efforts to improve organizational performance by discouraging managers from considering administrative reforms that are thought to be inconsistent with Weber's ideal-type bureaucracy.

NOTES

1. Max Weber, *The Protestant Ethic and the Spirit of Capitalism,* translated by Talcott Parsons (New York: Charles Scribner's Sons, 1958).

2. Max Weber, *The Theory of Social and Economic Organization,* translated by A. M. Henderson and Talcott Parsons (New York: Oxford University Press, 1947), 124.

3. Weber, *Theory of Social and Economic Organization,* 324.

4. Max Weber, "Politics as a Vocation," in H. H. Gerth and C. W. Mills (eds.), *From*

Max Weber: Essays in Sociology (New York: Oxford University Press, 1958), 78.

5. Weber, "Politics as a Vocation," 115.

6. Weber, "Politics as a Vocation," 95.

7. Brian R. Fry and Lloyd G. Nigro, "Max Weber and U.S. Public Administration: The Administrator as Neutral Servant," *Journal of Management History 2* (No. 1, 1996), 40.

8. Weber, *Theory of Social and Economic Organization,* 328.

9. Part I of *Wirtschaft und Gesellschaft* is found in Weber, *Theory of Social and Economic Organization.* The discussion of bureaucracy in Part III is found in Gerth and Mills, *From Max Weber.*

10. Weber, *Theory of Social and Economic Organization,* 337.

11. Weber, *From Max Weber,* 198.

12. Henry Mintzberg, *Structure in Fives: Designing Effective Organizations* (Englewood Cliffs, NJ: Prentice-Hall, 1983), 34.

13. Gerth and Mills, *From Max Weber,* 216.

14. Weber, *Theory of Social and Economic Organization,* 339.

15. Weber, *From Max Weber,* 216.

16. Weber, *Theory of Social and Economic Organization,* 337.

17. See, as examples, Stanley H. Udy, "Bureaucracy" and "Rationality" in Weber's "Organization Theory: An Empirical Study," *American Sociological Review 24* (December 1959), 791–95; Richard H. Hall, "The Concept of Bureaucracy: An Empirical Assessment," *American Journal of Sociology 69* (July 1963), 32–40; Charles

M. Bonjean and Michael D. Grimes, "Bureaucracy and Alienation: A Dimensional Approach," *Social Forces 48* (March 1970), 365–73.

18. Donald P. Warwick, *A Theory of Public Bureaucracy: Politics, Personality, and Organization in the State Department* (Cambridge, MA: Harvard University Press, 1975), 183.

19. Dwight Waldo, *Perspectives on Administration* (Birmingham, AL: University of Alabama Press, 1956), 36.

20. Dwight Waldo, "Development of Theory of Democratic Administration," *American Political Science Review 46* (March 1952), 100.

21. David Osborne and Ted Gaebler, *Reinventing Government: How the Entrepreneurial Spirit Is Transforming the Public Sector* (Reading, MA: Addison-Wesley, 1992), 11–16. See also, Ralph P. Hummel, *The Bureaucratic Experience: A Critique of Life in the Modern Organization* (New York: St. Martin's Press, 1994).

22. Elliott Jacques, "In Praise of Hierarchy," *Harvard Business Review 68* (January–February 1990), 127.

23. Jacques, "In Praise of Hierarchy," 128.

24. Jacques, "In Praise of Hierarchy," 133.

25. Weber, *From Max Weber,* 214.

26. Weber, *From Max Weber,* 228.

27. Dennis W. Organ and Charles N. Greene, "The Effects of Formalization on Professional Involvement: A Compensatory Process Approach," *Administrative Science Quarterly 26* (June 1981): 237–52.

28. Weber, *Theory of Social and Economic Organization,* 324.

5

Scientific Management Theory

Frederick W. Taylor

rederick W. Taylor, a machinist and engineer by training, is widely regarded as the father of scientific management. Possessed of a keen sense of
moral purpose and enormous self-discipline, Taylor did more than any
other single individual to systematize industrial production in the early 1900s.
He put all managers on notice, with no particular tact, that it was their duty to
standardize every aspect of production, identify and eliminate all sources of
waste, and base all decisions on careful scientific study. During the 1880s and
1890s he developed a variety of techniques for increasing production that
came to be known as the Taylor system or, alternatively, scientific management.
Understood as a theory of organizational effectiveness, **scientific management** calls for increasing output by systematizing work processes, dividing
work into narrowly defined tasks, determining the "one best way" to perform
each task, training workers in the "one best way," measuring their performance, and offering economic incentives for surpassing daily production quotas. As we shall see, this is essentially a prescriptive theory for directing,
motivating, and controlling work performance.

Whereas Weber's analysis focused on the organization's administrative
structure, Taylor's focused primarily on the shop floor. Despite this difference
in focus, certain similarities in their work emerge on closer examination. Taylor embodied the rationalistic spirit that Weber believed was transforming
modern society. Aware of Taylor's experiments across the Atlantic, Weber
viewed the Taylor system as the deliberate application of reason to the analysis
of work and the management of workers. Both Weber and Taylor perceived

---

Frederick W. Taylor 1856–1915

Taylor was born in Germantown, just outside Philadelphia, in 1856.[1] From his earliest days he had a passion for inventing better ways of doing things. Instead of becoming a lawyer like his father, Taylor chose to become a machinist. He began working at Midvale Steel Company in 1878 at the age of 22. He rose rapidly through the ranks as lathe operator, gang boss, machine shop foreman, and chief engineer for the entire steel works. He studied engineering in the evenings and received a bachelor's degree in mechanical engineering from the Stevens Institute of Technology in 1883. It was during his twelve years at Midvale that Taylor developed the core elements of his system of scientific management.

In 1893 Taylor went into business as a "consulting engineer." During the next several years he refined his management techniques, presenting a paper to the American Society of Mechanical Engineers (ASME) entitled "A Piece-Rate System" in 1895 and one entitled "Shop Management" in 1903. Between 1898 and 1901 he worked exclusively for the Bethlehem Steel Company, systematizing operations and introducing his system of piece rates. Suddenly dismissed in 1901, Taylor chose to retire from paid employment at the age of 45.

Having made lucrative investments, Taylor was able to devote the rest of his life to promoting the cause of scientific management. Taylor helped his longtime associates, Barth, Gantt, Cooke, and Hathaway, introduce scientific management in several organizations, and in 1911 he published *Principles of Scientific Management.* He also invited individuals from all over the world to his home just outside Philadelphia and regaled them with two-hour lectures on the merits of scientific management. Returning from a speaking engagement in Cleveland in 1915 he caught pneumonia and died suddenly at the age of 59.

---

organizations as rational instruments for accomplishing collective goals and both viewed organizational structure as the key to controlling what takes place within them. Their writings share an underlying premise that an efficient organization is one whose parts, both physical and human, are systematically controlled so that goods and services are produced with wondrous precision.

This chapter describes the core components of the Taylor system and assesses Taylor's contributions to organization theory. It closes with an analysis of the relevance of scientific management theory for public management and government performance.

INDUSTRY AND MANAGEMENT IN 1878

When Taylor began working at the Midvale Steel Company in 1878, large-scale industrial production was still in its infancy and management often operated in a state of "near-total confusion."[2] Taylor was one of several far-sighted individuals who recognized that changes in the size and complexity of industrial production called for parallel changes in the structure and practice of management. His ideas for systematizing production and rationalizing management were shaped by the conditions that then prevailed in American industry.

A key characteristic of industry at the time was the absence of middle managers and technical support staffs in the production units. Management was highly decentralized, with the workers and their foremen largely determining what took place in these units. An administrative structure entailing a clear chain of command and an explicit division of responsibilities between line and staff departments was yet to be developed. Administrative support staffs were kept to a bare minimum because they were viewed as "nonproductive" workers and an unwarranted drag on profits. As a consequence, no one was responsible for systematic planning, productivity measurement, or cost accounting. No one was charged with ensuring that raw materials were on hand to fill current orders, that the work was scheduled so that deadlines could be met, or that unnecessary costs were identified and eliminated.

A second characteristic was the inability of managers to exercise effective control over employee productivity. Gang bosses and foremen directed workers in what needed to be accomplished but generally did not presume to tell workers how to accomplish their tasks. This was true particularly for skilled workers who had trained for years to learn a particular craft or trade. It was widely assumed that these workers, not their supervisors, best understood what level of quality and quantity of production was required. The inability to exercise effective supervision was compounded by the fact that managers did not have a clear idea of what defined a fair day's work. Because they did not know how long it should take for a worker to complete a task, supervisors could not rightfully insist upon a particular level of productivity. Their only recourse was to keep continual pressure on employees in an effort to exact as much work as possible.

A third characteristic was the rising level of conflict between labor and management caused by poor working conditions, low pay, and long hours. Facing intense competition, employers believed they could not afford to pay more than subsistence wages or invest in better working conditions. As a result, a growing number of workers joined labor unions and strikes became increasingly common. The violent railroad strike of 1877 was a harbinger of many more to come. Even the most progressive managers found it difficult to succeed in an environment characterized by open warfare between capital and labor.

These three factors—the absence of middle managers and technical staffs to ensure systematic planning, supervisors who exercised little control over the quality and quantity of production, and increasing labor unrest—help define the social and institutional context in which Taylor developed his ideas in the years after 1878. The problems caused by these factors led many individuals to think deeply about how to improve administrative structures and work processes. Unlike most of his contemporaries, however, Taylor developed a unique set of management techniques that were given purpose and coherence by his deeply felt social philosophy.

SCIENTIFIC MANAGEMENT
AS A SOCIAL PHILOSOPHY

Like many Americans, Taylor was genuinely troubled by the poverty, class conflict, and constraints on social mobility associated with advanced industrialization. Taylor's system of scientific management was partly a product of his search for solutions to these problems. The remedy he seized upon was to increase industrial wealth through greater technical efficiency and better management. He believed that increased wealth would translate into higher wages for workers, higher returns on investment for owners, and lower prices for consumers. Everyone stood to benefit; no one stood to lose. Under scientific management, according to Taylor, owners and workers would concentrate on increasing the economic surplus rather than fighting over its division. Managers and workers alike would take their instructions from the scientifically determined best way to perform each task and supervisors would no longer need to resort to coercion.

Although capitalists and socialists alike found Taylor's remedy for reconciling class interests hopelessly naive, Taylor's social philosophy struck a chord with the American public. The efforts of Taylor and others who had entered the field of scientific management came to the attention of the public as the result of the Eastern Rate Case of 1910–11. This case involved a set of hearings held by the Interstate Commerce Commission to determine whether railroads along the east coast would be allowed to raise their rates. Future Supreme Court justice Louis Brandeis represented those opposed to the rate increases. Brandeis seized upon a unique and ultimately successful strategy for defeating the rate increase. Rather than argue about whether the railroads deserved the increase, Brandeis focused the debate on whether they truly needed the increase. He assembled eleven experts to testify that through the elimination of waste the railroads could easily remain profitable without raising rates. Before the hearings began Brandeis asked those testifying to reach an agreement regarding what their system should be called. Taylor had referred to his work at various times as functional management, task management, scientific time study, and scientific management. Others had referred to it as the Taylor system. Those testifying agreed that *scientific management* held the broadest appeal and Taylorism has been known under that name ever since.[3]

The hearings were closely reported in the press and, when Harrington Emerson testified that through the elimination of waste the railroads could "save a million dollars a day," scientific management suddenly became a household word. Hundreds of articles on the subject appeared in the technical and popular press in the months following the hearings. As a result, "Taylorism was transformed overnight from an obscure obsession of certain middle-class engineers to an amazing and highly publicized nostrum for all the ills of society."[4] It had become no less than a social movement. Efficiency societies dedicated to the elimination of waste sprang up in dozens of cities. The American public warmly embraced Taylor's philosophy that eliminating waste is both a moral duty and the key to economic prosperity and social harmony.

THE TAYLOR SYSTEM

If Taylor was not the first to propose a science of management, he was certainly the first to introduce the scientific method into management "as a matter of all-around, consistent, every-day cultivation and practice."[5] Over a period of several years Taylor developed a set of tools and techniques for improving production that he later offered to interested clients as an integrated management system. He did not begin with a particular theory of management, nor did he set out to develop one. Rather, his ideas emerged incrementally as he searched for remedies to the problems he faced as a manager and the social problems of the day.

One such problem was "soldiering," the tendency on the part of workers to work at a slower pace than they were capable of. After being promoted from lathe operator to gang boss, Taylor undertook a three-year battle to obtain a fair day's work from his workers. Although he ultimately succeeded through coercion, punitive fines, and higher pay for those who agreed to increase output, the daily battle nearly destroyed his health. Realizing that there must be a better way to increase individual productivity, Taylor began his search for answers. The problem as he saw it was the absence of performance standards defining a fair day's work. Management simply did not know how long it should take a worker to complete a particular task. In response Taylor experimented with using stopwatches to determine how long it should take to complete a task. He also experimented with various incentive systems for inducing workers to complete the task in the allotted time. The results of these experiments were presented in "A Piece-rate System" at an ASME meeting in 1895.[6]

Taylor also experimented for more than 20 years to determine the proper feed and speed for operating a lathe, given any possible combination of twelve variables. These were true scientific experiments. Taylor held all other variables constant while investigating the effects of one variable on the efficiency with which metals could be cut. As reported in "On the Art of Cutting Metals" in 1906, these experiments resulted in the invention of the Barth slide rule that allowed lathe operators quickly to determine the correct speed and feed for the particular task at hand.[7] During the course of these experiments Taylor and a metallurgist named Maunsel White also invented high-speed steel. They discovered that by heating the new tungsten-chromium steel to extremely high temperatures and then cooling it under a blast of cold air they could produce cutting tools that retained their hardness even when they became red-hot during use. This discovery allowed machines to run at 2 to 4 times their usual speeds, thereby greatly increasing the nation's industrial production.

As a consultant, Taylor tried to convince his clients to adopt his system as a whole. He believed that each and every component was essential to fulfilling his promise of higher output and lower labor costs. For this reason he asked clients to give him at least 3 years to complete the conversion to scientific management. In essence, his system involved getting the right tools and materials to the right place at the right time, providing workers with written instructions for each task, specifying the exact time allowed to complete each element of work, and providing economic incentives to induce workers to complete their tasks in the allotted times. In those rare instances where a client agreed to adopt the Taylor system as a whole, the individual components of the system were implemented in a carefully prescribed way. These components are described in the sections that follow.

Systematization of the Production Process

Upon signing a contract to implement his system Taylor first undertook to systematize the production line. He performed a detailed analysis of the physical layout of the plant and the flow of work through it. Taylor laid out sequentially the steps in the production process so that the product could be routed from one department to the next as quickly and efficiently as possible. Machines performing similar kinds of work were grouped together so that a single foreman could oversee them. The workers were sometimes rearranged as well. In a ball-bearing inspection unit, for example, the inspectors were physically separated from one another so that they could not converse or otherwise disrupt each other's concentration.

Scheduling systems were also introduced to help put production on a more systematic basis. Prior to the introduction of scientific management, production often came to a halt because the storerooms lacked the necessary inventories of raw materials or parts. To address this problem Taylor's associates developed charts for tracking the progress of products as they moved through each step in the production process. Whether presented on paper or on an enormous bulletin board, these charts specified where a product should be at any given time and how long it should take to complete a particular operation before moving to the next stage. By consulting these charts supervisors could easily determine the deadlines they were to meet and the person in charge of the storerooms could easily determine what supplies needed to be delivered to each work station and when. Records were also kept of all incoming and outgoing stock so that the person in charge of the stores could determine what additional supplies to purchase. As a result, time was no longer lost as workers searched for needed materials or waited for them to be purchased.

Systematization of Tools

Taylor or one of his associates also systematized the tool room so that every tool had a stated purpose and was designed and maintained to rigid standards. Instead, a specialist was put in charge of the tool room to make sure that tools were properly stored, maintained, and distributed to workers according to their assigned tasks. Although his critics believed this introduced too much complexity, Taylor insisted that "It is far simpler to have all of the tools in a standardized shop ground by one man to a few simple but rigidly maintained shapes than to have, as is usual in the old style shop, each machinist spend a portion of each day at the grindstone, grinding his tools with radically wrong curves and cutting angles, merely because bad shapes are easier to grind than good."[8]

Standardization of Work

Work standardization involved determining the best way to perform each task and then communicating it to workers through on-the-job training and daily written instructions. Machinists, for example, were issued instructions regarding what tasks to perform, what feed and speed to use, and how long it should take to complete each task. All work was to be performed as prescribed by management. Taylor's intent was to safeguard the quality and quantity of production from procedural mistakes, failures of memory, and ignorance of how best to perform specific tasks. Scientifically determined work standards provided supervisors a means of holding workers accountable for the quality and quantity of their work.

Work standardization was accomplished through task setting and time study. **Task setting**, as Taylor and Gantt used the term, is the process of defining what a worker is expected to do and how long it should take to do it. For example, Taylor "set the task" for pig iron handlers at 47 tons per day, for lathe operators at 10 steel forgings per day, and for sewing machine operators at two garments per minute. **Time study** refers to the use of the stopwatch to make these determinations. The first step is to identify through observation the elementary motions that comprise a job, and the second is to establish the appropriate unit times for each element. For example, Taylor identified the elements and unit times for pig iron handling as follows:[9]

Pig Iron Handling

Work elements	Unit times
1. Picking up the pig from the ground or pile	time in hundredths of a minute
2. Walking with it on a level	time per foot walked
3. Walking with it up an incline	time per foot walked
4. Throwing the pig down	time in hundredths of a minute
5. Walking back empty to get another load	time per foot walked

The third step in time study is to determine the "standard time" for each element. This is the "quickest time" in which an element can be accomplished by a "first-class man." Taylor typically selected one or two of the best workers for the time-study experiments and induced them to participate by offering significantly higher rates of pay. They were then instructed to perform work elements while a time-study specialist repeatedly recorded the times for each element. The standard time for the task as a whole was determined by taking the average time to complete each element, adding the times for all of the elements together, and adding an additional amount of time for rest breaks and unavoidable delays. In this way it was determined that by carrying pigs in the standard time all day long a worker could move 47 tons without experiencing long-term fatigue. Since pig iron handlers at the Bethlehem Steel Company had previously carried about 12 tons per day on average, this represented nearly a 300 percent increase in productivity.

Taylor believed that tasks should be "set" at the highest possible level without causing cumulative fatigue in the worker. At Bethlehem Steel, for example, the "tasks were all purposefully made so severe that not more than 1 out of 5 laborers (perhaps even a smaller percentage than this) could keep up."[10] In practice, productivity increased 350 percent because only the strongest and quickest workers continued to work as pig handlers. The others quit or were reassigned to other duties. Although Taylor considered this a form of scientific selection, it was also a form of natural selection.[11] Under the Taylor system, only the strongest, quickest, or most dexterous tended to survive. When Gantt set the task for the ball-bearing inspectors at the Simonds Company, for example, many of the most dependable workers were laid off simply because they were not among the most dexterous.[12]

Wage Incentive Systems

Many companies had adopted piecework systems in the 1870s to motivate employees to be more productive. Taylor concluded that these systems actually discouraged higher productivity because workers knew that employers tended to reduce the price per piece over time to keep labor costs low. This was the primary cause of what Taylor called **systematic soldiering**. To eliminate soldiering Taylor developed his differential piecerate system. Believing that both the carrot and the stick were needed to motivate employees, his system promised a high wage when a task was finished in the allotted time and without defects, and a low wage when the task was not finished in the allotted time or had imperfections. For example,

> Under the differential rate system, if a workman finishes 20 pieces per day, and all of these pieces are perfect, he receives, say, 15 cents per piece, making his pay for the day 15 × 20 = $3. If, however, he works too slowly and turns out, say, only 19 pieces, then, instead of receiving 15 cents per piece he gets only 12 cents per piece, making his pay for the day 12 × 19 = $2.28, instead of $3 per day. If he succeeds in finishing 20 pieces, some of which are imperfect, then he should receive a still lower rate of pay, say 10 cents or 5 cents per piece, according to the circumstances, making his pay for the day $2, or only $1, instead of $3.[13]

Workers who completed their tasks in the allotted times were rewarded with wages that were 30–100 percent above the prevailing wage, those who produced anything less than the assigned task received less than the prevailing wage, and those whose work contained defects received a wage below the subsistence level. As intended, the latter either quit or asked for reassignment.

Taylor claimed that his system determined a fair day's work through scientific experimentation rather than guesswork. This, he claimed, is what made his system unique. Employers no longer had cause to reduce the price per piece because they knew through scientific study how long it should take to perform a task. By inducing significantly higher levels of productivity from workers, employers could afford to pay significantly higher wages in return. The latter was indispensable, according to Taylor, because "men will not do an extraordinary day's work for an ordinary day's pay."[14] In Taylor's words, the differential piecerate system "makes each workman's interests the same as that of his employer, pays a premium for high efficiency, and soon convinces each man that it is for his permanent advantage to turn out each day the best quality and quantity of work."[15] Further, the system promotes "a most friendly feeling between the men and their employers, and so renders labor unions and strikes unnecessary."[16]

Despite these claims, Taylor offered employers a rather severe system of rewards and punishments, a system reflecting his own stringent moral views. He believed that requiring the absolute best from workers builds moral character, whereas allowing them to do less than their best contributes to their moral decay. He also believed that paying them too much contributes to moral decay. Whereas higher pay is necessary to induce workers "to become and remain ambitious and energetic,"[17] and causes them "to save money, become more sober, and work more steadily,"[18] too much money can have the opposite effect:

> It is the writer's judgment . . . that for their own good it is as important that workmen should not be very much over-paid, as it is that they should not be under-paid. If over-paid, many will work irregularly and then to become more or less shiftless, extravagant and dissipated. It does not do for most men to get rich too fast.[19]

In practice, the differential rate system was rarely implemented. Employers and workers alike viewed it as overly severe because it mandated punitive wage cuts for any level of production beneath the scientifically determined level. In the example cited above, the worker who produced 19 pieces—significantly more than had been produced in the past—received no economic reward because he had missed the mandated target by one. For this reason Gantt's task and bonus system was adopted by employers much more often. Under this plan economic bonuses began at the average worker's level of output and became progressively greater with higher levels of output. It was much less punitive because workers never received less than the standard daily wage.

Functional Foremanship

Once the tools, methods, and processes were standardized and incentive systems put in place, the Taylor system charged managers with enforcing the "natural laws of production." Taylor believed that this responsibility was so broad in scope that no single supervisor could fulfill it. He believed that in practice supervisors attended only to those aspects of management that they were most comfortable with and neglected the rest. Consistent with the specialization principle, Taylor advocated replacing the military type of organization with its single chain of command with a functional type in which workers received daily orders from eight different bosses. "Functional management," Taylor said, "consists in so dividing the work of management that each man from the assistant superintendent down shall have as few functions as possible to perform. If practicable the work of each man in the management should be confined to the performance of a single leading function."[20]

Under the Taylor system, four line supervisors provided direct and immediate supervision, making sure that plans were quickly and fully executed but performing no planning or clerical duties themselves. The **gang boss** prepared the work setting by making sure that required materials were available and that each worker understood how best to perform the assigned task. The **speed boss** made sure that the proper tools and methods were used so that the task could be performed in the quickest time possible. The **inspector** made sure that quality standards were met, and the **repair boss** saw to it that each worker kept his machines properly maintained.

The other four foremen were staff supervisors who worked out of the planning department and communicated with workers primarily through written instructions. Under the Taylor system workers and bosses alike had to be taught to provide strict obedience to instructions from the planning staff, something not required of them under the military conception of line-staff relationships. The **routing clerk** instructed workers and supervisors regarding the exact order in which the work was to be done by each class of machines and workers so that all production remained on schedule. The **instruction card clerk** provided daily written instructions to each worker regarding the details of task performance, including the tools to use, the procedures to follow, the quota to be made, and the bonus to be paid. The **time and cost clerk** provided daily forms to workers on which they recorded how much they produced and in what length of time. Finally, the **shop disciplinarian** imposed appropriate sanctions on workers who violated workplace rules.

Taylor believed that functional foremanship prevented important elements of management from falling between the cracks. In practice, however, this system never caught on, both because it blurred the boundaries between line and staff authority and because eight separate supervisors were not truly needed. But, although it was never instituted as described in Taylor's essay on shop management, many employers did establish technical staffs to assist traditional supervisors perform the full range of their managerial responsibilities.

The components of the Taylor system described above represented a basic model for implementing scientific management. Taylor understood that his system must be adapted to the unique conditions and requirements of each company. Rarely, however, did clients commit themselves to the 3 to 5 years that it took to implement the system and the enormous expenses it required. More often they allowed some modest efforts at standardization to occur and then insisted that a piecerate system be introduced. Under pressure from boards of directors and investors, factory superintendents needed to show results immediately. Because Taylor and his associates resisted introducing ad hoc reforms, they unintentionally created enormous business opportunities for other "efficiency engineers" who were willing to do what their clients asked, whether or not it entailed an integrated system of management.

TAYLOR'S IMPLICIT THEORY OF ORGANIZATIONAL EFFECTIVENESS

During the last twelve years of his life Taylor's friends pleaded with him to articulate his underlying theory for the benefit of posterity. Trained as an engineer, Taylor was not comfortable with theorizing. Nonetheless, he wrote *Principles of Scientific Management* in 1909 with this purpose in mind and published it in 1911. Although it does not present a comprehensive theory of management, it does identify four basic principles:

> *First.* The development of a true science. *Second.* The scientific selection of the workman. *Third.* His scientific education and development. *Fourth.* Intimate friendly cooperation between the management and the men.[21]

Taylor later described the first principle as "the deliberate gathering together of the great mass of traditional knowledge which, in the past, has been in the heads of the workmen, recording it, tabulating it, reducing it in most cases to rules, laws, and in many cases to mathematical formulae, which, with these new laws, are applied to the cooperation of the management to the work of the workmen."[22] Here he refers to the use of time-and-motion study and other forms of scientific experimentation to establish what he called the natural laws of production. The second and third principles call for selecting workers based on their ability to perform the assigned task and training them in the proper methods. The final principle reflects Taylor's belief that the planning of work must be separated from its execution. Accordingly, management must take responsibility for planning the work, including what needs to be done, when, and how, and workers must take responsibility for executing the work as directed. To Taylor, this was a fair, just, and mutually beneficial division of labor.

Implicit in Taylor's four principles are six concepts that help define his underlying theory of organizational effectiveness. As introduced at the beginning of the chapter, Taylor's theory holds that effectiveness—defined primarily in terms of productivity and total output—is achieved by narrowly dividing work, standardizing how each task is performed, training workers in the "one best way," paying them bonuses for surpassing daily production quotas, and instituting centralized planning. Most of these concepts were not new at the time Taylor wrote. What was new was the particular way that Taylor melded them into a unique theory of management colored by his own ideological biases.

Task Specialization

Taylor theorized that task efficiency is the primary determinant of industrial output and he took it for granted that narrowly divided work provided the basis for efficient task performance. In 1776 Adam Smith described how dividing pinmaking into eighteen narrowly defined operations, and requiring workers to perform one or two of these operations all day long, caused productivity to increase dramatically.[23] When Taylor began developing his theory of management a century later he simply took the advantages of task specialization for granted. When asked by a special committee of the U.S. House of Representatives in 1912 whether scientific management advocated fragmenting work into narrowly defined tasks, Taylor responded that it advocated no greater fragmentation than found in most manufacturing firms at that time. Although critics charged that scientific management destroyed craftsmanship, including the personal pride and quality of work that comes from applying skills, exercising discretion, and producing an entire piece of work, the truth is that the Industrial Revolution had undermined craftsmanship long before Taylor came on the scene.[24] Rightly or wrongly, Taylor accepted task specialization as a necessary feature of the industrial age.

Although the general concept was taken for granted, Taylor took special interest in one aspect of task specialization. In 1832 Charles Babbage described how significant savings in labor costs could be achieved by taking all routine tasks away from skilled craftsmen and reassigning them to unskilled laborers.[25] This allowed factories to employ fewer craftsmen and hire cheap, unskilled laborers in their place. It was this practice that Taylor adopted whenever possible. He felt justified in doing so not only because it reduced labor costs but also because he believed craft expertise was highly overrated, being based on "the rule of thumb" or pure guesswork rather than science.

Work Standardization

Viewed from a theoretical perspective, if task specialization created the potential for efficient task performance, work standardization provided the means for realizing that potential. In his early days at Midvale, Taylor noticed that there was no uniformity in the way tasks were performed, even among skilled craftsmen. He thus set out to standardize work by determining the most efficient way to perform each task and then reducing it to standard operating procedures and performance standards. As an element in Taylor's larger theory governing ways to control human effort and maximize industrial productivity, work standardization promises three constructive results. First, it promotes consistency and predictability. Supervisors can expect good work from employees day in and day out because the best practices in every line of work have been carefully prescribed for them. Product variability due to inexperience and human error is kept to a minimum. Second, Taylor's theory depersonalizes the authority relationship between supervisors and workers. At least in theory, instances of arbitrary or autocratic supervision should no longer occur because supervisors as well as workers take their guidance from the "one best way." Finally, a standardized task coupled with a standardized time for completing it provide the foundation for inducing motivation through the use of economic rewards.

Economic Rewards

A cornerstone of Taylor's theory of management is the use of economic rewards to induce higher levels of productivity. Although he recognized that many factors affect motivation, including fair treatment and opportunities for advancement, Taylor believed that only economic incentives are sufficiently powerful to bring an end to soldiering. Maximum output cannot be achieved, he argued, simply by exhorting employees to work harder or by instilling them with fear. Rather, soldiering can be eliminated only by appealing to individual self-interest by promising significantly higher wages in exchange for achieving the highest possible level of output. Without the use of individual economic incentives, Taylor argued, workers will collude to restrict productivity and the output of the most slothful will become the standard for the work group as a whole. In Taylor's theory of scientific management, cooperation was something to be purchased and group solidarity something to be destroyed.

Performance Measurement

With production goals set and the methods of task performance systematically prescribed, mechanisms were still needed to ensure that desired results were being achieved. Part of Taylor's theory included the belief that hard data should provide the basis for making management decisions. Taylor deserves much of the credit for introducing performance measurement systems into management, not only to measure individual performance but also the performance of the organization as a whole. He found it deeply troubling that production managers in the late 1800s relied almost exclusively on instinct, common sense, and experience. Taylor believed that all management questions should be determined on the basis of factual data. So that this might become a matter of routine, Taylor developed several performance measurement systems. Workers were given cards on which to record at the end of the day how much they had produced and in what amount of time. Not only was this information used to determine each worker's daily wage, it was also used for productivity measurement and cost accounting. Individual productivity data, for example, were recorded on bar charts. By analyzing these charts supervisors could quickly determine when workers were having trouble earning their bonuses and could intervene to identify and redress the causes.

For Taylor, performance measurement was more than a management tool. It was an integral part of his theory of human and institutional control: everything must be carefully pre-planned, with performance measurement being the vehicle for determining whether actual results match desired results. If they do not, managers must take steps to close the performance gap. And, because somebody must be responsible for performance planning, data collection, and corrective action, Taylor's theory called for centralized planning with its attendant separation between planning and doing work.

Centralized Planning and Control

At the heart of scientific management theory lies the idea that operations can and should be centrally planned and controlled by experts using scientific methods. "The problem which faces modern scientific management," Taylor once said, "is the daily control and the direction of what at first appears to be an almost uncontrollable multitude of movements of men, of machines, of small implements, of materials, and of parts in process."[26] He understood very well that it is one thing to discover the natural laws of production and quite another thing to enforce them. The latter requires the exercise of intense control. Consequently, the Taylor system called for a central planning office comprising planners, efficiency experts, engineers, and clerks dedicated to standardizing and controlling every aspect of production. Taylor intended that once these systems were in place control would be exercised as a matter of routine, largely independent of the managers themselves.

At issue was not simply *how* to control the various aspects of production but *who* should do the controlling. The Taylor system was explicitly designed to take control of production away from the workers. Taylor states in his essay on shop management that "we propose to take all of the important decisions and planning which vitally affect the output of the shop out of the hands of the workmen, and centralize them in a few men, each of whom is especially trained in the art of making those decisions and seeing that they are carried out. . . ."[27] Although Taylor's critics appreciated the importance of increased efficiency, many of them objected strongly to the principle that workers should be totally excluded from planning and decision making. Taylor insisted, however, that his control-centered view of the employment relationship was justified by the fact that workers possessed neither the knowledge nor the will to discover the natural laws of production.

Overview of Scientific Management Theory

Taken together, these concepts represent a top-down, control-oriented approach to management in which workers are told exactly how to do their jobs by management specialists and are rewarded financially for working as quickly and efficiently as possible. According to his contemporary critics, as well as later generations of organization theorists, it is an approach that encourages a culture of distrust—distrust of the workers' commitment to organizational goals and distrust of their ability to decide for themselves how best to do their jobs. When put into practice it redistributes power in the workplace so that workers have less and managers more.

Although Taylor's critics were quick to point out the human and institutional costs flowing from a top-down, control-oriented approach, scientific management was undeniably successful in boosting industrial production in the early 1900s and was quickly adopted by industrialists in Europe, Japan, and Leninist Russia. Because Taylor's theory possesses a certain internal logic, it continues to influence management thinking today, not just in factories but in office settings. It makes a certain amount of sense, after all, to set goals, systematize operations, prescribe ways to perform tasks, set standards, measure performance, and reward effort. An important question addressed in later schools of thought is whether the more valuable methods of scientific management might not be applied to advantage in a less distrustful, less top-down and control-oriented manner.

CRITICISMS OF
SCIENTIFIC MANAGEMENT THEORY

Scientific management theory has been criticized on both theoretical and practical grounds, and by contemporaries of Taylor as well as more recent theorists. The sections that follow discuss four of these criticisms: that it robbed workers of human dignity by treating them as extensions of the machine, that it was hostile to the values and goals of organized labor, that it constituted no more than pseudoscience, and that it was overly obsessed with control at the expense of human needs.

Workers as Cogs in the Industrial Machine

Schools of thought are sometimes distinguished by a particular metaphor or image that captures how theorists view organizations.[28] Trained in mechanical engineering, Taylor tended to view organizations as inert, rational machines and workers as cogs in the larger industrial apparatus. His more humanistic critics argued that scientific management treated workers and machines in the same way, standardizing both and running them as fast as possible. That Taylor intended to speed up the pace of work was clear to everyone who read his work, despite his frequent denials. At various times Taylor described scientific management as achieving "maximum speeds," "quickest times," and "the maximum productivity of each machine and man."

For humanistic critics both then and now, treating workers as things to be "engineered" like any other aspect of production dehumanizes and enslaves them by robbing them of autonomy and personal dignity. As will be seen in later chapters, many of the organization theorists that came after Taylor emphasized the human and institutional costs arising from a mechanical view of organizations. These concerns notwithstanding, the idea that organizations can and should be designed to operate as well-oiled machines is a powerful one, one that continues to shape management thinking today.

Organized Labor's Counterattack

Members of organized labor criticized scientific management both because of its dehumanizing aspects and because it threatened their immediate interests. The industrial harmony that Taylor had promised never materialized. Scientific management evoked a counterattack from labor leaders for several reasons. First, it threatened to reduce the scope of collective bargaining. The natural laws of production, according to Taylor, were not subject to debate. With wages, methods, and output determined by the planning room, scientific management left little for workers to bargain over. Second, scientific management put people out of work. Taylor was quite explicit about the savings in labor costs that accrue as one worker is induced to accomplish what had previously been accomplished by two. Third, scientific management threatened to destroy the trade and craft unions. High wages for craftsmen could not be maintained if management succeeded in replacing them with unskilled workers. Fourth, labor leaders believed that by denying workers an opportunity to learn a trade, scientific management condemned them to a monotonous routine and deprived them of initiative and a sense of achievement.[29]

These concerns, taken together, caused labor leaders to view scientific management as far more than a technical innovation. To them it represented a new system of authority and control, one that dehumanized workers, greatly reduced their involvement in management decisions, and threatened to destroy unions altogether. Thus, when scientific management rose to national prominence during the Eastern Rate Case of 1911, labor leaders decided they had no choice but to counterattack. They focused their efforts on several government-owned arsenals that were implementing the Taylor system. Labor leaders feared that if Taylorism was allowed to succeed in government it would quickly catch hold in the private sector. Accordingly, they demonized scientific management in labor publications and encouraged workers in government arsenals to resist the introduction of the Taylor system. Late in the summer of 1911 several molders at the Watertown Arsenal outside of Boston went on strike for more than a week as a protest against the introduction of time study.[30]

The molders at Watertown took their case directly to the House of Representatives, which immediately appointed a committee of three congressmen to investigate the Taylor system. Hearings were held from October 4, 1911 to February 12, 1912, with Taylor testifying for four days in late January. The committee's final report identified problems with the use of the stopwatch but concluded that the adoption of any particular management system was an administrative decision. There was no reason to recommend corrective legislation. Labor leaders nonetheless maintained pressure on Congress, and in 1915 they succeeded in securing amendments to the Army and Navy appropriations bills that outlawed the use of the stopwatch in government installations. This prohibition continued in effect until 1949.

After Taylor's death in 1915 scientific management advocates gradually made peace with organized labor. Although Taylor believed that industrial democracy and scientific management were inherently opposed, most of his followers did not. In the aftermath of the Watertown strike they applauded the government arsenals for allowing collective bargaining over piecerates, setting up labor-management committees, and establishing formal grievance systems. By the 1920s the Taylor Society had become the foremost advocate of union-management cooperation.[31]

Scientific Management as Pseudoscience

Scientific management was also criticized in the early 1900s as being far from scientific. In 1914 the U.S. Commission on Industrial Relations, a study commission created by Congress, appointed Robert F. Hoxie to investigate the apparently irreconcilable claims of organized labor and scientific management. During the early months of 1915 Hoxie visited thirty-five shops where scientific management had been introduced. His final report documented the enormous gulf between theory and practice. Hoxie concluded that, although scientific management claimed to establish a code of natural laws equally binding upon employers and workers through careful scientific study, it generally failed to do so in practice. The methods used to select workers, determine the time to complete tasks, and establish a fair day's wage were not truly scientific in nature. Tainted by value judgments, questionable inferences, and measurement errors, they amounted to little more than pseudoscience.

For example, Hoxie found the centerpiece of the Taylor system, time study and task setting, to be much less scientific than its advocates claimed. Hoxie concluded that "far from being the invariable and purely objective matters that they are pictured, the methods and results of time study and task setting are, in practice, the special sport of individual judgment and opinion, subject to all the possibilities of diversity, inaccuracy, and injustice that arise from human ignorance and prejudice."[32] First, Hoxie wrote, even if time study can accurately measure the time in which a task could be performed, it cannot determine the time in which a task should be performed. The latter always calls for a value judgment. Taylor believed that all workers should meet the standard set by a "first-class worker," but others believed work standards should be based on an "average, steady man." Value decisions such as these determined the pace at which individuals had to work to earn their bonuses.

Hoxie also concluded that time study cannot determine with any degree of accuracy the time in which a task could in fact be performed. For time study to be truly scientific the investigator's judgment must not affect the results. Yet Hoxie identified seventeen variables that may undermine scientific objectivity. One of these is the investigator's level of knowledge about the work under study. Dwight Merrick, the time-study specialist at the Watertown Arsenal, possessed no knowledge of the work performed in the arsenal's foundry. In the wake of the Watertown strike he was asked how he had determined that the task under investigation could be performed in 24 minutes when it traditionally had taken 53 minutes. His response was that he had simply guessed at which motions were unnecessary or wasteful: "I was more or less at a loss to know what time to set upon the job, but I am very confident that I didn't get a true observation. . . . I felt that 30 minutes was too long a time for it, and I made a guess at 24 minutes."[33]

Lastly, Hoxie found that the economic surplus resulting from increased production was not divided between employers and workers on the basis of science. Productivity often increased between 200 and 300 percent, whereas wages were set at between 30 and 100 percent above prevailing market wages. In practice, wage setting seemed to reflect a clear value judgment: Wages should be set at the lowest level at which full cooperation from workers could be secured. As noted earlier, Taylor believed high wages only encouraged moral decay.

Hoxie's characterization of scientific management as pseudoscience was not intended to discredit the theory itself. He personally believed that the destruction of craft unions was inevitable, that scientific management offered a relatively progressive approach to management, and that new social-science

techniques would be developed to place management on a more rational basis. To a certain extent Hoxie simply documented the failure of employers to
implement scientific management in accordance with Taylor's instructions.
Nonetheless, his findings tended to undermine key aspects of the theory itself.
For example, if the best ways to perform work cannot be reduced to scientifically determined laws without entailing fundamental value judgments, then
the justification for refusing to involve workers in policy and operational decisions is greatly undermined.

Taylor's Obsession with Control

An early biography of Taylor written by Frank Copley paints a vivid picture of
a personality defined by a strong work-centered morality and an obsession
with control.[34] Taylor clearly placed a high value on hard work, self-discipline,
and orderliness. Whether gardening, playing golf, or managing a factory, Taylor
sought to reduce every aspect of his life to a well-ordered system for accomplishing his purposes. He also tended to embrace ideas with the fanaticism of
an extremist. His obsession with rationality and control no doubt influenced
his theory of scientific management. It is apparent, for example, in the establishment of a planning room to coordinate and control every aspect of production, in the use of eight functional foremen to enforce the natural laws of
production, in reliance upon an especially punitive pay-for-performance system to induce maximum individual productivity, in an absolute refusal to give
voice to workers except as isolated individuals, and in an insistence that clients
adopt every element of his system.

For Taylor, simplifying, standardizing, and systematizing were necessary but
not sufficient conditions for maximizing output. In addition, workers had to
be made to work at their "quickest speeds." Tasks were to be set at levels at
which workers had to concentrate hard and continuously on the task at hand.
Workers were to be prohibited from speaking to each other so as not to inter-
rupt each other's concentration. And, because workers were inclined to restrict
output and were generally ignorant of how to perform their tasks well, all control had to reside with management.

Unfortunately, Taylor's personality and training as an engineer created blind
spots regarding basic human needs. Approaching every problem from a technical orientation, he "saw no reason for introducing psychological, humanistic,
or philosophic factors into a system which he considered as complete and sufficient."[35] His responses to questions put to him by members of the Special
House Committee investigating Taylorism showed little appreciation for the
potential human costs of dividing work narrowly, increasing the pace of work,
and refusing to allow employees to participate in decision making. Taylor's
work-centered morality and obsession with control were responsible for much
of the resistance to scientific management by labor unions and humanists.

It is important to emphasize, however, that Taylor's personal obsession with
control was not a defining characteristic of the larger scientific management
movement. Other advocates, most of whom were also trained as engineers, did

not share Taylor's emphasis on control, maximum work pace, and hostility to labor unions. Nor did they pursue changes in the workplace with an all-or-nothing attitude; any improvements were cause for rejoicing.

Frank and Lillian Gilbreth offered the clearest alternative to Taylorism. To the Gilbreths, motion study was superior to time study in both purpose and principle. Frank Gilbreth succeeded in increasing productivity dramatically in his clients' firms simply through the elimination of unnecessary motions. Frank and Lillian believed that workers did not need to be speeded up. Fewer motions, rather than quicker motions, was the key. Productivity could be increased significantly, they argued, by selecting good workers, showing them how to perform their tasks efficiently, and turning them loose to use their skills to best advantage. Although their approach also involved systematizing the workplace, the value toward which their efforts aimed was, first and foremost, efficiency rather than control. In short, Taylorism and scientific management were not altogether synonymous. Many progressive reformers of the early 1900s could see beyond Taylor's personal obsession with control to those aspects of scientific management that represented long-overdue and constructive management reforms.

SCIENTIFIC MANAGEMENT
IN THE PUBLIC SECTOR

In the early 1900s progressive reformers seized upon scientific management as a means of reducing graft, corruption, and waste in government. When the reform mayor of Philadelphia asked Taylor to head the city's public works department in 1911, Taylor recommended Morris L. Cooke for the job. Cooke saw this as an opportunity to showcase scientific management and to demonstrate the relevance of Taylor's four principles to government.[36] But, whereas the Taylor system of shop management centered on the elimination of soldiering, scientific management in the public sector emphasized standardization, fact-based decision making, and the search for better work methods. At the public works department, for example, Cooke studied how to pave streets and remove snow more efficiently. He also collected data to show that the utility companies were not satisfying their contractual obligations to the city. Taylor and Cooke viewed efficiency as an important value, but only as a means to an end. In the factory the goal was to increase production. In the public agency, by contrast, the goal was to improve the agency's responsiveness to public demands, including the demand for a certain level of service delivered in an efficient and effective manner. Being responsive required systematic and scientific study of how to deliver services better and how to measure agency performance. In short, Cooke viewed scientific management as a vehicle for fulfilling the promises of democracy.

The impact of scientific management in the public sector may have been much smaller had it not been for the Progressive reform movement and the municipal research bureaus. The first of these bureaus, the New York Bureau of Municipal Research, was established in 1906. Others soon followed in Chicago, Cincinnati, Milwaukee, and Philadelphia. The leaders of these bureaus were strong advocates of scientific management. They worked to systematize and standardize government operations using scientific methods much as Taylor had done in manufacturing firms. Their primary aim was to conduct the kind of research, and gather the kind of information, that would improve government efficiency and allow citizens to hold elected officials accountable for government's performance. The innovations they helped introduce into government are numerous. They include standardized accounting procedures, standardized job descriptions and salary structures, individual performance appraisal techniques, agency performance standards, standardized statistical reporting of performance data, centralized purchasing of supplies, comprehensive planning, management training, survey research, and systematic policy analysis and program evaluation.

Originally designed "to drive waste out of city government and to make graft unprofitable,"[37] these innovations soon became standard features of public management. The interest in maximizing efficiency spread quickly to the state and federal levels as well. In 1910 President Taft established the Commission on Economy and Efficiency to improve the transaction of public business in all federal departments, and many state and local governments established similar commissions.

SCIENTIFIC MANAGEMENT THEORY
IN PERSPECTIVE

It became fashionable among scholars in the late 1940s to demean Taylor's contribution to organization theory because of his patronizing attitude toward workers, his rather limited understanding of human psychology, his vehement opposition to unions, his obsession with control, and his blindness to the dehumanizing effects of simplifying and standardizing work.[38] Prior to this time, scientific management had generally been viewed as a modern approach to management, one which was quite progressive in its concern for doing things more efficiently, training and developing workers, and replacing autocratic management with the rule of law. The advocates of scientific management who attended Taylor Society meetings were willing to separate Taylor's core concepts—standardization of work, performance measurement, pay-for-performance, elimination of waste, and centralized planning—from his personal and philosophical prejudices. Today there are many who continue to regard these core concepts as important contributors to organizational performance.

Nonetheless, when scientific management is viewed as a set of value-laden ideas rather than value-neutral methods, it begins to appear in a much less progressive light. Understood as a theory of management, scientific management calls for centralized planning and control, routinization of work, withholding of discretion and initiative, and reliance on extrinsic motivators. And it rests on the assumption that everything can and should be managed. The final question for us to consider is whether this top-down, control-oriented theory of management holds any relevance for public agencies.

RELEVANCE FOR PUBLIC MANAGEMENT

The remainder of this chapter explores the relevance of scientific management theory for public management and agency performance using the three analytical frameworks introduced in Chapter 3.

Models of Organizational Effectiveness

As indicated by the shaded quadrants in Exhibit 5.1, scientific management theory emphasizes the values associated with the rational goal and internal process models, most notably efficiency, productivity, and predictability. Located at the bottom of Quinn's framework, these quadrants are clearly biased toward control at the expense of flexibility. The **rational goal model** emphasizes planning and goal setting as means, and efficiency and productivity as ends. This model is reflected in Taylor's beliefs that planning and goal setting must be centralized in the hands of management and that every aspect of work must be designed to increase output.

The values associated with the **internal process model** are also apparent in Taylor's theory of scientific management. As indicated in Exhibit 5.1, this model emphasizes the use of formal communications and information management systems to ensure that work processes are carried out in a rational and predictable manner. This model is reflected in Taylor's efforts to maximize predictability by systematizing internal processes, routinizing work, and monitoring work performance. The development and use of information management systems is one of scientific management's most enduring contributions to management practice.

Although efficiency, productivity, and predictability are important values, scientific management's emphasis on the goal attainment and integrative functions is troubling in two respects. First, managers who focus on integration and goal attainment may do so at the expense of the adaptive function. For example, standard operating procedures defining the one best way often create rigidities that undermine the organization's ability to adapt successfully to changing circumstances. Taylor's theory showed little awareness of the environment outside of the organization or the importance of individual discretion in helping organizations adapt to change. A theory that aims to make man and machine operate like clockwork has limited applicability for public agencies because they often function in turbulent and politicized environments in which goals, technologies, and situational factors are constantly changing. In such environments it is very difficult to standardize work and formalize rules and still maintain the capacity to adapt successfully to changing conditions.

**Exhibit 5.1 The Competing Values Framework:
Four Models of Organizational Effectiveness**

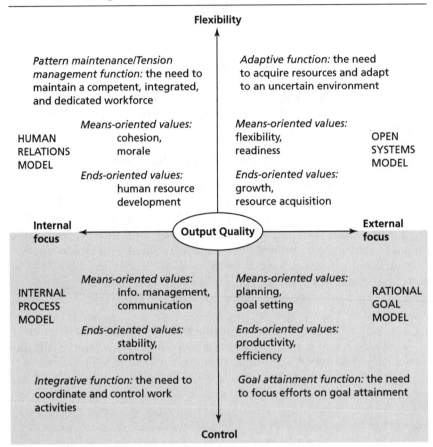

SOURCE: Adapted with permission from Figures 3 and 4, Robert O. Quinn and John Rohrbaugh, "A Spatial Model of Effectiveness Criteria: Towards a Competing Values Approach to Organizational Analysis," *Management Science* 29 (March 1983): 363–373. Copyright 1983, The Institute of Management Sciences, now the Institute for Operations Research and the Management Sciences (INFORMS), 901 Elkridge Landing Road, Suite 400, Linthicum, Maryland 21090-2909 USA.

Second, managers who focus on the integration and goal attainment functions may do so at the expense of the pattern maintenance/tension management functions. More specifically, efficiency and productivity may be achieved at the expense of openness, trust, and social cohesion. Although Gantt, Cooke, and the Gilbreths recognized the importance of pattern maintenance and tension management, the same cannot be said for Taylor. Inclined to take a purely technical view of management, Taylor demonstrated little understanding of human needs or the importance of creating a supportive social environment at work. While he stressed employee competence, he largely ignored cohesion and commitment. He believed, rather naively, that if he could induce cooperation through economic rewards, employee relations would be free of conflict and other institutional tensions. Scientific management's inattention to the values of openness, trust, and social cohesion limit its relevance for most organizations, public and private.

Mechanisms for Coordinating and Controlling Work Activities

As indicated in Exhibit 5.2, scientific management relies on **standardization of work processes** to coordinate and control work activities. Work is programmed in advance of its execution by developing standard operating procedures specifying how each task is to be performed. Workers are expected to follow the mandated procedures to the letter. Coordination is built into the work process itself and control is exercised by strictly limiting each worker's discretion, so that mistakes are kept to a minimum and workers do not flounder about trying to determine how best to perform their assigned tasks. Although the chain of command is very much in evidence, the use of impersonal controls such as standard operating procedures reduces the need for direct supervision and, at least in theory, reduces conflict between supervisors and workers.

Exhibit 5.2 Six Mechanisms for Coordinating and Controlling Work Activities

Mutual adjustment	Workers consult with each other informally about what needs to be accomplished and how. Responsibility for coordination and control rests with those who do the work.
Direct supervision	A supervisor is assigned to take responsibility for a group of workers and a managerial hierarchy is established to integrate the efforts of all work groups. The supervisor issues personal instructions and monitors individual performance.
Standardization of work processes	Work is programmed in advance of its execution by developing rules and standard operating procedures specifying how everyone is to perform assigned tasks. Coordination is built into the work process itself and control is achieved by strictly limiting each worker's discretion.
Standardization of work outputs	Work outputs are programmed in advance by providing each work group with product specifications or performance goals and allowing members considerable latitude in determining how to achieve them. Control is exercised by collecting output data, requiring corrective action when needed, and rewarding and sanctioning workers based on results achieved.
Standardization of worker skills	Workers are employed who possess the knowledge and skills needed to make appropriate decisions. Educational institutions and professional associations are relied upon to provide standardized training. Professionally trained workers are largely self-coordinating and self-controlling.
Standardization of values	Organizational leaders communicate and act upon a clear vision of what the organization exists to do, where it should be headed, and what values should guide it. Coordination and control is facilitated by commitment of organizational members to shared, internalized values and ideals.

SOURCE: Based in large part on Henry Mintzberg, *Structure in Fives* (Prentice-Hall, 1993, 3–7).

Standardization of work processes is most relevant to those agencies that Wilson calls production agencies. In these agencies conditions are stable and the work is simple, routine, and predictable. Work includes such things as determining the eligibility of public assistance applicants, generating Social Security checks, processing tax returns, and reviewing applications for licenses and permits. The work performed in most public agencies, however, is complex and nonroutine, and requires considerable independent judgment. It is not the kind of work that can be preprogrammed and routinized without undermining organizational effectiveness. In addition, much government work is performed in ambiguous and uncertain environments in which the machine metaphor breaks down completely, further limiting the relevance of this mechanism of coordination and control.

Scientific management also relies on **standardization of work outputs** as a mechanism of coordination and control. The efficiency expert not only determines how to perform tasks efficiently but also how long it should take to produce a certain amount of work output. When this analysis is completed, workers are given production quotas that they are expected to meet, as well as performance standards relating to product or service quality. According to the logic of scientific management, the accomplishment of each individual's performance standards then contributes in coordinated fashion to the attainment of the organization's overall objectives. Control is exercised by collecting performance data and mandating corrective action to close any gaps between actual and desired levels of performance.

Standardization of work outputs is much more relevant for public agencies than standardization of work processes because it is better suited to complex tasks requiring high levels of discretion. Often mandated for use in government today under the banner of managing for results, it involves identifying desired outputs or outcomes and measuring how well they are attained. Unfortunately, it tends to be effective only where the agency's outputs and outcomes are readily observable, a criterion that many agencies cannot satisfy. Thus, although standardization of work outputs is appropriate for complex tasks requiring high levels of discretion, it is not equally relevant to all public agencies and may have the effect of steering behaviors toward those things that are easily measured at the expense of those that are not (see Chapter 10 for examples).

Motivational Strategies

As indicated in Exhibit 5.3, scientific management relies primarily on the **instrumental rewards strategy** to motivate employees. Pay bonuses are distributed to workers who meet or exceed performance standards. Taylor believed pay is important to workers because it is instrumental in helping them achieve their personal goals, goals that lie primarily outside of the workplace. Management can take advantage of this fact, Taylor believed, by making pay contingent on performance. Although he recognized that other factors influence motivation, he insisted that only monetary incentives have the power to eliminate soldiering. He characterized the pay bonus as "a plum for [workers] to climb after."[39] For Taylor the plum symbolized an appeal to self-interest and

Exhibit 5.3 Four Motivational Strategies

Legal Compliance

Using rules, formal directives, and sanctions to direct and control employee behavior. Employees may come to work, comply with rules, and satisfy minimum role requirements, either because they accept the legitimacy of organizational authority or fear being sanctioned.

Instrumental Rewards

Using rewards to induce desired behaviors.

Rewards for Performance

Distributing pay, promotions, and recognition based on individual performance. Employees may meet or exceed role expectations because they value the material and psychological satisfactions that money, advancement, and recognition can provide.

Considerate Leadership

Adopting a leadership style based on being attentive to employees and considerate of their needs. This strategy may improve morale. It might also induce those who value the respect, support, and approval of persons in authority to meet or exceed their role requirements.

Group Acceptance

Creating a work environment that allows employees to socialize, form group bonds, and enjoy the approval of their peers. This strategy may induce those who value affiliation and peer approval to meet or exceed role requirements, assuming that group norms are consistent with organizational objectives.

Job Identification

Offering work that is interesting, challenging, and responsible. Employees may come to work, meet or exceed role requirements, and possibly exhibit greater creativity and innovativeness. They may do so because they identify with the jobs and find their work intrinsically rewarding.

Goal Congruence

Hiring employees whose goals and values are congruent with the organization's and/or socializing employees so that they internalize organizational goals and values. Employees may come to work, remain with the organization, meet or exceed role requirements, and exhibit greater creativity, innovativeness, and institutional loyalty. They may do so because they identify with the organization's mission and values and because contributing to them reinforces their own self-concept.

SOURCE: Based in large part on Daniel Katz and Robert L. Kahn, *The Social Psychology of Organizations* (Wiley, 1966), pp. 336–68.

ambition. He believed it alone could create the essential identity of interest between workers and employers in keeping output as high as possible.

Although pay-for-performance has been adopted by a growing number of public agencies in recent years, there are limits to its use and effectiveness as a motivational strategy. First, there is the threshold issue of whether an agency has the authority to offer pay bonuses. As noted in Chapter 2, agencies operate within larger authority systems. They can do only what the law allows them to do and with the resources that are made available to them. Although the recent managing-for-results movement has increased the number of pay-for-performance systems in use, most agencies still do not have the necessary authority or resources.

Second, pay-for-performance has its greatest relevance in those agencies where outcomes are readily observable and measurable. These are primarily the agencies that James Q. Wilson calls production and craft agencies. In other agencies it is very difficult to develop fair and accurate performance appraisal systems. Morale quickly deteriorates where employees cannot see a clear relationship between what they accomplish and the pay that is distributed as rewards for performance.

Third, there is some evidence that the use of extrinsic rewards actually diverts attention from intrinsic satisfactions. Based on laboratory experiments, Edward Deci concluded that the greater the use of extrinsic rewards, the greater the decrease in intrinsic motivation.[40] As noted in Chapter 2, most public agencies comprise large numbers of well-educated, technical and professional employees who often desire growth, autonomy, and the intrinsic rewards that come with task accomplishment. Pay-for-performance may not be the most effective strategy for motivating these employees.

Scientific management theory places secondary emphasis on the **legal compliance strategy**. According to Taylor, workers under scientific management are expected to obey orders and instructions promptly. They are expected to obey, however, not so much because supervisors possess formal authority but because the orders and instructions encompass the natural laws of production. If everyone takes their guidance from these laws, the legal compliance strategy need not degenerate into an authoritarian form of management. Supervisors need not insist on obedience simply because they are "the boss." And "the whip" need not be required to back up "the plum." Nonetheless, Taylor's reliance on instrumental rewards and legal compliance reflected a pessimistic view of human nature. He assumed, for example, that most workers will not provide a fair day's work unless they are induced to do so. As we shall see in Chapters 12 and 13, human resources theorists would find this assumption particularly troublesome.

SUMMARY

Understood as a theory of organizational effectiveness, scientific management theory asserts that work output and productivity can be increased by systematizing work processes, dividing work into narrowly defined tasks, determining the "one best way" to perform each task, training workers in the "one best way," setting performance standards, measuring actual performance, and offering economic incentives for surpassing daily production quotas. Among the most important implications of Taylor's theory for public management and organizational performance are the following:

- **Elimination of waste**. Productivity can be increased by ferreting out and eliminating waste from all work processes and procedures. This con-

clusion is one of the most enduring contributions of scientific management. In the early 1900s the municipal research bureaus and President
Taft's Commission on Economy and Efficiency demonstrated the value of
eliminating wasted time, effort, and resources in public agencies.

- **Putting management on a "rational" basis.** Reflecting the values of
the rational goal and internal process models of effectiveness, scientific
management theory emphasizes the importance of planning, goal-setting,
scheduling, systematizing, measuring, and monitoring. These remain standard elements in many textbook discussions of "good management" and
thus represent an enduring contribution to both public and private organizations. However, several of the schools of thought discussed in later
chapters emphasize the problems that arise when rational values are pursued at the expense of human values.

- **Standardization of work.** Scientific management theory relies heavily
on standardization of work as a method of control. Although this remains
an option for public agencies, its usefulness is probably limited to those
situations where employees are relatively uneducated, work is simple and
routine, and the external environment is more or less stable. As we will see
in later chapters, some schools of organization theory are vehemently opposed to the principle of separating planning from doing. In their view,
work standardization prevents workers from exercising discretion, denies
them opportunities to participate in decision making, and thus robs them
of the intrinsic rewards that participation and the exercise of discretion
can bring.

- **Economic rewards.** Scientific management theory advocates the use of
economic rewards as a means of inducing maximum individual productivity.
Although other schools of thought place greater faith in the use of intrinsic
rewards for purposes of motivation, the use of economic rewards remains a
viable option for public agencies. Because the logic behind their use is compelling, many public agencies chose to adopt pay-for-performance systems
in the wake of the recent managing-for-results movement.

Some students of organization theory find it easy to reject, even condemn,
scientific management theory. Others admit to a certain ambivalence. Because
scientific management can be understood in more than one way, both kinds of
responses are understandable. Viewed as a **general business orientation**, scientific management calls for systematizing operations, ferreting out waste,
searching for better ways of doing things, and using performance data to keep
the organization on track. From this perspective scientific management is a
way of doing things that transcends the factory setting in which the Taylor system was born, a way of doing things that has relevance and value for all organizations. In the early 1900s, for example, advocates of scientific management
reduced corruption in government and made agencies more responsive to the
people by introducing standardized classification and pay systems, modern accounting and budgeting procedures, and more efficient and less wasteful work
operations.

However, scientific management can also be viewed as a prescriptive, value-laden **theory of management**. Because of ideological biases such as distrust of human motives and insistence on orderliness and control, this view is much more controversial and its relevance and value for public agencies much less certain. It calls for narrow division of labor, routinization of work, limited discretion, and use of extrinsic rewards. In the opinion of many, these structural elements tend to discourage initiative, deny workers opportunities for personal growth, rob the organization of the full value of its human resources, and undermine the organization's capacity to adapt successfully to change.

As a general business orientation, scientific management is almost synonymous with "good management practice" and consequently has much to offer public agencies. But as a prescriptive theory of management, orthodox Taylorism may create the same problems as Weberian orthodoxy. Managers who are steeped in the assumptions of scientific management theory may find it difficult to imagine that self-direction and self-management are possible, or that employees can be motivated without either pushing from behind or pulling from in front. In the final analysis, scientific management theory encourages a top-down, control-oriented approach to management that may have limited relevance for public agencies because of the political uncertainties they face, the ambiguity of their goals, the complex nature of their tasks, the unique characteristics of their workforces, and the difficulties inherent in measuring their outputs and outcomes.

NOTES

1. Frank B. Copley, *Frederick W. Taylor: Father of Scientific Management* (New York: Harper and Brothers, 1923).

2. Judith A. Merkle, *Management and Ideology: The Legacy of the International Scientific Management Movement* (Berkeley: University of California Press, 1980), 21–22.

3. Copley, *Frederick W. Taylor*, vol. 2, 372.

4. Merkle, *Management and Ideology*, 58.

5. Copley, *Frederick W. Taylor*, vol. 1, 222.

6. Frederick W. Taylor, "A Piece-rate System," *Transactions of the American Society of Mechanical Engineers 16* (1895), 856–83.

7. Frederick W. Taylor, "On the Art of Cutting Metals," *Transactions of the American Society of Mechanical Engineers 28* (1906), 31–35; Carl G. Barth, "Slide Rules for the Machine Shop as a Part of the Taylor System of Management," *Transactions of the American Society of Mechanical Engineers 25* (1904), 49–62.

8. Taylor, "On the Art of Cutting Metals," 55.

9. Frederick W. Taylor, "Shop Management," *Transactions of the American Society of Mechanical Engineers 24* (1903), 1358.

10. Taylor, "Shop Management," 1361–62.

11. H. L. Gantt, *Industrial Leadership* (New Haven: Yale University Press, 1916), 89.

12. Frederick W. Taylor, *The Principles of Scientific Management* (New York: Norton, 1967), 90.

13. Taylor, "A Piece-rate System," 872.

14. Taylor, "A Piece-rate System," 873.

15. Taylor, "A Piece-rate System," 856.

16. Taylor, "A Piece-rate System," 858.

17. Taylor, "Shop Management," 1348.

18. Taylor, "Shop Management," 1346.

19. Taylor, "Shop Management," 1346.

20. Taylor, "Shop Management," 1391.

21. Taylor, *Principles of Scientific Management,* 130, note 1.

22. Frederick W. Taylor, "The Principles of Scientific Management," in Jay M. Shafritz and J. Steven Ott, *Classics of Organization Theory* (Orlando, FL: Harcourt, 2001), 65.

23. Adam Smith, *The Wealth of Nations* (New York: Random House, 1937), 3–10.

24. John E. Kelly, *Scientific Management, Job Redesign and Work Performance* (London: Academic Press, 1982), 19–24.

25. Babbage, *Economy of Manufacturers and Machinery.* See discussion in Copley, *Frederick W. Taylor,* vol. 1, 278.

26. Taylor, quoted in Copley, *Frederick W. Taylor,* vol. 1, 358.

27. Ibid.

28. Gareth Morgan, *Images of Organization* (Thousand Oaks, CA: Sage, 1997).

29. Robert Franklin Hoxie, *Scientific Management and Labor* (New York: D. Appleton and Company, 1918), 15.

30. Hugh G. J. Aitken, *Taylorism at Watertown Arsenal* (Cambridge: Harvard University Press, 1960).

31. Aitken, *Taylorism at Watertown Arsenal,* 237.

32. Hoxie, *Scientific Management and Labor,* 40.

33. Quoted in Aitken, *Taylorism at Watertown Arsenal,* 147.

34. See Copley, *Frederick W. Taylor,* vol. 1.

35. L. P. Alford, *Henry Laurence Gantt: Leader in Industry* (New York: American Society of Mechanical Engineers, 1934), 130.

36. Morris L. Cooke, "Scientific Management of the Public Sector," *American Political Science Review 9* (August 1915), 488–95.

37. Henry Bruere, "Efficiency in City Government," *Annals of the American Academy of Political and Social Sciences 41* (May 1912), 15.

38. See discussion in Hindy Lauer Schachter, *Frederick Taylor and the Public Administration Community: A Reevaluation* (New York: State University of New York Press, 1989).

39. Quoted in Copley, *Frederick W. Taylor.* vol. 1, 321–22.

40. Edward L. Deci, *Intrinsic Motivation* (New York: Plenum Press, 1975).

6

Administrative Management Theory

Fayol, Mooney, and Gulick

A s Frederick Taylor was developing his system for rationalizing task performance on the shop floor, other theorists were searching for ways to rationalize the design and management of the organization as a whole. These theorists constituted a highly diverse group of individuals, including a French coal-mining executive, a vice president at General Motors, and a professor of public administration at Columbia University. The theory of organizational effectiveness implicit in their writings calls for a highly formalized administrative structure characterized by clear lines of authority and responsibility running from top to bottom, a clear and distinct division of labor among departments, and delegation of power and authority to administrators commensurate with their responsibilities.

This chapter examines three closely related literatures that capture the essence and evolution of administrative management theory. The first centers on the search for fundamental principles of management and administrative structure. It is represented by Henri Fayol's *General and Industrial Management* (1916) and James D. Mooney and Alan C. Reiley's *Onward Industry!* (1931). A second literature applies the principles identified by Fayol and Mooney to the organization and management of government's executive branch. It is represented by Luther Gulick's "Notes on the Theory of Organization," which was published in 1937. A third literature draws on the efforts of government research bureaus to formulate basic administrative principles for public agencies in general. The chapter closes with analysis of the relevance of administrative management theory for public management and organizational performance.

Henri Fayol 1841–1925

Henri Fayol was born in France in 1841.[1] After graduating from the National School of Mines at St. Etienne in 1860, he was hired by the coal-mining firm of Commentry-Fourchambault as a mining engineer. He remained with this company throughout his career, becoming director of a group of pits in 1872 and managing director of the entire company in 1888. Fayol brought the company back from the brink of bankruptcy and oversaw its continued growth through the end of the First World War. He attributed his success to adherence to a few basic principles which he described in *General and In-dustrial Management,* a lengthy paper published in French in 1916 but not widely available in English until 1949. After retiring in 1918 at the age of 77, Fayol founded the Center of Administrative Studies to spur development of an authoritative literature dealing with general management. Fayol also undertook to apply his principles of administration to the public sector. He released the results of his investigation of the Department of Posts and Telegraphs in 1921 and was engaged in a study of the government-owned tobacco industry at the time of his death in 1925 at the age of 84.

HENRI FAYOL'S THEORY OF GENERAL MANAGEMENT

The growing size and complexity of public and private institutions in the late 1800s and early 1900s created a simultaneous awareness in Europe and the United States of the importance of establishing management as a distinct profession supported by a body of research-based knowledge. In 1886 Henry Towne urged the American Society of Mechanical Engineers to establish a special section for developing such a body of knowledge.[2] Across the Atlantic a business executive in the coal-mining industry named Henri Fayol also recognized the importance of developing a body of knowledge to support the training of professional managers.

Fayol was appalled that general managers, typically trained in specialized fields such as engineering, had to learn for themselves how to manage complex organizations. No authoritative set of principles or bodies of knowledge existed to guide them. Nor were the educational institutions in France doing anything to equip future leaders to carry out their managerial responsibilities. Even in the colleges of civil engineering, syllabi contained no reference to management. Professional training could not begin, Fayol concluded, until a widely accepted theory of management was developed:

> The real reason for the absence of management teaching in our vocational schools is absence of theory; without theory no teaching is possible. Now there exists no generally accepted theory of management emanating from general discussion. There is no shortage of personal theorizing, but failing any accepted theory each one thinks that he has the best methods and

everywhere there may be observed—in industry, the army, the home, the state—the most contradictory practices under the aegis of the same principle. . . . The situation might be quite otherwise were there an accepted theory, that is to say, a collection of principles, rules, methods, procedures, tried and checked by general experience.[3]

Although a busy executive, Fayol took it upon himself to develop such a theory—a theory specifying sound administrative principles and the methods for putting them into practice. He published his theory in 1916 under the title *General and Industrial Management* and in 1918 he established the Center of Administrative Studies to encourage ongoing discussion of management issues. Today Fayol is generally regarded as one of the great pioneers in the field of management. Not only did he define management as a function common to all forms of human association, but he also developed the first general theory of management. As outlined in the following, Fayol's theory is comprised of four components: organizational activities, management functions, administrative principles, and methods for putting principles into operation.

Organizational Activities

Governing an organization, Fayol wrote, is not the same as managing it. Governing involves six kinds of activities, and **managerial activities** comprise only one of these six. Among industrial concerns, the other five are **technical activities** (relating to the production of goods and services), **commercial activities** (relating to buying and selling), **financial activities** (relating to raising and expending capital), **security activities** (relating to the protection of property and persons), and **accounting activities** (relating to the tracking of profit and losses). The nature of these activities, Fayol acknowledged, varies somewhat according to the type of organization. Most government agencies, for example, do not manufacture and sell products but they do enter into exchange relationships of some kind. Similarly, they may not raise capital but they do need to secure funding.

Of these six sets of activities, Fayol found managerial activities to be especially important. It is through management that the other sets of activities are harmonized, thereby facilitating the accomplishment of organizational objectives.

Managerial Functions

In Fayol's words, "to manage is to forecast and plan, to organize, to command, to coordinate and to control."[4] This brief statement encapsulates the first modern statement of management's essential functions. **Planning**, according to Fayol, means forecasting future events or trends that may impact the organization and making provision for them in the organization's plan of action. This plan provides for the optimal use of the organization's resources and identifies the methods for achieving organizational objectives. It ensures unity of direction for all organizational members. **Organizing** means establishing the structure of the undertaking, both material and human. Among other things, organizing involves dividing work among members, creating appropriate organizational units, and building a hierarchy of authority in which managers at each level supervise an appropriate number of subordinates, all based on the size and needs of the organization.

Commanding means keeping the organization moving down the path toward the realization of organizational objectives. According to Fayol, this requires communicating goals, motivating employees to perform assigned tasks diligently and enthusiastically, and discharging those found to be incompetent. **Coordinating** means unifying and harmonizing all activity and effort. This requires making sure that every worker has an assigned task, every unit has an assigned function, and the efforts of every individual and unit contribute harmoniously to achieving organizational objectives. The "excellent" organization, Fayol states, is one whose "interrelated parts move in unison toward the same end."[5] Finally, **controlling** means seeing to it that everything occurs in conformity with established rules, directives, plans, and schedules. Managers, according to Fayol, must monitor the work of those below them and hold them accountable without encroaching on their delegated spheres of authority.

Fayol insisted that these functional responsibilities do not belong to a single individual such as the chief executive. Rather, they belong to all persons serving in a supervisory capacity. The higher the position in the hierarchy of authority, the more the supervisor's time is allocated to one or more of these functional responsibilities. According to Fayol, the ability of managers as a group to fulfill these responsibilities constitutes the key to organizational success. In his words, "The chief features of an efficient administration are almost exclusively managerial in character. It is acknowledged, indeed, that when foresight, organization, command, coordination, and control are effectively exercised throughout the concern, all duties will be duly performed and the running of the concern assured."[6]

Administrative Principles

To initiate the much-needed dialogue about managerial effectiveness, Fayol identified fourteen principles that had served him well as a chief executive. These principles are identified in Exhibit 6.1 along with summary statements intended to capture Fayol's meaning.

To assess his theory fairly, it is necessary to ask what Fayol meant by the term *principle*. Because the term often refers to a fundamental truth or rule of correct conduct that allows individuals to make appropriate choices in various situations, some commentators concluded that Fayol intended his fourteen principles as universal truths capable of generating solutions to problems in all organizations and in all situations. It appears, however, that Fayol viewed these principles as universal truths only in the sense that they can provide guidance to all managers in all organizations. He did not view them as prescribing universal solutions. For example, he believed that all complex organizations must divide work if they are to achieve their objectives with any degree of efficiency, but he did not claim that the division of work principle could prescribe *how* to divide work or *what degree* of specialization to adopt. He understood that the application of a principle depends upon the situation

Exhibit 6.1 Fayol's Fourteen Administrative Principles

1. **Division of work.** All complex organizations must assign fixed tasks to its members to profit from the advantages of specialization.
2. **Authority and responsibility.** Authority gives rise to responsibility; good leaders must exercise both formal and personal authority and must sanction those who do not fulfill their assigned responsibilities.
3. **Discipline.** Leaders must maintain discipline if the organization is to function efficiently and effectively; obedience, loyalty, and dedication must be obtained from all members in accordance with employer-employee agreements.
4. **Unity of command.** An employee should receive orders from only one superior, his or her immediate supervisor; dual command undermines authority, discipline, and order.
5. **Unity of direction.** There should be one leader and one plan for a group of activities having the same objective.
6. **Subordination of individual interest to general interest.** The interests of any member or group of members must not be allowed to prevail over the interests of the organization as a whole; ways must be found to reconcile individual and general interests.
7. **Remuneration of personnel.** Employees must receive remuneration that is fair and encourages productive work effort.
8. **Centralization.** Directives must always come from a central source, but the optimal balance between centralization and decentralization must be determined for each organization separately; this is a question of how much discretion to allow members at each level.
9. **Scalar chain.** Complex organizations require a chain of superiors from the highest to lowest levels of authority; communications normally must ascend and descend through each level, although authorized exceptions may be made in the interest of speed.
10. **Order.** Smooth organizational functioning requires a place for everything and everyone, and everything and everyone in its appointed place.
11. **Equity.** Retaining devoted and loyal employees requires that they be treated with kindliness and fairness.
12. **Stability of tenure of personnel.** Smooth organizational functioning is impossible when personnel, especially management personnel, are constantly coming and going; steps must be taken to obtain as much stability as possible.
13. **Initiative.** It is essential to encourage individual initiative because it stimulates motivation; this is achieved by allowing employees freedom to propose and carry out their own ideas, within the limits of authority and discipline.
14. **Esprit de corps.** Every effort must be made to establish and maintain cohesion among personnel; dividing enemy forces is clever, but dividing one's own team is a grave error.

---

at hand. In his words, "Therefore, principles are flexible and capable of adaptation to every need; it is a matter of knowing how to make use of them, which is a difficult art requiring intelligence, experience, decision and proportion."[7]

Although from today's perspective Fayol's fourteen principles seem to offer a strange mix of concepts for organizing and managing personnel, it must be remembered that his was a pioneering effort. His goal was simply to "endow management theory with a dozen or so well-established principles, on which it is appropriate to concentrate general discussion."[8]

Administrative Methods

Having adopted the machine metaphor often found in classical theory, Fayol argued that top managers must develop an administrative apparatus for implementing administrative principles on a daily basis.[9] This apparatus comprises methods that keep the organization on track and facilitate administrative improvements. The **survey** is an investigation that produces a description of the organization's history, its current resources and needs, and the prevailing social, political, and economic circumstances that are likely to affect it in the future. This last part of the survey requires forecasting future events that are likely to affect each component of the organization. Those events can then be provided for in the organization's long-term plan. The **action plan** establishes the direction of the organization, its objectives, and the general means by which it intends to achieve them. Given the difficulty of foreseeing the future, the longterm plan must be adjusted annually. Once it is in place the plan builds unity of direction, Fayol's fifth principle, by communicating shared objectives and the reasoning behind administrative decisions. It is interesting to note that the survey and the action plan resurfaced in the 1970s as key elements in strategic planning.

Daily, monthly, and yearly **statistical reports** allow administrators to determine whether the plan is being carried out and its stated objectives achieved. These reports are essentially control mechanisms. If the reports reveal problems, administrators may demand corrective action from those responsible. **Minutes** are the records of the weekly meetings of the various department heads through which coordination is achieved. They record discussions of results obtained and difficulties encountered in each department. Chief executives can refer to these records to obtain insights about what is occurring in the various work units. Finally, the **organization chart** illustrates the hierarchy of organizational units, establishing the functions performed by each unit and clarifying who reports to whom. These charts, according to Fayol, also provide important clues about structural faults, such as duplication of effort, overlapping responsibilities, unstaffed functions, and lack of functional unity in the services provided by a particular unit.

Taken together, these methods represent a systematic approach to management that was very rare in the early 1900s. Although the benefits of these methods are now well established, administrators often fail to take full advantage of them even today.

An Overview of Fayol's Theory of Management

As illustrated in Exhibit 6.2, the four components of Fayol's theory comprise an integrated whole. The hypothesized means-ends relationships among these components may be stated as follows: administrative principles (bottom of Exhibit 6.2) guide functional decisions (center column), and administrative methods (righthand column) provide the means for carrying them out. The implicit dependent variable is organizational effectiveness. Fayol believed that administrators who perform the five management functions,

Exhibit 6.2 An Overview of Fayol's Theory of Management

Organizational activities	Managerial functions	Administrative methods
Technical	Planning (examining the future and drawing up the plan of action)	Organizational survey
Commercial		
Financial	Organization (building up the dual structure: material and human)	Action plan
Security		
Accounting	Command (maintaining required activity among personnel)	Statistical reports
Managerial		
	Coordination (binding together, unifying and harmonizing all activity)	Minutes
	Control (seeing that everything occurs in conformity with established rules and expressed commands)	Organization chart

Administrative Principles: Division of work, authority and responsibility, discipline, unity of command, unity of direction, subordination of individual interests to the general interest, remuneration, centralization, scalar chain, order, equity, stability of tenure of personnel, initiative, esprit de corps

follow sound administrative principles in doing so, and use appropriate methods will meet with greater success than those who do not.

JAMES D. MOONEY'S THEORY OF ORGANIZATION

Fayol's fourteen principles dealt with psychological and behavioral as well as structural issues. Equity and esprit de corps, for example, relate to management's responsibility for establishing positive employee relations. By contrast, administrative management theory in the United States tended to focus more narrowly on organizational structure. The most comprehensive presentation of organizational principles is found in James D. Mooney and Alan C. Reiley's *Onward Industry! The Principles of Organization and Their Significance to Modern Industry,* which was published in 1931. Mooney, a vice president at General Motors, and Reiley, who assisted with much of the historical research, shared with other administrative management theorists the belief that organizational structure is governed by universal principles. "The entire book," Mooney and Reiley wrote, "is based on the thesis that there are fundamental principles of organization, structural in character, which may be identified in every form of

---

James D. Mooney 1884–1957

James D. Mooney was born in Cleveland on February 25, 1884. After completing high school, Mooney studied mechanical engineering at the Case School of Applied Science in Cleveland for four years. He then held a series of jobs in mining, publishing, and sales before being hired by Alfred P. Sloan at General Motors to turn around a failing subsidiary plant in Anderson, Illinois.[10] He did so well that he was promoted to general manager of the General Motors Export Company in 1921 and immediately set about building assembly plants and purchasing other automobile companies all over the world. Known for his energy, negotiating skills, and ability to inspire loyalty, Mooney was promoted to vice president in 1923 and quickly became a key member of GM's top management team. While at General Motors, Mooney completed the requirements for his Bachelor of Science degree at New York University and then asked the Case School to assess the possibility of completing his mechanical engineering degree. Case responded that the degree would be awarded if he could successfully write and defend a thesis. Case was so pleased with his "Principles of Industrial Organization" that it awarded him the doctor of engineering degree as well. Mooney subsequently hired Alan C. Reiley as a research assistant to help him expand his thesis into a book. This work, first published as *Onward Industry!* in 1931, is now recognized as a significant contribution to administrative management theory.

---

human association, and that the orderly correlation of these principles furnishes the key to their more efficient application in all fields of collective human effort."[11] The purpose of their book was to "expose the principles of organization" by analyzing historical examples, including the Roman Republic, the Catholic church, and the French and German armies. Frederick Taylor had shown how to increase production line efficiency, but this alone, according to Mooney and Reiley, could not guarantee success. Principles of efficiency must be applied to the structure of the entire organization. Only by establishing a formal structure based soundly on universal principles can an organization hope to coordinate its internal activities efficiently and effectively and protect itself from the forces of disintegration.

Mooney and Reiley began their analysis by clarifying their definition of organization. In popular usage, *organization* refers to a group of individuals who work together to achieve a common purpose. They noted, however, that a mob has a common purpose but no organization. This led them to identify a second meaning of organization, one relating to the degree and kind of order imposed on group activities. *Organization* in this sense refers to the specific form adopted by an enterprise to attain its purpose. More specifically, it refers to the formal structure—the sum total of institutionalized relationships, methods, and procedures—that allows an enterprise to coordinate and control its internal activities. Because organizational performance depends upon achieving a good fit between form and purpose, structural decisions must be guided by fundamental organizational principles. While acknowledging that principles cannot solve all organizational problems, Mooney and Reiley nonetheless believed that "it is of decisive advantage to know exactly what the principles are that we are striving to apply."[12] Their research led them to identify three universal principles: coordinative, scalar, and functional.

The Coordinative Principle

Although management is "the vital spark which actuates, directs and controls the plan and procedure of organization,"[13] a formal structure consistent with the organization's essential purpose must exist before the vital spark can be applied. This is accomplished by organizing according to certain principles, the most fundamental of which is the coordinative principle. All complex organizations must coordinate the activities of many individuals if they are to attain their objectives. According to Mooney and Reiley, coordination is the all-inclusive, master principle; all others are the principles through which coordination is achieved.

Mooney and Reiley define **authority** as the source of coordinating power. It resides with chosen leaders who are responsible for issuing rules and procedures and directing a truly coordinated effort. Coordination is achieved largely through the exercise of formal authority up and down the chain of command.

The Scalar Principle

All complex organizations must have a means by which the supreme coordinating authority can operate from the top to the bottom of the organizational structure. This is the scalar principle, or the principle of hierarchy. As Fayol had done earlier, Mooney and Reiley refer to the vertical division of labor as a **scalar chain** because it comprises a scale of duties graduated according to degrees of authority and corresponding responsibilities. The scalar chain is made up of a series of superior-subordinate relationships arranged vertically throughout the organization and through which communications flow up and down.

The scalar chain is created through the process of delegation. This entails conferring a specific grant of authority by a higher official upon a lower official. According to Mooney and Reiley, higher officials must delegate authority and responsibility when their workload becomes too great to handle themselves, but they always remain accountable to their superiors for the actions of their subordinates. In their words, "The subordinate is always responsible to his immediate supervisor for doing the job, the superior remains responsible for getting it done, and this same relationship, based on coordinated responsibility, is repeated up to the top leader, whose authority makes him responsible for the whole."[14]

Delegated authority usually includes the right to command persons at the next lower level of authority. In such instances an official not only delegates functional responsibilities but also the right of delegation itself. This is what creates and lengthens the scalar chain. However, within each organizational unit, and in the organization as a whole, the scalar chain eventually comes to an end. This is the point "where authority ceases to delegate its own authority over others and simply delegates or assigns specific functions."[15] The scalar chain ultimately exists to allow for the coordination of these functional activities.

The test of a true leader, according to Mooney and Reiley, lies in the way authority is delegated. One type of leader delegates authority so easily that he or she effectively abdicates all responsibility. A second type refuses to delegate any real authority for fear of losing control over task performance. Such individuals are finally "crushed and fail under the weight of accumulated duties that they do not know and cannot learn how to delegate."[16] The third type, the true leader, understands the necessity of delegating but remains ever conscious of the fact that the ultimate responsibility of office cannot be delegated. These leaders delegate tasks as soon as the total task begins to exceed their own unaided powers and then hold subordinates accountable for the performance of their delegated responsibilities.

Mooney and Reiley also identified a specific principle governing the superior-subordinate relationship. Discussed at length by Frederick Taylor, and called by others the **exception principle**, it states that subordinates should refer only the few unusual and difficult problems to their superiors while handling all easy and routine problems themselves. However, just as leaders vary in their willingness to adhere to the delegation principle, subordinates vary in their willingness to adhere to the exception principle.

The Functional Principle

Whereas the scalar principle calls for vertical differentiation based on degrees of authority, the functional principle calls for horizontal differentiation based on kinds of duties. To use an analogy suggested by Mooney and Reiley, the difference between generals and colonels is scalar, whereas the difference between infantry and artillery is functional. In practice the functional principle involves dividing the organization's work into discrete activities according to their functional purposes and assigning those activities to specific organizational units. Mooney and Reiley concluded that functional differentiation is a universal feature of complex organizations. It is a means of ensuring that the work activities of each individual and organizational unit mesh with all other work activities. Functional differentiation clarifies the nature of each person's duties and how those duties contribute to the attainment of organizational goals. Once the functional framework is established it is the responsibility of those in the scalar chain to coordinate work activities efficiently. "Reason and evidence," according to Mooney and Reiley, "combine to prove that exactitude in functional definition is a necessity in the creation of a true collective harmony."[17]

One aspect of functional differentiation facilitates both vertical and horizontal coordination. Mooney and Reiley refer to this as the staff phase of functionalism or the **line and staff principle**. It refers to the creation of staff units to advise or support line authorities in the performance of their duties. Their functional roles are to inform line managers of things they should know before making their decisions, advise them based on that information, and supervise the details of implementation. So as not to violate the unity-of-command principle, Mooney and Reily insisted that staff units not be delegated command authority over line units. In their words, "The line plans, the line executes, the line does everything. In the line alone rests the authority to determine plans, the authority to execute such plans, and the responsibility for what is done."[18] The staff units merely function to assist and support the line in these matters.

Mooney and Reiley were compelled to acknowledge, however, that a complete separation of line and staff duties exists only in the conceptual realm. In practice it tends to apply only to purely advisory bodies, such as a citizens' advisory board, or to purely support staffs, such as the Army's quartermaster corps. Modern staff units are more likely to comprise technical specialists than general counselors. Part of their task in highly centralized administrative systems is to help upper-level administrators exercise control over lower-level officials. As Gulick later noted, overhead staff agencies such as budget, personnel, and purchasing offices exercise functional authority over line units and are therefore line units themselves according to a strict interpretation of the line-staff principle.

Onward Industry! offered perhaps the most comprehensive and internally consistent theory of organization yet developed. At a time when management was still in the process of being defined as a distinct profession and field of study, Mooney and Reiley reminded administrators that they were struggling with the same problems of organizational design with which administrators throughout history have struggled and that management's primary task is to find the optimal balance between the horizontal division of labor and the vertical division of authority required to maintain coordination. Their work also provided researchers and administrators with core concepts for thinking through problems of organizational design.

Mooney and Reiley's work contains the theoretical proposition that organizational effectiveness is highly dependent on the fit between structural arrangements and organizational purpose. Rather than claiming that there is "one best way" to organize, they insisted that different purposes call for different structural arrangements. They described, for example, how the ancient Romans developed a vertically and horizontally decentralized administrative system to maintain control over their expanding empire, while the early Catholic church, by contrast, adopted a highly centralized structure so that it could integrate all churches into a single spiritual system.

Although Mooney and Reiley were not familiar with Fayol and his writings, they reached a similar conclusion: coordination, hierarchy, and functional differentiation may be universal principles but their application is not. As Mooney and Reiley put it, "The discovery and identification of these principles will not of course solve all problems of organization. Principles, as such, must be ever present, and are certain to be applied in some fashion, but their efficient application is the task of the organizer."[19]

LUTHER GULICK'S ADMINISTRATIVE MANAGEMENT THEORY

The movement in the early 1900s to reform the structure of government and introduce business methods into public administration was spearheaded by research bureaus such as the New York Bureau of Municipal Research and the Institute for Government Research located in Washington, D.C. By

1936 their contributions to government reform were so widely recognized that President Roosevelt appointed a study committee to "suggest a comprehensive and balanced program for dealing with the overhead organization and management of the executive branch."[20] Administrative management theory takes its name from the official title of this committee, the President's Committee on Administrative Management. In its original meaning, *administrative management* referred to the role played by overhead staff agencies in assisting the chief executive manage the administrative agencies of government.

The President's committee, more commonly known as the Brownlow Committee, was comprised of Louis Brownlow, Charles E. Merriam, and Luther Gulick, three well-known figures in the field of public administration. Finding that the existing literature on administrative theory was unavailable in Washington, Gulick wrote a briefing paper for the committee entitled "Notes on the Theory of Organization." He and Lyndall Urwick, a British management consultant, subsequently included this paper in a collection of articles published under the title *Papers on the Science of Administration*.[21] This collection included papers by Henri Fayol and Mary Parker Follett (see Chapter 7), as well as those by Gulick and Urwick. At least one commentator has cited the work of the President's Committee and the publication of the *Papers* as the zenith of the field of public administration's reputation and influence.[22] Those working in the field were widely consulted by business and government alike for their knowledge of administrative structure and management.

Gulick's contribution to organization theory is threefold. First, his "Notes on the Theory of Organization" provided a very readable synthesis of the ideas of theorists such as Henri Fayol and James Mooney. His purpose in writing was not to articulate his own theory but to bring together and make accessible the ideas of others. Because a synthesis of this kind did not then exist, and because the works of many theorists were unavailable or difficult to read and comprehend, publication of Gulick's paper was itself a valuable contribution. Second, "Notes on the Theory of Organization" applied administrative principles specifically to government. Gulick expanded upon the basic theoretical framework provided by Fayol and Mooney and Reiley by adding his own conceptual distinctions. One of these, for example, stated that government agencies can be departmentalized on the basis of purpose, process, persons, or place. By drawing out the implications of administrative principles for government's organizational structure, Gulick initiated an important second phase in the evolution of administrative management theory. Finally, through his work as director of the Institute of Public Administration (formerly the New York Bureau of Municipal Research), as well as his work on the Brownlow Committee, Gulick was able to demonstrate the applicability of theory to practice. As discussed in the following, many of the recommendations contained in the Brownlow Committee's report and subsequently adopted by the president were derived from or supported by Gulick's analysis of administrative principles.

Luther H. Gulick 1892–1993

Luther Gulick, often called the dean of public administration, was born in Osaka, Japan, in 1892.[23] The son of missionary parents, he spent much of his youth in Japan before his family returned to the United States in 1904. Gulick earned an A.B. in political science and an M.A. in philosophy from Oberlin College in Ohio before entering Columbia University in 1915 to study public law and political science under Charles Beard. As a graduate student he attended courses at the Training School for Public Service operated by the New York Bureau of Municipal Research. After a year in the army Gulick was appointed director of the Training School in 1918, completed his Ph.D. requirements at Columbia in 1920, and became director of the New York Bureau of Municipal Research in 1921, a position he would hold for over 40 years. Gulick also began teaching courses at Columbia in 1921, was appointed Eaton Professor of Municipal Science and Administration in 1931, and continued to teach at Columbia until 1942. Over a long and distinguished career in public service Gulick served on numerous government commissions. One of the most important of these was the President's Committee on Administrative Management (1936–37) which recommended expanding the White House staff and restructuring the executive branch. In 1954 Gulick was appointed the first city administrator of New York City, a post he held for three years. He remained actively involved in public service in later years and was appointed chairman emeritus of the Institute of Public Administration (formerly the New York Bureau) at the age of 90. Luther Gulick died in 1993 at the age of 100.

Applying Administrative Principles to Government

Gulick recognized that governments face special problems of organizational design and that these had not been given sufficient consideration by earlier theorists. Governments are responsible for carrying out many complex tasks, tasks that are highly dissimilar in nature, ranging from national defense to regulation of the economy. This led some theorists to suggest a basic similarity between governments and private holding companies.[24] According to this view, the administrative departments of government produce distinct goods or services, much like the divisions of General Motors. For this reason each department could be treated as an independent, largely autonomous unit within the larger holding company known as government. But the analogy does not stand up under closer scrutiny, Gulick argued, because democracy requires chief executives to hold departments accountable to the will of the people. Not only is this a fundamentally different matter than holding a division of General Motors accountable, but in the absence of profits as a measuring stick the chief executive has no clear way of ensuring accountability other than to rely on systemwide personnel and accounting systems. In short, chief executives must exercise closer supervision over administrative departments than the heads of holding companies. There is also a greater need for coordination because there is a greater degree of interaction between departments of government than between corporate divisions.

A good theory of administration, Gulick believed, must recognize and take into account differences of this kind. He understood, however, that such a theory did not yet exist. As he noted in the foreword to *Papers on the Science of Administration,* theory building was still at an early stage:

> It is the hope of the editors that the availability of these papers will advance the analysis of administration, assist in the development of a standard nomenclature, encourage others to criticize the hypotheses with regard to administration herein set forth and to advance their own concepts fearlessly, and to point the way to areas greatly in need of exploration. If those who are concerned scientifically with the phenomena of getting things done through cooperative endeavor will proceed along these lines, we may expect in time to construct a valid and accepted theory of administration.[25]

Coordination Through Organizational Structure

Gulick expanded upon the conceptual framework proposed by Mooney and Reiley by beginning his analysis with a discussion of the division of labor. Coordination is indeed the essence of organization, he wrote, but it is the division of labor that necessitates it. To achieve their complex tasks, all but the smallest and simplest of organizations must divide labor. This not only ensures that one or more individuals is responsible for a necessary part of the organization's overall task, but it also allows the organization to benefit from the advantages of specialization described by Adam Smith. But, once having divided the larger task among many individuals and work units, coordinating their work becomes an institutional imperative. As Gulick put it, "If subdivision of work is inescapable, coordination becomes mandatory."[26]

The task of organizational design is made more difficult by the fact that these two master principles are opposing in nature. As Gulick put it, "the more the work is subdivided, the greater is the danger of confusion, and the greater is the need of overall supervision and coordination."[27] For Gulick, this reality defines the essence of organization theory. In his words, "The theory of organization, therefore, has to do with the structure of coordination imposed upon the work–division units of an enterprise. Hence it is not possible to determine how an activity is to be organized without, at the same time, considering how the work is to be divided. Work division is the foundation of organization; indeed, the reason for organization."[28] From this perspective, organizational structure may be understood as the sum total of ways in which labor is divided and coordination is achieved among the divided parts.

Following Mooney and Reiley's lead, Gulick focused his analysis on the way coordination may be achieved through the joint application of the functional and scalar principles. "Organization as a way of coordination," he wrote, "requires the establishment of a system of authority whereby the central purpose or objective of an enterprise is translated into reality through the combined efforts of many specialists, each working in his own field at a particular time and place."[29]

In the public sector this generally entails four steps: identifying a basic task such as providing pure water, appointing a director to see that the task is carried out, determining the number and nature of specialized work units into which the task will have to be divided, and establishing and perfecting the structure of authority between the director and the ultimate work subdivisions. The third of these step reflects the functional principle at work and is often referred to by Gulick as part of the process of **departmentalization**. The final step reflects the scalar principle at work and is illustrated by an organization chart showing the span of control of each manager and indicating who reports to whom in the organizational hierarchy.

Organizational design is clearly important. By definition, good design enhances the organization's ability to achieve its goals and bad design reduces its ability. The difficulty lies in determining *how* to divide work and *how* to coordinate work activities to best advantage. Like Fayol, Gulick believed organizational design should be guided in part by the **span of control principle**. According to this principle, the number of individuals reporting to a superior should be limited to the number he or she can supervise effectively, given limited time and energy. Gulick noted, however, that there can be no one correct span of control for all superior-subordinate relationships. The optimal span necessarily varies with the unique abilities of the superior, the nature of the work, the size of the organization, and the level of authority.

Second, Gulick agreed with Fayol that design decisions should be guided by the **unity of command principle**. As defined by Fayol, this principle states that each worker should receive orders from only one superior. Like Fayol, Gulick criticized Taylor for setting up separate foremen to deal with machinery, materials, machine speed, and discipline, each with the power of giving orders directly to individual workers. Gulick acknowledged that the rigid adherence to the principle of unity of command may have its absurdities but he maintained that "these are, however, unimportant in comparison with the certainty of confusion, inefficiency and irresponsibility which arise from the violation of the principle."[30]

Third, Gulick believed design decisions should be guided by the **homogeneity principle**. This principle states that work should be divided so that the work of a single organizational unit is as homogenous in character as possible. Gulick believed that an organizational unit that is assigned work that is nonhomogenous in nature, technology, or purpose "will encounter the danger of friction and inefficiency."[31] Gulick also noted that the span-of-control and homogeneity principles are somewhat opposed. The first emphasizes limiting the number of subunits reporting to each superior, whereas the second tends to increase the total number of subunits. The homogeneity principle thus creates pressures toward a very tall hierarchy and increases demands for coordination. A designer who begins by applying the span-of-control principle to the top of the organization will produce a different set of recommendations from one who begins by applying the homogeneity principle at the bottom of the organization. The answer, Gulick suggested, is to plan from the top downward and from the bottom upward simultaneously and to reconcile the two principles at the center of the hierarchy:

> . . . . In planning the first subdivisions under the chief executive, the principle of the limitation of the span of control must apply; in building up the first aggregates of specialized functions, the principle of homogeneity

must apply. If any enterprise has such an array of functions that the first subdivisions from the top down do not readily meet the first aggregations from the bottom up, then additional divisions and additional aggregates must be introduced, but at each further step there must be a less and less rigorous adherence to the two conflicting principles until their juncture is effected.[32]

Gulick provided an example drawn from his experience with the New York City Charter Commission of 1934. Because the number of departments, based on the application of the homogeneity principle, could not be reduced to less than twenty-five, and because the mayor could not possibly supervise twenty-five directors effectively, Gulick reconciled the two principles by recommending the creation of three or four assistant mayor positions to which supervisory responsibilities could be delegated. Consistent with the principle that politics should be separated as much as possible from administration, Gulick also recommended that the assistant mayors exercise political supervision over department heads but not participate in the administration of programs.

Finally, Gulick believed organizational design should be guided by the **line-staff principle**, although he found the conventional definition of a staff agency highly misleading. According to the traditional definition, staff agencies are created to advise and support line agencies, and are never authorized to issue commands. Gulick believed that this distinction is useful in relation to planning offices because it underscores the importance of "refusing to inject any element of administrative authority and control into such an agency."[33] Budgeting, purchasing, and personnel offices, however, exist for a different purpose, that is, to exercise administrative direction and control. Thus, although they may be referred to as staff agencies, according to a strict interpretation of the line-staff principle, they are not. As Gulick noted, "When administrative responsibility and power are added to any staff function, that function thereby becomes immediately and completely a line function."[34]

POSDCORB: Core Management Functions

Another of Gulick's contributions to administrative management theory was his reformulation of Fayol's statement of managerial functions. As shown in the following, Gulick identified seven management functions using the acronym POSDCORB:

Core Management Functions

Henri Fayol	Luther Gulick
Planning	Planning
Organization	Organizing
	Staffing
Command	Directing
Coordination	Coordinating
Control	Reporting
	Budgeting

Gulick argued that if these functions represent core management responsibilities, then it makes sense to create overhead staff agencies to help the chief executive carry them out. This argument found a central place in the Brownlow Committee report.

Putting Theory into Practice

President Roosevelt forwarded the Brownlow Committee's report to Congress on January 12, 1937. Although Congress rejected Roosevelt's initial proposals, fearing that they would concentrate too much power in the hands of the president, it did pass the Reorganization Act of 1939, authorizing the president to appoint up to six administrative assistants and to draw up plans for restructuring the executive branch. President Roosevelt's Reorganization Plan 1, which went into effect when Congress raised no objection to it, transferred the Bureau of the Budget and the Natural Resources Planning Board to the Executive Office. The Executive Office of the President (EOP) thus evolved into an umbrella organization containing staff agencies charged with helping the president manage the widely dispersed and divergent activities of the executive bureaucracy. This was no small matter. As Donald Stone has written, "Creation of the EOP and its connotation of the president as chief executive as well as head of state is, without doubt, the most significant development in federal administration since the founding of the Republic."[35]

The work of the Brownlow Committee demonstrated the power of ideas and the importance of theory. Each of its recommendations was derived from, or at least supported by, Gulick's analysis of administrative principles. Two recommendations—to provide the president with staff assistants and to establish staff agencies within the Executive Office—were supported by POSDCORB and Gulick's analysis of the line-staff principle.[36] Similarly, Gulick's analysis of the functional principle, specifically the homogeneity principle, supported the committee's recommendation to assign each of the 100 independent agencies to one of twelve executive departments. Each department, Gulick had said in his briefing paper, should be organized around a distinct function or task for which government is responsible. To do otherwise invites confusion, duplication of effort, and inefficiency, and undermines the ability of congress and the president to manage them effectively. This recommendation, too, was backed by theory, even though Congress chose not to act on it.

THE RESEARCH BUREAUS'
CANONS OF INTEGRATION

Textbooks usually limit their treatment of administrative management theory to the writings of Fayol, Mooney and Reiley, and Gulick and Urwick. There is, however, another important body of literature pertaining to administrative principles, one that helped establish public administration as a dynamic and influential field of study in the early 1900s. The writers who contributed to this literature, including Luther Gulick, worked for or were closely associated with the research bureaus that sprang up after the New York Bureau of Municipal Research was founded in 1906.[37] These bureaus, which were supported primarily by philanthropists, provided research and consulting services to government clients. Schooled in the principles of scientific management, they initially concentrated on promoting efficiency and economy by introducing "business methods" to government, including the latest budgeting, accounting, purchasing, and personnel techniques. As noted in Chapter 5, their aim was to eliminate graft, corruption, and the waste associated with inefficient management practices and procedures.

Each time a research bureau completed another study new lessons were learned, thereby adding to an evolving body of knowledge about government's "administrative branch." These were exciting times for researchers in the field of public administration. Understanding the importance of their work, bureau directors took it upon themselves to publish their findings so that others might benefit from them. Often they referred to their findings as "principles." The Institute for Government Research in Washington, D.C., for example, published the following works soon after its formation in 1916: Lewis Meriam's *Principles Governing the Retirement of Public Employees* (1918); A. G. Thomas' *Principles of Government Purchasing* (1919); Francis Oakey's *Principles of Government Accounting and Reporting* (1921); and Arthur W. Proctor's *Principles of Public Personnel Administration* (1921).

The research bureaus soon broadened their scope from introducing business methods into government to reorganizing the government itself. Their aim was to enhance executive leadership and eliminate overlapping responsibilities and duplication of effort by creating a single, integrated piece of administrative machinery. The theme of **integration**, which played a prominent role in the Brownlow Committee Report of 1937, first appeared in the reports of President Taft's Commission on Economy and Efficiency in the years between 1910 and 1913. In transmitting one of the commission's reports to Congress, President Taft wrote:

> . . . .This vast organization has never been studied in detail as one piece of administrative mechanism . . . . At no time has the attempt been made to study all of these activities and agencies with a view to the assignment of each activity to the agency best fitted for its performance, to the avoidance of duplication of plant and work, to the integration of all administrative agencies of the government, so far as may be practicable, into a unified organization for the most effective and economical dispatch of public business.[38]

That the same theme, and sometimes the same language, should characterize government reform efforts for over 30 years is not surprising because most of the key participants were associated with the research bureaus. Taft's Commission on Economy and Efficiency included, among others, Frederick A. Cleveland, codirector of the New York Bureau of Municipal Research, W. F. Willoughby, a professor of political science at Johns Hopkins and future director of the Institute for Government Research in Washington, D.C., and Frank Goodnow, a professor of administrative law at Columbia University who had authored the groundbreaking *Politics and Administration* in 1900. Luther Gulick, who became director of the New York Bureau of Municipal Research in 1918, carried forward the theme of integration in his work on the Brownlow Committee in the 1930s. In the latter instance, however, he chose to support the theme of integration with the universalistic principles identified by Henri Fayol and James Mooney. He did so, perhaps, in the belief that this would give the committee's recommendations even greater credibility.

Although the work of the bureau researchers was largely applied and atheoretical, their recommendations regarding government reorganization rested on a particular theory of democracy that they developed during the course of their research. According to this theory, the chief executive, as the person primarily responsible for executing the public will, must direct and control a single, integrated administrative structure. Otherwise, neither the public nor the legislature can know who to hold accountable for administrative actions. This theory found formal expression in 1915 when the New York Bureau of Municipal Research was asked to conduct a study of the government of New York State. In the early 1900s political authority tended to be highly fragmented by state constitutions, with governors having little control over the many elected department heads and independent boards and commissions. Having concluded that executives must have authority commensurate with their responsibilities, Charles A. Beard and Frederick A. Cleveland presented a set of recommendations for constitutional reform in a report entitled *The Constitution and the Government of the State of New York*. Described by one commentator as a "landmark in the study of public administration," the Bureau's report laid out principles of organizational design that antedated the ones identified by Fayol in 1916 and Mooney and Reiley in 1931.[39] These principles, which came to be known as the canons of integration, may be summarized as follows:[40]

1. The chief executive should be directly elected by and responsible to the voters or their representatives and should serve as chief administrator as well as head of state.

2. All administrative agencies should be consolidated into a relatively small number of executive departments and each department should be organized around, and responsible for, one clear and distinct government function.

3. The power to discharge each administrative function should be vested in a single administrative officer and the lines of responsibility from subordinates to superiors should be definitely fixed.

4. The power of each department head and bureau chief should be commensurate with his or her responsibilities.

5. Chief executives should have at their disposal overhead staff agencies to assist them with planning, budgeting, and staffing, as well as the overall coordination of executive agencies.

6. Chief executives should be responsible for preparing the budget and proposing needed legislation.

7. The legislature should limit its administrative involvement to exercising oversight through investigations, reports and audits.

Although these canons were offered as an antidote to the fragmented and disorganized administrative structures then existing at all levels of government, they also reflected the Progressive party's desire for strong executive leadership. They rested on the belief that neither the legislature nor the public can rightfully hold a chief executive accountable for administrative actions unless he or she is fully responsible for those actions and is given the authority and tools necessary to oversee and manage executive agencies. Only when executives are given authority commensurate with their responsibilities, bureau researchers argued, can democracy and efficiency flourish together. Not every one, however, shared this view of democracy. As discussed in the following, the canons of integration rested on a set of values and a model of centralized control that, in the view of many, served more to undermine democracy than to strengthen it.

TWO CRITIQUES OF ADMINISTRATIVE MANAGEMENT THEORY

The administrative management literature largely defined the content and scope of the newly emerging discipline of public administration during the first half of the twentieth century. In the late 1940s, however, two critiques of administrative management theory were published that helped steer the discipline in new directions. One was penned by Herbert Simon, the other by Dwight Waldo.

Herbert Simon's Critique: Principles as Proverbs

In 1946 Herbert A. Simon, a political scientist at the Illinois Institute of Technology, published a now well-known critique of administrative management theory.[41] Gulick's "Notes on the Theory of Organization" constituted his primary target. The principles identified by Gulick, Simon wrote, are nothing more than proverbs and, like most proverbs, they occur in mutually contradictory pairs. The specialization principle, for example, states that administrative efficiency is increased by dividing work among specialized work units, and the span of control principle says efficiency is increased by limiting the number of people reporting to each supervisor. Yet, as the number of specialized units increases, so too does the span of control of each supervisor. Given this inherent contradiction, Simon wrote, it is not clear which principle an administrator should apply or what trade-offs to accept. In practice, Simon insisted, "Mutually incompatible advantages must be balanced against each other, just as an architect weighs the advantages of additional closet space against the advantages of a larger living room."[42]

Whereas Simon's critique was accurate, it was not entirely fair. Most administrative management theorists recognized the inherent contradictions among the principles they identified. While they believed organizations are characterized by certain universal dynamics, such as vertical and horizontal differentiation, they viewed administrative principles, as Simon did, as criteria for describing and diagnosing administrative situations. They also understood the dilemmas involved in applying them. Gulick, for example, focused a large part of his analysis on the trade-offs between organizing according to purpose, process, clientele, or place.

If Fayol, Mooney, and Gulick did not actually suggest that administrative principles could provide solutions to administrative problems, what was the purpose of Simon's attack? As a behavioral scientist, Simon was put off by the claims of administrative management theorists that they were engaged in developing a science of administration. The idea that principles of administration could be discovered in the same way as laws of science and nature was viewed with considerable skepticism by many social scientists. Even if such laws could be discovered, Simon criticized the bureau researchers for failing to state their principles in terms of causal relationships that could be verified through scientific testing.[43] Administrative theory, he argued, must be based less on personal experience and logical reasoning and more on scientific investigation, and it must be capable of providing administrators with effective guidance in designing and operating their respective organizations.

In 1937 Gulick wrote of the importance of proceeding with the development of a theory of administration of the kind that Simon would later describe.[44] This suggests that the similarities in their views were much greater than their differences. Nonetheless, Simon's critique tended to discredit the contributions of administrative management theorists in the eyes of future generations of public administration students. According to Thomas Hammond, Simon's essay "marked the beginning of the end for the study of the 'principles of administration.' Gulick's essay, and the school of thought it supposedly represented, gradually fell into disrepute, his essay seen as representing an interesting—though fatally flawed—approach to the study of organization."[45]

Dwight Waldo's Critique: Principles as Prescriptions

Dwight Waldo's critique of administrative management theory is found in *The Administrative State*, a revised version of his doctoral dissertation published in 1948.[46] According to Waldo, Gulick's paper on administrative principles, the recommendations of the Brownlow Committee, and the writings of the various "reformers and reorganizers" were heavily influenced by the social and political values of the Progressive Era. Consequently, their principles represent value-based prescriptions rather than value-free scientific findings. Waldo argued that before a science of administration can be developed researchers must acknowledge their value assumptions and treat their prescriptions as testable hypotheses.

Among the Progressive Era value assumptions Waldo associated with administrative management theory are these: that humans are capable of reshaping society for the better; that government is the appropriate instrument for achieving social progress; that policy makers should rely on the expertise of trained professionals; that the powers of chief executives should be increased so that they can exercise effective leadership; and that centralized staff agencies should be created so that chief executives can hold administrative agencies accountable for results. In Waldo's view, the democratic philosophy of the Progressive reformers reversed the nineteenth-century belief that democracy is achieved by dispersing rather than centralizing the powers and functions of government.

Waldo's critique brought to everyone's attention the values underlying what had often been presented as objective, scientific principles. Because of their ideological underpinnings, the canons of integration must be viewed as prescriptions—prescriptions favoring executive leadership, centralized control, and decision making based on expertise. Whereas bureau researchers had offered the canons as a general blueprint for constitutional and organizational reform, Waldo emphasized that they represented a desirable blueprint only for those who accepted the values that underlie them. Waldo's purpose in writing, like Simon's, was not to disparage the study of administration but to place it on firmer foundations. Waldo concluded that this could be achieved only if researchers were willing to state their value assumptions explicitly. Although there are probably no universal principles that are both scientifically and ethically valid, this does not mean that propositions cannot and should not be subjected to scientific study. Theory can advance, Waldo concluded, only if we acknowledge and clarify the frame of reference from which it is offered.

ADMINISTRATIVE MANAGEMENT THEORY
IN PERSPECTIVE

Fayol, Mooney, and Gulick brought the same rational approach to the design of administrative structure that Taylor brought to the shop floor. If their ideas now seem naive or overly prescriptive, the importance of their contribution to organization theory has not been lessened by the passage of time. As management scholar Harold Koontz once observed, "Those who feel that they gain caste or a clean slate for advancing a particular notion or approach often delight in casting away anything which smacks of management principles. Some have referred to them as platitudes, forgetting that a platitude is still a truism and a truth does not become worthless because it becomes familiar."[47]

Henri Fayol offered a general theory of management at a time when organizations were growing rapidly in size and complexity and old ways of doing things no longer sufficed. He emphasized the importance of management education at a time when management was not yet conceived as a distinct profession. Finally, Fayol's statement of management functions—planning, organizing, commanding, coordinating, and controlling—continues to provide the conceptual core around which many management textbooks are organized today.

James D. Mooney and Alan C. Reiley isolated those aspects of organizing that are universal in nature. Drawing upon examples from the past, they described how organizers throughout history had divided work horizontally and vertically to accomplish unique purposes under varying conditions. If the three universal principles they identified do not provide immediate answers about how to divide work, delegate responsibilities, and coordinate work activities, they do provide a valuable framework for thinking about these important questions.

Gulick and others in the research bureau movement brought sorely needed improvements to administrative structures and methods by applying the canons of integration to government. Despite exaggerated claims to scientific objectivity and a propensity to refer to the canons as universal truths, their ideas had positive impacts. If the administrative controls they introduced are now seen as imposing excessive constraints on managerial discretion, this does not diminish their contribution. It only underscores the fact that the task of organizing is never completed. Administrators must continually reassess how best to divide work and coordinate work activities without stifling discretion and initiative.

RELEVANCE FOR PUBLIC MANAGEMENT

The remainder of this chapter explores the relevance of administrative management theory for public management and organizational performance. This exploration is guided by the three analytical frameworks identified in Chapter 3.

Models of Organizational Effectiveness

As indicated in Exhibit 6.3, administrative management theory emphasizes the values associated with the **internal process model**, including information management, stability, and control. This model asks managers to fulfill the organization's integrative function by serving as monitors and coordinators. In administrative management theory, as in Weber's theory of bureaucracy, the scalar chain provides the primary means by which the many specialized activities occurring within the organization are monitored and coordinated. If a conflict occurs at any level of the hierarchy, it is referred upwards until a manager is found with authority over all of the disputing parties. Administrative management theory is particularly concerned with the ability of top administrators to manage the organization as a whole. It calls for a single, integrated administrative apparatus, and it emphasizes the use of overhead staff agencies to assist the chief executive in carrying out planning, budgeting, and staffing responsibilities.

To a lesser extent, administrative management theory also emphasizes the values associated with the **rational goal model**, including planning, goal setting, and administrative efficiency. This model asks managers to help accomplish the organization's goal-attainment function by serving as directors and producers. Forecasting and planning, for example, are key elements in Fayol's theory of management. Similarly, administrative management theorists in the United States advocated strengthened administrative capacity in government so that chief executives might formulate and carry out comprehensive plans addressing the nation's social and economic problems.

Exhibit 6.3 The Competing Values Framework: Four Models of Organizational Effectiveness

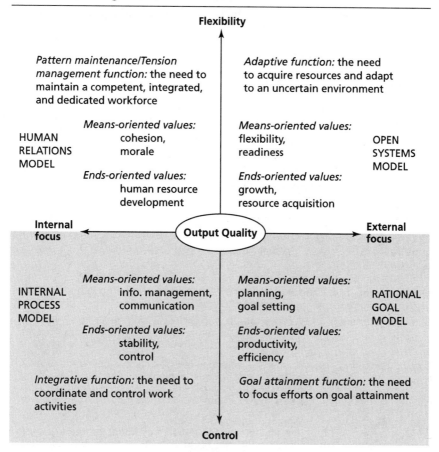

SOURCE: Adapted with permission from Figures 3 and 4, Robert O. Quinn and John Rohrbaugh, "A Spatial Model of Effectiveness Criteria: Towards a Competing Values Approach to Organizational Analysis," *Management Science* 29 (March 1983): 363–373. Copyright 1983, The Institute of Management Sciences, now the Institute for Operations Research and the Management Sciences (INFORMS), 901 Elkridge Landing Road, Suite 400, Linthicum, Maryland 21090-2909 USA.

Although organizations must seek stability to the extent that it is possible in a turbulent environment, managers who focus heavily on integration may achieve stability and predictability at the expense of internal flexibility and external adaptability. Insisting upon strict adherence to the chain of command, for example, may produce red tape and delays that undermine the organization's ability to respond quickly and successfully to changing circumstances. Similarly, managers who focus on the integration and goal-attainment functions may do so at the expense of the pattern maintenance/tension management functions. Fayol's references to the importance of initiative and esprit de corps notwithstanding, the values of cohesion and morale, and the effects of structure on human behavior, receive little attention in administrative management theory. Like scientific management theory and Weber's theory of bureaucracy, administrative management theory tends to view workers impersonally, as role incumbents to be coordinated and controlled rather than as human beings with needs to be satisfied.

Mechanisms for Coordinating and Controlling Work Activities

As indicated in Exhibit 6.4, administrative management theory relies upon **direct supervision** for purposes of coordination and control. Although references are made to psychic coordination and the power of shared ideas, by far the greatest amount of attention is given to the direct supervision of lower officials by higher officials through a highly formalized chain of command. Indeed, administrative management theorists have often been derided for their fixations with organization charts and reporting relationships. Nonetheless, there is not quite the same emphasis on close supervision and standardization of work processes that is found in the writings of Frederick Taylor. Nor is there quite the same emphasis on strict discipline that is found in Weber's theory of

Exhibit 6.4 Six Mechanisms for Coordinating and Controlling Work Activities

Mutual adjustment	Workers consult with each other informally about what needs to be accomplished and how. Responsibility for coordination and control rests with those who do the work.
Direct supervision	A supervisor is assigned to take responsibility for a group of workers and a managerial hierarchy is established to integrate the efforts of all work groups. The supervisor issues personal instructions and monitors individual performance.
Standardization of work processes	Work is programmed in advance of its execution by developing rules and standard operating procedures specifying how everyone is to perform assigned tasks. Coordination is built into the work process itself and control is achieved by strictly limiting each worker's discretion.
Standardization of work outputs	Work outputs are programmed in advance by providing each work group with product specifications or performance goals and allowing members considerable latitude in determining how to achieve them. Control is exercised by collecting output data, requiring corrective action when needed, and rewarding and sanctioning workers based on results achieved.
Standardization of worker skills	Workers are employed who possess the knowledge and skills needed to make appropriate decisions. Educational institutions and professional associations are relied upon to provide standardized training. Professionally trained workers are largely self-coordinating and self-controlling.
Standardization of values	Organizational leaders communicate and act upon a clear vision of what the organization exists to do, where it should be headed, and what values should guide it. Coordination and control is facilitated by commitment of organizational members to shared, internalized values and ideals.

SOURCE: Based in large part on Henry Mintzberg, *Structure in Fives* (Prentice-Hall, 1993, 3–7).

bureaucracy. Rather, the importance administrative management theorists attached to individual initiative, and their preference for leaving administrative decisions to technical experts, indicates a willingness to rely on standardization of worker skills as well as direct supervision for purposes of coordination and control. Workers who possess the knowledge and skills required to perform their duties effectively require less formal supervision.

Motivational Strategies

As indicated in Exhibit 6.5, administrative management theory tends to assume the use of the **legal compliance** strategy. Through the scalar chain, superiors are delegated formal authority to issue commands and apply sanctions

Exhibit 6.5 Four Motivational Strategies

Legal Compliance

Using rules, formal directives, and sanctions to direct and control employee behavior. Employees may come to work, comply with rules, and satisfy minimum role requirements, either because they accept the legitimacy of organizational authority or fear being sanctioned.

Instrumental Rewards

Using rewards to induce desired behaviors.

Rewards for Performance

Distributing pay, promotions, and recognition based on individual performance. Employees may meet or exceed role expectations because they value the material and psychological satisfactions that money, advancement, and recognition can provide.

Considerate Leadership

Adopting a leadership style based on being attentive to employees and considerate of their needs. This strategy may improve morale. It might also induce those who value the respect, support, and approval of persons in authority to meet or exceed their role requirements.

Group Acceptance

Creating a work environment that allows employees to socialize, form group bonds, and enjoy the approval of their peers. This strategy may induce those who value affiliation and peer approval to meet or exceed role requirements, assuming that group norms are consistent with organizational objectives.

Job Identification

Offering work that is interesting, challenging, and responsible. Employees may come to work, meet or exceed role requirements, and possibly exhibit greater creativity and innovativeness. They may do so because they identify with the jobs and find their work intrinsically rewarding.

Goal Congruence

Hiring employees whose goals and values are congruent with the organization's and/or socializing employees so that they internalize organizational goals and values. Employees may come to work, remain with the organization, meet or exceed role requirements, and exhibit greater creativity, innovativeness, and institutional loyalty. They may do so because they identify with the organization's mission and values and because contributing to them reinforces their own self-concept.

SOURCE : Based in large part on Daniel Katz and Robert L. Kahn, *The Social Psychology of Organizations* (Wiley, 1966), pp. 336–68.

and thereby motivate compliance on the part of their subordinates. And yet
Fayol, Mooney, and Gulick were very clear about the limitations of this strategy. Gulick wrote that, "Human beings are compounded of cognition and
emotion and do not function well when treated as though they were merely
cogs in motion. Their capacity for great and productive labor, creative cooperative work, and loyal self-sacrifice knows no limits provided the whole man,
body-mind-and-spirit, is thrown into the program."[48] Gulick wrote in a similar vein that "the task of the administrator must be accomplished less and less
by coercion and discipline and more and more by persuasion."[49] For the most
part, however, administrative management theory focuses on administrative rationality and has little to say on the subject of employee motivation.

SUMMARY

Administrative management theory emphasizes the importance of finding a
good fit between administrative structure and organizational purpose. Understood as a theory of organizational effectiveness, it holds that administrative efficiency is enhanced by clear lines of authority and responsibility running from
top to bottom, a clear and distinct division of labor among departments, and
delegation to administrators of power and authority commensurate with their
responsibilities. Fayol, Mooney, and Gulick restricted their analysis to structural
variables, knowing that other important variables, such as the "human factor,"
would be left out of consideration. They did so because they believed a well-
ordered administrative structure is a prerequisite for the successful attainment
of both individual and organizational objectives. Among the most important
implications of administrative management theory for public management and
organizational performance are the following:

- **Organizing.** Administrative management theory reminds public managers that organizing is a core management responsibility. This responsibility requires finding a good fit between the organization's formal structure
  and its central purpose. Formal structure refers to all institutionalized relationships, methods, and procedures that allow an agency to coordinate and
  control its internal activities.

- **Organizing by function.** Administrative management theory alerts
  public managers to the advantages of organizing by function. When agencies and their subunits are organized around a single basic task they can
  concentrate attention and resources on what the task demands and avoid
  duplication of effort and overlapping responsibilities. And when agencies
  are assigned to one of a small number of executive departments based on
  shared functions it is easier for the chief executive to provide oversight
  and maintain accountability. Of course application of this principle in
  practice calls for considerable judgment. Situations may arise, for example,
  where duplication of effort and overlapping responsibilities are politically
  or administratively advantageous.

- **Clear lines of authority.** Administrative management theory also reminds public managers of the advantages of clarifying the scope of each official's authority and establishing who reports to whom. This aspect of administrative rationality is typically captured in an organization chart. Although agencies operating in an environment of rapid change cannot afford to maintain rigid role descriptions and chains of command, it is still important to clarify basic lines of authority and responsibility.

The implications of administrative management theory are so general in nature that the reader may be forgiven for wondering what guidance this body of theory can provide to the practicing public manager. Aside from the rare situation where senior administrators are asked to participate in a major restructuring of government, this body of theory provides little day-to-day guidance. Nonetheless, this literature is rich in conceptual distinctions that can evoke thoughtful analysis of some of the most important questions in public administration, including how to centralize administrative direction and oversight without unduly constraining managerial discretion, how to delegate authority and responsibility to subordinates without losing control over their actions, whether reliance on formal authority provides an adequate basis for engaging and motivating employees, and to what extent managers should insist upon strict adherence to the formal chain of command. If administrative management theory does not provide definitive answers to these questions, it does provide much food for thought.

Administrative management theory also holds relevance for the larger debates over government reform. Although recent advocates of the entrepreneurial management paradigm argue that the canons of integration are obsolete in today's turbulent environments, political scientists Ronald Moe and Robert Gilmour respond that nothing could be farther from the truth.[50] The purpose of organizing executive departments by function, putting a single administrator in charge of each of them, establishing clear lines of authority running from top to bottom, and maintaining central staff agencies is not only to ensure coordination and control but also political accountability. Because public administration is grounded in public law, structural means must be found to hold those responsible for carrying out the law accountable for their actions. According to Moe and Gilmour, those who champion the entrepreneurial management paradigm, with its emphasis on contracting out and creating public-private partnerships, simply do not understand the threat their paradigm poses for democratic accountability.

NOTES

1. Henri Fayol, *General and Industrial Management* (London: Pitman & Sons, 1949), vi–x.

2. Henry R. Towne, "The Engineer as Economist," *Transactions of the American Society of Mechanical Engineers* vol. 7,

reprinted in Jay M. Shafritz and J. Steven Ott, *Classics of Organization Theory* (Orlando, FL: Harcourt, 2001).

3. Fayol, *General and Industrial Management,* 14–15.

4. Fayol, *General and Industrial Management,* 6.

5. Fayol, *General and Industrial Management,* 57.

6. Fayol, *General and Industrial Management,* 72.

7. Fayol, *General and Industrial Management,* 19.

8. Fayol, *General and Industrial Management,* 41.

9. Fayol, *General and Industrial Management,* x–xii.

10. See *Saturday Evening Post 210* (Oct. 30, 1937), 22; and *Fortune 33* (March 1946), 170.

11. James D. Mooney and Alan C. Reiley, *Onward Industry! The Principles of Organization and their Significance to Modern Industry* (New York: Harper & Brothers, 1931), ix.

12. Mooney and Reiley, *Onward Industry!,* xx.

13. Mooney and Reiley, *Onward Industry!,* 13.

14. Mooney and Reiley, *Onward Industry!,* 37.

15. Mooney and Reiley, *Onward Industry!,* 44.

16. Mooney and Reiley, *Onward Industry!,* 39.

17. Mooney and Reiley, *Onward Industry!,* 57.

18. Mooney and Reiley, *Onward Industry!,* 62.

19. Mooney and Reiley, *Onward Industry!,* xx.

20. President's Committee on Administrative Management, *Report with Special Studies* (Washington, DC: United States Government Printing Office, 1937), 3.

21. Luther Gulick and L. Urwick (eds.), *Papers on the Science of Administration* (New York: Institute of Public Administration, Columbia University, 1937).

22. Nicholas Henry, *Public Administration and Public Affairs* (Upper Saddle River, NJ: Prentice Hall, 1999), 29–30.

23. Lyle C. Fitch, "Luther Gulick," *Public Administration Review 50* (November–December 1990): 604–608.

24. See, for example, W. F. Willoughby, "The National Government as a Holding Corporation: The Question of Subsidiary Budgets," *Political Science Quarterly 32* (December 1917): 505–521.

25. Gulick and Urwick (eds.), *Papers on the Science of Administration,* Foreword.

26. Luther Gulick, "Notes on the Theory of Organization," in Gulick and Urwick, *Papers,* 6.

27. Gulick, "Notes," 6.

28. Gulick, "Notes," 3.

29. Gulick, "Notes," 6–7.

30. Gulick, "Notes," 9.

31. Gulick, "Notes," 10.

32. Gulick, "Notes," 12.

33. Gulick, "Notes," 31.

34. Gulick, "Notes," 31.

35. Donald C. Stone, "Administrative Management: Reflections on Origins and Accomplishments," *Public Administration Review 50* (January-February 1990), 5.

36. James. W. Fesler, "The Brownlow Committee Fifty Years Later," *Public Administration Review 47* (July–August 1987): 291–96.

37. Luther H. Gulick, "Reflections on Public Administration, Past and Present," *Public Administration Review 50* (November-December 1990): 599–603.

38. *Message of the President of the United States on Economy and Efficiency in the Government Service,* January 17, 1912. 62d Cong. 2d sess. House Doc. 458. Serial No. 6296. (Washington, DC: Government Printing Office, 1912), 4.

39. Jane S. Dahlberg, *The New York Bureau of Municipal Research* (New York: New York University Press, 1966), 96.

40. See, for example, Luther Gulick, "Principles of Administration," *National Municipal Review 14* (July 1925): 400–403.

41. Herbert A. Simon, "The Proverbs of Administration," *Public Administration Review 6* (Winter 1946), 53–67.

42. Simon, "The Proverbs of Administration," 62.

43. See also Edwin O. Stene, "An Approach to a Science of Administration," *American Political Science Review 34* (December 1940), 1124.

44. Luther Gulick, "Science, Values and Public Administration," in Gulick and Urwick (eds.), *Papers,* 191–95.

45. Thomas H. Hammond, "In Defense of Luther Gulick's 'Notes on the Theory of Organization'," *Public Administration 68* (Summer 1990), 144.

46. Dwight Waldo, *The Administrative State* (New York: Ronald Press, 1948).

47. Harold Koontz, "The Management Theory Jungle," *Academy of Management Journal 4* (December 1961), 184.

48. Gulick, "Notes," 37.

49. Gulick, "Notes," 37, 39.

50. Ronald C. Moe and Robert S. Gilmour, "Rediscovering Principles of Public Administration: The Neglected Foundation of Public Law," *Public Administration Review 55* (March-April 1995): 135–46.

7

Pre-Human Relations Theory

Mary Parker Follett

Trained almost exclusively in mechanical engineering, the scientific management theorists left behind a rather mechanistic, coldly impersonal philosophy of management. Those trained in the behavioral sciences, by contrast, offered a very different organizational perspective and management philosophy. They viewed the workplace as a social environment peopled by warm-blooded human beings, focused their analysis on interpersonal relations and the social and psychological determinants of morale and motivation, and used the results of their behavioral research to challenge many of the core assumptions of scientific management. From their work emerged two major schools of organization theory: human relations (Chapter 8) and human resources (Chapters 12 and 13).

The origins of human relations theory is generally traced to the Hawthorne studies of the late 1920s. However, the human-centered approach to organizational analysis did not spring forth all at once. Efforts to "humanize" scientific management had begun in the earliest days of the movement. This chapter examines the contributions of Mary Parker Follett, an early pioneer in human relations whose work preceded by several years that of Elton Mayo and Fritz Roethlisberger at the Hawthorne plant. As a theory of organizational effectiveness, Follett's theory holds that organizational performance is enhanced by depersonalizing the authority relationship between supervisor and subordinate and by engaging in collective problem solving. The chapter closes with an analysis of the relevance of this theory for public management and organizational performance.

SCIENTIFIC MANAGEMENT'S TREATMENT
OF THE HUMAN FACTOR

It is often said that Taylorism neglected the human factor in the productivity equation. Taylor's theory suffered from many deficiencies, but neglect of the human factor was not one of them. Despite the engineer's fixation with machines, tools, operating systems, and task definition, Taylor clearly understood that output depended upon the well-being and commitment of the workers. His biography, as well as his own writings, reveal a sincere concern for developing moral character through hard work, facilitating the worker's fullest potential through careful job placement and training, and raising the economic status of workers through a fairer distribution of profits.

The issue is not one of neglect but of flawed assumptions. Taylor's understanding of human needs and the factors that motivate human behavior was shallow and unsophisticated. He underestimated, for example, the importance of the workers' need to affiliate with each other and to seek membership in informal and formal work groups. His experiences with soldiering and labor unions caused him to view work groups as impediments to management control and a chief cause of restricted output. A primary aim of his approach to scientific management was to destroy group solidarity. He intended that managers relate to workers as isolated individuals—defining individual tasks, selecting appropriate individuals to perform them, and rewarding them based on their individual contributions. Holding to the "economic man" theory of motivation that prevailed at the time, Taylor was confident that economic self-interest would prevail over any natural tendency toward human affiliation or group solidarity. Commitment, loyalty, and interest in work were things to be purchased through fatter paychecks.

Taylor's faith in financial incentives, and his belief in the necessity of destroying all forms of group solidarity, were not shared by other scientific management theorists. Henry Gantt, Taylor's closest associate, as well as the Gilbreths, were highly uncomfortable with the coldly rational, patronizing, "slave-driving" aspects of Taylorism. They believed that human beings are not simply an important factor in the productivity equation—they are the most important factor. Whereas Taylor sought to adjust human beings to the needs of the production process, Gantt and the Gilbreths sought to adjust the production process to the needs of human beings. In a passage laden with significance, Lillian Gilbreth wrote that scientific management "has demonstrated that the emphasis in successful management lies on the *man*, not on the *work*; that efficiency is best secured by placing emphasis on the man, and modifying the equipment, materials, and methods to make the most of the man."[1] This, for Taylor, was an unwarranted reversal of priorities. Threatened by the implication that human needs must be placed ahead of technical rationality, Taylor broke off relations with some of his strongest supporters. The seeds of human relations theory are thus to be found in the works of Gantt and the Gilbreths.

The humanizing influence of social science on scientific management was apparent from the beginning. While completing requirements for her doctoral degree in psychology, Lillian Gilbreth wrote and subsequently published *The Psychology of Management*. It summarizes the key elements of scientific management—understood as a synthesis of Frank Gilbreth's motion study and Frederick Taylor's time study—and describes the positive effects of scientific management on the human mind. Scientific management, she argued, focuses the worker's attention, sharpens the senses, strengthens memory, reduces stress, promotes a sense of personal accountability, raises self-confidence, and forms positive work habits. "The ultimate result of all this physical improvement, mental development and moral development," she wrote, "is increased capacity, increased capacity not only for work, but for health, and for life in gen-

Mary Parker Follett 1868–1933

Mary Parker Follett, noted social worker, author, and lecturer, was born September 3, 1868 in Quincy, Massachusetts.[2] In 1888 she entered what would later be known as Radcliffe College and spent two years studying English, political economy, and history. She continued her studies at Newnham College, Cambridge, England, for nearly a year before her mother's ill health necessitated her return to the United States. She attended Radcliffe College periodically while caring for her mother and graduated summa cum laude in 1898. While an undergraduate she wrote and published *The Speaker of the House of Representatives*, which Theodore Roosevelt described as "indispensable to every future student of congressional government."[3] Supported by an inheritance from her grandfather, Follett dedicated the next twenty-five years of her life to social reform programs in the Boston area. She founded and managed social, recreational, and educational clubs for young boys and vocational guidance and job placement programs for teenagers. The Roxbury League, which she founded in 1902, was the first educational and recreational program in the United States to use school buildings for community activi-

ties after hours. School-based community centers soon caught on across the nation and Follett was elected vice president of the National Community Center Association. Follett also dedicated her life to scholarship. Her experiences as a social worker led her to publish *The New State* in 1918 and *Creative Experience* in 1924. Through her work on various public boards and commissions, Follett came in contact with many progressive business leaders. Impressed with their innovative thinking, Follett became interested in management problems, joined the Taylor Society, and began a second career as a lecturer in the field of management. Four of her earliest lectures were sponsored by the Bureau of Personnel Administration in New York City in 1925. Follett chose to live in England during the last five years of her life and her final lectures were delivered at the London School of Economics in early 1933. Later in the year she returned to the United States, where she died of cancer at the age of 65. A fresh and innovative thinker, Follett's ideas were far ahead of her time. Although her ideas had little immediate impact on management practice, her influence on administrative theory has steadily increased with the passage of time.

eral."[4] Although the tone of the book was highly respectful of Taylor, her analysis emphasized the human side of the productivity equation over the technical side, including the foreman's role as a teacher, fair treatment of employees, the development of human capacity, recognition of differences in individual personality and fitness, elimination of fatigue, and maintenance of a supportive, nondistracting work environment. Human happiness was a constant theme.

Unfortunately, Lillian Gilbreth's training in individual psychology diverted her attention away from group dynamics and interpersonal relations. Her analysis was limited primarily to the effects of scientific management on the mind. As did other scientific management theorists, she viewed the workplace as a physical setting rather than a social environment. The variables requiring adjustment were predominantly physical and physiological in nature. If humans are motivated by a desire to satisfy basic social and psychological needs, Lillian Gilbreth's analysis does not reveal what those needs are. Nor is there a clear understanding of the social context of work and how that context affects human behavior. In short, despite the important contributions of the Gilbreths to a human-centered view of management, it was left to later theorists to conceive of the workplace as a social environment and to isolate the social and psychological factors that shape group as well as individual behavior in the workplace. Among the first theorists to do so was Mary Parker Follett.

MARY PARKER FOLLETT'S CONTRIBUTIONS
TO ORGANIZATION THEORY

Mary Parker Follett had little or no influence on Elton Mayo and the human relations school of thought that emerged soon after her death. Nonetheless, like the human relations theorists that followed her, Follett played an important role in steering the theory and practice of scientific management in a more humanistic direction. Her lectures and books have had a lasting impact on organization theory for three reasons. First, she helped put a human face on scientific management, emphasizing that morale and motivation depend on how well the personal needs of workers are satisfied. Second, she exposed the limitations of the structural, organization-chart view of organizations. Her analysis revealed that the principles of administrative management—including formal authority, delegation, and hierarchically ordered chains of command—tell us next to nothing about how to manage people effectively. Finally, she identified a new form of human association and anticipated a time when societal institutions would resolve differences by integrating the needs of all parties and encouraging the fullest development and use of human capacity. Her ideas continue to influence organization theory and management practice precisely because they were so far ahead of their time.[5] Through her books and lectures, Follett laid down the philosophical and theoretical groundwork for many management innovations, including participative management, cross-functional work teams, interest-based bargaining, and diversity management. The analysis that follows focuses on core concepts in her writings, including democracy, integration, power and authority, and leadership.

Follett's Theory of Democracy

Influenced by the German philosopher Georg Hegel, Follett believed that the factual world is a reflection of the collective minds and purposes of past and present generations of human beings. As reflections of mind and purpose, human institutions are dynamic and self-developing. Despite occasional setbacks, they are evolving toward higher states of liberty, or true democracy. This evolution is driven by an underlying force that tends to unify all differences, and that force is the creative power of each individual. In *The New State*, first published in 1918, Follett provided evidence that the effects of this unifying force are beginning to manifest themselves. The New State refers to what the political community will look like when human beings learn how to achieve and sustain True Democracy. It will come into existence when individuals learn to participate in community groups at increasingly more inclusive levels—neighborhood, city, state, regional and national—to determine the collective will of each group at each level. As these collective wills are integrated at successively higher levels, the state comes into being. To Follett, the neighborhood associations she helped organize in Boston, and the resulting national movement, indicated that the unification process was well under way.

Follett found the American conception of representative democracy inherently flawed for two reasons. First, it demands passive consent rather than active involvement. Neither the individual nor society is benefited, Follett argued, by a process in which lone individuals go to voting booths and turn their sovereign right of self-government over to elected officials. True Democracy, as she conceived it, requires the full participation of each and every citizen so that the collective will might be discovered and so that humanity's fullest potential might be realized. Follett believed that the potential that lies in each individual and in society as a whole can be realized only when all citizens contribute their unique talents, perspectives, and expertise—everything that makes them different from everyone else—to the deliberative process.

Second, representative democracy mobilizes particularistic rather than community interests. Instead of integrating the interests of everyone, representative democracy simply counts votes. In Follett's view, the collective will cannot be determined in this way. The interests of the majority are rarely the interests of the citizenry as a whole. Most often, one set of particularistic interests finds majority support and the interests of the rest are simply ignored. According to Follett's theory of democracy, the collective will can only be achieved by integrating individual perspectives and interests. With each person contributing to the deliberative process, a synthesis of differences is eventually achieved. It is this synthesis, reached through the involvement of everyone, that defines the collective will.

Follett believed that humans have an inherent need to associate with others, develop social bonds, and participate in a collective life with all of its obligations. This is a need for self-expression and for self-realization. These needs can be satisfied only through group involvement. In Follett's words, "The craving we have for union is satisfied by group life, groups and groups, groups ever widening, ever unifying, but always groups."[6] Thus it is the group that emerges as the basic political unit in Follett's theory of democracy. As a social worker in Boston, Follett helped organize several neighborhood associations. Members of these associations brought in experts to discuss the pressing issues of the day, organized social and recreational activities for children and adults, and deliberated on how to improve conditions within the community. Having come to view these associations as the nucleus of the New State, Follett proposed that people "should organize themselves into neighborhood groups to express their daily life, to bring to the surface the needs, desires and aspirations of that life, that these needs should become the substance of politics, and that these neighborhood groups should become the recognized political unit."[7]

For Follett, the neighborhood association functioned as a vehicle for satisfying the wants of the community and a forum for uniting differences. "Neighborhood organization," she wrote, "gives us the best opportunity we have yet discovered of finding the unity underneath all our differences, the real bond between them—of living the consciously creative life."[8] Follett believed that by participating in group life individuals develop their fullest potentials as human beings and make their sovereign right to self-government manifest. Responding to those who believed she was advocating a collectivist doctrine, Follett argued that group life liberates rather than suppresses individuality. According to Follett, "We find the true man only through group organization. The potentialities of the individual remain potentialities until they are released by group life. Man discovers his true nature, gains his true freedom only through the group."[9]

Follett understood that her vision of True Democracy represented an ideal, but she believed the tendency in nature to unify all differences was transforming this ideal into reality. Especially relevant to organization theory was her belief that this unifying process calls for an *entirely new form of human association,* one based on collective deliberation. It is not participation in group life itself that is important, Follett emphasized, but the particular way that human beings relate to each other in the act of participating. The integration of differences requires a commitment to deliberately working out problems together. The ideal is reached when people come together not to compare ideas or to vote but to create a common idea through the full involvement of everyone. All of this entails a process of collective deliberation, one in which group satisfaction is understood to be paramount to individual satisfaction. "We must learn to think of discussion," she wrote, "not as a struggle but as an experiment in cooperation. We must learn cooperative thinking, intellectual teamwork."[10] The process of reaching a group decision requires the continuous intermingling of everyone's ideas until something new is created—the collective will or group idea. Each individual then wants what the group wants. Individuals will not always agree with the final decision, but by participating in deliberations they help produce the best possible decision for the group. According to Follett, they may disagree with, even violate, the group decision but they must nonetheless demonstrate their loyalty to the group by continuing to participate, continuing to work to change that with which they disagree.

Resolving Conflict Through Integration

Integration, or the uniting of differences, is the central theme in all of Follett's work. In *The New State* Follett described how integration allows community groups and government bodies to determine their collective wills. In *Creative Experience* Follett extended the concept of integration to all human settings by defining it as a means of resolving conflict. Whether manifested in the home, politics, or workplace, conflict is dealt with in one of three ways: domination, compromise, or integration. **Domination** entails victory of one side over the other. It occurs when one party to a dispute has the means to force its will on the other party. Although domination is often the easiest and quickest way to settle disputes, it holds clear disadvantages in the long run. It fails to resolve the underlying causes of conflict, requires the winning party to expend considerable resources in maintaining its dominance, and legitimizes the right of the other party to dominate in its turn. Although it was the method of choice among heads of state and captains of industry in the 1800s, Follett believed a growing awareness of its disadvantages was turning attention to the virtues of compromise. She did not, however, expect domination to wither away any time soon. It would continue to flourish as long as the American culture glorified battle and the thrill of conquest.

Compromise, by contrast, entails each side giving up some of what it wants to obtain a temporary peace. Compromise, Follett wrote in 1924, is now the socially approved way of resolving conflict, especially in the business sector. In collective bargaining, for example, two countervailing powers, business and organized labor, are encouraged to come to the bargaining table to work out whatever compromises they can. Because collective bargaining reduces incidences of labor violence, Follett endorsed it as a temporary expedient while advocating integration in its place. Compromise, like domination, holds clear disadvantages. Each side is required to make sacrifices, individual perspectives are not altered, the underlying conflict is not resolved and, as a result, no social progress is made. Further, a tendency to think in either-or and us–versus–them terms continues to polarize the two sides.

Integration, which Follett believed is nature's way of unifying differences, involves arriving at a solution in which the desires of both sides find a place. It is the most difficult and challenging means of resolving conflict because it requires approaching deliberations with an open mind, engaging in often lengthy fact-finding exercises, searching for a synthesis, and creating an as–yet unimagined solution. Nonetheless, it is the most constructive of the three means of dealing with conflict, in Follett's view, because it creates something new, something which in satisfying the interests of both parties adds value to society.

The secret to the success of integration is what Follett called **interpenetration**. The ideas and perspectives of each party interpenetrate or intermingle as concerns are discussed. A change in thinking occurs as all participants come to view each other and the total situation in a new light. Mutual understanding and a sense of interdependence are created, thereby motivating participants to search for new ways to integrate their interests. In Follett's words, "Through an interpenetrating of understanding, the quality of one's own thinking is changed; we are sensitized to an appreciation of other values. By not interpenetrating, by simply lining up values and conceding some for the sake of getting the agreement necessary for action, our thinking stays just where it was. In integration all the overtones of value are utilized."[11]

Because some people found her concept of integration too abstract, Follett offered several concrete examples in the course of her writing and lecturing. Her simplest illustration involved a personal experience:

> . . . . In the Harvard Library one day, in one of the smaller rooms, someone wanted the window open, I wanted it shut. We opened the window in the next room, where no one was sitting. This was not a compromise because there was no curtailing of desire; we both got what we really wanted. For I did not want a closed room, I simply did not want the north wind to blow directly on me; likewise the other occupant did not want that particular window open, he merely wanted more air in the room.[12]

Follett also cited an example of integration achieved through legislation. Workmen's Compensation laws integrate the interests of workers and employers by extending disability benefits to injured employees and shielding employers from lawsuits arising from on-the-job accidents. In the language of a later period, laws of this kind create win-win situations. Follett explained the value-adding aspect of integration as follows:

> The illustration just given of the Workmen's Compensation Act shows the important thing about integration. The moment you try to integrate loss, you reduce loss; as when you try to integrate gain, you increase gain. This is the whole claim of integration over either domination or compromise, the three ways of dealing with conflict. In either of the latter you rearrange existing material, you make quantitative not qualitative adjustments, you adjust but do not create. In the case of the Workmen's Compensation Act, you have done more than distribute loss, you have prevented loss. This is creating. You have not balanced or weighed interests, those of industry, workers and community. By integrating these interests you get the increment of the unifying.[13]

Follett gave substance to the concept of integration by clarifying how it might unfold in practice. In most instances integration occurs through conference. She emphasized, however, that not every meeting constitutes a "genuine" conference. Whether the context is a board meeting, a legislative committee, or a labor-management committee, "A conference should not merely record existing differences of opinion, nor should it be a fight, with the vote registering the outcome of the struggle, but a sincere attempt to find agreement."[14] Open-mindedness is a prerequisite. If participants try to push through something already decided on, "then it is not a genuine conference." In addition, a genuine conference calls for a new understanding of what it means to be a representative, as in the case of a labor-management committee. Because the intermingling of ideas constantly creates a new situation, the representative, according to Follett,

> . . . should go back to his constituents not merely to bring information to them, not only to receive fresh instruction from them, but to take back to them whatever integrations of ideas and interests have been made in the representative body in order to unite these again with the ideas and wishes of his constituents. For in the representative body his ideas have been enlarged by all he has discovered of the objections to what he has presented to his fellow representatives, with all that he has heard of the possible consequences of the legislation he is proposing, with all that he has learned of the advantages of other plans, etc. Then, turning back to his constituents, he should unite all his with their developing ideas and wishes, and again go to meet his confreres in assembly or conference reinforced now by the larger point of view thus gained. Our relation to the people we are representing is interweaving at every moment with our relation to the new group.[15]

Once the conference begins, the first step is to bring all differences into the open so that the parties can ascertain the true nature of the conflict and comprehend the entire situation. This stands in sharp contrast to the process of collective bargaining in which each side's true interests and most pressing demands are kept hidden for fear of losing strategic advantage. In Follett's words, "The first rule, then, for obtaining integration is to put your cards on the table, face the real issue, uncover the conflict, bring the whole thing into the open."[16] Full disclosure prompts each side to reevaluate demands in light of their new understanding of the situation. The second step, according to Follett, is to "take the demands of both sides and break them up into their constituent parts."[17] Having isolated each party's underlying concerns, or all of the subproblems relating to the controversy, participants may then engage in problem solving.

Follett acknowledged that formidable obstacles stand in the way. Integration does not come naturally because it is a new concept to most people and all but a few lack the requisite skills. Successful adoption of integration requires acceptance of the concept of integration itself, the strength to break longstanding habits premised on domination or compromise, and a willingness to develop new skills. Because integration entails a new way of relating to each other, skill development is critical to its success. Participants must learn how to think collectively and how to cooperate as a team. They must learn how to synthesize various points of view, how to search for creative solutions, and how to exercise team leadership. In the workplace, for example, much will have to change. Workers and managers must find new ways of relating to each other, their attitudes toward each other must change, and training in teamwork must be provided to everyone.

Follett believed that the acceptance of integration must begin with the acceptance of conflict itself. In her view, conflict is merely the manifestation of differences and thus an inevitable part of the natural order: "We may wish to abolish conflict but we cannot get rid of diversity. We must face life as it is and understand that diversity is its most essential feature."[18] Anticipating the themes of the diversity management literature by over fifty years, Follett argued that differences are not something to be suppressed or feared but something to be valued. "As long as we think of difference as that which divides us, we shall dislike it; when we think of it as that which unites us, we shall cherish it. Instead of shutting out what is different, we should welcome it because it is different and through its difference will make a richer content of life. . . Give *your* difference, welcome *my* difference, unify *all* differences in the larger whole—such is the law of growth."[19]

The conflicts that arise from diversity, Follett added, provide opportunities for constructive social change. Like friction, it can be made to work for us. "It is possible," Follett wrote, "to conceive of conflict as not necessarily a wasteful outbreak of incompatibilities, but a *normal* process by which socially valuable differences register themselves for the enrichment of all concerned. One of the greatest values of controversy is its revealing nature. The real issues at stake come into the open and have the possibility of being reconciled. A fresh conflict between employers and employees is often not so much an upsetting of equilibrium, really, as an opportunity for stabilizing."[20]

The foregoing review of Follett's theory of integration provides the necessary foundation for understanding Follett's views on management, views that are discussed in the sections that follow. Although *Creative Experience* received a favorable response from the more progressive members of the business community, there were still many who found the concept of integration hopelessly idealistic. They challenged her belief that opposed interests are not necessarily incompatible interests, arguing that interests are often inherently opposed and win–win situations are extremely rare. Follett responded by saying ". . . I want to say definitely that I do not think integration is possible in all cases. . . . All that I say is that if we are alive to its advantages, we could often integrate instead of compromising."[21] For her, the ideal is possible much more often than we think, and the reasons for making the effort are compelling.

Follett's Theory of Power and Authority

After publishing *Creative Experience* in 1924, Follett began addressing her ideas specifically to questions of business management. Impressed with the innovative thinking taking place in management circles, she had already joined the Taylor Society when Henry Metcalf, director of the Bureau of Personnel Administration in New York, asked her to speak at a series of conferences for business executives and personnel directors. Accepting his invitation, Follett delivered more than a dozen lectures between 1925 and 1928, with a final lecture presented in

1932.[22] In the course of applying her theory of integration to questions of management, a fresh and intriguing understanding of organizational life and management practice emerged. Power and authority in the workplace provided the subjects of her earliest lectures, including "The Giving of Orders," "Business as an Integrative Unity," and "Power."

As earlier chapters indicated, those who study organizations from a structural perspective tend to emphasize the use of formal authority to coordinate and control the multitude of organizational functions created in the wake of increased specialization. Coordination and control, according to the classical theorists, is achieved by issuing orders to subordinates through the chain of command. Follett, by contrast, having approached the study of organizations from a behavioral perspective, concluded that the exercise of formal authority contributes very little to organizational effectiveness. Worse yet, she believed, the emphasis on formal authority in classical theory actually encourages an autocratic, domination-based approach to management. Greatly troubled by this possibility, Follett devoted her earliest lectures to reassessing the prevailing view of power and authority.

Follett concluded that superior work performance has little to do with the exercise of formal authority and much to do with functional authority, or authority based on expertise. Each member of the organization, manager and worker alike, has a distinct function to perform. Each develops specialized expertise in the performance of duties. For this reason, the authority that matters in the workplace is not the formal authority attached to a person's place in the hierarchy but the authority inherent in the job itself. Functional authority is what allows organizational members to exercise power effectively. In practice, Follett observed, managers often respond to the suggestions of subordinates because they recognize their functional expertise, and subordinates respond to the suggestions of managers for the same reason.

Follett also observed that formal authority is rarely exercised in progressive organizations. Decisions are made based on the needs of the situation and in accordance with policies and operating procedures, not in response to formal orders issued by superiors. Further, communications in progressive organizations are reciprocal, moving in both horizontal and vertical directions, as persons with functional responsibilities pursue their mutual concerns. From Follett's point of view, the suggestion that the exercise of formal authority through the chain of command is a universally sanctioned means of controlling and coordinating only serves to legitimize a command-and-control approach to management. The concept itself tends to encourage managers to think of themselves as perched atop existing hierarchies for the sole purpose of imposing control over all those beneath them. Acceptance of the alternative approach to management—a participative, integration-based approach—becomes all the more difficult to achieve where the exercise of formal authority is viewed as a universal principle.

Follett acknowledged that many supervisors still issue orders and expect to have them obeyed without question. Nonetheless, the shrewd supervisor understands that "to demand unquestioning obedience to orders not approved, not perhaps even understood, is bad policy."[23] It is bad policy, Follett argued, because it is inconsistent with the lessons of psychology. Ordering, exhorting, or even reasoning with employees, according to Follett, seldom produces the desired results. By issuing orders, the supervisor emphasizes the status inferiority of those receiving the orders, robs them of self-respect, and reduces personal autonomy. In Follett's view, autonomy, or the "wish to govern one's own life is, of course, one of the most fundamental feelings in every human being."[24] Most humans do not want to feel subordinate to another. As employees, they want to work *with* others, not *under* others. Follett emphasized that "It is often the order that people resent as much as the thing ordered. People do not like to be ordered even to take a holiday."[25]

These realities led Follett to distinguish "power-over" from "power-with." In her words, "whereas power usually means power-over, the power of some person or group over some other person or group, it is possible to develop the conception of power-with, a jointly developed power, a co-active, not a coercive power."[26] Power-with arises through integration, as workers are encouraged to develop and contribute their unique talents in the course of performing their jobs and resolving differences with others. It encapsulates what today is referred to as empowerment.

Follett's analysis of power and authority established the importance of human relationships as an organizational variable. Success, she believed, is tightly linked to the character of human relations within the organization. She concluded, for example, that a system of human relations premised on the formal superior-subordinate relationship tends to produce negative "habit-patterns." This was to become a central theme in human relations theory: how workers view their jobs, management, and the workplace is colored by the emotions, beliefs, and habits of mind evoked by how they are treated. The manner in which orders are given provides a telling example:

> . . . . Probably more industrial trouble has been caused by the manner in which orders are given than in any other way. . . . What happens to a man, *in* a man, when an order is given in a disagreeable manner by a foreman, head of department, his immediate superior in store, bank or factory? The man addressed feels that his self respect is attacked, that one of his most inner sanctuaries is invaded. He loses his temper or becomes sullen or is on the defensive; he begins thinking of his "rights"—a fatal attitude for any of us. In the language we have been using, the wrong behavior pattern is aroused. . . .[27]

As the foregoing passage suggests, the way human relationships are structured clearly influences behavior, but not always in positive directions. Follett believed that positive habit patterns will replace negative ones only when managers and employees agree to relate to each other in an entirely new way. Managers can take the first step in improving human relations, Follett suggested, by joining with all other employees in learning to obey the law of the situation.

Obeying the Law of the Situation

Follett believed all organizations must coordinate and control work activities, but she parted company with classical theorists regarding how this is best accomplished. Follett's unique contribution to organization theory lies in the application of her theory of integration to the subject of coordination and control. The key to the latter, she concluded, entails *obeying the law of the situation*. In every work situation, she explained, there is a problem to be solved or a need to be addressed. Obeying the law of the situation simply means doing what needs to be done according to principles or methods discovered through joint investigation by those involved, including both workers and supervisors. In Follett's words, "One *person* should not give orders to another *person,* but both should agree to take their orders from the situation. If orders are simply part of the situation, the question of someone giving and someone receiving does not come up. Both accept the orders given by the situation. . . ."[28] In this new way of relating, coordination and control are accomplished behaviorally rather than structurally; coordination occurs automatically through cross-functional consultation and problem solving, and control is achieved by commanding facts rather than people.

Follett emphasized that integration is not a utopian concept. Observing that officials at the same level of authority relate to each other in this way routinely, Follett asked why the same should not be true for individuals at different levels, such as supervisors and workers. Human relations will improve, Follett believed, as soon as supervisors learn "to depersonalize the giving of orders, to unite all concerned in a study of the situation, to discover the law of the situation and obey that."[29] Personal autonomy and self-respect will be preserved, and the resentments that cause negative habit-patterns will be greatly reduced. According to Follett, depersonalizing authority relationships has the added advantage of encouraging workers to take personal responsibility for their work. Involving employees in problem solving, and encouraging them to exercise judgment in carrying out their duties, causes employees to take greater interest in their work. Conversely, employees who are expected to follow orders passed down from above have no reason to take personal responsibility. If anything goes wrong, they can safely say they had done as they were told.

Most workers, Follett believed, are capable of self-management. Organizations can take advantage of this by developing the capabilities of their workers and providing opportunities for them to fully utilize their talents. Follett credited scientific management with depersonalizing authority by substituting standard operating procedures for individual orders but faulted Taylor for insisting upon the strict separation of managing and doing. Workers, Follett argued, should participate in the development of policies and procedures and should have considerable discretion regarding their application. This allows them to develop pride in their work and to gain in self-respect. The organization in turn is able to utilize its human resources much more efficiently. Follett believed that nearly all employees have some managerial ability, even if only a little, and opportunity should be given to them to exercise their ability on the job. Initiative, creative imagination, and executive ability, she emphasized, are not qualities found among managers alone. Her willingness to put trust in workers, to trust their common sense and capacity for self-development, was a breath of fresh air at a time when organization theory was imbued with elitist and paternalistic overtones.

If workers and supervisors are capable of integrating their differences by obeying the law of the situation, is the same true for labor and management as a whole? In her lecture "Business as an Integrative Unity" Follett extended the concept of integration from the worker-supervisor relationship to the relationship between labor and management in the aggregate. True functional unity, she argued, cannot be achieved unless management and labor confer jointly over all matters relating to the productive efficiency of the organization. All business records should be open to employee scrutiny, the fears and concerns of both parties should be discussed openly, and differences should be resolved through integration rather than compromise or concession. Further, this should apply to both labor-management committees established for purposes of collective bargaining and employee-management committees built into the structure of every organizational unit. The most effective method for unifying a business, she stated, is to involve workers in departmental decision making. Doing so creates a crucial identity of interests. In her words, "When you have made your employees feel that they are in some sense partners in the business, they do not improve the quality of their work, save waste in time and material, because of the Golden Rule, but because their interests are the same as yours."[30]

Obeying the law of the situation, a concept encompassing a new and distinct way of relating, provided the foundation for the theory of participative management articulated by Rensis Likert forty years later (Chapter 12). By applying her theories of integration and true democracy to the workplace, Follett developed an alternative vision of the way work should be organized and managed. In *The New State* Follett argued that the potential that exists in each human being can be realized only when each contributes his or her unique talents, perspectives, and expertise to group decisions. Representative democracy, resting as it does on passive consent, denies citizens the opportunity to participate and robs society of the value of their contributions. In her business lectures Follett made it clear that the same is true in the economic realm. Value is added only through the direct involvement of everyone. Workplace relations in Follett's alternative vision are highly participative and egalitarian, demanding a high degree of employee involvement and cooperation among equals.

Follett's Theory of Leadership

As noted earlier, Follett found the prevailing view of power seriously flawed. In her mind, power is not a fixed commodity possessed by top administrators who delegate portions of it to their subordinates. It is instead the capacity to produce results. As she put it, "*We can confer authority; but power or capacity, no man can give or take.*"[31] Although managers cannot delegate power to subordinates, they can and should give subordinates opportunities for developing their own power—that is, the capacity to perform their functions successfully. This is not a matter of sharing power but of creating and exercising power jointly.

Once power is understood in terms of human capacity a new conception of leadership inevitably emerges. The leader is no longer a person who gains the consent of others through force or persuasion but one who successfully builds a team by developing the capacities of its members and securing their fullest contributions. In Follett's words,

> . . . . Power is now beginning to be thought of by some as the combined capacities of a group. We get power through effective relations. This means that some people are beginning to conceive of the leader, not as the man in the group who is able to assert his individual will and get others to follow him, but as the one who knows how to relate these different wills so that they will have a driving force. He must know how to create a group power rather than to express a personal power. He must make the team.[32]

Follett emphasized that the leader may or may not be the member of the group with the highest rank. The leader is simply the one who is able and willing to play a facilitative role: "Now that we are recognizing more fully the value of the individual, now that management is defining more exactly the function of each, many are coming to regard the leader as the man who can energize his group, who knows how to encourage initiative, how to draw from all what each has to give."[33]

Follett's lectures on leadership anticipated the team-building literature of the 1980s by over fifty years. Speaking in 1927, she acknowledged that businesspeople were only beginning to sort out what this new understanding of team leadership might look like in practice. Teamwork, she concluded, is neither democratic nor autocratic. It is integrative. It involves bringing together people performing different functions in an interdependent environment, discussing each other's needs, and reaching agreement about how to integrate differences. Order giving is replaced by joint consultation, and control is exercised not over workers from above but over situations arising at all levels through cross relations between department heads, staff experts, and other involved employees. The purpose of this participative, integration-based approach, Follett emphasized, is not industrial peace as such but progress toward mutual goals.

Follett's Four Principles of Organization

To sharpen the contrast between her understanding of coordination and control and that of the classical theorists, Follett identified four fundamental principles of organization:

1. Coordination by direct contact of the responsible people concerned.
2. Coordination in the early stages.
3. Coordination as the reciprocal relating of all the factors in a situation.
4. Coordination as a continuing process.[34]

Coordination, in Follett's view, is achieved most effectively through the unfolding process of integration. These principles, she told her audience, are already "at work in some of our best managed industrial plants." The first principle emphasizes that integration occurs laterally rather than vertically as all persons who exercise responsible authority in the matters concerned meet to confer and adjust their differences. Because these matters often spill over functional boundaries, consultation must involve managers and workers with relevant expertise from all affected departments.

The second principle stresses that direct contact must occur at the earliest stages of the problem solving or policy making process. If a problem arises on the shop floor, for example, supervisors should immediately involve their workers in factfinding, investigation, and diagnosis of the problem. An interpenetration of their views must occur from the outset if the law of the situation is to be determined. Similarly, if a policy problem arises at the strategic level of an organization, department heads should be involved in deliberations from the outset. Agreement is difficult to secure where department heads are asked to comment after a policy has already been drafted. Policy forming and policy adjusting, Follett believed, must be part of the same process.

The third principle suggests that the process of mutual adjustment must take into account everyone's concerns and the effects the process itself is having on the participants. Peoples' views shift as they deliberate, creating new situations in a continuous fashion. The final decision must reconcile these intermingling and interpenetrating views in a way that adds value to the group and the individuals involved.

The final principle emphasizes that coordination is something that is never achieved once and for all. Situations constantly change. For this reason coordination must be viewed as a continual and necessary process of deliberative problem solving. Follett suggested establishing permanent mechanisms by which problem solving can take place on a continual basis, much like what are now called continuous improvement teams. As we shall see in Chapter 14, the similarities between Follett's four principles and those espoused by quality management theorists in the 1980s are striking.

Follett's Enduring Contributions

Warren Bennis observed in 1995 that "Just about everything written today about leadership and organizations comes from Mary Parker Follett's writings and lectures."[35] Indeed, it is difficult to exaggerate or overstate the value of her insights.

First, Follett humanized scientific management by steering it in a more worker-centered direction. In general she believed scientific management was on the right track. She approved of fact-based decision making, the development of standardized operating procedures, and the elimination of waste. However, she rejected Taylor's separation of managing and doing, and she was among the first to recognize that rational planning and technical efficiency could not guarantee success. Once all competitors had adopted the latest technological and managerial innovations, the continuing pursuit of competitive advantage would cause them to turn their attention to the one critical variable remaining: their human resources. By adopting a behavioral approach to organizational analysis, Follett was able to demonstrate the fundamental importance of human relations as a subject of study. She believed that most institutional problems are essentially problems of human relations. She also believed that there is sufficient commonality in human reactions to similar situations to permit the development of administrative principles pertaining to the behavioral dimensions of organizational life.[36] Accordingly, she called for the scientific study of human relations and chided social scientists for failing to go into the factory, store, town meeting, and congress to study people interacting in specific social contexts.[37]

Second, Follett simultaneously deepened and broadened the prevailing view of the workplace by characterizing it as a social and psychological setting rather than a purely physical one. She concluded that any attempt to understand issues of morale and motivation must begin, not with the lone individual, but with the interrelationships among individuals. This in turn led her to reject individual psychology's stimulus–response model of human behavior. Behavior, she said, is not a response to a single, isolated stimulus but rather a response to a continually evolving situation. She observed, for example, that a boy does not merely respond positively or negatively to school but to his own response to school. The same is true for workers. Above all else, it is perceptions that matter. Because the roles of boss and subordinate are already pregnant with meaning, managers must consider how workers perceive their respective roles and the treatment they receive. Although Follett did not articulate a needs-based theory of motivation, she identified certain basic human needs, including the needs for self-respect, self-expression, and personal autonomy, and established that perceptions regarding the satisfaction of these needs greatly affect employee motivation and morale.

Third, Follett was among the first to envision an alternative to the bureaucratic paradigm implicit in the works of Weber, Taylor, Fayol, and Gulick. As Follett shifted the frame of reference from structure to human relations, the understanding of organizations changed in fundamental and remarkable ways. In contrast to classical theorists, Follett stressed task interdependence rather than independence, reliance upon personal and functional authority rather than formal authority, integration rather than domination, fact control rather than person control, joint consultation rather than unilateral commands, collective responsibility rather than individual responsibility, and teamwork rather than individual action.

It is often said that Follett rejected the bureaucratic paradigm, but it is perhaps more accurate to say that she rejected the prevailing view of what should take place within the bureaucratic shell. For her the key issue was not whether to reject structural principles but how to implement them most advantageously. For example, she did not suggest that the use of formal authority should be avoided altogether, only that it should be exercised sparingly and carefully, with managers relying primarily on personal and functional authority. She did not suggest that hierarchy should be abolished, only that supervisors avoid emphasizing status differences. Nor did she suggest that chains of command are unnecessary, only that they should not stand in the way of cross-functional communication and deliberation. In short, the alternative vision she offered had less to do with formal structure and more to do with the character of worker-management relations within it. Ultimately, she offered an egalitarian and participative approach to management in place of the prevailing command-and-control approach. Although the issue is not discussed by Follett, adopting a different managerial approach is likely to have structural consequences, with hierarchies becoming flatter as formal authority is deemphasized and teamwork is encouraged.

That Follett's alternative paradigm captured something fundamental is suggested by the "rediscovery" of her ideas by three subsequent schools of thought: the participative management school of the 1950s and 1960s, the quality-of-work-life school of the 1970s, and the empowerment and team-building school of the 1980s and 1990s.[38] Having never grown obsolete, her ideas serve to capture the essence of contemporary thinking remarkably well. Debate continues, however, about the viability of Follett's alternative vision. Some commentators believe that, however desirable an egalitarian, participative, integration-based workplace might be, Follett offered a romantic ideal that cannot be achieved—or at least cannot be sustained for long.

Nitin Nohria, for example, suggests that Follett's ideal ultimately runs afoul of Michel's "iron law of oligarchy," which states that all organizations tend to become divided into a minority of directors and a majority of directed.[39] As long as people seek power, either as a means to an end or as an end in itself, it will be hard to sustain a system based on the concept of power-with. Nohria also notes that many situations are truly zero-sum in nature, making integrative solutions impossible. "A classic case," he wrote, "is downsizing. It is hard to arrive at a decision to lay off 20 percent of a workforce through a participative process."[40] Paul Lawrence has offered a slightly more optimistic view.[41] In his view we do not yet know whether the iron law of oligarchy is universal and inevitable. Over time we may see a gradual, episodic progress toward the attainment of Follett's ideal.

Follett's considerable influence on later generations of theorists is now well-established, but her influence on her contemporaries in the business community was slight. Although her ideas were well-received among the more progressive members of the business community, they had no discernible impact on management practice. Why her ideas failed to fall on fertile ground until much later has been the subject of considerable speculation. Rosabeth Moss Kanter suggests that her ideas were ignored in part because they had been expressed by a woman.[42] Peter Drucker, by contrast, argues that her ideas were simply too far ahead of their time.[43] Management lacked the language, the structural mechanisms, and the mental mindset to put her theory of integration into practice. This was a time, after all, when managers were struggling to implement the structural innovations endorsed by scientific and administrative management theorists, including the departmental form of organization, clear chains of commands, planning staffs, and standardized operating procedures. It was also a time when management and labor alike believed in the inevitability of class warfare and thus viewed the concept of integration as hopelessly naive. They were not yet ready or able to follow through on the implications of a behavioral theory calling for team-based consultation and less reliance on formal authority. Although the extent to which Follett's ideas can be put into practice remains to be seen, for many her vision serves as an ideal toward which to strive. The important thing, Follett said, was to strive for something better. Human progress depends on it.

RELEVANCE FOR PUBLIC MANAGEMENT

The remainder of this chapter explores the relevance of Follett's theory of integration for public management and government performance. This exploration is guided by the three analytical frameworks identified in Chapter 3.

Models of Organizational Effectiveness

As indicated in Exhibit 7.1, Follett's theory of integration emphasizes the values associated with the **human relations model**, including cohesion, morale, and human resource development. This model focuses on accomplishing the organization's pattern maintenance and tension management functions. By serving as facilitators and mentors, managers can help maintain cohesive social relations in the workplace and keep to a minimum the tensions and conflicts that inevitably arise in organizational settings. Follett's adoption of the human relations model may be seen in her concern for depersonalizing the authority relationship, safeguarding individual autonomy and self-respect, and searching for ways to satisfy the wants of workers and supervisors alike through collective deliberation and problem solving. Her theory asks managers to exercise personal leadership in developing the unique talents of all workers and melding them together into a cohesive work team.

One of the most interesting aspects of Follett's theory of integration is that it goes farther than perhaps any other theory of organization toward achieving a workable balance among the many effectiveness values cited in Quinn's competing values framework. As indicated in Exhibit 7.1, Follett's theory embraces the **rational goal** and **internal process** models as well as the human relations model. Her theory of integration calls for an entirely different set of means for directing the attention of workers to what needs to be accomplished (the goal attainment function) and for coordinating and controlling their efforts (the integration function), means that are more compatible with the values associated with the human relations model than those endorsed by the classical theorists. Follett's theory of integration asks supervisors at all levels to rely upon their formal authority and status in the hierarchy as little as possible, relying instead on the authority inherent in each situation. Stated more concretely, her theory asks managers to invite all persons familiar with or affected by a particular organizational problem to deliberate together, drawing upon their collective expertise and knowledge to determine what the situation calls

Exhibit 7.1 The Competing Values Framework: Four Models of Organizational Effectiveness

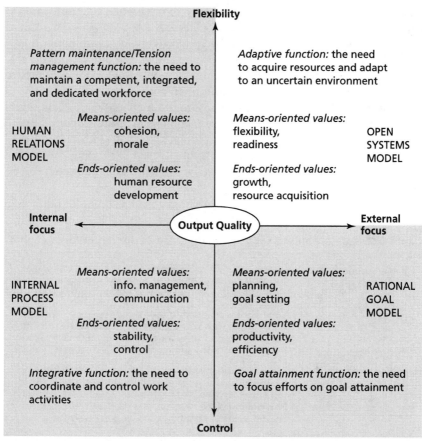

Flexibility

Pattern maintenance/Tension management function: the need to maintain a competent, integrated, and dedicated workforce

Adaptive function: the need to acquire resources and adapt to an uncertain environment

HUMAN RELATIONS MODEL

Means-oriented values: cohesion, morale

Means-oriented values: flexibility, readiness

OPEN SYSTEMS MODEL

Ends-oriented values: human resource development

Ends-oriented values: growth, resource acquisition

Internal focus ← Output Quality → **External focus**

INTERNAL PROCESS MODEL

Means-oriented values: info. management, communication

Means-oriented values: planning, goal setting

RATIONAL GOAL MODEL

Ends-oriented values: stability, control

Ends-oriented values: productivity, efficiency

Integrative function: the need to coordinate and control work activities

Goal attainment function: the need to focus efforts on goal attainment

Control

SOURCE: Adapted with permission from Figures 3 and 4, Robert O. Quinn and John Rohrbaugh, "A Spatial Model of Effectiveness Criteria: Towards a Competing Values Approach to Organizational Analysis," *Management Science* 29 (March 1983): 363–373. Copyright 1983, The Institute of Management Sciences, now the Institute for Operations Research and the Management Sciences (INFORMS), 901 Elkridge Landing Road, Suite 400, Linthicum, Maryland 21090-2909 USA.

for and then working together to carry out the resulting decision. This allows goals to be attained and work activities coordinated, all without sacrificing job satisfaction and self-respect in the process.

Follett's approach to management provides a stark contrast to the top-down, command–and–control approach often reflected in classical theory. Rather than formulating orders and directives at the top and passing them down the chain of command for disciplined implementation at the bottom, Follett's theory calls for delegating as much decision-making authority as possible to those closest to the problem, thereby showing a greater concern for flexibility and empowerment than predictability and control.

Mechanisms for Coordinating
and Controlling Work Activities

As indicated in Exhibit 7.2, Follett's theory of integration relies on **mutual adjustment** to coordinate and control work activities. Although she believed that all complex organizations must be internally divided and hierarchically ordered to carry out their mandated responsibilities, she did not believe that orders issued through the chain of command represented the most effective means of ensuring coordination and control. In her view the resulting costs in terms of reduced cohesion and morale were too high and entirely unnecessary. She believed a much more effective method is to invite workers from all organizational units and all hierarchical levels to consult with each other as needed to determine the law of the situation. Instead of viewing control as a static management function, Follett viewed it as a continuous, dynamic process of mutual adjustment.[44]

Exhibit 7.2 Six Mechanisms for Coordinating and Controlling Work Activities

Mutual adjustment	Workers consult with each other informally about what needs to be accomplished and how. Responsibility for coordination and control rests with those who do the work.
Direct supervision	A supervisor is assigned to take responsibility for a group of workers and a managerial hierarchy is established to integrate the efforts of all work groups. The supervisor issues personal instructions and monitors individual performance.
Standardization of work processes	Work is programmed in advance of its execution by developing rules and standard operating procedures specifying how everyone is to perform assigned tasks. Coordination is built into the work process itself and control is achieved by strictly limiting each worker's discretion.
Standardization of work outputs	Work outputs are programmed in advance by providing each work group with product specifications or performance goals and allowing members considerable latitude in determining how to achieve them. Control is exercised by collecting output data, requiring corrective action when needed, and rewarding and sanctioning workers based on results achieved.
Standardization of worker skills	Workers are employed who possess the knowledge and skills needed to make appropriate decisions. Educational institutions and professional associations are relied upon to provide standardized training. Professionally trained workers are largely self-coordinating and self-controlling.
Standardization of values	Organizational leaders communicate and act upon a clear vision of what the organization exists to do, where it should be headed, and what values should guide it. Coordination and control is facilitated by commitment of organizational members to shared, internalized values and ideals.

SOURCE: Based in large part on Henry Mintzberg, *Structure in Fives* (Prentice-Hall, 1993, 3–7).

Under mutual adjustment, responsibility for coordination and control rests with those who do the work. This means that for mutual adjustment to be effective managers must genuinely believe that workers are capable of self-management and self-control and that they don't need to be told what to do or be threatened with sanctions to ensure compliance. Mutual adjustment requires a philosophy based on management-by-trust rather than management-by-fear, and this, Follett acknowledged, is a difficult prerequisite to satisfy.

Whereas direct supervision and work standardization may be appropriate mechanisms of coordination and control in production and procedural agencies where the work is routine, outputs measurable, and the environment stable, mutual adjustment may be more appropriate in those agencies that James Q. Wilson calls craft and coping agencies. In these agencies the work typically requires considerable independent judgment and outputs and outcomes are difficult to measure. Where these conditions prevail, top-down control through direct supervision and work standardization is unlikely to be effective. Developing the talents of each worker, expanding the scope of each worker's discretion, and encouraging cross-functional problem solving may prove to be far more effective in these agencies if the prerequisite noted above can be satisfied. As Follett observed, managerial employees consult with each other all the time without any particular concern about their position in the hierarchy. She saw no reason why the same cannot be true for relations between managerial and nonmanagerial personnel.

Motivational Strategies

In contrast to theorists such as Frederick Taylor, Follett did not believe that humans respond primarily to economic incentives. In what might be recognized today as an early statement of a needs-based theory of motivation, Follett wrote at length about the value workers place on personal autonomy and self-respect. Their perceptions of how they are being treated and their feelings of self-worth influence their degree of job satisfaction and motivation. Although Follett did not endorse any particular motivational strategy, her analysis is consistent with the considerate leadership, group acceptance, and job identification strategies.

As indicated in Exhibit 7.3, the **considerate leadership strategy** calls for motivating employees by being supportive, respectful, and attentive to their individual needs, and by distributing extrinsic rewards in the form of praise and approval. Similarly, the **group acceptance** strategy relies on the extrinsic rewards associated with affiliating with others, forming social bonds, and enjoying the approval of one's peers. Follett characterized group involvement as a fundamental human need.

The **job identification strategy**, by contrast, relies on the motivational power of intrinsic rewards. For example, if jobs are challenging and provide considerable autonomy, job incumbents may be motivated by the intrinsic rewards

Exhibit 7.3 Four Motivational Strategies

Legal Compliance

Using rules, formal directives, and sanctions to direct and control employee behavior. Employees may come to work, comply with rules, and satisfy minimum role requirements, either because they accept the legitimacy of organizational authority or fear being sanctioned.

Instrumental Rewards

Using rewards to induce desired behaviors.

Rewards for Performance

Distributing pay, promotions, and recognition based on individual performance. Employees may meet or exceed role expectations because they value the material and psychological satisfactions that money, advancement, and recognition can provide.

Considerate Leadership

Adopting a leadership style based on being attentive to employees and considerate of their needs. This strategy may improve morale. It might also induce those who value the respect, support, and approval of persons in authority to meet or exceed their role requirements.

Group Acceptance

Creating a work environment that allows employees to socialize, form group bonds, and enjoy the approval of their peers. This strategy may induce those who value affiliation and peer approval to meet or exceed role requirements, assuming that group norms are consistent with organizational objectives.

Job Identification

Offering work that is interesting, challenging, and responsible. Employees may come to work, meet or exceed role requirements, and possibly exhibit greater creativity and innovativeness. They may do so because they identify with the jobs and find their work intrinsically rewarding.

Goal Congruence

Hiring employees whose goals and values are congruent with the organization's and/or socializing employees so that they internalize organizational goals and values. Employees may come to work, remain with the organization, meet or exceed role requirements, and exhibit greater creativity, innovativeness, and institutional loyalty. They may do so because they identify with the organization's mission and values and because contributing to them reinforces their own self-concept.

SOURCE: Based in large part on Daniel Katz and Robert L. Kahn, *The Social Psychology of Organizations* (Wiley, 1966), pp. 336–68.

associated with higher self-esteem, greater personal growth, and opportunities for self-expression. Although Follett did not address this strategy explicitly, it is clearly consistent with her analysis of the satisfactions derived by participants as they engage in collective problem solving. Because public employees are typically well-educated, engaged in technical or professional lines of work, and desirous of personal and professional growth, a motivational strategy based on intrinsic rewards may be particularly effective in many public agencies.

SUMMARY

Lillian Gilbreth and Mary Parker Follett were among the first to explore questions of organizational design and management from a behavioral perspective. They helped nudge scientific management and administrative management theory in a more humanistic direction by challenging classical assumptions about human motivation and the necessity of coordinating and controlling human behavior through structural means. Their work provides evidence that the humanizing of scientific and administrative management theory was well underway when Elton Mayo and Fritz Roethlisberger first articulated their theory of human relations in the late 1920s.

Mary Parker Follett's theory of integration views conflict as a natural part of organizational life and suggests that it should be resolved through integration rather than domination or compromise. Understood as a theory of organizational effectiveness, it holds that organizational performance is enhanced by relying on functional and personal authority rather than formal authority and by engaging all members of the organization in collective problem solving. Among the most important implications of her theory for public managers are the following:

- **Depersonalizing authority.** Follett suggests that supervisors and managers should de-emphasize the differences in authority and status between themselves and their subordinates. As a corollary, they should avoid issuing orders or commands. The top-down, command-and-control approach to management violates deeply felt needs for self-respect and personal autonomy and thus succeeds only in producing "negative habit-patterns."

- **Collective problem-solving.** Follett also suggests that supervisors and managers should engage everyone affected by a problem in searching for an integrative solution in which the interests of all parties find satisfaction. This involves investigating the facts of the situation and agreeing to do what the situation seems to call for. By agreeing to "obey the law of the situation," participants experience personal autonomy, maintain self-respect, and develop "positive habit patterns," including heightened commitment to the decisions they help to craft. Further, a new, creative solution is brought into being which "adds value" to both the organization and those who work within it.

- **Participative management.** Rejecting Taylor's separation of planning and doing, Follett suggests that supervisors and managers should be entirely open about issues facing the organization and involve everyone in developing organizational policies and procedures. Anticipating human resources theory by forty years, she suggests that supervisors and managers should develop and utilize the unique talents of their workers and release the creative potential locked up in each and every individual through collective problem solving and participation in management decision making.

Mary Parker Follett's theory of integration was well ahead of its time. Even today it offers one of the clearest alternatives to the command-and-control approach to management and reliance on the scalar chain for purposes of coordination and control. It holds out the possibility that collective self-control is a viable option for those seeking to improve organizational performance. Although her writings were idealistic and prescriptive in tone and generally unsupported by available research findings, the basic outline of her theory would find support in several of the later schools of thought. The significance of her contributions to organization theory will become more apparent as the chapters unfold.

NOTES

1. L. M. Gilbreth, *The Psychology of Management: The Function of the Mind in Determining, Teaching and Installing Methods of Least Waste* (New York: The Macmillan Company, 1919), 3.

2. Edward T. James (ed.), *Notable American Women 1607–1950* vol. 1 (Cambridge: Harvard University Press, 1971), 639–41; Pauline Graham (ed.,) *Mary Parker Follett—Prophet of Management* (Boston: Harvard Business School Press, 1995), 11–32.

3. Theodore Roosevelt, "Follett: Speaker of the House of Representatives," *American Historical Review 2* (October 1896), 177.

4. L. Gilbreth, *The Psychology of Management,* 324.

5. Elliot M. Fox, "Mary Parker Follett: The Enduring Contribution," *Public Administration Review 28* (November/December 1968), 520–28; Pauline Graham (ed.), *Mary Parker Follett—Prophet of Management* (Boston: Harvard Business School Press, 1995).

6. Mary Parker Follett, *The New State* (New York: Longmans, Green, 1920), 6.

7. Follett, *The New State,* 96.

8. Follett, *The New State,* 201.

9. Follett, *The New State,* 6.

10. Follett, *The New State,* 97.

11. Mary Parker Follett, *Creative Experience* (New York: Longmans, Green, 1924), 163.

12. Mary Parker Follett, "Constructive Conflict," in Henry C. Metcalf and L. Urwick (eds.), *Dynamic Administration: The Collected Papers of Mary Parker Follett* (New York: Harper & Brothers, 1941), 32.

13. Follett, *Creative Experience,* 45–46.

14. Follett, *Creative Experience,* 200.

15. Follett, *Creative Experience,* 241–42.

16. Follett, "Constructive Conflict," 38.

17. Follett, "Constructive Conflict," 40.

18. Follett, *Creative Experience,* 301.

19. Follett, *The New State,* 39–40.

20. Follett, *Creative Experience,* 301.

21. Follett, "Constructive Conflict," 36.

22. These lectures are found in Metcalf and Urwick (eds.), *Dynamic Administration.*

23. Follett, "The Giving of Orders," in Metcalf and Urwick (eds.), *Dynamic Administration,* 51.

24. Follett, "The Giving of Orders," 61.

25. Follett, "The Giving of Orders," 61.

26. Follett, "Power," in Metcalf and Urwick (eds.), *Dynamic Administration,* 101.

27. Follett, "The Giving of Orders," 57.

28. Follett, "The Giving of Orders," 59.

29. Follett, "The Giving of Orders," 58.

30. Follett, "Business as an Integrative Unity," in Metcalf and Urwick (eds.), *Dynamic Administration,* 82.

31. Follett, "Power," 112.

32. Follett, "Leader and Expert," in Metcalf and Urwick (eds.), *Dynamic Administration*, 248.

33. Follett, "Leader and Expert," 247.

34. Follett, "Individualism in a Planned Society," in Metcalf and Urwick (eds.), *Dynamic Administration*, 297.

35. Warren Bennis, "Thoughts on 'The Essentials of Leadership,'" in Pauline Graham (ed.), *Mary Parker Follett—Prophet of Management*, 178.

36. Metcalf and Urwick, *Dynamic Administration*, 24.

37. Follett, *Creative Experience*, ix–x.

38. See, Nitin Nohria, "Mary Parker Follett's View on Power, the Giving of Orders, and Authority: An Alternative to Hierarchy or a Utopian Ideology?" in Graham (ed.), *Mary Parker Follett*, 159–60.

39. Nohria, "Mary Parker Follett's View," 160–61.

40. Nohria, "Mary Parker Follett's View," 161.

41. Paul R. Lawrence, "Epilogue," in Graham (ed.), *Mary Parker Follett*, 295.

42. Rosabeth Moss Kanter, "Preface," in Graham (ed.), *Mary Parker Follett*, xvi–xvii.

43. Peter F. Drucker, "Introduction," in Graham (ed.), *Mary Parker Follett*, 1–9.

44. L. D. Parker, "Control in Organizational Life," *Academy of Management Review* 9 (October 1984): 736–45.

8

Human Relations Theory

Elton Mayo and
Fritz Roethlisberger

Whereas scientific management theorists approached the study of organizations from a structural perspective, human relations theorists did so primarily from a behavioral perspective. This had the effect of shifting the focus of analysis from the technical to the human aspects of production, from economic and physiological determinants of behavior to social and psychological determinants, and from individuals working in isolation to groups of employees working together. The result was an approach to management that was much less impersonal and mechanistic than scientific management. But, as we shall see, human relations theorists did not ultimately repudiate scientific management theory. They contented themselves instead with challenging some of its assumptions and offering a few useful correctives. Understood as a theory of organizational effectiveness, human relations theory calls for maintaining a nurturing work environment, replacing close supervision with a more relaxed and sympathetic form of supervision, and encouraging the development of cohesive work groups.

The body of theory that came to be known as *human relations* grew out of a series of studies conducted at the Hawthorne Western Electric plant on the outskirts of Chicago between 1927 and 1932. This chapter describes the Hawthorne studies and the theory of human relations developed by Elton Mayo and Fritz Roethlisberger. It closes with an analysis of the relevance of human relations theory for public management and organizational performance.

Elton Mayo 1880–1949

George Elton Mayo, widely recognized as the father of human relations theory, was born in Adelaide, Australia, on December 26, 1880.[1] He studied medicine in Australia, Scotland, and England before deciding that the routine aspects of medicine were not to his liking. In 1905 he returned to Australia, entered the University of Adelaide in 1907, and received his A.B. degree in philosophy and psychology in 1911. He also began graduate studies at this time but did not receive his M.A. degree until he completed a thesis in 1926. As a professor of philosophy at the University of Queensland, Mayo began working with soldiers who had returned from World War I suffering from mental disorders known as shell shock. He found the task of treating patients and reporting his observations an exciting one and subsequently applied the clinical approach to his work in industrial relations. In 1922 he left Australia for England by way of the United States but was unable to continue to England due to lack of funds. Aided by a grant from the Laura Spelman Rockefeller Foundation, Mayo secured a temporary position as a research associate at the Wharton School of Commerce and Finance at the University of Pennsylvania. There he wrote a series of articles on the problems of life and work in industrial society. His work caught the attention of the dean of Harvard's Graduate School of Business Administration, who invited him to join the faculty in 1926 as associate professor and director of the newly created Department of Industrial Research.

Soon after Mayo joined the Harvard faculty, a business executive with the Western Electric Company asked him to assist with a study of working conditions at the Hawthorne plant on the outskirts of Chicago. Although the research was already underway, Mayo's interpretation of the data led company researchers to conduct additional studies centering on employee attitudes and group behavior. The first extensive report of the now-famous Hawthorne studies is found in Mayo's *The Human Problems of an Industrial Society* published in 1933. The findings of the Hawthorne studies received worldwide attention and the ideas and methods that Mayo brought to industrial research spurred the development of a new field of study known first as human relations and later as *organizational behavior*. The clearest statement of his ideas is found in *The Social Problems of an Industrial Society*, published in 1945. Mayo retired from Harvard in 1947 and died in England two years later at the age of 68.

MAYO'S THEORY OF SOCIAL DISORGANIZATION AND HUMAN IRRATIONALITY

Whereas Mary Parker Follett derived her ideas about human relations from Hegelian philosophy and keen personal observation, Elton Mayo derived his from clinical psychology. To understand Mayo's contribution to organization theory, it is necessary to begin with his theory of social disorganization, irrationality, and revery. The general outline of his theory was expressed in a series of articles published in *The Journal of Personnel Research* and *Harper's Magazine* soon after his arrival in the United States from Australia in 1922.[2]

Mayo believed that modern industrial societies are experiencing the adverse effects of **social disorganization**. These include international distrust, labor unrest, higher rates of suicide, higher numbers of people experiencing mental breakdowns, and a general sense of discontent. Mayo attributed social disorganization to the Industrial Revolution, which destroyed the social ties that once bound together the members of society. Individuals are no longer integrated with each other through family and kinship ties, shared norms about how to behave, and clearly defined social roles. Children leave home after completing high school and move from place to place seeking employment. Some find jobs in factories but are forced to perform monotonous and boring tasks without any sense of how they are contributing to the common interest. Mayo argued that although we cannot restore the conditions of earlier, more traditional societies we can and must discover new modes of social collaboration.

One sign of social disorganization is industrial unrest. Mayo believed that the causes of industrial unrest can be traced to the **irrational tendencies** of otherwise normal individuals and their incomplete adjustment to their environments. As part of the maturation process, all humans strive to develop a sense of self, come to terms with their childhood experiences, and adjust themselves to the physical and social environments of the adult world. But in a disorganized society, according to Mayo, individual adjustment is much more difficult. Extended kinship groups are rarely available to assist with personal development, social norms defining appropriate behaviors are much weaker, and the pace of technological change is much greater. Consequently, many people reach adulthood without having come to terms with, for example, a childhood preoccupation with death, an abusive or absent parent, or an overly strict upbringing. Burdened with unresolved personal fears and feelings of inadequacy, some individuals suffer mental breakdowns or are paralyzed by neurotic obsessions. Most, however, are maladjusted in relatively minor ways and continue to function reasonably well. They may exhibit eccentricities such as personal rituals and superstitions, or a tendency toward perfectionism or rebelliousness. They may also experience a reduced ability to relate to others in a healthy fashion due to their irrational beliefs, distorted perceptions, or personal delusions. According to Mayo, the more preoccupied individuals are with their unresolved fears and feelings the more strained their relationships become.

Mayo believed that researchers had missed the significance of this point. "What social and industrial research has not sufficiently realized as yet is that these minor irrationalities of the "average normal" person are cumulative in their effect. They may not cause "breakdown" in the individual but they do cause "breakdown" in the industry."[3] Mayo believed that labor-management conflicts are driven more by mistrust and misperception arising from unconscious fears than by objective facts or conditions. In short, Mayo's training in clinical psychology led him to view strikes and workplace disputes as products of individual maladjustment.

Workplace disputes occur, according to Mayo, because neither the complainer nor the person receiving the complaint is aware of what lies behind it.

For example, a worker's belief that she is not paid fairly may mask a deeper concern about her family's financial security. The worker's grievance is likely to persist despite a wage increase because the underlying fear has not been addressed. In short, fears tend to distort a person's understanding of objective reality. In Mayo's words, "Reveries born of imperfect adjustment to industrial conditions make the individual restless, dissatisfied, unhappy. He may think that "another ten dollars" would make him happy; and he may be quite wrong."[4] Because labor complaints of this kind are merely symptoms of underlying fears, feelings, and needs, responding to the complaint itself has no long-term benefit. For this reason Mayo urged industrial researchers to investigate the sources of maladjustment and help individuals come to terms with their unconscious fears and unacknowledged feelings.

Mayo understood that industrial unrest cannot be attributed to human irrationality alone; the factory system itself is largely responsible. From this perspective, industrial problems must be viewed as arising from the lack of fit between each individual's fears and needs and the system's ability to allay those fears and satisfy those needs. Indeed, Mayo believed that industrial methods actually exacerbate fears and prevent need satisfaction. He castigated researchers and managers alike for failing to comprehend this. Rather than adjusting working conditions to the needs of human beings, managers expect workers to adjust to the prevailing system, a system designed according to the cold, technical logic of industrial engineers. No one, Mayo wrote, has cared to ask how industrial methods and working conditions can be adjusted to human needs.

Arguing that we can no longer maintain "the vague hope that humanity will somehow adapt itself to any working conditions we see fit to impose," Mayo insisted "that a careful investigation of the human aspect of industrial organization is greatly needed."[5] His own study of employee turnover in a Philadelphia textile mill provided support for his thesis that the narrow division of labor creates boredom and monotony, and frustrates the basic human need to achieve something of importance in collaboration with others. In his view, performing narrowly defined tasks in relative isolation prevents workers from developing their capabilities and leaves them feeling defeated. Mayo introduced these themes in a 1924 article entitled "The Great Stupidity":

The human desire to achieve is essentially social; there is a fundamental urge not merely to stand well with one's fellows but also to collaborate with them in a social task. When this initiative is denied and turned aside, it only rarely finds another equally satisfactory outlet. More often than not it turns upon itself and manifests itself in the form of disintegrating moods of pessimism. There are few machine shops in America or elsewhere which do not run a noisy accompaniment to a rising tide of human defeat. This is not necessary; some enlightened employers have demonstrated that it can be avoided. But widely over the industrial field the assertion remains true. The machine shop is a potent agency of repression or perversion of human energy; that civilization disregards this fact is the great stupidity of our time.[6]

Mayo's theory of social disorganization does not offer a complete and convincing explanation of industrial unrest. The latter cannot be reduced so easily to a macro-level explanation (social disorganization), an intermediate-level explanation (industrial methods), and a micro-level explanation (individual irrationality). Even if the hypothesized relationships among these variables could be confirmed, many other causes of industrial unrest are excluded from the analysis. Mayo's theory is nonetheless important because it influenced the direction the Hawthorne studies would take and the interpretation of the results.

THE HAWTHORNE STUDIES, 1927–1932

In 1927 the Hawthorne Works of the Western Electric Company employed some 29,000 workers who manufactured the telephones, telephone lines, and central office equipment used by the companies of the Bell System. In the best tradition of scientific management, the research staff at the Hawthorne plant sought to isolate the conditions that minimized fatigue and maximized output. In November 1924 the research staff joined forces with the National Research Council of the National Academy of Sciences to study the effects of illumination on industrial productivity. This marked the beginning of a series of studies, each designed to address questions raised by the previous one.

A report of the Hawthorne studies was published in 1939 by Fritz Roethlisberger, a colleague of Mayo's at Harvard, and William J. Dickson, Chief of the Employee Relations Research Department at the Hawthorne plant. Because Mayo and his colleagues did not become involved until after the illumination experiments had ended, the account of the studies reported in Roethlisberger and Dickson's *Management and the Worker* covers only the five-year period between 1927 and 1932.[7] Nonetheless, because the results of the illumination experiments are a key part of the story, our discussion begins with them.

The Illumination Experiments

In the first illumination experiment the intensity of the lighting was increased at specified intervals in three manufacturing departments and changes in output were recorded.[8] In one department output bobbed up and down. In the other two departments output increased but not in direct proportion to the increases in lighting. Although other determinants of productivity seemed to be at work, the researchers had no idea what they were. In the second illumination experiment workers in one department were assigned to either a test group or a control group. The test group worked under three intensities of lighting, while the control group worked under constant lighting. The two groups were similar in all respects except for the variable of lighting, thus allowing for a test of its effect on output. To the astonishment of the researchers, however, production increased in both groups and at almost the same magnitude. Because the researchers suspected that the increase in daylight during the spring season may have contaminated the results, a third experiment was conducted using only artificial light. This time, however, the intensity of lighting was decreased rather than increased. Again, productivity actually increased in both groups until the lighting had been reduced to 3 foot-candles, at which point the workers could no longer see to work.

The puzzling results caused the researchers to question their own assumptions. They had assumed a simple cause-and-effect relationship between a change and the workers' response to that change. What they discovered was that the meaning attached to a change is more important in determining the workers' response than the change itself. The illumination experiments revealed what came to be known as the **Hawthorne Effect**: when people know they are part of an experiment, the meaning they attach to being a participant affects the results. As Roethlisberger put it, "If one experiments on a stone, the stone does not know it is being experimented upon—all of which makes it simple for people experimenting with stones. But if a human being is being experimented upon, he is likely to know it. Therefore, his attitudes toward the experiment and toward the experimenters become very important factors in determining his responses to the situation."[9] The conclusion that behavior is shaped by the meaning workers attach to their total situation was soon reinforced by the results of the relay assembly room experiments.

The Relay Assembly Test Room Experiments

At the close of the illumination tests in April 1927, the research team initiated another set of experiments designed to study the effects of fatigue on individual productivity. This time the researchers decided to study only five workers so they could eliminate the effects of factors such as the amount of work ahead of the operators, changes in type of work, and the introduction of inexperienced operators.[10] The chief architect of the relay assembly test room experiments was George A. Pennock, Superintendent of Hawthorne's Inspection Branch. The origins of human relations theory may be traced to a chance meeting between Pennock and Elton Mayo.[11] In the spring of 1927 Pennock attended a meeting of the National Industrial Conference Board at which Mayo gave a talk. Afterwards, Pennock told Mayo of the puzzling results of the illumination experiments and implored him to visit Chicago to take a look at the relay assembly experiments that were then underway. Mayo took him up on his offer the following year. Although Mayo did not initiate or direct the Hawthorne studies that followed, his informal advice and counsel did influence their design and the subsequent interpretation of the results.

To conduct these experiments, a small separate room was constructed in one corner of the large room where the relay assemblers worked. The assembly of telephone relays "consisted of putting together approximately thirty-five small parts in an "assembly fixture" and securing them by four machine screws."[12] Each relay took about 1 minute to assemble. The completed assembly was dropped into a chute beneath the workbench and was automatically tallied by means of a hole punched into a continuously moving paper tape. Six women with long experience as relay assemblers were selected to participate in the experiment, five to assemble the relays and a sixth to supply the necessary parts. One of the researchers performed the role of test room observer. His task was to record output, keep a log of everything that happened or was said in the test room that might affect output, and maintain friendly relations with the workers. The latter was deemed necessary so that hostility or resentment on the part of the workers would not adversely affect the experiment. For this reason, two workers were replaced after a few months because their negative attitudes were adversely affecting the group's output.

Because the researchers had learned from the illumination experiments that very little could be gleaned from studying a single variable, the relay assembly experiments were designed to introduce a variety of changes in working conditions, including rest breaks and shorter work hours. The intent was to find the intersecting point at which fatigue was lowest and output highest. Although the experiments continued for five years, it was the results of the first thirteen periods, covering two years, that were most widely reported.

In Period 1 output was measured while the workers were still in the main relay assembly department. This was done to obtain baseline data. In Period 2 the workers were moved to the test room, but no changes in working conditions were introduced. In Period 3 the system of financial incentives under which they worked was modified slightly. A piecerate was calculated for each completed relay so that they would take home the same amount of pay they had taken home previously for the same level of output. As before, individual pay was determined by the output of the entire group, but now the group was five workers rather than one hundred. This created a tighter link between individual effort and reward, thereby increasing the incentive to complete more relays. Period 4 marked the initiation of changes in working conditions. The assemblers received two 5-minute breaks in Period 4, two 10-minute breaks in Period 5, six 5-minute breaks in period 6, and a 15-minute break with food provided in the morning and a 10-minute rest break in the afternoon in Period 7. The number of hours worked was reduced during periods 8, 9, and 11.

The results through Period 11 were consistent with expectations. Each positive change in working conditions brought increases in average hourly output, although total productivity declined during periods 9 and 11 because the group was working 15 percent and 13 percent fewer hours. The initial results tended to confirm the hypothesis that rest breaks and shorter hours reduced fatigue, thereby increasing productivity. Expectations were confounded in Period 12, however, when the original conditions in Period 3 were restored (a 48-hour work week and no rest breaks). Hourly productivity declined slightly for 4 of 5 workers but everyone's output remained well above levels in Period 3 when conditions were presumably identical. And, because the workers were once again working full days without rests, total weekly output reached the highest level yet recorded. The workers made it clear, however, that they valued the rest breaks and, when they were restored in Period 13, all five workers achieved still higher levels of output. The unexpected continual upward trend in productivity demanded an explanation. To the researchers, the primary candidates were reduced fatigue, greater economic incentive, and improved morale.

Fatigue The researchers ultimately rejected the hypothesis that the increases in output were due to relief from fatigue caused by the introduction of rest breaks and shorter hours. In fact, they found no evidence of cumulative fatigue at all. Productivity did not decline during the week as would be expected if cumulative fatigue were present. Further, medical exams found no evidence of adverse affects on the workers' health. It seemed clear that the introduction of rest breaks had had a positive effect on productivity but, in the absence of evidence of fatigue, the researchers could not explain why. Scientific management assumptions had initially led them to view the worker "as essentially a physiological machine hindered and limited by his organic make-up and his physical surroundings."[13] This assumption no longer seemed warranted. The relay assembly experiments caused them to conclude that, except where heavy muscular work is involved, fatigue is not a major problem in industrial organizations.

Economic Incentives The researchers concluded that the initial spurt in productivity in Period 3 was due to the improved linkage between effort and reward. They also suspected that the reward system motivated workers to increase output as the hours of work decreased, so that their take-home pay did not suffer. But although the system of economic incentives could explain why productivity did not decline with each reduction in work hours, it could not explain why productivity continued to increase, nor why it reached the levels it did.

Employee Morale The researchers ultimately concluded that positive attitudes engendered by the group's social environment were the primary cause of increased productivity. In designing the experiment, they had sought to hold attitudes constant by maintaining friendly relations, but in doing so they had fundamentally altered the social environment. Not only had the six women become important players in an important experiment, but the traditional employee-supervisor relationship had been altered as well. Where previously they had been subject to close supervision and lived in fear of being berated for failing to achieve their daily production target, now they rarely saw their supervisor and the production target had been eliminated. As Mayo noted, the observer "took a personal interest in each girl and her achievement; he showed pride in the record of the group. He helped the group to feel that its duty was to set its own conditions of work, he helped the workers to find the "freedom" of which they so frequently speak."[14]

The Hawthorne researchers concluded that improved morale in the test room was the single most important factor governing employee productivity, but they could only guess at the specific determinants of morale. Several possibilities were raised. First, the relay assemblers may have responded favorably to **relaxed supervision** and the resulting freedom from fear and anxiety. According to Roethlisberger and Dickson, the researchers received the clear impression "that freedom from rigid and excessive supervision was an important factor in determining the girls' attitude toward their work in the experimental room."[15]

A second possibility is that the observed increases in output resulted from increased **social cohesion or solidarity** as the workers coalesced into a well-integrated work group. This explanation was supported by an increased amount of social activity among the test room operators outside of working hours, an increased amount of social conversation during the day, and a willingness to help one another for the common good of the group.[16] It was also supported by Mayo's theory of social disorganization. Believing that people have a basic human need to collaborate in pursuit of collective goals, he predicted that teamwork would result in higher job satisfaction and often higher productivity.

A third possibility is that the workers responded favorably to **personal attention and sympathetic treatment**. According to the researchers, the relay assemblers seemed to respond positively when the observer showed a personal interest in them, listened to their personal concerns, responded sympathetically to their needs, and praised them for their achievements. This, too, was supported by Mayo's theory of social disorganization. He predicted that job satisfaction would improve as workers became better adjusted to their work environments and experienced a greater sense of personal security, although it was less certain that their productivity would increase as well.

A fourth possibility is that they responded favorably to **participative decision making**, that is, the opportunity to participate in making decisions relating to their work and working conditions. Again, this possibility is consistent with Mayo's belief that all people have a basic need for group involvement and collaborative effort.

Which of these possibilities is most likely? All of them may have played a role. In words reminiscent of Mary Parker Follett, the Hawthorne researchers concluded that workers respond to their total situation. The work breaks, for example, may have symbolized an interest on the part of management in the health and well-being of its workers. They may have meant an opportunity to get together and socialize, as well as a time for relaxation and relief from tension. All of these meanings may have been present simultaneously as part of the total situation to which the workers responded.

Mayo never developed an explicit theory of employee morale and productivity. He believed that much more research was needed before such a theory could be formulated. His working hypothesis was "that the locus of industrial maladjustment is somewhere in the relation between person-work-company policy rather than in any individual or individuals."[17] If no definitive theory emerged from the relay assembly room experiments, they nonetheless placed a spotlight on certain key variables, including supervisory style, social cohesion, and employee participation. These variables became the subject of extensive research by future students of human relations.

The Interviewing Program

Having concluded that the meanings workers attach to factors in their environment affect their morale, the Hawthorne investigators turned their attention to studying the workers themselves. The purpose of the interviewing program was "to secure a picture of their problems, worries, likes and dislikes, in relation to working conditions and supervision."[18] With such a picture in hand the researchers hoped to enhance morale by correcting identified problems. Sixteen hundred employees in the Inspection Branch were interviewed between September 1928 and February 1929. The program was subsequently expanded and by 1930 over 21,000 employees had been interviewed. Workers were initially asked a set of structured questions during a brief interview session. The results, however, were unsatisfactory. The workers seemed to want to talk about what they, rather than the interviewers, thought was important. At Mayo's suggestion, the interviewers adopted a nondirective approach similar to the kind used by clinical psychologists. Workers were encouraged to discuss any matters of concern to them for as long as 90 minutes. To encourage workers to share their feelings, the interviewers were trained to listen attentively and to say as little as possible. They were not to argue, give advice, offer moral judgments, or give any appearance of holding formal authority.

The interviewing program failed to achieve its goals because the researchers once again assumed a simple cause-and-effect relationship between the workers' feelings and objective conditions in the workplace. A few problems relating to physical working conditions, safety, and health were referred to the appropriate authorities for corrective action, and some complaints became topics of discussion in the supervisory training sessions. For the most part, however, problems could not be isolated and corrected as the researchers had hoped because no clear patterns of satisfaction or dissatisfaction emerged. As Roethlisberger and Dickson put it, "People working in similar surroundings did not react in the same way to those surroundings. Some expressed satisfaction, some dissatisfaction with similar plant conditions, wages, and working conditions."[19] Because there was no consensus among the workers about the objects of complaint, the researchers had to abandon their hope of obtaining a full and accurate picture of industrial conditions from employee comments.

If the interviewing program failed to achieve its goals, it nonetheless produced important findings. In the course of the interviews the researchers discovered a world inhabited by sentiments rather than facts. They found that workers perceive the same reality differently because their perceptions are filtered by their feelings and emotions. The latter in turn are shaped by differences in personality, unresolved childhood experiences, problems at home, and work-related interests that vary with age, marital status, and seniority. Consequently, to improve morale supervisors must look beyond the subjectively defined complaints to the sentiments that lie beneath them. They must distinguish the manifest content of the complaint from its underlying meaning for the worker.

Another important finding was that the interviewing program improved morale whether or not complaints were addressed.[20] Workers seemed to appreciate being recognized as individuals who had valuable comments to make. They also expressed appreciation for being allowed "to participate jointly with the company in its endeavor to improve working conditions and supervision."[21] For many, the interview also seemed to have a therapeutic or cathartic effect. These workers welcomed the opportunity to get grievances "off their chest" and reported feeling better after having done so. One worker even thanked an interviewer for improving the quality of food in the cafeteria when she had in fact done no such thing.

In another instance a worker insisted that his supervisor was a bully, and yet no other member of the unit expressed the same complaint. The interview revealed that the worker had recently lost a daughter to meningitis and his wife had to be hospitalized for a mental breakdown. He was highly anxious because he lacked the money to send her to a sanitarium, and he was resentful that his supervisor made him work at night when his wife needed him at home. The worker eventually laid out his complaints to the boss and the latter seemed nicer to him thereafter. The researchers concluded that the supervisor had not actually been mean or hostile to the worker, but that the latter, because of the stress he was experiencing, perceived him to be. According to Roethlisberger and Dickson, such cases involved "distorted thinking" in which there is "a tendency on the part of the complainant to project all of his troubles on one object and in such terms to overthink his situation."[22]

According to Mayo and his colleagues, understanding a worker's total situation requires knowledge of the worker's personal history, social situation at work, and the sentiments that shape responses to workplace conditions. But is it realistic to expect supervisors to acquire knowledge of each worker's total situation? Although many found this an unrealistic expectation, Mayo and his colleagues believed that the interview technique provided the necessary means. Whether conducted by a professional counselor as part of an ongoing program or by well-trained supervisors on a daily basis, Mayo and his colleagues believed that the interview process enables workers to achieve a higher level of self-awareness and, consequently, a greater degree of adjustment to their work environment. It also enables supervisors to understand the emotional significance of particular events and objects to workers and to respond with sympathetic understanding rather than unilateral commands and sanctions.

In many cases all that is required is what Roethlisberger and Dickson called **active listening**. Referring to two specific cases, they concluded, "Had either supervisor listened sympathetically and attentively to his subordinate, he might have found out what the trouble was. Instead, the supervisors delivered futile ultimatums, which had little result other than to make any kind of effective working together impossible."[23] As discussed later, this "new method of human control" constituted a central but highly controversial element of human relations theory.

The Bank Wiring Observation Room Study

Sociological explanations of behavior began to replace psychological ones as the Hawthorne studies proceeded. Mayo's training in clinical psychology had led him to overemphasize human irrationality. During the course of investigating employee complaints it became increasingly apparent that very few cases involved distorted thinking or neurotic obsessions rooted in the individual psyche. Nor were attitudes toward work determined primarily by problems at home. More often, complaints seemed to be grounded in social relations at work. The emerging hypothesis was that complaints reflect a mismatch between the needs and desires of individual workers and the ability of the workplace to satisfy them. Most of these needs and desires seemed to be social in nature, involving each worker's relationships with colleagues and supervisors. This new sociological point of view guided the final stage of the Hawthorne studies.

The bank wiring study was designed to learn more about social relations at work. Fourteen workers from the Bank Wiring Department were placed in a separate room and studied while they performed their usual task of assembling switches for central office telephone systems. Each "bank" had either 100 or 200 terminals. One worker threaded wires to the terminals, one soldered the wires to the terminals, and one inspected the completed work. In contrast to the relay assembly test room, the observer was instructed to give no special attention or recognition to the workers. Nor were any experimental changes introduced. The goal was simply to identify formal and informal patterns in social relationships through careful observation. The study lasted from November 1931 until May 1932.

The test room observer quickly discovered that the piecework system, in which each person's pay was determined by the department's weekly output, did not work as intended. Soldiering, as described by Frederick Taylor forty years earlier, still flourished in the Bank Wiring Department. Because the workers feared the piece rate would be cut if they worked at full capacity, they set their own productivity target and paced themselves accordingly. A key finding of the study was that output is sometimes determined more by group norms than individual effort and skill. In the bank wiring room, the majority pressured the fastest and slowest members to stay within the group's output norms. Those who refused to do so were socially ostracized. This finding was significant. It meant that the prescriptions of scientific management—rigorous selection, training, and incentive pay systems—do not always produce the desired results.

The test room observer also discovered two social cliques, one at the front of the room and one at the back. Workers at the front tended to have more years of experience. Within each clique, wiremen held more status than soldermen. The inspectors enjoyed the highest status but they did not call the shots because as employees of the Inspection Branch they were viewed as outsiders. In short, the test room was stratified by occupation and experience. The observer also discovered that not every worker belonged to a clique. Only those willing to abide by group norms were accorded membership status. Group norms included the following: don't be a rate-buster (doing too much); don't be a chiseler (doing too little); don't squeal to supervisors about things that will hurt individual or group interests; and don't try to maintain too much social distance (being too aloof). In the observer's view, the men had developed "spontaneously and quite unconsciously, an intricate social organization around their collective beliefs and sentiments."[24] This social organization performed a twofold function. It protected the group from internal indiscretions, such as working too hard or too fast, and it protected the group from outside interference by dealing with problems internally. The same mechanisms—sarcasm, ridicule, and social ostracism—often served to fulfill both functions.

The researchers did not believe that the prevailing theory of class warfare could explain the group's restricted output. The workers showed no hostility toward management, nor could their behavior be defined as rebellious. They simply behaved differently than those who designed the piecerate system expected them to behave. These observations led the researchers to conclude that the workers were simply being self-protective. Group solidarity had produced positive results in the relay assembly test room because the worker's fears and anxieties had been allayed. In the bank wiring test room, by contrast, fears and anxieties (however unfounded) had not been allayed. Restricted output was the result.

These findings challenged two fundamental assumptions of scientific management. First, they challenged the assumption that economic incentives are sufficient motivators. The bank wiring study indicated that group norms and personal loyalties also affect individual motivation. Second, they challenged the assumption that workers can be adjusted to the needs of industrial production in the same way that machines and work processes can be adjusted. The bank wiring study indicated the importance of mutual adjustment. If it is necessary for humans to adjust to workplace methods and conditions, the latter must also be adjusted to the social and psychological needs of the workers. Mayo and his colleagues concluded that management innovations, such as work simplification and wage incentive schemes, often fail to work as intended because they "have consequences other than their logical ones, and these unforeseen consequences tend to defeat the logical purposes of the plan as conceived."[25]

These unforeseen consequences include altered interpersonal relationships, reduced opportunities to develop and demonstrate craftsmanship, decreased autonomy, and reduced social status. From the workers' sentiment-based, "nonlogical" perspective, industrial engineers are a source of interference and constraint. Workers have every reason to fear the consequences of their actions and to resort to self-protective behaviors. For Mayo and his colleagues the lesson for management was clear. Technical innovations should not be introduced until their potential human consequences have been studied fully.

The bank wiring study confirmed what Frederick Taylor had already discovered: that productivity levels are sometimes determined more by group norms than individual skills. Taylor's solution was to break up group solidarity by relying upon individual rewards and sanctions. Mayo and his colleagues proposed a different solution: nurture constructive human relations by addressing the causes of self-protective behaviors and by integrating individual and organizational needs.

HUMAN RELATIONS AS A FIELD OF STUDY

Essentially a social philosopher at heart, Mayo left the task of establishing human relations as a field of study to his Harvard colleague, Fritz Roethlisberger. Roethlisberger understood that, for human relations to be viewed as something other than a subfield of industrial psychology or a paltry effort to humanize scientific management, it must have a clear subject matter, appropriate research methods, and a conceptual framework to guide the organization and interpretation of data.

Subject Matter and Research Methods

Roethlisberger believed the new discipline should focus on human interactions and investigate the following kinds of problems: "(1) general problems of communication and understanding between individuals, between individuals and groups, and between groups under different conditions and varying relationships, (2) general problems of securing action and cooperation under different conditions and in varying formal organizations, and (3) general problems of maintaining individual and organizational equilibrium through change."[26] He also believed interviewing and observational techniques provided the most appropriate methods for conducting research in these areas.

Organizations as Social Systems

Acting on a suggestion from one of his colleagues, Lawrence J. Henderson, Roethlisberger chose the concept of a social system as the basis for organizing and interpreting data. A system is an entity that must be studied and comprehended as a whole because each of its parts is interdependent with every other part. A change in one part necessarily produces change elsewhere in the system. A **social system** is that type of system containing human as well as physical components. Organizations clearly fall into this category. As the Hawthorne researchers discovered, the human and physical components of the plant were highly interdependent. Changes in working conditions and management methods, for example, produced changes in social relationships, personal satisfactions and, ultimately, individual and group behaviors. Because organizations are made up of human components, those who manage them cannot afford to think and act in terms of logical relationships alone. The Hawthorne researchers learned that sentiments, feelings, beliefs, and perceptions must be taken into account.

Work groups may also be viewed as social systems. Workers in the bank wiring observation room, for example, perceived the incentive pay system as a threat to their financial and job security. They coped with the resulting tensions by organizing and engaging in self-protective behaviors. The systems concept helps explain why such behaviors occur. Good intentions notwithstanding, changes introduced by management often alter the distribution of financial, status, and social rewards, thereby provoking resistance among those adversely affected.

Roethlisberger's conceptual framework held clear implications for management practice. It suggested that managers should listen to, and become better acquainted with, the sentiments of their employees. They should learn to view complaints as the "creakings and groanings" of their own social structures. Finally, they should continually assist in adjusting the organization's human and technical components. All of this is required because, as Elton Mayo often said, collaboration is not something than can be left to chance. Nor can it be secured through logical contrivances such as collective bargaining. According to Roethlisberger, only by exercising skill in human relations, only by attending to sentiments arising from social relations at work, can collaboration be achieved and maintained.

Formal and Informal Organization

The discovery that behavior in the bank wiring observation room was socially organized led Roethlisberger and Dickson to develop a conceptual distinction between formal and informal organization. **Formal organization** refers to all the factors that are deliberately designed to shape social relationships at work. It includes the systems, policies, rules, and regulations that prescribe what the relations of one person to another are supposed to be in order to achieve organizational tasks. It also refers to the patterns of interaction that result from these formal mechanisms of control. **Informal organization** refers to the personal relationships and patterns of interaction that develop among individuals at work that are not the intended products of the formal organization. The social cliques or groups that sometimes come into being to satisfy the social needs and sentiments of workers are components of the informal organization. These groups sometimes work in tandem with the prescriptions of the formal organization, as in the relay assembly test room, and sometimes they develop in opposition to the prescriptions of the formal organization, as in the bank wiring observation room.

note difference Frederick Taylor viewed informal groups as pathological and sought to break them up by controlling workers with individual carrots and sticks. Roethlisberger, by contrast, argued that informal groups are natural phenomena that can serve the needs of workers and managers alike. They provide members with a sense of security, belonging, and affiliation (being part of something important), and the more satisfactions of this kind workers obtain, the more likely they are to cooperate with management in working to achieve organizational goals. Consequently, a better method of securing cooperation than the one proposed by Taylor is to remove the sources of employee resistance and facilitate the simultaneous satisfaction of individual and organizational needs. From this perspective, group cohesion is something to be encouraged. As Roethlisberger and Dickson put it, "What the Relay Assembly Test Room experiment showed was that when innovations are introduced carefully and with regard to the actual sentiments of the workers, the workers are likely to develop a spontaneous type of informal organization which will not only express more adequately their own values and significances but also is more likely to be in harmony with the aims of management."[27]

The findings of the Hawthorne studies and Roethlisberger's early efforts to define human relations as a field of study encouraged many other scholars to gravitate toward the study of human relations in the 1930s and 1940s; chief among them were W. Lloyd Warner, Burleigh Gardner, and William Foote Whyte. But, despite the value of Roethlisberger's conceptual framework for human relations research, the integrity of human relations as a field of study was greatly undermined by the way organizations chose to incorporate the findings of the Hawthorne studies into management practice.

HUMAN RELATIONS IN PRACTICE

The Hawthorne studies not only established a new field of study, they also spawned a new management movement. The human relations movement that swept through industry in the 1940s and 1950s called for the adoption of two closely related innovations: human relations training for supervisors and counseling programs for employees. Unlike scientific management theorists, human relations theorists did not believe cooperation can be secured through authoritative commands, programmed work, and economic incentives alone. A "new method of human control" was needed. Mayo and Roethlisberger referred to it as active listening, or the interview method, and suggested that it should form the basis of both human relations training and employee counseling programs.

The aim of this method is to help workers achieve a state of personal equilibrium with their work environments. Mayo and Roethlisberger believed that complaints, resistance, and other forms of uncooperative behavior are caused by a mismatch between what workers demand of their jobs (e.g., a certain level of pay, opportunities for advancement, fair treatment, and social recognition) and what their jobs actually offer them.[28] Active listening provides the means for addressing this mismatch. Through active listening managers can identify the needs and expectations of workers and adjust workplace conditions to better satisfy those needs and expectations. Similarly, through active listening supervisors or counselors can help workers view themselves and their work situations more objectively, thereby causing them to adjust their own demands. In short, active listening can be used to adjust formal structure to satisfy the needs of human beings and to adjust human beings to satisfy the needs of the formal structure.

Human Relations Training

The conclusion that supervisors were failing to take human sentiments into account led to the widespread adoption of training programs for supervisory personnel. The purpose of these programs was to teach supervisors how to obtain cooperation and understanding from workers in face-to-face situations.

Workers are not machine parts

The underlying assumption was that the exercise of human relations skills would produce greater harmony in the workplace. The typical training program encouraged supervisors to think of workers as human beings rather than labor commodities, to be more sympathetic toward their personal situations, to seek to understand complaints from the worker's point of view, and to adopt a counseling-centered approach to supervision. In Mayo's words, cooperation in the workplace requires "the introduction of a new method of supervision—a method which does away with personal criticism and the giving of orders, and substitutes for these a sympathetic and careful technique of listening."[29]

Supervisor training

In practice, supervisory training programs rarely followed the approach advocated by Mayo and Roethlisberger. Supervisors were urged to treat their workers more sympathetically and with greater sensitivity, but emphasis was placed on defusing emotions rather than making structural adjustments to better accommodate human needs. Training seldom involved more than providing supervisors with platitudes about how better to relate to workers. In addition, it quickly became apparent that human relations skill is highly complex, not easily communicated or learned, and not readily transferable to the work unit. Human relations training programs became very popular in industry in the 1940s and 1950s, but enthusiasm soon waned when the expected benefits failed to materialize.

Although some of the blame must be attributed to the poor quality of the training programs, Roethlisberger also concluded that the counseling-centered method of supervision was too idealistic. Because supervisors are human beings, they cannot be expected to approach every dispute objectively, without anger or resentment, and without falling back on their formal authority. Nor is it realistic to expect them to be comfortable discussing feelings with workers or sharing their own feelings openly. Most people, according to Roethlisberger, are inclined to rationalize their feelings and disguise them as logic. He also observed that skill in interpersonal relations tends to be personal and intuitive; if you don't come by it naturally, it is difficult to develop on the job. Roethlisberger concluded, reluctantly, that it may be easier for administrators to change working conditions and other structural aspects of the work environment than to change supervisory and managerial behavior.

Employee Counseling Programs

From the outset, the Hawthorne researchers entertained doubts about the ability of supervisors to adopt a counselor-centered approach. Supervisors at the Hawthorne plant had many other duties to perform besides investigating each worker's personal situation and sentiments, they were not sufficiently trained to act as counselors, and their role as authority figures caused them to be viewed by workers with suspicion and distrust. The alternative to relying on supervisors was to create a new category of personnel specialist trained to interview employees and help them achieve better self-awareness and personal adjustment. The final chapter of Roethlisberger and Dickson's report on the Hawthorne studies describes the personnel counseling program that the Western Electric Company adopted in 1936. Personnel counselors were assigned fulltime to specific units to observe workplace behaviors and counsel employees as needed. Each counselor was responsible for approximately three hundred workers.

Interviews were conducted on a strictly confidential basis. To maintain trust with the workers, counselors were prohibited from reporting to management what they learned during their interviews. Their role was limited to encouraging workers to talk about what was bothering them, helping them to clarify their feelings, and assisting them to achieve the level of self-awareness needed to make their own decisions about their immediate problems. In carrying out this role, counselors were expected to abide by the rules developed in the earlier interviewing program. They were not to argue, give advice, offer judgments, or give any appearance of holding formal authority.

Other companies adopted employee counseling programs but, as in the case of supervisory training programs, enthusiasm soon waned. After the Western Electric Company ceased operating its counseling program in 1956, Roethlisberger and Dickson were asked to conduct an evaluation of the program. The results of their study were published in 1966 in a report entitled *Counseling in an Organization: A Sequel to the Hawthorne Researches.* This report highlighted three inherent problems with the counseling program. First, the program was expensive. At its peak the program employed fifty-five counselors at considerable expense. Second, relatively few workers benefited from the program. A study conducted between 1948 and 1951 found that only 36 percent of employees expressed serious concerns about work or their personal situations, and only 10 percent of all employees were helped in resolving their concerns. Third, the program injected an additional player into the work unit who lacked the authority to resolve problems and was prohibited from communicating useful employee feedback to unit supervisors. Since the counselor had no authority to adjust workplace conditions, the program seemed to require the workers to do all of the adjusting. What was missing, Roethlisberger and Dickson concluded, was an integrated attack by all managerial and staff personnel on the causes of employee dissatisfaction. Because of these inherent difficulties, employee counseling programs came to be viewed as unjustified expenses and soon fell out of favor, although vestiges of them still exist in employee assistance programs.

Human relations training and employee counseling programs represented two lines of attack on problems of industrial relations suggested by the Hawthorne studies. Neither Mayo nor Roethlisberger viewed them as panaceas or comprehensive solutions. They understood that they did not address all of the factors contributing to job dissatisfaction and industrial unrest. For this reason they were not particularly troubled by their disappointing results. Nonetheless, critics were quick to point out an apparent contradiction in Mayo's prescriptions. Given Mayo's intense concern about the harmful effects of industrial methods on human beings, something he referred to as the Great Stupidity, why didn't the innovations most closely associated with human relations theory focus on changing those methods? This criticism and others are discussed in the following section.

CRITICISMS OF
HUMAN RELATIONS THEORY

The human relations school of thought associated with Elton Mayo and his Harvard colleagues stirred up considerable controversy among members of the academic community. Two bodies of criticism are reviewed in the following sections. The first finds human relations theory tainted by a conservative ideology, and the second asserts that the aim of practicing human relations skills is to manipulate workers into being content with their subordinate status.[30]

Neglect of Structural Change

According to the first body of criticism, members of the Mayo group failed properly to analyze the structural causes of industrial unrest, especially the external causes embedded in industrial society. The Hawthorne researchers analyzed complaints and disputes in terms of unresolved fears, personal preoccupations, problems at home, and frustrated expectations at work. In doing so they generally ignored the underlying structural causes of unrest, including economic struggles over the distribution of profits, social struggles between classes, and power struggles between managers and workers. According to this second line of criticism, the quest to understand concrete social interactions led human relations theorists to study the most superficial, least important causes of conflict, including interpersonal misunderstandings, poor communications, and perceived threats to social status and security. It also caused them to highlight behavioral rather than structural remedies. For example, there is much discussion in the human relations literature about how to foster better communications and how to resolve interpersonal conflicts but very little discussion about how to establish self-managed work teams.

In fairness, a field of study committed to studying human behavior cannot be expected to give equal attention to all of the structural and contextual forces that influence behavior. Most researchers, by necessity, take some variables as givens while concentrating analysis on another set of variables. Roethlisberger and Dickson, for example, referred occasionally to the impacts of the Great Depression on human behavior, but the central focus of their research was a set of variables that had been previously neglected: the sentiments of workers, including their hopes and fears and sense of fair play. It was appropriate for them to choose the variables they wished to study.

This line of criticism, however, went much deeper than the neglect of structural forces. It held that human relations theory is tainted by a conservative ideology that serves the interests of the managerial class at the expense of workers. According to Koivisto, Mayo injected values into a purportedly objective field of study by suggesting that cooperation and harmony are good, and conflict and disharmony are bad.[31] Mayo's rhetoric implies that "good" social relations are those relations that contribute to the efficient, frictionless functioning of the organization. This is the same value espoused by scientific management. As C. Wright Mills put it, it is the workers who must do the co-

not all of taylor's work discredited

operating, with cooperation defined as the efficient and compliant pursuit of "managerially approved ends."[32] As did Taylor, Mayo entrusted the pursuit of social harmony to a managerial elite whose prerogatives remain unchallenged.

Mayo also injected values into the study of human relations, according to his critics, by assuming an identity of interests between managers and workers. Mayo believed that both are benefited by the collaborative pursuit of organizational objectives. There is no need to accommodate diverse and divergent interests because the latter do not exist. There is no need for labor unions for the same reason. Mayo's critics, by contrast, maintained that the interests of workers and managers are inherently opposed, that management is driven by cost and profit imperatives that limit their ability to satisfy human needs, and that labor unions have an important and necessary role to play in industrial relations. As Daniel Bell put it, "The question of how to distribute increased income resulting from higher productivity, for example, cannot be flim-flammed away as a problem of verbal misinterpretation."[33]

For these critics, a conservative bias was apparent in the remedies spawned by the Hawthorne studies. Human relations training and employee counseling programs were designed to achieve better personal adjustment. They entailed no structural changes in authority relations or the design of work. Individuals working under a human relations regime remained in the same powerless, subordinate position performing the same unsatisfying tasks. Mayo's critics wondered why more attention wasn't given to the concept of self-directed, socially cohesive work teams, since this is what seemed to have produced such positive results in the relay assembly room. According to his critics, the team concept received little attention because it required structural reforms, including a fundamental redistribution of power and authority, and the conservative orientation of Mayo and his colleagues precluded them from moving in this direction.

It is true that Mayo's social theory led him to dismiss political and economic struggles as phenomena that would disappear when spontaneous cooperation was restored. And yet the changes in industrial methods that Mayo favored were not entirely conservative. His conclusion in a later study of the aircraft industry was that the solution to high levels of absenteeism and turnover, as well as poor morale, was the deliberate creation of integrated, cohesive, and partly self-directing work teams.[34] Supervisors, he argued, must become facilitators and team builders. They must establish and maintain trust with members of the work group, carefully integrate new members, encourage workers to socialize and establish social bonds, consult them about changes, and act on their advice. It is likely that Mayo did not push this remedy more vehemently because he knew that, with prosperity returning and labor tensions easing, few business organizations were interested in making the required changes. Mayo retired in 1947, and Rothlisberger, although he did not retire until 1967, was much more interested in interpersonal communications than structural reforms. Consequently, it was left to the human resources theorists (see Chapters 12 and 13) to follow up on the structural implications of the Hawthorne studies.

A Strategy of Manipulation

Another group of critics was troubled by the implications of *practicing* human relations, a term which seemed to imply doing something to others. Malcolm McNair, for example, insisted that the term *human relations skill* has "a cold-blooded connotation of proficiency, technical expertness, calculated effect."[35] These critics feared that employers were adopting training and counseling programs to manipulate workers into being complaisant, compliant, and generally contented with their subordinate position in the organization. According to this line of criticism, supervisors were being trained to co-opt workers by pretending they were sympathetic and caring, and counselors were being hired to defuse hostilities by allowing workers opportunities to vent. Supervisors were also being taught, according to these critics, to obtain feedback from workers before introducing policy or technological changes but not to give their comments much weight. The purpose of doing so was to secure the workers' acceptance of change without a true integration of their needs.

Whereas Roethlisberger's conceptual framework called for mutual adjustment, human relations in practice seemed to require adjustment only on the part of the workers. As Koivisto put it, "Research in human relations in industry seems not to take the individual as given but rather attempts to alter his psychological state to fit the work situation, which, instead, is taken as given."[36] For Daniel Bell, human relations in practice is nothing but a "feel good" strategy designed to produce contented cows. As he put it, "The gravest charge that can be leveled against these researchers is that they uncritically adopt industry's own conception of workers as *means* to be manipulated or adjusted to impersonal ends. The belief in man as an end in himself has been ground under by the machine, and the social science of the factory researchers is not a science of man, but a cow-sociology."[37]

Yet another attack on human relations came from Malcom McNair, one of Roethlisberger's colleagues at the Harvard Business School. He objected vehemently to the idea that human relations skill was something to be taught and practiced. Although he believed awareness of human relations was an essential aspect of a manager's job, he saw awareness of human relations and the conscious effort to practice human relations on other people as two very different things. The latter, he believed, amounts to manipulating people for one's own ends. As he put it, "Consciously trying to practice human relations is like consciously trying to be a gentlemen. If you have to think about it, insincerity creeps in and personal integrity moves out."[38] According to McNair, integrity is lost as students are taught, in effect, to practice amateur psychiatry, invade the privacy of workers, and develop a love for managing other peoples' lives. Integrity is also lost as students are taught conversational strategies, such as "This is what I think I hear you saying." McNair found such strategies highly patronizing and demeaning. Finally, McNair argued that teaching human relations skill encouraged "sloppy sentimentalism." It encouraged workers and managers alike to look for personal factors to excuse poor work performance. By emphasizing the need to investigate the human sentiments behind each complaint or dispute, workers are allowed to save face but at the expense of personal responsibility and organizational performance. In short, McNair believed that the ability to look at problems from multiple human perspectives is very much needed, but packaging it as a set of manipulative techniques is extremely dangerous. As he put it, "Let's treat people like people, but let's not make a big production of it."[39]

This body of criticism, as well as the way human relations was being practiced, inevitably tarnished Mayo's and Roethlisberger's contributions to organizational analysis. Many came to view human relations as a manipulative approach to managing workers even though Mayo and his colleagues intended no such thing and had no control over how employers chose to interpret and use their findings. Certainly Mayo and Roethlisberger opened the door to this view of human relations by referring repeatedly to the interviewing technique used by supervisors and counselors as a new method of human control. Although they conceived of control as an objective management function and viewed the counseling method as a humanistic alternative to current practice, their choice of words often made them sound as authoritarian, coercive, and patronizing as their predecessors in the scientific management movement. Consequently, Roethlisberger dropped the term *human relations* in the early 1950s in favor of the less value-laden term *organizational behavior*.

HUMAN RELATIONS THEORY
IN PERSPECTIVE

Although they raise legitimate concerns, these criticisms do not diminish Mayo and Roethlisberger's contributions to organization theory. First, they pioneered in the application of social-science methods to the study of concrete organizations, and in doing so they initiated a new, multidisciplinary field of study. The Hawthorne studies are still widely regarded as the most extensive, systematic, and exhaustive study of employees in an industrial setting ever conducted.[40] The studies introduced many important variables that remain the subject of organizational research today, including employee morale, job satisfaction, social cohesion, informal group behavior, interpersonal communication, supervisory style, and employee participation.

Second, Mayo and his colleagues administered an important corrective to scientific management theory without rejecting it altogether. By highlighting the flawed assumptions and limited perspectives of scientific management they were able to develop a more complete and balanced understanding of organizations. For example, they challenged the assumption that there is "one best" set of working conditions, discoverable through scientific study, for maximizing productivity. The Hawthorne studies indicated that workers perceive and respond to working conditions differently because their perceptions are colored by their unique life experiences and personal desires. They also challenged the assumption that people are driven primarily by rational self-interest and that workers respond best to economic incentives. The Hawthorne studies indicated that workers are just as likely to be motivated by human sentiments and the underlying desire to satisfy their social and psychological needs. Finally, Mayo and his colleagues challenged the assumption that human behavior can be rationally ordered or programmed by introducing technological improvements, standardizing work, and systematizing work operations. The Hawthorne studies indicated that workers will resist the best-laid plans of managers and their technical specialists if those plans fail to take human sentiments into account.

Third, Mayo and Roethlisberger developed a conceptual scheme that is still a valuable guide for researchers engaged in organizational analysis and for administrators seeking to comprehend the interpersonal and group dynamics they experience on a daily basis. Viewing organizations as social systems, for example, focuses attention on social relations and the interrelated and interdependent nature of those relations. It emphasizes that workers are social creatures rather than isolated individuals and that they respond to informal group norms as well as formal incentives. It tells the researcher that organizational behavior can be comprehended only in terms of the total situation of human, technical, and structural factors, and it reminds administrators that their responses to specific problems must be contingent upon all of the facts contained in the situation.

Finally, Mayo and his colleagues helped humanize management by defining workers as human beings rather than costs of production and by raising awareness of human relations in general. Although they sometimes left the impression that practicing human relations is more important than organizing, planning, and directing, they nonetheless established the importance of employee morale to organizational performance. They acknowledged that better morale may not boost productivity directly, but it can reduce the frustrations that undermine motivation and contribute to absenteeism and turnover.

RELEVANCE FOR PUBLIC MANAGEMENT

The remainder of this chapter explores the relevance of human relations theory for public management and government performance. This exploration is guided by the three analytical frameworks identified in Chapter 3.

Models of Organizational Effectiveness

As indicated in Exhibit 8.1, human relations theory emphasizes the values associated with the **human relations model**, including social cohesion, morale, and development of human resources. By serving as mentors and facilitators, managers can help fulfill the organization's pattern maintenance and tension management functions—that is, the means by which organizations ensure employee commitment and address the interpersonal tensions that inevitably arise. From the human relations perspective, being a facilitator entails fostering teamwork, mediating interpersonal disputes, and establishing the workplace conditions that allow workers to satisfy their individual needs by contributing to organizational goals. Similarly, being a mentor involves listening attentively when employees voice concerns, helping them develop their abilities, support-

Exhibit 8.1 The Competing Values Framework: Four Models of Organizational Effectiveness

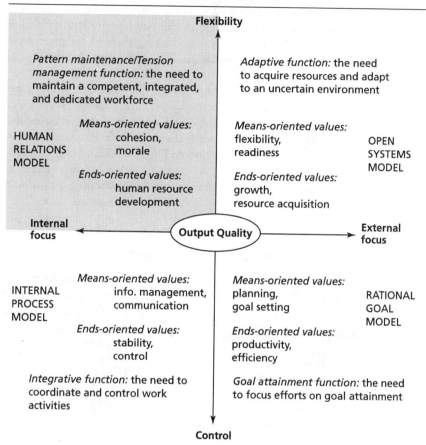

Flexibility

Pattern maintenance/Tension management function: the need to maintain a competent, integrated, and dedicated workforce

HUMAN RELATIONS MODEL

Means-oriented values: cohesion, morale

Ends-oriented values: human resource development

Adaptive function: the need to acquire resources and adapt to an uncertain environment

Means-oriented values: flexibility, readiness

Ends-oriented values: growth, resource acquisition

OPEN SYSTEMS MODEL

Internal focus ← **Output Quality** → **External focus**

INTERNAL PROCESS MODEL

Means-oriented values: info. management, communication

Ends-oriented values: stability, control

Means-oriented values: planning, goal setting

Ends-oriented values: productivity, efficiency

RATIONAL GOAL MODEL

Integrative function: the need to coordinate and control work activities

Goal attainment function: the need to focus efforts on goal attainment

Control

SOURCE: Adapted with permission from Figures 3 and 4, Robert O. Quinn and John Rohrbaugh, "A Spatial Model of Effectiveness Criteria: Towards a Competing Values Approach to Organizational Analysis," *Management Science* 29 (March 1983): 363–373. Copyright 1983, The Institute of Management Sciences, now the Institute for Operations Research and the Management Sciences (INFORMS), 901 Elkridge Landing Road, Suite 400, Linthicum, Maryland 21090-2909 USA.

ing legitimate requests for assistance, showing respect and being sympathetic to them as human beings, and recognizing their accomplishments.

Although the human relations model and its associated values receives the greatest attention in human relations theory, the importance of two other quadrants is recognized as well. These are the rational goal and internal process models. Mayo and Roethlisberger were among the first to emphasize that organizational performance cannot be enhanced by focusing narrowly on the effectiveness criteria of any one model. Focusing on social cohesion and commitment alone, for example, may undermine management's ability to achieve desired results; it may produce contented but not necessarily productive workers. Conversely, they criticized scientific management theorists for failing to see how a narrow emphasis on goal attainment pursued solely from a rational, logical perspective undermines satisfaction of the organization's pattern maintenance/tension management function. They maintained that organizations have both an economic function and an employee relations function and that organizational success depends on achieving them in an interrelated and interdependent fashion. This means that goal-setting and directing (goal attainment function), and coordinating and controlling (integrative function), must be carried out in a way that satisfies individual needs and thereby increases cohesion and commitment (pattern maintenance/tension management function). This concept of integrating individual and organizational needs and balancing several effectiveness-related values simultaneously represents an important contribution to organizational theory. The only organizational function that does not receive attention is the adaptive function. Human relations theory remains internally focused, concerned more with stabilizing social and productive relations than adapting to forces in the external environment.

Mechanisms for Coordinating
and Controlling Work Activities

As shown in Exhibit 8.2, human relations theory, like scientific management and Weber's theory of bureaucracy, relies on **direct supervision** as a mechanism of coordination and control. The hierarchical structure of authority is taken for granted. In this respect, human relations theory differs from classical theory only in terms of how supervision is exercised. It is to be exercised in a more relaxed and sympathetic manner, taking into account the social and psychological needs of workers and the unique personal problems with which they are struggling.

Mayo and Roethlisberger understood that organizations have purposes, and to secure those purposes structural controls are required. Certain work activities have to be performed, certain roles have to be assigned and prescribed, and certain standards of performance have to be set. They also understood, however, that structural controls can easily upset the equilibrium of the organization as a social system and make matters worse rather than better. They believed that conflict often arises when individuals are forced to adjust to the needs of the organization. For this reason, control and coordination must be achieved through more integrative methods, including relaxed supervision, sympathetic treatment, employee counseling, and perhaps even a measure, however small, of employee participation in decision making.

The concept of integrating individual and organizational needs has relevance for all complex organizations, including public agencies. But, as later schools of organizational theory would point out, relaxed supervision and sympathetic treatment are not sufficient by themselves to create and sustain a high-performing organization. Whereas positive human relations may increase morale and job satisfaction, it cannot guarantee high levels of competence or individual productivity. Depending on the nature of their work and their external environments, public agencies must rely on mechanisms of coordination and control other than direct supervision.

Exhibit 8.2 Six Mechanisms for Coordinating and Controlling Work Activities

Mutual adjustment	Workers consult with each other informally about what needs to be accomplished and how. Responsibility for coordination and control rests with those who do the work.
Direct supervision	A supervisor is assigned to take responsibility for a group of workers and a managerial hierarchy is established to integrate the efforts of all work groups. The supervisor issues personal instructions and monitors individual performance.
Standardization of work processes	Work is programmed in advance of its execution by developing rules and standard operating procedures specifying how everyone is to perform assigned tasks. Coordination is built into the work process itself and control is achieved by strictly limiting each worker's discretion.
Standardization of work outputs	Work outputs are programmed in advance by providing each work group with product specifications or performance goals and allowing members considerable latitude in determining how to achieve them. Control is exercised by collecting output data, requiring corrective action when needed, and rewarding and sanctioning workers based on results achieved.
Standardization of worker skills	Workers are employed who possess the knowledge and skills needed to make appropriate decisions. Educational institutions and professional associations are relied upon to provide standardized training. Professionally trained workers are largely self-coordinating and self-controlling.
Standardization of values	Organizational leaders communicate and act upon a clear vision of what the organization exists to do, where it should be headed, and what values should guide it. Coordination and control is facilitated by commitment of organizational members to shared, internalized values and ideals.

SOURCE: Based in large part on Henry Mintzberg, *Structure in Fives* (Prentice-Hall, 1993, 3–7).

Motivational Strategies

As indicated in Exhibit 8.3, human relations theory relies primarily on the **instrumental rewards strategy** to motivate employees, with special emphasis on **considerate leadership** and **group acceptance**. The results of the relay assembly room test seemed to underscore the importance of these strategies. The assemblers appeared to respond positively both to the attention, praise, and approval given by the assembly room observer and to the extrinsic rewards they received from forming social bonds and enjoying the approval of their peers.

The considerate leadership strategy entails adopting a leadership style based on being attentive to employees and their needs. It holds that workers will increase their level of performance in order to obtain the respect, support, and approval of persons in authority. Mayo and Roethlisberger believed that workers value social recognition and appreciation of their work efforts, prefer to be praised rather than blamed, desire to be independent rather than

Exhibit 8.3 Four Motivational Strategies

Legal Compliance

Using rules, formal directives, and sanctions to direct and control employee behavior. Employees may come to work, comply with rules, and satisfy minimum role requirements, either because they accept the legitimacy of organizational authority or fear being sanctioned.

Instrumental Rewards

Using rewards to induce desired behaviors.

Rewards for Performance

Distributing pay, promotions, and recognition based on individual performance. Employees may meet or exceed role expectations because they value the material and psychological satisfactions that money, advancement, and recognition can provide.

Considerate Leadership

Adopting a leadership style based on being attentive to employees and considerate of their needs. This strategy may improve morale. It might also induce those who value the respect, support, and approval of persons in authority to meet or exceed their role requirements.

Group Acceptance

Creating a work environment that allows employees to socialize, form group bonds, and enjoy the approval of their peers. This strategy may induce those who value affiliation and peer approval to meet or exceed role requirements, assuming that group norms are consistent with organizational objectives.

Job Identification

Offering work that is interesting, challenging, and responsible. Employees may come to work, meet or exceed role requirements, and possibly exhibit greater creativity and innovativeness. They may do so because they identify with the jobs and find their work intrinsically rewarding.

Goal Congruence

Hiring employees whose goals and values are congruent with the organization's and/or socializing employees so that they internalize organizational goals and values. Employees may come to work, remain with the organization, meet or exceed role requirements, and exhibit greater creativity, innovativeness, and institutional loyalty. They may do so because they identify with the organization's mission and values and because contributing to them reinforces their own self-concept.

SOURCE: Based in large part on Daniel Katz and Robert L. Kahn, *The Social Psychology of Organizations* (Wiley, 1966), pp. 336–68.

subordinate, and like to be consulted about and participate in making decisions that affect them personally. The findings of the relay assembly room study tended to confirm Follett's belief that close supervision, the issuing of orders, and the threat of sanctions creates a level of fear and tension that is ultimately counterproductive. These findings led Mayo and Roethlisberger to conclude that the considerate leadership strategy is a better choice for purposes of motivating employees than the legal compliance strategy.

The group acceptance strategy calls for encouraging the development of social bonds among employees so that they may enjoy the approval of their peers and experience the rewards of group accomplishment. Mayo and Roethlisberger believed that morale, cooperation—and often, productivity—can be enhanced by satisfying each worker's inherent need for affiliation or belongingness. As Mayo put it, "Man's desire to be continuously associated in work with his fellows is a strong, if not the strongest, human characteristic. Any disregard for it by management or any ill-advised attempt to defeat this human impulse leads instantly to some form of defeat for management itself."[41] Much of Mayo's later work emphasized the importance of encouraging social cohesion through teamwork. Both Mayo and Roethlisberger believed that supervisors who seek to satisfy their workers' social needs obtain better results than those who supervise exclusively in terms of their productivity.[42]

Whereas human relations theory emphasizes the benefits of practicing a more relaxed and sympathetic style of supervision, it stops short of advocating a fundamental redistribution of power and authority. Similarly, although Mayo identified boring and monotonous work as the single greatest cause of employee discontent, human relations theory stops short of advocating the job identification strategy that calls for designing jobs so that they are intrinsically rewarding. The possibilities for redistributing power and authority and using intrinsic rewards for purposes of motivation were left for the human resources theorists to explore.

SUMMARY

Elton Mayo and his colleagues identified human behavior and interpersonal relations as important subjects for organizational analysis, pioneered in the use of social science methods for purposes of organizational research, and spurred the development of a new field of study that is now known as *organizational behavior*. By issuing stern warnings about the dangers inherent in designing organizational systems according to the cold, impersonal logic of industrial engineering, they also helped steer management theory and practice in a more humanistic, employee-centered direction. As a theory of organizational effectiveness, human relations theory calls for maintaining a nurturing work environment, replacing close supervision with a more sympathetic and relaxed form of supervision, and developing cohesive work groups. As such, it has general applicability to all public agencies. Among its most important implications for public management and organizational performance are the following:

- **Maintaining a positive work environment.** According to human relations theory, public managers should seek to remove the sources of employee dissatisfaction by adjusting policies, technologies, work processes, and methods of supervision to satisfy human as well as organizational needs. Doing so may not always increase productivity but it should improve organizational functioning by enhancing morale, increasing cooperation between workers and supervisors, and reducing absenteeism and turnover.

- **Personal attention and sympathetic treatment.** Human relations theory holds that workplace frictions can be decreased if supervisors are willing to get to know each worker personally, including his or her needs, wants, idiosyncrasies, and preoccupations, and treat each with sympathy and respect. When complaints or personal problems arise, supervisors should listen attentively, seek to understand the complaints or problems from the worker's perspective, and respond based on an assessment of the total situation. Sympathetic treatment may not always motivate workers to higher levels of productivity and effort but it can, according to human relations theory, enhance collegiality, cooperation, and organizational commitment.

- **Relaxed supervision.** Human relations theory holds that higher productivity is possible if close supervision is replaced with a more relaxed form of supervision. Whereas special attention and sympathetic treatment are important to morale, Mayo and Roethlisberger concluded that it was primarily the relaxed supervision in the relay assembly room that caused the continuing rise in output. The total situation was altered as general supervision replaced close supervision, personal authority replaced formal authority, consultation and face-to-face suggestions replaced commands, and praise replaced sanctions. Consequently, the workers experienced a sense of relief from the anxieties and fears associated with the traditional command-and-control approach to supervision. Although critics dismissed the concept of relaxed supervision as benevolent paternalism, it is possible for it to be practiced in a genuinely caring manner.

- **Cohesive work groups.** Human relations theory suggests that supervisors should encourage the development of cohesive work groups whenever possible. Mayo viewed workers as social creatures who wish to collaborate and enjoy the security, comradery, and heightened sense of self-worth that teamwork has to offer. In his study of the aircraft industry Mayo tells of supervisors who were particularly adept at taking total strangers and integrating them into the work team by orienting them to their jobs, showing them how their work contributed to the war effort, counseling them about their personal problems, and soliciting their feedback and acting on their advice. He argued that if "nonlogical factors" are present, such as a sense of belongingness and recognition of effort, then spontaneous cooperation will occur.

Human relations theory's primary deficiency as a theory of organizational effectiveness is that it focuses too narrowly on reducing interpersonal frictions and securing greater workplace cooperation. Although Mayo and Roethisberger made significant contributions to organization theory by emphasizing the importance of human relations, it must be acknowledged that constructive interpersonal relations is only one of many determinants of organizational performance. As we shall see, later schools of thought would take the most useful elements of human relations theory and integrate them into more comprehensive and sophisticated theories of organizational effectiveness.

NOTES

1. See George F. F. Lombard, "George El-
ton Mayo," in *Dictionary of American Biog-
raphy,* Supplement 4, 1946–50 (New York:
Scribner's, 1974), 564–66; Richard Tra-
hair, *The Humanist Temper: The Life and
Work of Elton Mayo* (New Brunswick, NJ:
Transaction Books, 1984); and J. H.
Smith, "The Enduring Legacy of Elton
Mayo," *Human Relations 51*(March
1998):221–49.

2. Elton Mayo, "The Irrational Factor in
Society," *Journal of Personnel Research 1* (no.
10, 1923), 419–26; "Irrationality and
Revery," *Journal of Personnel Research 1* (no.
11, 1923), 477–83; "Civilized Unreason,"
Harper's Magazine 148 (March 1924),
527–35; "Civilization—The Perilous Ad-
venture," *Harper's Magazine 149* (October
1924), 590–97; "The Great Stupidity,"
Harper's Magazine 151 (July 1925),
225–33; "Sin with a Capital S," *Harper's
Magazine 154* (April 1927), 537–45.

3. Mayo, "Irrationality and Revery," 482.

4. Mayo, "Irrationality and Revery," 482.

5. Mayo, "The Great Stupidity," 233.

6. Mayo, "The Great Stupidity," 230–31.

7. See F. J. Roethlisberger and William J.
Dickson, *Management and the Worker* (Cambridge: Harvard University Press, 1939).

8. Roethlisberger and Dickson, *Management and the Worker,* 14–17.

9. F. J. Roethlisberger, *Management and
Morale* (Cambridge, MA: Harvard University Press, 1941), 14.

10. G. A. Pennock, "Industrial Research at
Hawthorne," *Personnel Journal 8* (no. 5,
1930), 296–313.

11. "The Fruitful Errors of Elton Mayo,"
Fortune 34 (November 1946), 181.

12. Roethlisberger and Dickson, *Management and the Worker,* 20.

13. Roethlisberger and Dickson, *Management and the Worker,* 571.

14. Elton Mayo, *The Human Problems of an
Industrial Civilization* (New York: Macmillan, 1933), 71.

15. Roethlisberger and Dickson, *Management and the Worker,* 67.

16. Roethlisberger and Dickson, *Management and the Worker,* 154.

17. Mayo, *The Human Problems of an Industrial Civilization,* 116.

18. Pennock, "Industrial Research at
Hawthorne," 297.

19. Roethlisberger and Dickson, *Management and the Worker,* 373.

20. M. L. Putnam, "Improving Employee
Relations: A Plan Which Uses Data Obtained from Employees," *Personnel Journal
8* (no. 5, 1930), 314–25.

21. Roethlisberger and Dickson, *Management and the Worker,* 194.

22. Roethlisberger and Dickson, *Management and the Worker,* 313.

23. Roethlisberger and Dickson, *Management and the Worker,* 322–23.

24. Roethlisberger and Dickson, *Management and the Worker,* 524.

25. Roethlisberger and Dickson, *Management and the Worker,* 546.

26. F. J. Roethlisberger, *Man-in-
Organization: Essays of F. J. Roethlisberger*
(Cambridge: Harvard University Press,
1968), 82.

27. Roethlisberger and Dickson, *Management and the Worker,* 561–62.

28. Roethlisberger, *Management and
Morale,* 120–21.

29. Elton Mayo, "Changing Methods in
Industry," *Personnel Journal 8* (February,
1930), 327.

30. Landsberger identifies four general
areas of criticism. See Henry A. Landsberger, *Hawthorne Revisited* (Ithaca, NY:
Cornell University, 1958).

31. W. A. Koivisto, "Value, Theory, and
Fact in Industrial Sociology," *American
Journal of Sociology 58* (May 1953), 564–72.

32. C. Wright Mills, "The Contribution
of Sociology to Studies of Industrial Relations," in Industrial Relations Research
Association, *Proceedings of the First Annual
Meeting 1* (1948), 210.

33. Daniel Bell, "Adjusting Men to Machines," *Commentary 3* (January 1947), 88.

34. Mayo, *The Social Problems of an Industrial Society* (Andover, MA: Andover Press, 1945), Chapter 5.

35. Malcom P. McNair, "Thinking Ahead," *Harvard Business Review 35* (March–April 1957), 20.

36. Koivisto, "Value, Theory, and Fact in Industrial Sociology," 571.

37. Bell, "Adjusting Men to Machines," 88.

38. McNair, "Thinking Ahead," 28.

39. McNair, "Thinking Ahead," 39.

40. "Hawthorne Revisited: The Legacy and the Legend," *Organizational Dynamics 3* (Winter 1975), 66–80.

41. Mayo, *The Social Problems of an Industrial Society,* 111.

42. Roethlisberger, *Man-in-Organization,* 123.

9

⌘

The Natural Systems
Perspective

Chester I. Barnard

S ystems theory is not a distinct school of thought. It refers instead to a diverse range of studies often having little in common beyond a shared
commitment to a particular mode of analysis—systems analysis. As noted
in Chapter 8, a *system* is anything whose components are so interrelated and
interdependent that a change in one produces simultaneous changes in other
components, thereby altering the thing as a whole. The aim of systems analysis
is to understand the subject under study holistically, that is, as something more
than the sum of its parts. Researchers have applied systems analysis to the study
of such diverse subjects as tissue cells, living organisms, self-regulating machines, human societies, entire galaxies and, of course, complex organizations.
According to its advocates, systems analysis possesses greater diagnostic and explanatory power than other modes of analysis. It can aid researchers and practitioners alike in comprehending the reasons organizations behave as they do,
the complexities of organizational life, and the difficulties inherent in sustaining high levels of organizational performance.

Alvin Gouldner observed in the late 1950s that organizations have been studied from two different perspectives.[1] The **rational perspective** views organizations as deliberately conceived and planned instruments for achieving collective
goals. Emphasis is placed on the formal structures established to ensure that goals
are achieved efficiently and it is taken for granted that organizations are subject to
planned control. The primary metaphor is that of a well-oiled machine whose
parts can be designed and manipulated so that each contributes to the efficient
attainment of organizational objectives. This perspective is reflected in the approach to organizational analysis taken by Weber, Taylor, Fayol, and Gulick.

The **natural systems perspective,** by contrast, relies explicitly on systems analysis. It views organizations as living organisms seeking to survive in uncertain and often hostile environments. Their internal components are seen partly as products of rational planning and partly as spontaneous, adaptive responses to threats to the system's equilibrium. From this perspective the organization is not simply a means to an end but also an end in itself. It abandons old goals and adopts new ones as needed to ensure its continued survival. This perspective stresses the interdependence of the system's components. Where interdependence is high, efforts to achieve planned change produce unanticipated consequences, thereby creating new problems for those seeking to control organizational activities in a deliberate fashion. This perspective is reflected in the approach to organizational analysis taken by Elton Mayo and Fritz Roethlisberger (Chapter 8), Robert Merton (Chapter 10), and Chester Barnard, whose work is discussed in this chapter.

At the time Gouldner offered this distinction other theorists were already engaged in defining a third approach to organizational analysis. Like the natural systems perspective, the **open systems perspective** views organizations as living creatures seeking to survive in an uncertain and often hostile environment. The key difference is that the natural systems perspective focuses on the organization's internal stresses and strains and its adaptive responses to them, whereas the open systems perspective focuses on the external environment and the exchanges between it and the organization. The latter perspective assumes that organizations must respond appropriately to external opportunities and threats, including changes in mandates, markets, and technologies, if they are to maintain a steady state. The open systems perspective also emphasizes the dynamic and aggressive nature of organizations. Whereas the natural systems perspective characterizes organizations as rather defensive or reactive in their adaptive responses, the open systems perspective views them as ready to transform themselves completely if necessary and to alter environmental conditions whenever possible. From this perspective management's primary task is not simply to regulate internal activities but also to manage the environment so that the organization as a whole can maintain a steady state of functioning. The open systems perspective, which is examined in Chapter 11, is reflected in the approach taken by such theorists as Joan Woodward, Emery and Trist, and Lawrence and Lorsch.

This chapter describes the evolution of the systems concept and reviews the work of Chester I. Barnard, a corporate executive and theorist who analyzed organizations from the natural systems perspective. The chapter closes with an analysis of the relevance of natural systems theory for public management and government performance.

SYSTEMS THEORY AS
A MODE OF ANALYSIS

Scholars working in a variety of disciplines in the early 1900s reached a similar conclusion. Their methods of analysis precluded them from understanding complex phenomena as unified wholes. Not only did their methods encourage them to study specific parts of the whole in isolation, they also encouraged them to view observed behaviors as products of linear cause-and-effect relationships. In the field of psychology, for example, the stimulus-response model of human behavior required researchers to trace specific behaviors to specific stimuli. This ignored the fact that humans do not experience reality as a series of stimulus-response relationships; they experience reality as a complex web of factors interacting simultaneously, and they respond to it accordingly. This conclusion led to the development of Gestalt psychology, which relies on systems analysis to comprehend human behavior holistically.

Organization theorists reached a similar conclusion at about the same time. Following the dictates of the scientific method, the Hawthorne researchers designed experiments to isolate the effects of one variable on another, such as the effects of lighting on productivity. It soon became apparent, however, that workplace variables are so interrelated and interdependent that outcomes cannot be understood in terms of linear cause-and-effect relationships. Where complex social and psychological phenomena are at issue, rarely does a change in one thing cause a direct change in another unmediated by other factors. Consequently, many organization theorists turned to systems analysis as a way of understanding human behavior and organizational dynamics in a more accurate and holistic fashion.

In systems analysis each researcher is responsible for identifying the boundaries of the system under study, including the level of analysis and the system's primary components. This is because systems do not have a concrete existence. They are simply conceptual frameworks created by researchers to aid in understanding the phenomena they are studying. A researcher may decide, for example, to study a particular subsystem of society (e.g., public organizations) rather than society as a whole. Regardless of the level of analysis chosen, social systems are typically defined as comprising people whose actions are shaped by structural, technical, and social forces. Emphasis is placed on understanding the complex interrelationships among these forces. Once developed, the conceptual framework serves as a guide in designing research and interpreting results.

As a mode of analysis systems theory holds certain advantages. It provides a means of understanding organizations as more than the sum of their parts, and it encourages us to think in terms of simultaneous interactions rather than linear cause-and-effect relationships. But despite these advantages, systems theory raises some troubling questions about the ability of social science to generate meaningful conclusions regarding "the simultaneous variations of mutually dependent variables."[2] The number of variables may be too great and the nature of their interactions too complex to be reduced to useful generalizations, let alone mathematical equations. This means that managers may have to rely on intuition as much as science when responding to concrete problems. It is unlikely, for example, that science can predict all of the effects of a managerial intervention on other system variables. Especially where system variables are tightly interdependent, the number of unanticipated consequences of an otherwise well-reasoned decision is likely to be enormous, creating new problems to be dealt with in turn. Such troubling implications are addressed more fully later in this and the following two chapters.

THE CONCEPT OF SYSTEM EQUILIBRIUM

A basic premise of systems theory is that the relationships among system variables are not random but patterned. The elements of the system act and interact with each other in a structured way. It is this quality of "systematic coherence" that gives each system its distinctive identity.[3] Systems theory raises the possibility that these patterns can be discovered through research and reduced to mathematical equations defining how a change in one variable affects all of the others. Structured patterns exist, according to systems theory, because system variables tend toward a state of balance or **equilibrium.** Whereas a system is a conceptual framework bearing only an approximate relationship to the subject under study, most systems theorists view equilibrium as a natural phenomenon. Unfortunately, there is little agreement about the definition or nature of this phenomenon. The following discussion demonstrates how system equilibrium has come to mean something quite different, depending on whether the subject under study is a planetary system, chemical mixture, biological organism, complex organization, or human society.

During the course of the nineteenth century, the use of systems analysis gradually extended from the physical sciences to the biological sciences and finally to the social sciences. In the field of physics the concept of system equilibrium conveys a mechanical image of physical forces at work. According to Newton's principles of thermodynamics, there is a constant amount of energy in the world in the form of heat and mechanical energy. Energy is dissipated continuously until a given physical or mechanical system reaches a state of equilibrium at which no further work can be done. This continuous dissipation of energy is called **entropy.** The solar system, for example, will eventually come to rest when all energy is consumed. Similarly, a kicked football will come to rest when the energy conveyed by the foot is used up and a machine will come to rest when its fuel is spent. In short, in the field of physics, equilibrium is defined as a state of rest where no further action can occur.

The field of physical chemistry also adopted a mechanical understanding of system equilibrium. An American physicist, Josiah Willard Gibbs, worked out equations in the 1870s defining the thermal and mechanical properties of chemical systems at rest. He described how chemicals dissolved in water at a given temperature and placed in a stoppered bottle comprise a physical-chemical system. The system's properties include temperature, pressure, and the concentration of the chemicals involved. Because they exist in a state of mutual interdependence, a change in one element produces a direct change in the others. For example, if the stopper is pushed further into the bottle, pressure increases, causing gas to change to liquid and the temperature to decrease. As in the field of thermodynamics, equilibrium is defined as a state of rest, and the interrelationships among elements, because they are few in number and follow physical laws, can be reduced to mathematical equations.

As biologists began using systems analysis they found they had to replace the mechanical view of system equilibrium with an organic one. The problem they encountered was that living and nonliving systems are fundamentally different. This led to the realization that system equilibrium cannot be defined as a state of rest for purposes of biological analysis. Unlike physical and chemical systems, biological systems constantly import energy in order to survive. Given these fundamental differences, biologists redefined the concept of system equilibrium as a state of "dynamic equilibrium" in which the living organism seeks a "steady state" of continued functioning. This dynamic equilibrium is not achieved by happenstance but by natural forces at work in all living things. As early as 1865 the French physiologist Claude Barnard described the systems of the human body in terms of an internal mechanism that works to maintain the organism in a state of health. In 1932 Walter B. Cannon coined the term **homeostasis** to refer to the self-regulating properties of living organisms that Barnard had described. *Homeostasis* refers to the dynamic equilibrium achieved when the organism is able to regulate or adjust its internal environment sufficiently well to be able to adjust as a whole to its external environment. If blood is lost through a wound, for example, the blood begins to clot and the blood vessels begin to constrict as forms of self-regulating adaptation. More generally, any conscious or unconscious need signals a temporary failure of adjustment and stirs the organism or one of its subsystems to restore equilibrium. In short, *equilibrium* in the field of biology came to mean a state of internal stability rather than a state of rest.

Wishing to bring greater theoretical rigor to their work, social scientists began applying the concept of system equilibrium to the study of society, including complex organizations, in the early 1900s. At first it seemed perfectly appropriate to apply the organic model of biology to social systems because they, like biological systems, seek to adapt to their environments to ensure their continued functioning. But on closer examination social scientists found themselves confronting two troubling questions. First, does equilibrium refer to a specific, definable state or condition such that we can say when it has been achieved? Second, are organizations and societies driven by an inexorable natural force to achieve that state of equilibrium?

Many natural systems theorists, past and present, have answered these questions in the affirmative. Society and its subsystems function as organic wholes whose separate parts mesh together to maintain a steady state. Any threat or disturbance, such as a revolution in the case of society or a budget cut in the case of an organization, creates pressures to restore a state of equilibrium. The latter is typically defined as a state in which conflicts and strains among its component parts are reduced to a minimum. Many, but not all, natural systems theorists also hold that societies and organizations are driven by homeostatic forces to achieve and maintain dynamic equilibrium.

Other social scientists have been less willing to answer these troubling questions in the affirmative. Critics doubt that terms such as *healthy functioning* or *steady state* can be defined objectively in terms of a specific set of conditions. Second, whereas the striving of biological organisms to return to a state of healthy functioning reflects an inherent tendency built into their genetic codes, many social scientists question whether there is any such force at work in social systems. The successful adjustment of organizations to their external environments, for example, may be a matter of good fortune or wise managerial decisions rather than the workings of some inexorable force. Third, some critics are troubled by the normative implications, reflected particularly in the natural systems perspective, that stability is good and conflict bad. Consequently, many social scientists now view equilibrium not as an objective, definable state to which organizations are driven but as a useful concept for thinking about and studying social phenomena. The concept of equilibrium can be used, for example, to think through how organizations and the individuals within them satisfy needs and respond to strains. Although this means giving up the hope that relationships among system variables can be reduced to mathematical equations, there is still every reason to believe that through the use of systems analysis researchers can discern basic patterns of organizational behavior and that better understanding of these patterns can lead to enhanced organizational performance.

ORIGINS OF THE
NATURAL SYSTEMS PERSPECTIVE

The natural systems perspective emerged in the1930s and held sway among systems theorists until it was eclipsed by the open systems perspective in the 1960s. This section reviews the origins of the natural systems perspective as it developed in the United States. A subsequent section examines the work of Chester I. Barnard, a corporate executive whose highly influential theory of organization relied heavily upon the natural systems perspective.

    Among the first to apply systems analysis to the formal study of society was the Italian economist Vilfredo Pareto. Initially trained as an engineer, Pareto was familiar with the systems concept as it applied to mechanical systems. Later, as a professor of economics at the University of Lausanne, he extended the systems concept to marketplace relations and succeeded in developing a mathematical model describing a state of equilibrium among price, supply, and demand. In doing so, Pareto described a closed system comprising a small number of variables—one which assumed rational, economic decisions by buyers and sellers. Recognizing that social actions are more often of a nonlogical sort, Pareto next sought to extend the systems concept to society as a whole by developing a model embracing nonlogical as well as logical behaviors. In doing so he immediately confronted the fact that the components of society and the forces that impact them represent dozens of interdependent variables that cannot be identified and reduced to a mathematical model in the same way as the variables in an economic system. He was forced to acknowledge that the development of scientific propositions in the social sciences would be a formidable task.

Despite the apparent difficulties, Pareto set out to develop a conceptual scheme for studying society as a social system. He understood that this scheme would not allow social scientists to predict behavior with precision but he believed it could bring greater clarity to the forces at work in society. Pareto published his systems model of society in *Treatise on General Sociology* in 1916. The components of his model were economic interests, residues, and derivations. He defined *residues* as the expressions of human sentiments and *derivations* as the laws and customs that rationalize sentiments. Pareto's model also introduced the idea of circulating elites. Members of society, according to Pareto, regularly overthrow the ruling elites in order to restore an equilibrium that better serves the interests of society as a whole. When one set of ruling elites inevitably betrays its trust, it is replaced by a new set and the cycle continues.

Pareto's conceptual model provided a point of departure for a group of social scientists who were then turning their attention to the study of complex organizations. That Elton Mayo, Fritz Roethlisberger, Robert Merton (Chapter 10), and Chester Barnard all applied systems analysis to the study of organizations was no accident. It was a direct consequence of their affiliation with Lawrence J. Henderson, the Harvard biochemist who transferred from Harvard's chemistry department to the business school in 1927 to operate the Fatigue Laboratory in collaboration with Elton Mayo.[4] Henderson was intimately familiar with the systems concept as it applied to biological systems and had relied upon it extensively in his own studies of the body's circulatory system. His work at the Fatigue Laboratory awakened him to the psychological as well as physiological factors governing human behavior. In 1928 a friend convinced him to read Pareto's treatise, and he immediately recognized its importance. Henderson became so enthralled with the potential contributions of systems analysis to social science that he organized a course on Pareto's work for colleagues and graduate students in 1932. Roethlisberger attended as an interested colleague and Merton attended as a graduate student in sociology. In 1938 Henderson developed a course for undergraduates entitled Sociology 23 that focused on systems analysis of concrete social behavior. Mayo, Roethlisberger, and Chester Barnard were among those who offered case studies for students to analyze.

Thus, terms such as *systems, equilibrium, nonlogical action,* and *sentiments* appeared in the writings of Mayo, Roethlisberger, Merton, and Barnard from Pareto by way of Henderson. Many of the next generation of organization theorists, including George C. Homans and William F. Whyte, were also introduced to systems analysis through Henderson. Henderson's impact on organization theory, although indirect, was substantial. As Cynthia Eagle Russett has written, "Henderson may have given greater impetus to the diffusion of equilibrium concepts among American social scientists than any other single individual. To a whole generation of Harvard students he passed on his conception of scientific method, of social science methodology, and specifically of the place of equilibrium analysis in social science."[5]

Chester I. Barnard 1886–1961

Chester Irving Barnard was born in Malden, Massachusetts, on November 7, 1886.[6] He completed the requirements for a major in economics at Harvard but left after three years because his preparatory training had not equipped him to pass the required courses in chemistry and physics. In 1909 Walter Gifford, an acquaintance of Barnard's, offered him a job at American Telephone and Telegraph (AT&T). Barnard's forty-year career with AT&T began in the statistical department, where he developed considerable expertise in foreign and domestic phone rates. In 1922 Barnard left Boston to become assistant vice president and general manager of the Bell Telephone Company of Pennsylvania. Five years later, at the age of 41, he was named president of the New Jersey Bell Telephone Company, a position he held until he retired in 1948.

Barnard possessed an intellectual and practical disposition that allowed him to move comfortably among the worlds of business, public service, and academia. In 1931 the governor of New Jersey asked Barnard to organize and direct the New Jersey Emergency Relief Administration. Barnard later presented a case study on the "Riot of the Unemployed" in Henderson's Sociology 23 course at Harvard. Henderson was so impressed with a speech delivered by Barnard at Princeton in 1936 that he arranged for him to give a series of eight lectures at Harvard sponsored by the Lowell Institute. These lectures, delivered during November and December of 1937, were the basis of Barnard's book, *The Functions of the Executive*, published in 1938. Although it was the only book Barnard wrote, its impact on subsequent generations of organizational analysts has been enormous.[7]

Barnard remained actively involved in public service, both while serving as president of New Jersey Bell and after his retirement. At the age of 65 he became chair of the National Science Board of the National Science Foundation and continued to work with the board until 1956. Barnard died June 7, 1961, a few months short of his seventy-fifth birthday.

BARNARD'S NATURAL SYSTEMS
VIEW OF ORGANIZATIONS

Barnard found that the existing literature on organizations did not capture the realities of organizational life in the way he experienced them as a business executive.[8] Whereas much had been written about organizational structure and the exercise of formal authority, little attention had been given to the actual processes of coordination and decision. Consequently, Barnard set out to develop a conceptual scheme for understanding organizations that was more behavioral than legalistic in nature, one that he hoped would prove to be "a useful tool" for studying the problems of concrete organizations.[9] The resulting scheme was published in *The Functions of the Executive* in 1938. With the possible exception of Weber's ideal-type model of bureaucracy, Barnard's conceptual scheme represented the first truly comprehensive theory of organization. Roethlisberger had developed a similar conceptual scheme for interpreting the results of the Hawthorne studies but it was much less comprehensive in scope. Key components of Barnard's conceptual scheme include the definition of organizations as cooperative systems, his inducements-contributions theory, and his view of the functions of executives.

Organizations as Cooperative Systems

Barnard conceptualized concrete institutions—churches, governments, businesses, civic associations, and families—as **cooperative systems.** A cooperative system, he wrote, "is a complex of physical, biological, personal, and social components which are in a specific systematic relationship by reason of the cooperation of two or more persons for at least one definite end."[10] Barnard's definition emphasized that organizations exist to achieve important purposes, that those purposes can only be achieved through cooperative effort, and that cooperative effort is not effective unless the relationships among the organization's various components are deliberately structured. Humans enter into cooperative arrangements so that they can accomplish together what they cannot accomplish alone. In doing so they sacrifice a certain amount of freedom to achieve a shared purpose.

Far from being self-contained and independent, organizations must obtain resources from the outside world and adjust to changes occurring in their external environments if they are to survive. As Barnard put it, external forces "both furnish the materials which are used by organizations and limit their action. The survival of an organization depends upon the maintenance of an equilibrium of complex character in a continuously fluctuating environment of physical, biological, and social materials, elements, and forces, which calls for readjustment of processes internal to the organization."[11] Barnard's use of biological terms such as *survival* and *equilibrium* is consistent with the natural systems perspective. From this perspective organizations are viewed as living organisms seeking to survive in an uncertain and often hostile environment. Barnard referred to organizations as being "alive," much in the same sense that human beings are alive.[12] As living things, organizations must continuously adjust to changes taking place in their environments that limit effective cooperation.

Barnard was among the first to recognize that organizations have **maintenance needs.** They must obtain "surplus" resources from their environments and use them to induce contributions from their members, minimize internal frictions, and cope with external threats. If resources are not committed to maintaining themselves as viable organisms, then questions about how to achieve stated purposes become moot. Often, Barnard noted, organizations must commit more energy to maintaining themselves than to achieving goals, much like an engine whose "losses of energy through internal friction and heat transfer are much greater than the energy actually converted to useful work."[13] Organizations may, for example, create overhead staff agencies and install new management systems to promote system maintenance, only to have them become sources of friction and inefficiency themselves.

The Concept of Formal Organization

Barnard hoped social scientists would use his conceptual scheme to develop propositions about how to manage organizations effectively. He understood, however, that useful propositions could not be generated from a systems model that attempted to include all of the physical, biological, and social variables encompassed by concrete, natural systems. For this reason he narrowed the scope of his analysis to one major component of cooperative systems, the **formal organization.** Barnard defined *formal organization* "as a system of consciously coordinated activities or forces of two or more persons."[14] In Barnard's conceptual scheme, the formal organization is a subsystem of the more inclusive cooperative system; other subsystems include the physical, biological, and psychological subsystems. In leaving the physical, biological, and psychological components out of his conceptual model, Barnard did not mean to say that these components are unimportant for understanding organizational behavior. He simply wished to isolate the consciously coordinated activities or forces as the central component under study.

Although Barnard restricted his analysis primarily to the formal organization, he noted that informal organizations inevitably arise within the formal structure. These he defined as any set of interactions that occur without conscious joint purpose but which tend to become organized or systematized nonetheless. Barnard's treatment of informal groups is generally favorable. He viewed them as functioning to facilitate communication, maintain cohesiveness, and promote feelings of personal integrity and self-respect. Because informal organizations are distinct from the consciously structured formal organization, with its hierarchy of authority and impersonal objectives, they provide an essential antidote to the tendency of formal organizations to rob participants of their individuality.[15] Informal groups provide freedom of choice and action, and an opportunity for individuals to structure group relations to their own liking.

A key element in Barnard's conceptual scheme is the premise that formal organizations comprise sets of activities that are consciously structured. They are structured primarily by managers seeking to satisfy the requirements of the system as a whole. Barnard thus created a conceptual scheme similar to Weber's ideal-type. Both schemes direct analysis to the impersonal, instrumental nature of organizations. A key difference, however, is that Barnard used the concept of subsystems to emphasize how the formal organization is impacted by physical, biological, and psychological factors. By including human sentiments in his conceptual scheme Barnard was able to explain organizational behavior in ways that adherents to the rational perspective could not.

Barnard's Inducements-Contributions Theory

System equilibrium, according to Barnard, refers to two sets of interrelated processes. The first aims to achieve an equilibrium, or fit, between the organization's internal characteristics and its external environment. The second aims to achieve an equilibrium, or balance, between the contributions that individuals make to the organization's collective purpose and the satisfactions they receive in exchange. Much of Barnard's theory of organization relates to the latter meaning of equilibrium. It is, as March and Simon have noted, essentially a theory of motivation.[16] This theory holds that organizational members make contributions to the organization in exchange for inducements, and that each continues to participate only as long as the inducements received are greater than the contributions he or she is asked to make.

Consistent with the pleasure-pain principle of motivation, Barnard viewed humans as striving to maximize their satisfactions. They cooperate only to satisfy their individual motives. From this premise he developed unique definitions of efficiency and effectiveness, two conditions that determine whether a cooperative system will survive. The cooperative system is **efficient** if the net satisfaction of all contributors is higher than the net dissatisfactions. Individuals who believe they will not experience sufficient satisfaction will withhold their contributions to the system, thereby reducing the efficiency of the system, possibly to the point where survival is no longer possible:

> . . . . If the individual finds his motives being satisfied by what he does, he continues his cooperative effort; otherwise he does not. If he does not, this subtraction from the cooperative system may be fatal to it. If five men are required and the fifth man finds no satisfaction in cooperating, his contribution would be inefficient. He would withhold or withdraw his services, so that the cooperation would be destroyed. If he considers it to be efficient, it is continued. Thus, the efficiency of a cooperative system is its capacity to maintain itself by the individual satisfactions it affords. This may be called its capacity of equilibrium, the balancing of burdens by satisfactions which results in continuance.[17]

A system is **effective** to the degree its purpose is achieved. In Barnard's conceptual scheme, effectiveness depends in large part on the efficiency of the inducements-contributions equilibrium. Only when a critical mass of contributors are receiving net satisfaction and are therefore continuing to contribute can the organization attain its goals. Being efficient in this sense means distributing just enough inducements to satisfy each individual, assuming that higher levels of satisfaction are not available elsewhere. This is a different meaning of efficiency than the technical efficiency espoused by Frederick Taylor. Although Barnard believed that an organization must be efficient in the technical sense to generate the surplus resources it needs to satisfy human motives, it is human satisfaction that ultimately determines effectiveness. By satisfying human motives the organization is able to compensate each participant for the lost freedoms they experience upon joining the organization. It is the net advantages they receive that induces them to contribute to the attainment of organizational objectives.

Also in contrast to Taylor, Barnard believed that nonmaterial inducements are more powerful motivators than material ones. Although some organizations may succeed in motivating members primarily through material inducements,

Barnard believed that it is "utterly contrary to the nature of man" to be induced to contribute by material or monetary considerations alone. True efficiency, he argued, is achieved by offering nonmaterial inducements such as recognition, prestige, personal power, pride of craft, and accomplishment.[18]

According to Barnard, organizations can get away with a degree of inefficiency or ineffectiveness and still survive for a time, but in the long run both efficiency and effectiveness are necessary to system survival. If efficiency is a prerequisite for effectiveness, effectiveness is also a prerequisite for efficiency. Ineffectiveness is a matter for concern because those who are motivated by goal attainment are unable to obtain personal satisfaction when goals are not attained and because an ineffective organization is less able to generate the surplus resources needed to induce the cooperation of those who are not motivated by goal attainment.

In practice the desired inducement-contribution equilibrium is achieved by simultaneously offering positive inducements, such as wages, and reducing negative burdens, such as hours of work. Unfortunately, it is impossible to determine objectively whether system equilibrium is being maintained. Much depends on what members perceive as burdensome and the value they place on available inducements. For this reason managers must remain attentive to signs that the desired equilibrium no longer exists—signs such as increased turnover, reduced productivity, and heightened levels of conflict.

The Altering of Motives

Early in his book Barnard notes that people can be viewed either as subjects to be satisfied or objects to be manipulated. The first expands individual choice by offering inducements from which to choose, whereas the second limits choice by shaping the individual's values, attitudes, or state of mind. Barnard's lengthy discussion of material and nonmaterial incentives seems to suggest that treating individuals as subjects to be satisfied is the preferred course of action. But later in his book Barnard acknowledged that some organizations lack the material and nonmaterial inducements needed to secure contributions and therefore must seek to shape each individual's state of mind, including what they value, so that they will desire the inducements the organization has to offer. Individuals, as the basic strategic factor in organizations, must be induced to cooperate, but it turns out that there are two ways of doing so: by offering incentives to satisfy existing motives (the incentive method) or by altering the motives themselves (the persuasion method). Barnard makes this distinction as follows:

> . . . . Given a man of a certain state of mind, of certain attitudes, or governed by certain motives, he can be induced to contribute to an organization by a given combination of these objective incentives, positive or negative. It often is the case, however, that the organization is unable to offer objective incentives that will serve as an inducement to that state of mind, or to those attitudes, or to one governed by those motives. The only alternative then available is to change the state of mind, or attitudes, or motives, so that the available objective incentives can become effective.[19]

The second method of inducing cooperation, which Bernard labeled the persuasion method, has three forms. The first is persuasion by coercion. Individuals may be persuaded to comply with directives through the threat of force, including discharge, ostracism, or the withholding of benefits. The second form is persuasion by propaganda. Individuals may be persuaded to contribute to organizational success by indoctrinating them in the importance of organizational mission, service, or product. Here participants are told that the organization exists to achieve an important collective purpose and that they will receive personal satisfaction from contributing to its attainment. The underlying strategy is to get individuals to identify with the organization's purpose, so that helping to accomplish it becomes a motive for cooperating. Military, religious, and patriotic organizations, according to Barnard, rely heavily on this form of persuasion. The third form of persuasion is the inculcation of motives. This involves educating individuals in religious beliefs, patriotic ideals, or professional values so that they are conditioned to behave in prescribed ways. In practice, according to Barnard, organizations use a combination of these forms of persuasion, with the mix varying according to their natures and circumstances. They generally proceed by trial-and-error to discover the optimal balance between the costs of providing these kinds of inducements and the benefits they receive in terms of heightened contributions.

Limits on the Exercise of Formal Authority

Like the administrative management theorists, Barnard believed that the hierarchical structure of authority is a universal feature of all complex organizations.[20] It is the primary vehicle by which purpose is communicated throughout the organization and by which coordination is secured. But, if each executive position carries with it the authority to issue formal directives, this does not mean that those who receive the directives are powerless. Barnard viewed compliance with institutional directives as a special form of contribution and noted that formal authority is often ineffective in securing it. Like Follett, Barnard believed authority rests on consent. Formal directives, including orders, rules, and regulations, are not effective unless they are accepted as legitimate by those who receive them. Here, too, individuals must be induced to cooperate, that is, induced to accept the legitimacy of institutional directives. For compliance to occur, four conditions must be satisfied: a person must understand the directive, believe that it is consistent with the organization's purpose, believe that it is compatible with his or her personal interests, and be able to comply with it mentally and physically.[21] In practice most organizations are able to satisfy these conditions for three reasons. First, most managers are astute enough to avoid issuing directives that are clearly inconsistent with organizational purpose and individual self-interest; second, most members do not wish to disturb the prevailing social equilibrium by challenging authority; and, third, most members have a rather broad "zone of indifference."

According to the latter concept, individuals accept most orders without consciously questioning them because whether they comply is a matter of

indifference to them. This, Barnard observed, is something organizations can manipulate. They can establish broad zones of indifference by ensuring that inducements continue to exceed burdens and sacrifices. Otherwise, if the balance
between inducements and burdens is perceived as negative, members will resign,
malinger, or behave in generally undependable ways. This helps explain why
coercion-based management generally fails. Although individuals may comply in
the short run to avoid sanctions, coercion adversely affects the inducement-
burden equilibrium. "In the last analysis," Barnard wrote, "the authority fails
because the individuals in sufficient numbers regard the burden involved in
accepting necessary orders as changing the balance of advantage against their interest, and they withdraw or withhold the indispensable contributions."[22]

The Process of Decision

The Functions of the Executive offered an analysis of the process of decision,
something that earlier works in organization theory had not done. Barnard
emphasized that the way individuals make decisions is a very different question from how organizations make decisions. In his view it was as important
to understand the latter as the former.

According to Barnard, decisions are the means by which organizations regulate the relations between purpose and environment. Organizations respond
to problems thrown up by their internal and external environments by deciding to change either their environments or their purposes. The decision
process is thus a process of adaptation. Given a particular set of circumstances,
the first step in the process is to identify the primary **strategic factor** in the
internal or external environment that is limiting the organization's ability to
accomplish its purpose, either by its presence or absence. How to cope with
the identified limitation becomes the next strategic factor for analysis. Relying
on experiential, logical, and factual analysis, alternative courses of action are
identified and a decision reached, with purpose serving as the general criterion for choice. After one strategic factor has been addressed, another takes its
place and is addressed in turn. The process of decision is thus an iterative one
in which broad purposes are achieved through many successive decisions, involving many different persons, and occurring both simultaneously and sequentially. Sometimes, however, strategic factors prove to be insurmountable
and it becomes necessary to change purpose rather than environment. The
newly agreed upon purpose brings with it a new environment, one defined by
different internal and external factors, and all subsequent decisions must take
this new environment into account.

The Functions of the Executive

Executives, in Barnard's conceptual scheme, are those responsible for maintaining the cooperative system in a state of internal and external equilibrium. They
are responsible for making the decisions that connect means to ends, as well as
those that regulate the relations between purpose and environment. In maintaining the cooperative system, the executive organization does not manage the

system as much as it serves to direct it. Barnard develops this point by drawing an analogy with the human body's nervous system: "The functions with which we are concerned are like those of the nervous system, including the brain, in relation to the rest of the body. It exists to maintain the bodily system by directing those actions which are necessary more effectively to adjust to the environment, but it can hardly be said to manage the body, a large part of whose functions are independent of it and upon which it in turn depends."[23]

The general task of maintaining the cooperative system, according to Barnard, involves the performance of three interrelated executive functions. The first is developing and maintaining a system of communication. This involves defining the hierarchy of authority, or structural scheme, through which communications are to flow. It includes defining executive positions, filling them with competent personnel, and inducing their loyalty and interest. The second executive function is inducing individuals to join the organization and contribute to accomplishing its purposes. This function encompasses the maintenance of morale, including maintenance of the systems of inducements and deterrents, supervision and control, and education and training.[24] The third executive function is defining the purposes and objectives of the organization. This includes delegating authority to the units and positions that are to be assigned responsibility for specific aspects of the overall purpose. It also involves making those decisions that guide the translation of purpose into concrete actions at all levels of the organization. According to Barnard, executives must "indoctrinate" those working at the lower levels of the organization with general purposes "so that they remain cohesive and able to make the ultimate detailed decisions coherent. . . ."[25] But Barnard emphasized that executives must also be attentive to information filtering up from below so that they can adjust purpose effectively. "Without that up-and-down-the-line coordination of purposeful decisions," he wrote, "general decisions and general purposes are mere intellectual processes in an organizational vacuum, insulated from realities by layers of misunderstanding."[26]

Barnard argued that system maintenance requires the ability to sense the organization as a whole and the total situation relevant to it. This ability relies heavily on intuition and is acquired by "persistent habitual experience." The difficulties inherent in sensing organizations holistically led Barnard to view system maintenance as more an art than a science.

The Moral Aspect

Organizations, according to Barnard, are inherently moral in nature because they exist to accomplish a collective purpose. To induce cooperation they develop their own moral codes. These reflect organizational expectations and norms of behavior, the most basic of which is the expectation that members will place the good of the organization first. A morally responsible person is one who holds to moral obligations in the face of temptations to act in a contrary fashion. Because everyone has multiple codes and obligations, organizations seek to establish the primacy of the organizational code over other, more personal codes.

Executives have their own organizational codes. The moral code of a department head, for example, typically includes obedience to the system of authority, commitment to advancing the general purpose of the department, commitment to advancing the good of the organization as a whole, informal norms such as acting like a lady or gentleman, and norms associated with a specific profession. If these should clash with personal religious, political, or familial codes, the organizational code will demand priority. This creates a moral dilemma. In some instances the department head may feel compelled to resign.

The executive is also responsible for creating moral codes for others. As Barnard put it, "This is the process of inculcating points of view, fundamental attitudes, loyalties, to the organization or cooperative system, and to the system of objective authority, that will result in subordinating individual interest and the minor dictates of personal codes to the good of the cooperative whole."[27]

Morals of this kind are inculcated through education and training or the natural process of socialization by which new members learn the norms and behavioral expectations that prevail in the workplace. Employees who are educated or socialized to feel a sense of dedication to their work are more likely than others to abide by the organizational code. Barnard cited an example of a switchboard operator who remained at her post as she watched the house where her invalid mother lived burn down. Organizations, he wrote, depend on this kind of dedication, and it is the responsibility of executives to foster it by altering the motives of organizational members. As he put it, "Executive responsibility, then, is that capacity of leaders by which, reflecting attitudes, ideals, hopes, derived largely from without themselves, they are compelled to bind the wills of men to the accomplishment of purposes beyond their immediate ends, beyond their times."[28]

Barnard acknowledged that demanding allegiance to the organization's moral code is sometimes taken to unwarranted extremes. Employees are sometimes asked to violate professional norms of good practice or to sacrifice their personal integrity for the good of the organization. He believed, however, that responsible executives will seek to minimize the number of situations where employees are asked to sacrifice their personal values and sense of integrity to serve the interests of the organization as a whole.

BARNARD'S CONTRIBUTIONS
TO ORGANIZATION THEORY

Drawing upon his experience as a corporate executive, Barnard proceeded logically and analytically, one concept at a time, to build a conceptual scheme for understanding organizational behavior. By doing so he produced the first truly comprehensive theory of organization. He conceptualized organizations as social systems and sought to understand them as organic wholes. Like Mayo and Roethlisberger, he used the concepts of formal and informal organization to illustrate how human sentiments as well as rational calculation influence individual and organizational behavior. He also used the concept of an inducements-contributions equilibrium to shift attention from coercing employees to satisfying their needs. Although the process of exchanging inducements for contributions was still one between unequals, and although the final bargain was still struck on management's terms, Barnard nonetheless tempered classical theory's emphasis on the exercise of formal authority and top-down control. Finally, he was among the first to analyze the way decisions are made within organizations and to define the functions of executives in terms of systems maintenance as well as goal attainment. His influence on subsequent generations of theorists has been substantial.

CRITICISMS OF BARNARD'S THEORY

Although Barnard's contributions to organization theory are widely acknowledged, his ideas have not escaped criticism. William G. Scott, for example, views *The Functions of the Executive* as an ideological defense of managerialism and the administrative state.[29] **Managerialism** is an ideology that justifies concentrating power in the hands of a managerial elite and establishing an activist state that plans for the rational attainment of the public good. It arose in the early 1900s as management was emerging as a distinct profession and as managers were replacing capitalists as the new ruling class. Among its beliefs are the following: that managers represent a benign ruling class because they are apolitical, morally responsible, and concerned only with promoting efficiency; that they are uniquely qualified to hold positions of leadership because of their technical expertise and commitment to scientific rationality; that they possess specialized tools for the effective coordination and control of people and work activities; and that by pursuing the interests of their organizations they promote the collective interests of society. These beliefs were buttressed by traditional Progressive values, including efficiency, faith in science, competence, moral integrity, and rational stewardship. In short, managerialism as it developed in the United States promised peace, prosperity, and progress through the efforts of its new guardian class. Whereas Taylor, Fayol, and Gulick had articulated the values of scientific rationality and managerial control, and Mayo and Roethlisberger had introduced the idea of "managing" human sentiments using behavioral techniques, the fullest expression of managerial values, according to Scott, is found in the work of Chester Barnard.

Scott finds Barnard's theory of organization troubling for several reasons. First, it accepts the legitimacy of the hierarchical structure of authority espoused by classical organization theorists. This means that the power to set policies is concentrated at the top of the organization and in the hands of a small elite group. Those at the top are viewed as qualified to make fundamental policy decisions because of their superior education and expertise, and those at the bottom are expected to offer their loyalty and obedience. Second, according to Scott, Barnard's theory espouses an antidemocratic approach to management. Not only are the governed excluded from participating in setting organizational policies but they also have few means by which to check potential abuses of power.

Third, Barnard's theory of organization offers a thinly disguised justification for the social control of employees. According to Scott, Barnard's theory encourages the use of management techniques derived from the behavioral sciences to secure employee compliance. These include techniques for distributing inducements and manipulating values, such as pay-for-performance and orientation sessions for new employees. Scott finds especially repugnant the idea that managers should seek to alter human motives by creating moral codes and indoctrinating employees in organizational ideals. To him, management by persuasion is management by deceit and manipulation. It is "the deliberate attempt by people with power to alter the perceptions of objective situations by others without their awareness of alternative interpretations, choices, or values."[30] The purpose is to expand each person's zone of indifference by causing them to value what they might not otherwise value.

It is often the case that criticisms of another person's work are overly broad, expressing more about the critic's values than the theorist's intent. In this instance, Scott's criticisms are fair but only up to a point. It is true, for example, that Barnard believed that hierarchies of authority are universal features of complex organizations. He viewed them as the primary structural means by which coordination is achieved. It is also true that he believed that organizations, unlike political systems, cannot be governed in a democratic fashion. In his view democracy is a process that allows individuals to express their views, so that general policy directions can be set by the majority of participants. It is perfectly well suited to the requirements of a political system. But complex organizations, he insisted, are entirely different entities. Their survival depends on well-informed, detailed decisions made by a small group of executives acting swiftly but deliberately, and requiring the consent of most if not all members. In view of the needs of complex organizations, the democratic process of decision is far too slow, far too divisive, results in a very abstract understanding of what is to be done, and rests on the consent of as few as 51 percent of its participants. Different kinds of systems, Barnard concluded, have different needs, and "experience shows that a final test of any system of governance is the survival of the organization in which it is used."[31]

Barnard did not believe, however, that managerial power is absolute and without checks. Executives are constrained by the knowledge that their directives are not authoritative unless they are accepted as such by those who receive them. They are also constrained by the fact that employees are free to leave the organization or otherwise withhold cooperation if they fail to provide net satisfaction. Moreover, Barnard argued that, whereas fundamental decisions regarding system maintenance are the responsibility of top management, operational decisions should be pushed downward to the point where action is required. Those at the top, he believed, cannot hope to exercise complete control over what takes place elsewhere in the organization. In short, if Barnard's theory did not encourage broad employee involvement, neither did it absolutely preclude delegation of responsibility and meaningful opportunities for empowerment.

It is also true, as Scott suggests, that Barnard believed organizations require a high degree of obedience and conformity. Cooperative effort, Barnard argued, cannot be effective if members are rowing in different directions or pursuing interests that run contrary to those of the organization. Nonetheless, Barnard was very concerned that the integrity of the individual not be lost in the process. Echoing the views of Mayo and Roethlisberger, Barnard argued that effective cooperation cannot be achieved unless management is willing to treat employees as individuals with human needs and emotions. "My own belief," he wrote, "is strong that the capacity, development, and state of mind of employees as individuals must be the focal point of all policy and practice relating to personnel."[32] This commitment to individual development, he added, must be completely genuine, not a matter of tactics or symbols. Further, he did not find this inconsistent with the executive's use of indoctrination to alter individual motives. He viewed indoctrination not as something hidden and deceitful but as a process of openly communicating organizational purpose and ideals to employees, thereby inculcating in them a sense of loyalty, dedication, and responsibility. The survival of any organizational system, he argued, depends on getting people to work together wholeheartedly for common purposes only remotely related to their individual purposes. In his view accomplishing this through persuasion is preferable to accomplishing it through coercion or the issuing of explicit instructions.

If Barnard was an articulate spokesman for managerialism as Scott contends, it is important to note that his brand of managerialism was much more progressive and humanistic in character than the neo-Taylorian and market-oriented brands that exist today.[33] Although a conservative businessman, Barnard embraced the Progressive values of moral responsibility, human dignity, and social progress. He believed that individual freedom and pursuit of the collective good represent opposing forces, forces that cannot ultimately be reconciled. He viewed social interdependence as a defining characteristic of modern society. So, too, is the establishment of complex organizations to accomplish shared purposes. As a result, the conflict between individual freedom and the collective good in modern society gives rise to inescapable tensions. When individuals join organizations they necessarily give up a measure of freedom and individuality. As members of organizations they are subject to the authority of some while exercising control over others; they are at once free and unfree, dependent and independent, possessing free will and experiencing limits on their choices.

Barnard noted that the tension between individual freedom and the collective good had given rise to two extreme faiths, one in individualism and the other in statism. He recognized that statism, which is premised on the value of cooperation, is fraught with dangers when taken to an extreme. Those who take this point of view, Barnard wrote, "are likely to advocate uncritically a vast regimentation, an endless subordination, a completeness of coordination, that in *their* unrestricted dogmatism would stifle all development of individuals beyond that found inescapable."[34] In contrast to many who embraced managerialist views in the 1930s and 1940s, Barnard warned of the dangers of centralized planning and statism.[35] Scott's criticisms notwithstanding, Barnard believed his theory of organization steered a middle course between these two extremes. Although cooperation is accomplished on management's terms, and although members experience the inevitable tensions between freedom and unfreedom, organizations are still places where people exercise choice in pursuit of collective purposes. Believing in the possibilities of a middle course between extreme individualism and statism, Barnard concluded his book with these words:

> . . . . I believe in the power of cooperation of men of free will to make men free to cooperate; that only as they choose to work together can they achieve the fullness of personal development; that only as each accepts a responsibility for choice can they enter into that communion of men from which arise the higher purposes of individual and of cooperative behavior alike. I believe that the expansion of cooperation and the development of the individual are mutually dependent realities, and that a due proportion or balance between them is a necessary condition of human welfare. Because it is subjective with respect both to a society as a whole and to the individual, what this proportion is I believe science cannot say. It is a question for philosophy and religion.[36]

CONTRIBUTIONS OF
NATURAL SYSTEMS THEORY

Natural systems theorists, including Elton Mayo, Chester Barnard, and Robert Merton (Chapter 10), produced one of the richest literatures in the field of organization theory. By conceptualizing organizations as social systems, they brought human behavior and its social and psychological determinants into the mainstream of organizational analysis. In doing so they exposed the limitations of the mechanistic view of organizations and they added flesh and blood to the structural skeleton described by classical management theorists. Second, they encouraged researchers to adopt systems analysis and managers to learn to think holistically. Those who did so were able to avoid the traps caused by linear cause-and-effect thinking and the tendency to investigate the parts without regard to the whole. Third, they identified maintenance needs that must be met if the system is to survive and they directed the attention of researchers to discovering the mechanisms by which those needs are satisfied. The concept of maintenance needs is useful in explaining, for example, why professional associations offer inexpensive insurance policies to their members (to induce new members to join and old members to remain), or why the National Foundation for Infantile Paralysis changed its name to the March of Dimes and committed itself to fighting a broad range of birth defects when the Salk vaccine essentially eliminated polio in the1950s (it sought to persist as an organization).[37]

But the natural systems perspective also has limitations. As Kast and Rosenzweig have observed, organizations may be systems but they are not necessarily natural systems.[38] The parallels between living organisms and social, man-made systems, although intriguing, are in fact quite limited. In contrast to living organisms, man-made systems are deliberately planned and structured. Kast and Rosenzweig feared that by overemphasizing the parallels we may fail to appreciate the differences between organizations and living things. They also noted that organizations do not merely adapt to their environments; they also take steps to alter them. Nor are all internal adaptations responses to external forces; many adaptations are responses to internal demands or needs. As will be seen in Chapter 11, many of these conceptual limitations were subsequently addressed by open systems theory.

RELEVANCE FOR PUBLIC MANAGEMENT

The remainder of this chapter explores the relevance of natural systems theory for public management and government performance. This exploration is guided by the three analytical frameworks presented in Chapter 3.

Models of Organizational Effectiveness

Barnard's natural systems theory emphasized the importance of all four sets of effectiveness values identified in Quinn's competing values framework, something that is very rare among theories of organization. The effective organization, according to Barnard, is one that succeeds in maintaining a state of external and internal equilibrium. Maintaining external equilibrium requires securing the resources the system needs to survive, adapting to external changes, and keeping the organization focused on its ultimate purpose, all of which requires careful and deliberate strategic planning. The effectiveness values associated with this external focus are encompassed by the **open systems model** and the **rational goal model.** Maintaining internal equilibrium, by contrast, requires coordinating work activities and balancing individual inducements and contributions, all of which requires constructing a formal organization that minimizes frictions while facilitating coordination and control. The effectiveness values associated with this internal focus are encompassed by the **internal process model** and the **human relations model.**

Barnard's theory offers an interesting blend of the rational and the natural systems perspective: Complex organizations are living organisms that engage in rational planning and decision making both to survive as institutions and to achieve their stated goals. Survival and goal attainment in turn depend on management's ability to pursue all four sets of effectiveness values in a balanced fashion, depending on the unique mix of internal and external forces at work in the organization's total situation.

The **human relations model** is highlighted in Exhibit 9.1 because it receives the greatest attention in Barnard's analysis. Although Barnard viewed complex organizations as cooperative systems by definition, he emphasized

Exhibit 9.1 The Competing Values Framework:
Four Models of Organizational Effectiveness

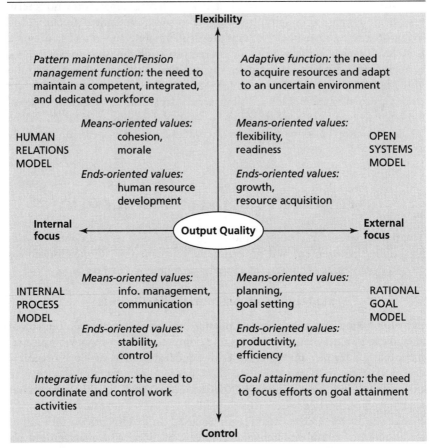

SOURCE: Adapted with permission from Figures 3 and 4, Robert O. Quinn and John Rohrbaugh, "A Spatial Model of Effectiveness Criteria: Towards a Competing Values Approach to Organizational Analysis," *Management Science* 29 (March 1983): 363–373. Copyright 1983, The Institute of Management Sciences, now the Institute for Operations Research and the Management Sciences (INFORMS), 901 Elkridge Landing Road, Suite 400, Linthicum, Maryland 21090-2909 USA.

that management must take deliberate steps to secure effective cooperation. Consequently, much of his analysis relates to fulfilling the organization's pattern maintenance and tension management functions. This is accomplished by ensuring that members receive net satisfactions through the various material and nonmaterial inducements that the organization has to offer. Whereas the rational perspective emphasizes material incentives for purposes of inducing cooperative effort, Barnard's natural systems perspective emphasizes the motivational power of nonmaterial incentives and the importance of goal attainment itself as a powerful source of motivation. The human relations model takes on special significance in Barnard's theory because maintaining an efficient internal equilibrium is the crucial prerequisite for effective goal attainment and institutional survival. Although strategic decision making by senior managers is also a crucial prerequisite, Barnard warned that any action by management that disrupts cooperation destroys the capacity of the organization to achieve its goals and adapt successfully to its environment. Consequently, Barnard's natural systems theory, like human relations theory, remained internally focused on questions of morale, motivation, and social cohesion. As we shall see in Chapter 11, the subject of how organizations adjust or adapt to their external environments was left for the open systems theorists to explore.

Mechanisms for Coordinating and Controlling Work Activities

Barnard's natural systems theory retains classical theory's emphasis on **direct supervision** as the primary mechanism for coordinating and controlling work activities. The formal chain of command in Barnard's conceptual scheme is the deliberately constructed means by which purpose is communicated throughout the organization, responsibilities are delegated and accountability maintained, and work activities are coordinated and controlled. Barnard warned, however, that, although compliance with directives is one of the contributions that supervisors hope to induce, reliance on formal authority and the threat of sanctions is rarely the best way to induce it. The wise supervisor works instead to establish the legitimacy of directives by emphasizing their connection with organizational purpose and individual self-interest. Success in doing so broadens each worker's zone of indifference and helps ensure that directives are followed as a matter of course.

Cooperative systems do not, however, rely on direct supervision alone. As indicated in Exhibit 9.2, Barnard's natural systems theory was among the first to draw attention to **standardization of values** as a mechanism of coordination and control. Barnard noted that many workers, especially those at the lower levels of the organizational hierarchy, do not identify with organizational purposes and consequently are not motivated by the intrinsic rewards associated with helping the organization achieve its goals. It falls to management, therefore, to alter the motives of these workers through indoctrination and propaganda so that an identity is created between what the individual and the organization values. This identity of values is achieved either by socializing members in the importance of the organization's mission, service, or product, or by socializing them in a specific set of values or ideals that conditions them to behave in prescribed ways. In either case, once values are internalized they establish the boundaries within which work-related decisions are made. Shared values thus serve to guide and coordinate the efforts of all organizational members, and control becomes, in part, a matter of self-control.

Despite the manipulative implications of Barnard's theory, standardization of values holds considerable promise for public agencies as a mechanism of coordination and control. It remains one of the few options for many agencies because government work tends to require considerable independent judgment. Work of this kind cannot be easily reduced to standardized routines.

Exhibit 9.2 Six Mechanisms for Coordinating and Controlling Work Activities

Mutual adjustment	Workers consult with each other informally about what needs to be accomplished and how. Responsibility for coordination and control rests with those who do the work.
Direct supervision	A supervisor is assigned to take responsibility for a group of workers and a managerial hierarchy is established to integrate the efforts of all work groups. The supervisor issues personal instructions and monitors individual performance.
Standardization of work processes	Work is programmed in advance of its execution by developing rules and standard operating procedures specifying how everyone is to perform assigned tasks. Coordination is built into the work process itself and control is achieved by strictly limiting each worker's discretion.
Standardization of work outputs	Work outputs are programmed in advance by providing each work group with product specifications or performance goals and allowing members considerable latitude in determining how to achieve them. Control is exercised by collecting output data, requiring corrective action when needed, and rewarding and sanctioning workers based on results achieved.
Standardization of worker skills	Workers are employed who possess the knowledge and skills needed to make appropriate decisions. Educational institutions and professional associations are relied upon to provide standardized training. Professionally trained workers are largely self-coordinating and self-controlling.
Standardization of values	Organizational leaders communicate and act upon a clear vision of what the organization exists to do, where it should be headed, and what values should guide it. Coordination and control is facilitated by commitment of organizational members to shared, internalized values and ideals.

SOURCE: Based in large part on Henry Mintzberg, *Structure in Fives* (Prentice-Hall, 1993, 3–7).

Standardization of values is also one of the few options for craft and coping agencies where outputs are not observable and thus cannot be standardized and measured. Where outputs are unobservable, direct supervision also tends to be ineffective as a control mechanism. Although Barnard emphasized propaganda and indoctrination as means for standardizing values, such overtly manipulative techniques are not always required to create an identity of values. Often an identity already exists due to professional training and personal commitment to the agency's mission and the ethic of public service.

Motivational Strategies

Barnard's inducements-contributions theory emphasizes the importance of offering a full range of material and nonmaterial incentives to induce cooperative effort. As indicated in Exhibit 9.3, his inducements-contributions theory highlights the importance of the **instrumental rewards** and **goal congruence** strategies. Barnard acknowledged the motivational power of

Exhibit 9.3 Four Motivational Strategies

Legal Compliance

Using rules, formal directives, and sanctions to direct and control employee behavior. Employees may come to work, comply with rules, and satisfy minimum role requirements, either because they accept the legitimacy of organizational authority or fear being sanctioned.

Instrumental Rewards

Using rewards to induce desired behaviors.

Rewards for Performance

Distributing pay, promotions, and recognition based on individual performance. Employees may meet or exceed role expectations because they value the material and psychological satisfactions that money, advancement, and recognition can provide.

Considerate Leadership

Adopting a leadership style based on being attentive to employees and considerate of their needs. This strategy may improve morale. It might also induce those who value the respect, support, and approval of persons in authority to meet or exceed their role requirements.

Group Acceptance

Creating a work environment that allows employees to socialize, form group bonds, and enjoy the approval of their peers. This strategy may induce those who value affiliation and peer approval to meet or exceed role requirements, assuming that group norms are consistent with organizational objectives.

Job Identification

Offering work that is interesting, challenging, and responsible. Employees may come to work, meet or exceed role requirements, and possibly exhibit greater creativity and innovativeness. They may do so because they identify with the jobs and find their work intrinsically rewarding.

Goal Congruence

Hiring employees whose goals and values are congruent with the organization's and/or socializing employees so that they internalize organizational goals and values. Employees may come to work, remain with the organization, meet or exceed role requirements, and exhibit greater creativity, innovativeness, and institutional loyalty. They may do so because they identify with the organization's mission and values and because contributing to them reinforces their own self concept.

SOURCE: Based in large part on Daniel Katz and Robert L. Kahn, *The Social Psychology of Organizations* (Wiley, 1966), pp. 336–68.

---

pay, promotions, and recognition for demonstrated performance, but tended to place greater faith in the nonmaterial incentives associated with the considerate leadership and group acceptance strategies. Although he did not address these strategies explicitly, he did discuss the role of informal organizations in promoting social cohesion, preserving feelings of personal integrity and self-respect, and protecting individuals from the tendency of the formal organization to rob participants of their individuality. Satisfying these needs is part of the system of providing net satisfactions to organizational members.

As discussed in the previous section, the goal congruence strategy is strongly implied in Barnard's discussion of moral leadership and individual persuasion. In Barnard's view, whether an identity of values already exists, or whether it is created through propaganda and indoctrination, it allows organizational members to receive intrinsic satisfactions from contributing to organizational ideals and purposes. Consequently, they experience a heightened sense of institutional loyalty and a greater willingness to comply with directives and to work hard on behalf of organizational purposes, sometimes even sacrificing their own personal interests in the process. This strategy has special relevance for public agencies because of the identity of values and goals inherent in public service. As a conscious management strategy, goal congruence may simply require nurturing and reinforcing an identity of values and goals that already exists.

SUMMARY

Unlike scientific management and human relations theory, Barnard's natural systems theory did not encompass a particular theory of management. Nor did it give rise to a particular management movement. Barnard's unique contribution to organization theory was the development of a conceptual framework for understanding complex organizations—one which many members of the academic community found to be highly useful. But if his work does not speak directly to practicing managers, it does offer an implicit theory of organizational effectiveness. This theory holds that cooperation is the essential prerequisite for both goal attainment and institutional survival, and that cooperation will not be forthcoming if members are asked to contribute more than they receive in net satisfactions. This theory holds several important implications for public managers, among which are the following:

- **The Value of systems thinking.** Systems theory encourages public managers to think about their world in more dynamic, holistic, and intuitive ways. This means thinking in terms of simultaneous interactions and complex webs of interdependence rather than linear cause-and-effect relationships. Systems thinking is not easy. It requires a high tolerance for ambiguity and a willingness to take action in the face of immense complexity. Although it seldom leads directly to solutions to perceived problems, systems thinking can help managers understand why actions have unanticipated consequences and why their best-laid plans often go astray. Buttressed by experience and intuition, systems thinking can also help managers gain a better sense of the primary factors at work in a particular situation, the basic patterns among them, and the probable consequences of taking particular courses of action.

- **Maintenance needs.** The natural systems perspective views organizations as living organisms seeking to survive in uncertain environments. As such, they have basic maintenance needs, including the need for a continuous supply of financial, material, and human resources, the need for external social and political support, the need to coordinate and control work activities, and the need to maintain morale and social cohesion among their members. Awareness of such needs provides a powerful antidote for those managers inclined to think in purely rational, instrumental terms. It reminds them that they must commit resources to maintaining the cooperative system itself as well as to pursuing organizational objectives. Although this is true of all public agencies, it is especially true for those agencies that lack natural political allies to come to their defense when they are threatened by hostile legislatures or powerful interests.

- **The Inducements–contributions equilibrium.** Edgar Schein has suggested that the inducements-contributions equilibrium results in an implicit psychological contract between employer and employees.[39] This contract matches what the *individual* will give with what the organization expects to receive and what the *organization* will give relative to what the individual expects to receive. If this psychological contract is broken by management, employees may leave the organization or withhold their contributions. This concept reminds public managers that employees have lives outside of work, that they have personal needs and expectations that do not always correspond to those of their agencies, and that organizational performance may suffer if a constructive psychological contract is not established and maintained.

- **Moral leadership.** Public agencies exist to accomplish important societal purposes and thus are inherently moral institutions. One of the primary functions of management, according to Barnard, is to exercise moral leadership by inculcating basic organizational values and purposes in members so that they are willing to put the interests of the organization ahead of their own when necessary. Although his references to "indoctrination" and the "altering of motives" held unfortunate connotations, Barnard was quick to emphasize that inviting members to join in pursuit of important organizational purposes need not entail brainwashing, deceit, or manipulation. It can be done in an open and honest manner. The importance of creating a shared sense of commitment to mission-related values reemerged as a central theme in organization theory in the 1980s and 1990s (See Chapters 14 and 15).

Perhaps the greatest deficiency in Barnard's theory is its conservative bias. It views organizations as cooperative, highly functional entities by definition, and it takes for granted the right of managers to govern over the cooperative system. Little is said about the coercive side of organizations, the inevitability of conflict between workers and managers, or the merits of allowing greater employee participation and involvement at all levels of the organization. As we will see, these are matters about which later theorists would have much to say.

NOTES

1. Alvin W. Gouldner, "Organizational Analysis," in Robert K. Merton, Leonard Broom, and Leonard S. Cottrell (eds.), *Sociology Today: Problems and Prospects* (New York: Basic Books, 1959), 400-28.

2. Lawrence J. Henderson, *Pareto's General Sociology: A Physiologist's Interpretation* (New York: Russell and Russell, 1935), 13.

3. Cynthia Eagle Russett, *The Concept of Equilibrium in American Social Thought* (New Haven: Yale University Press, 1966), 136.

4. Bernard Barber, "L. J. Henderson: An Introduction," in L. J. Henderson, *On The Social System: Selected Writings* (Chicago: University of Chicago Press, 1970).

5. Russett, *The Concept of Equilibrium in American Social Thought,* 117.

6. This biographical information is drawn from William G. Scott, *Chester I. Barnard and the Guardians of the Managerial State* (Lawrence, KS: University Press of Kansas, 1992); and William B. Wolf, *The Basic Barnard: An Introduction to Chester I. Barnard and His Theories of Organization and Management* (Ithaca: New York State School of Industrial and Labor Relations, Cornell University, 1974).

7. See, for example, Kenneth Andrews, "Introduction," in Chester I. Barnard, *The Functions of the Executive* (Cambridge, MA.: Harvard University Press, 1968).

8. Chester I. Barnard, *The Functions of the Executive* (Cambridge, MA: Harvard University Press, 1938), viii.

9. Barnard, *The Functions of the Executive,* 7.

10. Barnard, *The Functions of the Executive,* 65.

11. Barnard, *The Functions of the Executive,* 6.

12. Barnard, *The Functions of the Executive,* 79.

13. Barnard, *The Functions of the Executive,* 34.

14. Barnard, *The Functions of the Executive,* 73.

15. Barnard, *The Functions of the Executive,* 122.

16. James G. March and Herbert A. Simon, *Organizations* (New York: Wiley, 1958), 84.

17. Barnard, *The Functions of the Executive,* 57.

18. Barnard, *The Functions of the Executive,* 94, 144.

19. Barnard, *The Functions of the Executive,* 141.

20. Barnard, *The Functions of the Executive,* 160.

21. Barnard, *The Functions of the Executive,* 165.

22. Barnard, *The Functions of the Executive,* 165.

23. Barnard, *The Functions of the Executive,* 216–17.

24. Barnard, *The Functions of the Executive,* 231.

25. Barnard, *The Functions of the Executive,* 233.

26. Barnard, *The Functions of the Executive,* 233.

27. Barnard, *The Functions of the Executive,* 279.

28. Barnard, *The Functions of the Executive,* 283.

29. Scott, *Chester I. Barnard and the Guardians of the Managerial State.*

30. Scott, *Chester I. Barnard,* 79.

31. Barnard, *Organization and Management,* 27.

32. Barnard, *Organization and Management,* 6.

33. See C. Pollitt, *Managerialism in the Public Services* (Oxford: Blackwell, 1993); and Larry D. Terry, "Administrative Leadership, Neo-Managerialism, and the Public Management Movement," *Public Administration Review 58* (May/June 1998):194–200.

34. Barnard, *The Functions of the Executive,* 295.

35. See Barnard, *Organization and Management,* Chapters 6 and 7.

36. Barnard, *The Functions of the Executive,* 296.

37. David L. Sills, *The Volunteers* (Glencoe, IL: The Free Press, 1957), 254–64.

38. Fremont E. Kast and James E. Rosenzweig, "General Systems Theory: Applications for Organization and Management," *Academy of Management Journal 15* (December 1972): 447–65.

39. Edgar H. Schein, *Career Dynamics: Matching Individual and Organizational Needs* (Reading, MA: Addison-Wesley, 1978).

10

⌘

Structural-Functional Theory

Robert Merton

T he translation of Weber's writings into English in the 1940s caused many American scholars to turn their attention to the study of complex organizations. The Harvard sociologist Talcott Parsons is widely credited with introducing American scholars to Weber's work, but Parsons' depiction of organizations as social systems was considered by many to be too general and abstract to explain how and why organizations behave as they do. It was left to Robert Merton, a sociologist at Columbia University, to develop a "middle range theory" of bureaucratic behavior, and to his students—Philip Selznick, Alvin W. Gouldner, and Peter M. Blau—to flesh out his theory by conducting organizational case studies. Organization theory as a distinct field of sociological inquiry may be traced to the work of Merton and his students at Columbia in the late1940s and 1950s.[1]

Whereas Weber was content to examine bureaucratization as a historical phenomenon, Selznick, Gouldner, and Blau chose to study organizations empirically by relying on a combination of participant observation, interviews, and documentary evidence. Their work was spurred in part by the obvious contradiction between bureaucracy's presumed rationality and the dysfunctions apparent in existing institutions. Their purpose was not to supplant Weber's theory of bureaucracy but to build upon and modify it so that a richer and more complete understanding of complex organizations might be developed. In conducting their research they were guided, much like Mayo, Roethlisberger, and Barnard, by the natural systems perspective, but unlike their colleagues in human relations they relied heavily on structural-functionalism, a theory that Merton borrowed from anthropology and modified for purposes of organizational analysis.

This chapter examines Merton's structural-functional theory, the institutional case studies undertaken by his students, and the way their work both built upon and modified Weber's theory of bureaucracy. It closes with an analysis of the relevance of Merton's structural-functional theory for public management and organizational performance.

MERTON'S APPROACH TO THE
STUDY OF SOCIOLOGY

When Merton began writing in the 1930s, American sociology was still in its infancy and the relationship between theory and research was still being hotly debated. On one side were the empiricists who tested hypotheses and generated data with the hope that they might lead to interesting theoretical insights. Their approach was strong in method but weak in theory. On the other side

Robert K. Merton 1910–2003

Robert Merton was born in Philadelphia on July 4, 1910. After receiving his Ph.D. in sociology from Harvard in 1936, Merton taught at Harvard for a couple of years before accepting a position at Tulane University in 1939.[2] In 1941 he moved to Columbia University, where he remained for the rest of his distinguished career. A prolific scholar, Merton published several books and well over a hundred articles. The range of his sociological investigations was enormous, covering such diverse subjects as political bosses, juvenile delinquents, intellectuals, and babysitters. In 1949 many of his earlier articles were reprinted in a book entitled *Social Theory and Social Structure*. A new essay entitled "Manifest and Latent Functions," as well as his well-known article "Bureaucratic Structure and Personality," are found in this work. The ideas expressed in these articles led to doctoral dissertations on bureaucracy by three of his students. Philip Selznick began his study of the Tennessee Valley Authority before the war but was unable to complete it until 1947. It was published two years later as *TVA and the Grass Roots: A Study in the Sociology of Formal Organizations*. Alvin Gouldner's dissertation was reported in two monographs published in 1954, *Patterns of Industrial Bureaucracy* and *Wildcat Strike*. Both focused on labor relations in a gypsum plant in upstate New York. Peter Blau's *The Dynamics of Bureaucracy*, which examined interpersonal relations in a state employment agency and a federal law enforcement agency, appeared a year later in 1955. Each of these studies analyzed what Merton called the unanticipated consequences of social action. His students went on to distinguished academic careers-Selznick at the University of California, Berkeley, Gouldner at Washington University in St. Louis, and Blau at the University of Chicago and Columbia University.

were the general theorists, such as Talcott Parsons, who sought to develop a general theory capable of explaining social institutions and processes across the entire range of human experience with the hope that they might lead to testable propositions. Their approach was strong in theory but weak in method. Although Merton found Parson's theory useful, he believed sociology was not yet at the point where general theories could be formulated. As he put it,

> .... There are some who talk as though they expect, here and now, formulation of the sociological theory adequate to encompass vast ranges of precisely observed details of social behavior and fruitful enough to direct the attention of thousands of research workers to pertinent problems of empirical research. This I take to be a premature and apocalyptic belief. We are not ready. The preparatory work has not yet been done.[3]

Regarding the relationship between theory and research, Merton staked out a position halfway between narrow empiricism and general theory. He set for himself the task of developing what he called *middle range theories.* He defined these as "theories intermediate to the minor working hypotheses evolved in abundance during the day-by-day routines of research, and the all-inclusive speculations comprising a master conceptual scheme from which it is hoped to derive a very large number of empirically observed uniformities of social behavior."[4] Developing middle range theories, Merton believed, involves examining various aspects of social life, looking for common patterns, and defining basic sociological concepts that might help identify and explain those commonalities. In his own scholarship, Merton developed middle range theories relating to such subjects as anomie, deviance, science, and bureaucracy.

Like Weber, Merton set out to study social phenomena by examining the meanings people attach to their actions. But Merton found Weber's historical and comparative approach unsuited to generating middle range theories. A methodological approach known as structural-functionalism was in vogue in the 1930s, particularly among anthropologists. According to this approach, social *structures* can be understood by studying the *functions* they perform for the maintenance of the subsystems of which they are a part. Wedding ceremonies, for example, can be understood in terms of their role in legitimizing marriage and establishing the commitment necessary for the success of the family. Although Merton agreed that structural-functionalism held great promise as a methodological approach, he believed that it rested on three assumptions that must be modified or abandoned before it could usefully explain social phenomena. These assumptions are that social systems, like biological organisms, are self-regulating, always tending toward a state of equilibrium or stability; that every social practice contributes to the survival of the social system to which it belongs; and that every social practice is therefore indispensable, much as the heart and brain are indispensable to human beings. Although the analogy between living organisms and social systems may appear reasonable at first glance, Merton believed that the relevance of these assumptions to social realities cannot be supported upon closer examination.

The first of these assumptions Merton labeled the postulate of functional unity—the assumption that all parts of a social system work together harmoniously without producing persistent conflicts. Borrowed from the biological sciences, this postulate holds that social systems tend constantly toward a state of stability or equilibrium. Merton believed instead that the degree of integration in a social system is an empirical variable, one that can vary greatly from one society or institution to the next, and from one time to another. Similarly, Merton concluded that social practices are not necessarily functional for the entire social or cultural system. "That all human societies must have *some* degree of integration," he wrote, "is a matter of definition-and begs the question. But not all societies have that *high* degree of integration in which *every* culturally standardized activity or belief is functional for the society as a whole and uniformly functional for the people living in it."[5] Rather, they may be functional for some individuals and groups and dysfunctional for others in the same society. Religious practices, for example, can have functional consequences for some (such as the ruling elites who value religion's integrating and stabilizing effects) and dysfunctional consequences for others (such as nonbelievers or persons not of the dominant sect who find themselves persecuted by the majority).

Second, Merton questioned the postulate of universal functionalism. This is the assumption that *every* social practice fulfills some vital function in ensuring the system's survival. Merton argued instead that every practice *may* fulfill such a function but doubted that it *must*. He argued that it makes more sense for persisting social practices to have a net balance of functional consequences, either for the society as a whole or for powerful subgroups within it. In short, social practices have multiple consequences, some functional and some dysfunctional, and they persist only as long as the functional aspects outweigh the dysfunctional aspects.

Third, Merton questioned the postulate of indispensability. This is the assumption that *every* social practice is indispensable because it performs a necessary function. Merton suggests that any of several social practices may perform a particular function. Religion, for example, may help integrate members of society, but this does not make religion indispensable. Other practices may have integrating consequences as well. In Merton words, "just as the same item may have multiple functions, so may the same function be diversely fulfilled by alternative items."[6]

Manifest and Latent Functions

The purpose of Merton's critique of structural-functionalism was to rescue functional analysis from the belief that organizations are truly living organisms and to reshape it in a way that would be useful to the study of social phenomena. Complex organizations, for example, may not have inherent purposes, may not be inherently driven toward a state of equilibrium, may not be highly integrated and self-regulating, but their behaviors can be explained nonetheless through the careful application of functional analysis. According to Merton, functional analysis is simply "the practice of interpreting data by establishing their consequences for larger structures in which they are implicated."[7]

Merton's particular brand of functionalism marked a subtle but important shift in emphasis from the consequences of social practices for the survival of a social system to the consequences themselves. To enhance the value of functional analysis as a methodological tool, Merton drew a distinction between manifest and latent functions. In Merton's words, "*manifest functions* are those objective consequences contributing to the adjustment or adaptation of the system which are intended and recognized by participants in the system; *latent functions,* correlatively, being those which are neither intended nor recognized."[8] Consequences can also be functional or dysfunctional, depending on whether they work to the advantage or disadvantage of the system as a whole or certain groups within it.

An example may help clarify these concepts. Suppose management introduces a new pay-for-performance policy to increase productivity. The focus of functional analysis is the policy and the practices that follow from it. Now suppose that productivity in the agency subsequently increases. This is consistent with the manifest (intended) function of the policy and the consequences must be considered at least partially functional for the agency. But suppose analysis also reveals that the quantity of work increased at the expense of quality, thereby reducing public satisfaction with the agency's services. This is a latent (unintended) consequence, and one that is probably dysfunctional for officials and clients as well as for the agency as a whole. According to Merton's functional theory, the policy will remain in place only as long as the *net* consequences are positive for the agency or for a powerful subgroup. To summarize, functional analysis seeks to explain social practices by examining their consequences and determining for whom they are functional or dysfunctional.

The Structural Sources of Bureaucratic Dysfunctions

Although Merton applied functional analysis to a broad range of social phenomena in pursuit of middle range theories, that portion of his work most germane to the study of complex organizations is found in his essay "Bureaucratic Structure and Personality." First published in 1940, this essay offers one of the best-known analyses of bureaucratic dysfunctions. Taking Weber's theory of bureaucracy as his point of departure, Merton states that "a formal, rationally organized social structure involves clearly defined patterns of activity in which, ideally, every series of actions is functionally related to the purposes of the organization."[9] Merton then proceeds to analyze how one of the "patterns of activity" identified by Weber—reliance on impersonal systems of rules—produces serious unintended consequences, including goal displacement, institutional rigidity, and disgruntled clients.

The ideal-type bureaucracy achieves a high degree of efficiency because the application of rules to predetermined categories of cases precludes having to issue specific instructions for each specific case. It also achieves reliability of behavior by demanding a high degree of conformity to its rules. Conformity is reinforced in two ways. First, the professional training received by civil servants instills in them the importance of adhering to professional standards. They are taught that failure to adhere to the rules may expose them to charges of negligence or unprofessional conduct. Second, conformity is reinforced by organizational reward systems that reward and punish civil servants according to how well they demonstrate devotion to the rules. Officials quickly realize that their career aspirations may not be achieved unless they behave in a highly compliant fashion. In short, Merton describes how bureaucratic structure exerts continuous pressure on government employees to be, in Weber's words, "methodical, prudent, and disciplined."

There is a distinct danger, however, that these control mechanisms will lead to overconformity. Civil servants may become overly cautious, adhering blindly to the rules even when it is clear that an alternative course of action might produce a better outcome. Over time, according to Merton, there is a tendency for officials to internalize the rules and enforce them for their own sakes. In such cases, overconformity leads directly to **goal displacement,** a situation in which officials transfer their devotion from the aims of the agency to the particular behaviors required by the rules. Rules, originally conceived as means to an end, become ends in themselves. The extreme case, according to Merton, is the bureaucratic virtuoso "who never forgets a single rule binding his action and hence is unable to assist many of his clients."[10]

As an example, Merton related the story of Bernt Balchen, Admiral Byrd's pilot on the flight over the South Pole. The Bureau of Naturalization denied Balchen's application for citizenship on the grounds that he had failed to satisfy the rule that applicants must have five years' continuous residence in the United States. Although a resident for five years, Balchen had left the country briefly to participate in Byrd's expedition. In ruling that the pilot had technically failed to comply with naturalization law, the bureau failed to serve the needs of one of its clients. Its overarching purpose, processing the naturalization requests of individuals worthy of citizenship, was ignored to the benefit of no one.

The emphasis placed on reliable, predictable behavior not only undermines an agency's ability to fulfill its primary purpose, it also causes **institutional rigidity.** This occurs when rules that once produced desired outcomes no longer do so because objective conditions have changed. If the new conditions are not recognized as significantly different, the civil servant is likely to apply decision rules inappropriately. Similarly, blind adherence to rules reduces the likelihood that officials will look for alternative or innovative solutions to the problems they face. As a result, the organization as a whole loses its ability to adapt successfully to changes taking place in its external environment. Predictability may be achieved, but at the expense of the organization's ability to adapt to changing circumstances.

Finally, Merton describes how bureaucracy's emphasis on depersonalized relationships tends to produce **conflict** between bureaucrats and the public. Officials are trained to ignore the peculiarities of individual cases and to apply rules impartially to everyone. But clients, believing that the peculiarities of their individual cases are of the utmost importance, find the officials to be arrogantly indifferent to their needs. Such conflicts do not occur by accident, according to Merton. They are structurally induced.

It is important to note that what is a manifest or a latent function or dysfunction is for the researcher to determine based on the available evidence. The researcher must also specify for whom the structural pattern is functional or dysfunctional. In Merton's essay on bureaucracy, for example, the manifest functions are defined in terms of management's intent to advance the interests of the agency as a whole. The dysfunctions, by contrast, are arguably dysfunctional for the agency, for its clients, and for the officials who are allowed to exercise little discretion in applying rules to individual cases. It is also worth noting that Merton identified potential rather than inevitable dysfunctions. Other factors may mitigate against their development. Blau found, for example, that officials who enjoyed relatively high job security welcomed innovations that promised to improve service delivery and strongly resisted efforts to reduce their work to a matter of routine application of rules. In this instance, goal displacement and institutional rigidity did not occur.

THE INSTITUTIONAL CASE STUDIES
OF MERTON'S STUDENTS

Merton based his analysis of bureaucracy on his accumulated knowledge of bureaucratic behavior rather than on empirical investigation of specific organizations. His students carried forward the task of applying functional theory by conducting empirical case studies, relying on such techniques as participant observation, interviews, and review of internal documents. Their principal findings are summarized in the following sections.

Philip Selznick: Co-Optation and Its Consequences

Selznick's study of the Tennessee Valley Authority (TVA) examines the unintended and often dysfunctional consequences that occur when an agency provides services indirectly through local, well-established institutions.[11] Congress created the TVA in 1933 to construct dams in the Tennessee River valley and to produce electricity and fertilizer. A product of the New Deal, the TVA was unique in two respects. First, it was established as a public corporation to perform functions normally handled by private companies. Congress granted the TVA considerable autonomy from federal controls so that it would have the same degree of flexibility as private businesses. It was accountable, for example, neither to the Civil Service Commission nor the General Accounting Office. Second, the TVA was established as a regional planning agency to demonstrate that planning and democracy could coexist. Congress granted it authority to make decisions relating to flood control, soil erosion, forestry, and agriculture that cut across state and local jurisdictions.

Although its supporters hoped it would succeed as a model for other public corporations and regional planning agencies, the odds against the TVA's survival were high. Inhabitants of rural valleys in the South tended to view the federal government with suspicion. To make matters worse, the TVA had not been created at the request of local institutions and thus lacked legitimacy in the eyes of local residents. If the TVA was to succeed it would have to adjust itself to its external environment. To gain local support, the TVA's leadership developed an ideology grounded on the idea of "grassroots democracy." At every opportunity the TVA's board of directors espoused the doctrine that its programs would be administered with the democratic participation of those individuals and groups affected by its decisions. According to Selznick, this internal policy was deliberately adopted in response to the TVA's need to adjust itself to powerful institutions in its area of operation. This policy, and the practices that flowed from it, produced both functional and dysfunctional consequences.

The influence of the grassroots doctrine was most apparent in the TVA's agricultural programs. Rather than create its own system of field agents to distribute fertilizer and educate farmers, the TVA's agricultural relations department chose to deliver its programs through the federal Agricultural Extension Service administered by local land-grant colleges. The U.S. Department of Agriculture had provided funds to land-grant colleges to hire extension service agents since 1914. Working out of offices in each county, these agents educated farmers about new techniques for improving agricultural production. In 1935 the TVA negotiated a memorandum of agreement with the Department of Agriculture and the land-grant colleges. This agreement committed the TVA to providing grants-in-aid to the colleges for hiring additional field agents to distribute fertilizer to farmers for testing purposes and to educate them about controlling soil erosion. The Department of Agriculture also agreed that its other agricultural-assistance programs would not operate in the valley without the TVA's approval. By delivering its agricultural programs through the county extension service, the TVA became an ally of the American Farm Bureau Federation, an interest group representing local associations of farmers. According to Selznick, the TVA's willingness to enter into entangling alliances reflected a structural pattern of **informal co-optation.** This he defined as "the process of absorbing new elements into the leadership or policy-determining structure of an organization as a means of averting threats to its stability or existence."[12] The TVA deliberately pursued a strategy of co-optation to win consent in a situation where the legitimacy of its authority was open to question.

The dynamics of co-optation lies at the heart of Selznick's analysis. Whereas the decision to co-opt local institutions was functional in defusing local opposition to the TVA, it proved dysfunctional for TVA's policy goals and institutional character. The co-opted organizations became in effect the TVA's formal constituency, groups outside the organization to which the organization has a special commitment.[13] Co-optation proved to be a two-way street. When external groups made demands on TVA officials, these officials tended to take their concerns into account in formulating policy. Their field of choice in exercising administrative discretion narrowed as they felt constrained to make decisions acceptable to their institutional allies. Having once made institutional commitments, TVA officials also felt compelled to promote and protect the interests of their allies. As a result, they were dragged into jurisdictional and political disputes that they would rather have avoided and they abandoned many of the TVA's founding ideals to safeguard the status quo. In short, the institutional character of the TVA changed as a result of absorbing local elements into its policy-determining structure.

In one example Selznick described how institutional alliances deflected the TVA from serving the residents of the valley as a whole. TVA policy stated that farms chosen to participate in the fertilizer-testing program must be representative of all farms. In practice the larger farms were greatly over-represented. This occurred because the agricultural extension service worked primarily with the more prosperous farmers, those with the resources to implement new agricultural techniques. Extension agents naturally selected their clients to participate in the testing program. Similarly, the TVA was deflected from its goal of serving the needs of local residents because the extension service provided education rather than economic assistance. Blacks, poor farmers generally, and tenant farmers in particular, received little benefit from the TVA's agricultural programs. Those federal agencies providing direct assistance to farmers, such as the Soil Conservation Service and Farm Security Administration, were excluded from the Tennessee valley by the terms of the 1935 memorandum of agreement. In short, the nature of the local institutions through which the TVA channeled its agricultural programs—their educational focus and their bias toward the more prosperous farmers—had the effect of deflecting the TVA from its goal of assisting valley residents as a whole.

Functional analysis enabled Selznick to explain organizational dynamics that could not be explained by knowledge of the organization's goals alone. In Selznick's words,

.... The unacknowledged absorption of nucleuses of power into the administrative structure of an organization makes possible the elimination or appeasement of potential sources of opposition. At the same time, as the price of accommodation, the organization commits itself to avenues of activity and lines of policy enforced by the character of the co-opted elements. Moreover, though co-optation may occur with respect to only a fraction of the organization, there will be pressure for the organization as a whole to adapt itself to the needs of the informal relationship.[14]

For those seeking to understand organizational behavior, Selznick's analysis suggests that an organization's maintenance needs are often a better point of departure than its stated goals. In the present case the TVA's need to adjust itself to its environment helps explain why it adopted the grassroots doctrine, why it entered into entangling alliances, and why it ultimately experienced dysfunctional consequences.

Alvin W. Gouldner:
Authoritarian Management and Its Consequences

Gouldner's study of a gypsum plant in upstate New York focused on the consequences of close supervision and strictly enforced rules.[15] The appointment of a new factory manager provided Gouldner with an opportunity to analyze two distinct managerial patterns. The first manager, Old Doug, adopted a personal, folksy style of management. He allowed workers considerable autonomy in performing their duties and ignored rule violations that did not seriously jeopardize safety or production. He also permitted workers to socialize freely during slack periods and to take home gypsum board and other materials for personal use. Finally, he provided benefits that management was under no obligation to provide, such as light duty assignments for sick or injured employees. In short, his approach constituted what Gouldner labeled "an indulgency pattern." From the workers' perspective, Old Doug treated employees as they wished to be treated—as fellow human beings. Production was perhaps not as high as it might have been, but the workers trusted management and job satisfaction was high.

When Old Doug became ill and died, company executives sent a new manager to the plant and charged him with increasing productivity. Under pressure from headquarters, the new manager, Mr. Peele, adopted an impersonal style of management, enforced rules strictly, curtailed socializing, punished those who took materials home, and ended the practice of light-duty assignments. Gouldner labeled this a "bureaucratic pattern," a pattern consistent with Weber's emphasis on formal authority and strict obedience. Status distinctions were much more evident under the new manager, and if production increased, it did so at the expense of trust and job satisfaction.

Gouldner also examined the willingness of employees to comply with workplace rules. His analysis was driven in part by his belief that Weber had glossed over his own observation that rules can be initiated by imposition *or* by mutual consent. Gouldner found that workers obeyed rules voluntarily when they participated in their development, understood and accepted the rationale behind the rules, and believed that compliance served their interests. They complied with safety rules, for example, because they helped to formulate them at safety meetings and because they were the primary beneficiaries of enhanced safety. By contrast, workers generally resisted the no-absenteeism rule because neither the rationale behind it nor their interest in obeying it was clear to them. They believed production was not adversely affected by taking an occasional unpaid leave of absence. Mr. Peele took a different view and strictly enforced the no-absenteeism rule. Gouldner concluded that employees tend to resist workplace rules where there is lack of consensus among managers and workers regarding the values and interests at stake.

From these observations Gouldner identified two fundamental patterns of bureaucracy. The **punishment–centered pattern** is characterized by the unilateral imposition of rules, insistence upon obedience for its own sake, and strict punishment for those who violate them. Gouldner found, for example, that "when a supervisor investigated an absence, he did not do so in order to determine its causes. Instead he strove to extract obedience to the rule, without concern for the cause of the disobedience, and with the object of allocating blame and punishment."[16] Overt conflict resulted. The **representative pattern,** by contrast, is characterized by employee involvement in rule development, an emphasis on the instrumental value of the rules, and the use of education rather than punishment when rules are violated. Gouldner concluded that this pattern generates tensions but little overt conflict because it is consistent with the norms of a democratic society.

Significantly, Gouldner identified two ideal-typical patterns of bureaucracy, where Weber identified only one. Although the punishment-centered pattern is the one most clearly reflected in Weber's description of bureaucracy, Gouldner maintained that both patterns ultimately derive from Weber's distinction between authority based on formal position and authority based on expertise. The punishment-centered approach relies on the manager's formal authority and insists on obedience for its own sake, whereas the representative approach relies on the manager's personal knowledge and encourages voluntary compliance by emphasizing the rule's instrumental value. These two patterns thus represent alternative sets of management choices. Choosing the representative approach means, for example, that a degree of democracy is possible within complex organizations, a possibility that Weber tended to reject.

In response to those critical theorists who, relying on Weber's analysis, viewed bureaucracy as an inexorable force destructive of human freedom, Gouldner offered the following rebuttal: "If the world of theory is grey and foredoomed, the world of everyday life is green with possibilities which need to be cultivated."[17] But Gouldner cautioned that the representative approach does not offer a panacea. It is unlikely to be effective, for example, where common ground cannot be found between the values of supervisors and subordinates. According to Gouldner, voluntary consent "rests on the subordinate's belief that he is being told to do things congruent with *his own ends and values.*"[18] Situational factors also influence each manager's choice. The situation confronting Mr. Peele, for example, suggests that a new manager recruited from outside the organization and facing a succession crisis may feel compelled to rely on formal authority and the legitimating function of rules to obtain objectives.

Gouldner's analysis of the dysfunctional consequences of punishment-centered bureaucracy is especially relevant to organization theory. Gouldner concluded that Weber, in emphasizing the functional consequences of rules, ignored the important consequences that flow not from the rules themselves but from the *manner* in which they are initiated and administered. Driven by its own unique logic, punishment-centered bureaucracy leads to a "vicious cycle" of dysfunctional consequences. The cycle begins when workers are perceived as unmotivated and unwilling to do their jobs well. Supervisors respond by demanding strict adherence to the rules and relying upon punitive measures to secure compliance. This in turn increases employee resentment and resistance to rules. The cycle does not end here. Rules tend to depress performance by specifying the level above which employees can expect to escape punishment. As managers reveal a basic lack of trust, the tendency of subordinates to do only what the rules require of them increases. And, the more workers become aggressive toward their supervisors, and the more apathetic they become about their work, the more managers embrace close supervision as an adaptive response. The cycle then begins anew.[19]

According to Gouldner, rules can reduce tensions by substituting for close supervision and direct orders, but they cannot address the underlying causes of worker apathy. Gouldner's analysis lends support to Merton's observation that dysfunctions tend to persist as long as their underlying causes are not addressed.

Peter M. Blau: Quantitative Performance Records and Their Consequences

The thesis of Blau's study of two government agencies is that bureaucracy "contains the seeds, not necessarily of its own destruction, but of its own transformation."[20] Rather than exhibiting "Gibralter-like stability," bureaucracies are constantly changing.[21] Weber's methodology, according to Blau, prevented him from fully appreciating the dynamic character of bureaucracy:

> . . . . In his analysis of bureaucratic structure, Weber focused on official regulations and requirements and their significance for administrative efficiency. Of course, he knew that the behavior of the members of an organization does not precisely correspond to its blueprint. But he was not concerned with this problem and did not investigate systematically the way in which operations actually are carried out. Consequently, his analysis ignored the fact that, in the course of operations, new elements arise in the structure that influence subsequent operations.[22]

In practice, managers adjust, redefine, or amplify procedures in response to internal and external factors that are adversely affecting organizational performance. When a structural change is introduced, strains or dysfunctional disturbances are often created for those engaged in the agency's daily operations. In response, organizational members often adopt new behaviors or form new social relationships that alter subsequent operations. Change becomes a continuous event as one set of consequences begets another. In Blau's words, "The very innovation introduced to cope with one disturbance may in due course have consequences that create new problems and lead to new adjustments."[23] Organizational structure is constantly being redefined and transformed as a result.

One of Blau's examples of bureaucratic dynamics is found in his study of a state employment agency. When a job needed to be filled, agency policy required interviewers to screen all active applications to identify the most highly qualified job seeker. However, because the local textile mills also hired workers off the street, interviewers were under considerable pressure to fill each job vacancy with one of their clients before someone else could be hired. Consequently, they rarely reviewed the applications on file. Instead, they referred the first person they found who possessed the minimum qualifications. Agency policy notwithstanding, interviewers adapted agency procedures to better serve the needs of their clients in a period of job scarcity. Unfortunately, this held dysfunctional consequences for others, particularly for those qualified job seekers who were not in the office at the opportune moment.

Introduction of a new performance measurement system at the state employment agency enabled Blau to explore how policy changes affect interpersonal relations and how informal work groups adjust to such changes. The previous system measured only the number of clients interviewed, a practice that caused interviewers to be relatively unconcerned about successful placements. The new system provided statistical summaries of each interviewer's performance on eight measurable criteria, including number of successful placements. Department heads intended only to monitor what was occurring in each unit, but this did not preclude first-line supervisors from using the results to evaluate individual performance as well. Knowing that their supervisors would learn how many clients they had placed successfully caused interviewers to work harder at placing clients. The new system thus increased administrative control and productivity, enhanced adaptability by enabling managers to alter performance standards as changing circumstances warranted, and improved cordiality between supervisors and interviewers by reducing the need for close supervision. The new system also performed one latent function. Black and white clients were treated with equal impartiality as interviewers sought to place as many clients as possible.

But unanticipated, dysfunctional consequences occurred as well. Statistical reporting caused interviewers to concentrate on those factors most likely to affect their performance ratings. A form of goal displacement occurred as interviewers forgot about satisfying the needs of clients and focused instead on maximizing their scores on key statistical indicators. For example, because placing clients was what mattered most, interviewers spent less time ensuring that clients were referred to jobs for which they were well-suited. In addition, the preoccupation with productivity adversely affected interpersonal relations by inducing interviewers to compete with each other in filling the few available jobs. Many interviewers routinely monopolized job announcements by secreting them away on their desks so that others would not have access to them.

Blau discovered to his surprise that these dysfunctions occurred in one work unit and not in another. Whereas one group succumbed to competitive pressures, a second group succeeded in mitigating those pressures by insisting that members continue to behave in a cooperative fashion and by sanctioning those members who filled job orders without sharing information with their colleagues. Two situational factors helped in this regard. First, most members of this group had permanent civil-service status, making them less anxious about their ratings. Second, their supervisor made it clear he did not intend to base

their individual ratings on statistical indices alone. Blau also discovered that increases in individual productivity did not translate into increases in group productivity. Although the productivity of those who monopolized telephone
orders increased in the competitive group, productivity for the group as a
whole was lower than for the more collegial group. Competition had apparently weakened social cohesion, which in turn reduced operating efficiency
and ultimately productivity. In the more collegial group, by contrast, productivity increased in spite of, rather than because of, the competitive pressures introduced by the new system. Blau concluded that dysfunctional consequences
represent disturbances for those who experience them and that new social relationships are often formed in response, resulting in distinctly new organizational structures.

AN IMPLICIT THEORY OF
ORGANIZATIONAL CHANGE

The case studies of Selznick, Gouldner, and Blau were exploratory. Merton's
students used functional analysis to derive theoretical propositions that they
hoped would lead eventually to a general theory of organizational behavior.
Although they did not develop such a theory themselves, functional analysis
did lead them to similar conclusions about organizational change. The implicit
theory that emerges from their work is that managers act to defend their organizations in the face of internal and external threats and, in doing so, create institutional strains that lead to additional rounds of defensive responses by the
affected parties. The result is a continuous process of structural change inter-
rupted briefly by periods of relative stability. The sections that follow analyze
each of these theoretical components in turn.

Threats to Organizational Functioning

The process of structural change begins when managers perceive an internal
or external threat to organizational functioning. External threats confronted
each of the organizations studied by Merton's students. The TVA faced powerful institutions in the region whose cooperation could not be taken for
granted. The gypsum plant faced increased economic competition that threatened its very survival. And the state employment agency experienced a period
of job scarcity that affected its ability to place clients in a timely manner. These
organizations experienced internal threats as well. The gypsum company managers, for example, saw the rising power of the union as a threat to the plant's
operational stability.

   As defined by Merton's students, a *threat* is any factor, internal or external,
that interferes with the satisfaction of an organization's maintenance needs. As
noted in Chapter 9, maintenance needs are those basic things that organizations must do to maintain themselves as viable institutions. Maintenance

needs are not inherent to organizations in the same way that biological needs are inherent to living organisms. Rather, they are "stable systems of variables" that affect structure and behavior as organizations delegate tasks, coordinate work activities, and respond to forces in their external environments.[24] Although Merton and his students did not attempt to define or catalogue these variables, Selznick tentatively identified five maintenance needs in the course of his investigation of the TVA. They include the security of the organization as a whole in relation to social forces in its environment; the stability of the lines of authority and communication; the stability of informal relations within the organization; the continuity of policy and of the sources of its determination; and a homogeneity of outlook with respect to the meaning and role of the organization.[25]

The concept of maintenance needs is an important contribution to organization theory. First, it suggests that organizational charts and goal statements are not the best points of departure for understanding organizational behavior. In Selznick's words, "All formal organizations are molded by forces tangential to their rationally ordered structures and stated goals."[26] In adjusting to these forces they are easily deflected from their goals. This helps to explain why Weber's theory of bureaucracy fails to describe how bureaucracies behave in practice. Weber's ideal-type identifies only those technical prerequisites for instrumental goal attainment, those particular means by which bureaucracies delegate, coordinate, and control. According to Merton and his students, a theory that purports to explain organizational behavior must also take maintenance needs into account. Only then can it be determined why organizations look and behave differently than their formal blueprints and official doctrines indicate they should.

Second, the concept of maintenance needs suggests that organizations are best viewed as adaptive social structures. Although they are indeed rational instruments for accomplishing important purposes, each organization nevertheless has a life of its own. Its life is defined in large part by the way it responds to its maintenance needs. Accordingly, "The organization may be significantly viewed as an adaptive social structure, facing problems which arise simply because it exists as an organization in an institutional environment, independent of the special (economic, military, political) goals which called it into being."[27] Viewing organizations as adaptive social structures allowed Selznick, Gouldner, and Blau to explain aspects of organizational behavior that seemed inconsistent with stated goals. For example, it enabled Selznick to explain why the TVA failed to serve the interests of poor farmers, it enabled Gouldner to explain why management failed to address employee grievances, and it enabled Blau to explain why official procedures for filling job openings were routinely ignored. In each instance, management attended to the organization's maintenance needs at the expense of its stated goals and objectives. The task of managers is clearly a difficult one. They must help their organizations adjust to internal and external threats in order to maintain the integrity and continuity of the institutional machinery, and they must do so without allowing them to stray too far from their defined missions.

In short, management interventions represent adaptive responses to per-ceived threats. It is a basic premise of structural-functional analysis that organi-zations have basic needs and that structural patterns emerge, intentionally or unintentionally, to satisfy those needs. Most of the structural patterns analyzed by Selznick, Gouldner, and Blau were introduced by management. In Selznick's study, for example, co-optation of the land-grant colleges repre-sented an adaptive response to external threats to the TVA's stability and con-tinued existence. Similarly, management's decision to adopt a strict authoritarian style in Gouldner's study represented an adaptive response to the threat posed by increased economic competition. Some structural patterns, however, although adaptive in nature, are not the work of managers. For ex-ample, Blau describes structural changes introduced by employees as they adapted to threats posed by the new performance-measurement system. One group of interviewers chose to behave in a highly competitive manner, whereas a second group chose to perform their tasks in a more collegial man-ner. As discussed below, adaptive responses by nonmanagerial employees are another important component of the theory of organizational change.

Dysfunctional Consequences and Institutional Strains

The concept of adaptive responses is significant because it suggests that struc-ture is not simply a product of means-ends calculations regarding the most technically efficient way to achieve organizational goals. Rather, organizational structure is largely a product of adaptive responses by management to satisfy the organization's maintenance needs. These responses may or may not en-hance the organization's effectiveness in accomplishing stated goals. Although managers intend for their structural adjustments to enhance goal attainment, their actions sometimes produce dysfunctional consequences that they did not anticipate. For example, when managers at the gypsum plant replaced an in-dulgency pattern with a punishment-centered pattern, employee morale and motivation were adversely affected. Similarly, when managers at the state em-ployment agency introduced a new system of performance measurement, competition among interviewers increased and social cohesion decreased. From the perspective of the organization's ability to attain its goals effectively, these consequences were dysfunctional. They were also unanticipated.

The case studies of Selznick, Gouldner, and Blau suggest three reasons why managers fail to anticipate all of the consequences of their actions. First, it is inherently difficult to predict future events. Focused on their immediate ob-jectives, and with limited time and information for assessing probable out-comes, decision makers inevitably fail to perceive many of the consequences of their actions. Second, the commitments officials make have secondary con-sequences that are extremely difficult to anticipate. For example, when the agriculturalists at the TVA committed themselves to working with and through the land-grant colleges, they probably could not have anticipated how their decision would lead to deflection of goals, changes in institutional char-acter, and conflicts with other agencies. These eventualities occurred in part because all subsequent decisions by these officials were constrained by their initial commitments. Finally, unanticipated consequences occur because directing and controlling human behavior cannot be engineered with any degree of precision. Humans vary greatly in their individual characteristics, and the work situations they face are constantly changing. Such observations led Blau to conclude that "no system of rules and supervision can be so finely spun that it anticipates all exigencies that may arise."[28]

Whether or not they are anticipated, the consequences of managerial interventions inevitably affect organizational dynamics in one way or another. From the organization's perspective, consequences are functional when they help it adjust or adapt to internal and external factors that may interfere with proper organizational functioning. By contrast, consequences are dysfunctional when they produce institutional strains that impede the effective attainment of organizational objectives. In Merton's words, the concept of dysfunction "implies the concept of strain, stress, and tension on the structural level."[29] These stresses and strains are often manifested by increased conflict between internal and external groups, between managerial and nonmanagerial personnel, and among individual employees. When institutional strains are perceived as problems, either by management or some other group of organizational members, they create strong pressures for change aimed at reducing those strains. Institutional strains tend to persist as long as their underlying causes are not addressed. Sooner or later, according to Merton, dysfunctional consequences that are not dealt with successfully lead to serious institutional breakdowns.

But why do management's adaptive responses so often produce dysfunctional consequences? The most basic reason, which is evident in all three cases studies, is that individuals, formal subgroups, informal work groups, and even groups outside the organization are possessed of needs distinct from those of the organization. Accordingly, they will act to protect their respective needs, will resist being controlled by others, and will resent being treated merely as means to the organization's ends. Because managers must work with and through diverse individuals and groups, they must constantly cope with the recalcitrance of the human tools of action. In Selznick's words, "Social action is always mediated by human structures, which generate new centers of need and power and interpose themselves between the actor and his goal."[30] It is part of management's task to accommodate the needs of other human actors to the extent that it is reasonable to do so, but success in this regard is always uncertain.

A Continuing Cycle of Adaptive Responses

Perfect adjustment to internal and external threats is never achieved, according to Blau, because "the very practices instituted to enhance adjustment in some respects often disturbs it in others."[31] Further structural changes occur as affected parties respond defensively to the strains created by managerial interventions. A continuing cycle of adaptive responses is thus set in motion. This theoretical conclusion is supported by numerous examples in the three case studies. Beginning with Selznick's study, many local groups, feeling threatened by the potential for intrusive federal control, initially withheld their support. TVA directors, feeling threatened by the absence of local support, adopted a doctrine of grassroots democracy, and the agriculturalists similarly negotiated a memorandum of agreement with the local land-grant colleges. The American Farm Bureau Federation, feeling threatened by the direct assistance provided to farmers by other federal programs, insisted that the TVA join with it in keeping those programs out of the valley. The agriculturalists, also feeling threatened by direct-assistance programs, insisted that other subunits work with and through the land-grant colleges. The overall pattern is clear. Threats were perceived, adaptive responses were made, additional strains were created, and pressures for additional changes mounted. The agriculturalists accommodated the agency to the needs and interests of the land-grant colleges and local farm bureaus, but in doing so created institutional strains by violating the interests of other subunits and agencies. According to Selznick, it is precisely when organizational members seek to solve problems and adjust strains that they may allow the organization to be deflected from its primary goals.

In Gouldner's study of the gypsum plant the focus shifts to the management-employee relationship. Adoption of a punishment-centered style of management produced institutional strains because of the "status-threatening and deference-demanding" manner in which it was implemented. Originally introduced in response to heightened economic competition, the new approach violated employee expectations. They expected to be treated respectfully and personably and to be left alone as long as they were performing their jobs well. The new pattern of close supervision violated their need for self-respect and personal autonomy. Motivation declined as workers withdrew psychologically from a degrading work situation. Resentment and resistance increased. These dysfunctional consequences triggered additional adaptive responses from management. Bureaucratic rules were introduced to mitigate the strains caused by close supervision. The cycle of adaptive responses was driven in part by the fact that management's expectations had been violated as well. When workers voiced their grievances, most managers concluded that they were deliberately challenging their control and undermining their status as managers. Based on his analysis of a wildcat strike at the plant, Gouldner identified thirteen factors that seemed to increase or decrease tensions between employees and managers.[32] His general conclusion was that social relationships tend to be stable when each person knows the other's expectations, when each considers the other's expectations legitimate, and when each is motivated to conform to them.

A continuing cycle of adaptive responses was also apparent in Blau's study of the state employment agency. Management introduced a new performance-measurement system with the hope that it would enhance goal attainment by increasing the number of successful placements. In many ways it proved functional. It "increased productive efficiency, facilitated administrative control, helped in adapting operations to changing conditions, and improved the relations between officials and their immediate supervisors."[33] Nonetheless, interviewers felt threatened by the possibility that they would be sanctioned if they failed to reach some unspecified level of performance each month, and they responded in a defensive, self-protective fashion by sharing job information with colleagues less often. Increased competition produced institutional strains by undermining collegiality and reducing social cohesion. But, whereas one group adapted by becoming more competitive, another adapted in a way that allowed organizational adjustment to occur. They refused to give in to fear and insisted upon continued collegiality. As anxiety decreased and productivity increased, both their needs and the needs of the agency were served. Informal group norms had allowed successful adjustment to occur. This suggests that whether a structural pattern turns out to be functional or dysfunctional may depend in part on the informal norms that develop in response to it. Sometimes the cycle of change ceases temporarily as employees self-adjust or as managers and employees accommodate themselves to each other. Because each adaptive response generates counter-responses by those affected by it, Blau concluded that "the stable attainment of organizational objectives depends on perpetual change in the bureaucratic structure."[34] The assumption that bureaucratic structures tend toward a state of equilibrium simply is not supported by his empirical investigation.

Each case study thus revealed a similar dynamic. A dysfunction that interferes with operations is experienced as a disturbance by certain members of the organization, causing a chain reaction of adaptive responses. Managers, for example, perceive a **threat** to organizational functioning and alter organizational structure as an **adaptive response.** Because this in turn threatens the interests of affected parties, institutional **strains** are created and **additional rounds of adaptive responses** are initiated. Some of these are perceived as dysfunctional by managers, who intervene once again, causing the cycle of adaptive responses to continue. New patterns constantly supersede old patterns. The cycle continues until the interests at stake are mutually accommodated or the underlying causes of dysfunction are addressed. A brief period of

Exhibit 10.1 Merton's Implicit Theory of Organizational Change

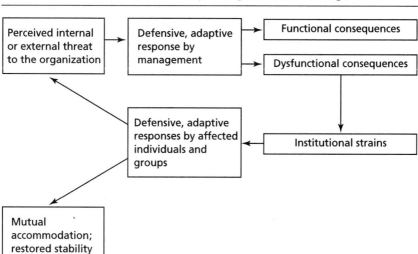

organizational stability may then result. This implicit theory of organizational change is shown schematically in Exhibit 10.1.

WEBER'S THEORY MODIFIED

The image of bureaucracy that emerges from Weber's writings is that of a vast mechanical apparatus that relentlessly cranks out goods and services with remarkable predictability and efficiency. It is characterized by "Gibralter-like stability."[35] Change seldom occurs. Indeed, officials timidly do what they can to resist change. Life within the bureaucracy is cold and impersonal. Individual discretion is severely limited and officials find that they cannot "squirm out of the apparatus" to which they are harnessed. Finally, personalities and behaviors are inexorably shaped by a bureaucratic structure over which officials have little control.

To comprehend the essence of bureaucracy, Weber deliberately restricted his analysis to the technical means by which bureaucracy attains its goals. Nonrational variables, such as emotions, individual needs, and politics, were intentionally left out. What emerges is a detailed picture of the organization's skeleton but without its flesh and blood. If there is an inherent flaw in Weber's theory of bureaucracy it is that the dynamic interaction between an organization's structure and its human inhabitants is largely ignored.

Having conducted field research, and having factored nonrational variables back into the equation, Merton's students offered a very different image of bureaucracy. Bureaucratic behavior is highly dynamic; change is the norm and stability the exception. Bureaucracy's internal life is much warmer and more personal than Weber's description indicates. Officials are much less rigidly controlled and less passive, and they often resist routinization and agitate for structural change. In addition, bureaucratic actions are not always related to the purposes of the organization. Sometimes their aim is to satisfy basic maintenance needs. Finally, there is no single bureaucratic pattern. Whereas reliance on formal authority and strict discipline represents one pattern, reliance on personal authority and interpersonal relations represents another.

Merton and his students were intrigued by the obvious contradiction between bureaucracy's presumed rationality and the dysfunctions apparent in existing institutions. They set for themselves the task of building upon and modifying Weber's theory so that a richer and more complete understanding of complex organizations might emerge. In this regard they succeeded exceptionally well. They left for future generations of managers and scholars a much better understanding of the dynamic interaction between organizational structures and the individuals who work within them.

RELEVANCE FOR PUBLIC MANAGEMENT

The remainder of this chapter explores the relevance of Merton's structural-functional theory for public management and organizational performance.

This exploration is guided by the three analytical frameworks presented in Chapter 3.

Models of Organizational Effectiveness

All of the quadrants in Exhibit 10.2 are highlighted because Merton and his students recognized all of the functional imperatives reflected in Quinn's competing values framework. They were also among the small number of theorists who recognized the competing nature of these effectiveness values. Selznick's study of the TVA, for example, described how values associated with the goal attainment model were sacrificed in order to achieve values associated with the

Exhibit 10.2 The Competing Values Framework: Four Models of Organizational Effectiveness

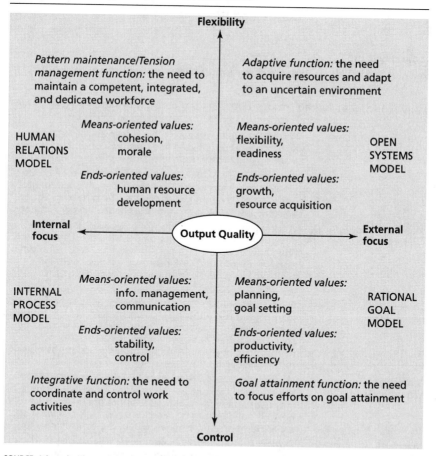

SOURCE: Adapted with permission from Figures 3 and 4, Robert O. Quinn and John Rohrbaugh, "A Spatial Model of Effectiveness Criteria: Towards a Competing Values Approach to Organizational Analysis," *Management Science* 29 (March 1983): 363–373. Copyright 1983, The Institute of Management Sciences, now the Institute for Operations Research and the Management Sciences (INFORMS), 901 Elkridge Landing Road, Suite 400, Linthicum, Maryland 21090-2909 USA.

open systems model, including flexibility, resource acquisition, and institutional survival. Similarly, Gouldner's study of a gypsum plant described how values associated with the human relations model, including social cohesion and interpersonal trust, were sacrificed in order to achieve values associated with the goal attainment model, including efficiency and productivity.

Although they acknowledged the importance of all four models of effectiveness, like other theorists relying on the natural systems perspective, Merton and his students focused most of their attention on the human relations model. By studying the functional and dysfunctional effects of structure on human behavior, they emphasized the strategic importance of employee relations to organizational performance, and the role of trust, commitment, and social cohesion in building and maintaining positive employee relations.

Mechanisms for Coordinating and Controlling Work Activities

No mechanism of coordination and control is highlighted in Exhibit 10.3. This is because Merton's structural-functional theory acknowledges that organizations may rely on any combination of these mechanisms to promote goal

Exhibit 10.3 Six Mechanisms for Coordinating and Controlling Work Activities

Mutual adjustment	Workers consult with each other informally about what needs to be accomplished and how. Responsibility for coordination and control rests with those who do the work.
Direct supervision	A supervisor is assigned to take responsibility for a group of workers and a managerial hierarchy is established to integrate the efforts of all work groups. The supervisor issues personal instructions and monitors individual performance.
Standardization of work processes	Work is programmed in advance of its execution by developing rules and standard operating procedures specifying how everyone is to perform assigned tasks. Coordination is built into the work process itself and control is achieved by strictly limiting each worker's discretion.
Standardization of work outputs	Work outputs are programmed in advance by providing each work group with product specifications or performance goals and allowing members considerable latitude in determining how to achieve them. Control is exercised by collecting output data, requiring corrective action when needed, and rewarding and sanctioning workers based on results achieved.
Standardization of worker skills	Workers are employed who possess the knowledge and skills needed to make appropriate decisions. Educational institutions and professional associations are relied upon to provide standardized training. Professionally trained workers are largely self-coordinating and self-controlling.
Standardization of values	Organizational leaders communicate and act upon a clear vision of what the organization exists to do, where it should be headed, and what values should guide it. Coordination and control is facilitated by commitment of organizational members to shared, internalized values and ideals.

SOURCE: Based in large part on Henry Mintzberg, *Structure in Fives* (Prentice-Hall, 1993, 3–7).

attainment and system survival. Gouldner's case study, for example, focused on direct supervision and alternative ways of exercising authority, whereas Blau's study focused on standardization of work output and the use of performance measurement systems. Instead of advocating or emphasizing a particular mechanism for coordinating and controlling work activities, structural-functional theory simply helps researchers and practitioners comprehend the functional purposes of such mechanisms and encourages them to anticipate the dysfunctional consequences that each type may produce. There is much public managers can learn from this literature's analysis of goal displacement, institutional rigidity, co-optation, inter- and intra-agency conflict, and the morale and motivation problems that follow from authoritarian management.

Motivational Strategies

Structural-functional theory does not advocate or emphasize a particular motivational strategy; Merton and his students assumed the use of a full range of strategies and limited themselves to investigating the functional and dysfunctional consequences of each. Although Gouldner and Blau paid considerable attention to legal compliance as a motivational strategy, it is not highlighted in Exhibit 10.4 because their purpose was not to endorse legal compliance but to explore its limitations.

Gouldner's study offers an interesting contrast in the use of motivational strategies. Below ground in the mines, where danger was ever-present, supervisors quickly learned that miners would rebel at the use of the legal compliance strategy. Miners routinely failed to show up for work, and yet supervisors did not enforce absenteeism rules or impose sanctions. They understood that under these conditions the legal compliance strategy, grounded on an expectation of unquestioned obedience, would not produce the desired results. The miners would simply walk off the job. Supervisors quickly learned to employ the group acceptance strategy. The resulting group solidarity and informal consultations that characterized work beneath the surface contributed to a relatively high level of coordination and productivity.

Above ground, by contrast, work was highly routinized and social relationships highly formalized. Supervisors maintained control over workers by relying on their formal authority. One particular example illustrates this point. The new plant manager, wishing to run "a tight ship," established a standardized warning notice that contained the sentence "This will confirm our conversation of today, in which you were informed of the following." This was followed by a checklist of possible offenses. Each supervisor was required to check all infractions, sign the form, and forward it to the plant manager for his signature. Similarly, the no-absenteeism rule was strictly enforced and unexcused absences led to suspensions.

Use of the legal compliance strategy in the manufacturing plant was effective in securing obedience but not in developing a highly motivated workforce. As indicated in Exhibit 10.4, the legal compliance strategy generally motivates workers only to satisfy minimum role requirements, including minimum standards for quantity and quality of performance. One of the bureau-

Exhibit 10.4 Four Motivational Strategies

Legal Compliance

Using rules, formal directives, and sanctions to direct and control employee behavior. Employees may come to work, comply with rules, and satisfy minimum role requirements, either because they accept the legitimacy of organizational authority or fear being sanctioned.

Instrumental Rewards

Using rewards to induce desired behaviors.

Rewards for Performance

Distributing pay, promotions, and recognition based on individual performance. Employees may meet or exceed role expectations because they value the material and psychological satisfactions that money, advancement, and recognition can provide.

Considerate Leadership

Adopting a leadership style based on being attentive to employees and considerate of their needs. This strategy may improve morale. It might also induce those who value the respect, support, and approval of persons in authority to meet or exceed their role requirements.

Group Acceptance

Creating a work environment that allows employees to socialize, form group bonds, and enjoy the approval of their peers. This strategy may induce those who value affiliation and peer approval to meet or exceed role requirements, assuming that group norms are consistent with organizational objectives.

Job Identification

Offering work that is interesting, challenging, and responsible. Employees may come to work, meet or exceed role requirements, and possibly exhibit greater creativity and innovativeness. They may do so because they identify with the jobs and find their work intrinsically rewarding.

Goal Congruence

Hiring employees whose goals and values are congruent with the organization's and/or socializing employees so that they internalize organizational goals and values. Employees may come to work, remain with the organization, meet or exceed role requirements, and exhibit greater creativity, innovativeness, and institutional loyalty. They may do so because they identify with the organization's mission and values and because contributing to them reinforces their own self concept.

SOURCE: Based in large part on Daniel Katz and Robert L. Kahn, *The Social Psychology of Organizations* (Wiley, 1966), pp. 336–68.

cratic dysfunctions identified earlier in this chapter is that rules tend to define minimum expectations. Workers in the gypsum plant, for example, remained relatively apathetic because they knew just how little they could do and still remain secure in their jobs.

If the legal compliance strategy is often counterproductive, why does it continue to be used? Gouldner concluded that supervisors turn to the legal compliance strategy when they believe workers are willfully failing to perform their roles dependably and when they have not established personal relationships based on trust. A deep distrust of their employees causes them to install new rules and insist on strict adherence. The more poor performance is perceived as deliberate, the more the supervisor uses sanctions to ensure strict obedience. As noted earlier, this leads to a vicious cycle in which supervisors become more authoritarian and workers become more resentful and rebellious.

Gouldner concluded that the coercive, punishment-centered form of legal compliance tends to fail for two reasons. First, it violates egalitarian norms that demand that all individuals be treated equally and respectfully. To insist upon obedience "because I am the boss" leaves workers with the impression that supervisors are deliberately exercising power to emphasize the workers' status inferiority. Employees may accept the right of supervisors to issue orders and impose sanctions, but if they feel consistently ill-treated they are likely to leave the organization in disgust. Second, the coercive, punishment-centered form of legal compliance tends to fail because it does not address the underlying problems that cause apathy. Indeed, Gouldner suggests that legal compliance, to the extent that it uses the punishment function of rules to exact obedience, should not be viewed as a motivational strategy at all. It is an approach taken by managers who have surrendered in the battle to motivate workers.

However, the legal compliance strategy need not be coercive and punishment-centered in application. Gouldner noticed, for example, that workers complied with safety rules without complaint or resistance. They did so because they had participated in their adoption and they understood the rationale behind them. Compliance with safety rules served the interests of management and labor alike. On closer examination, Gouldner found that workplace tensions are highest when rules are initiated and administered unilaterally, they do not appear to have a legitimate basis, their enforcement violates values held by workers, managers perceive deviance from rules as willful and deliberate, and enforcement of rules causes one group consistently to lose status relative to another.[36] Conversely, rules derived from the manager's expertise and reflecting a legitimate purpose are more likely to secure the workers' consent and reduce workplace tensions. As noted earlier, Gouldner believed that Weber failed to recognize the fundamental difference between authority based on expertise and authority based on formal position. Workers, Gouldner suggests, are much more likely to consent to the former.

Like Gouldner, Blau concluded that detailed rules and close supervision generate resentments among employees and that this greatly undermines motivation, particularly in an egalitarian culture such as that which prevails in the United States:

> . . . where independence of action and equality of status are highly valued, detailed rules and close supervision are resented, and resentful employees are poorly motivated to perform their duties faithfully and energetically. A striking contrast exists between the rigorous discipline employees willingly impose upon themselves because they realize their work requires strict operating standards, and their constant annoyance at being hamstrung by picayune rules that they experience as arbitrarily imposed upon them.[37]

Both Blau and Gouldner viewed egalitarian treatment as a prerequisite to social cohesion, commitment, and motivation. Further, both viewed an egalitarian approach as perfectly compatible with the exercise of bureaucratic authority. This approach, which Gouldner labels representative bureaucracy, emphasizes personal authority and informal relations and de-emphasizes formal authority and the use of rules and sanctions. In Gouldner's study the group acceptance strategy, as practiced in the mines and by Old Doug above ground, emerged as a clear alternative to legal compliance. In Blau's study of a government agency the goal congruence strategy, represented by reliance on shared professional norms, emerged as a clear alternative to legal compliance, reinforcing the suggestion in earlier chapters that goal congruence is an effective strategy among highly educated and professionally oriented employees of the kind typically found in the public sector. It is important to keep in mind, however, that their conclusions, although theoretically significant, were derived inductively from their empirical findings. Blau and Gouldner neither began with, nor developed, a distinct theory of motivation.

SUMMARY

During the 1940s and early 1950s Merton and his students established the boundaries of organization theory as a field of study and inspired other scholars to undertake empirical analyses of existing organizations. The result was an immensely valuable set of institutional studies, including David Sills' study of the Foundation for Infantile Paralysis, and Lipset, Trow, and Coleman's study of a labor union.[38] From these studies emerged an understanding of organizational dynamics that could not have been achieved through experimentation or secondary research alone. If their work does not provide a theory of organizational effectiveness, it does show how functional analysis can be used to diagnose and assess the kinds of situations facing public managers in daily practice. Among the most important implications of structural-functional theory for public managers are the following:

- **Adjusting structure in response to changing environmental conditions.** The necessity of responding to internal and external threats precludes organizations from being the fixed, deliberately planned, rational instruments described by Weber. Their structures are more a product of cumulative, adaptive responses to perceived threats than of deliberate planning. By implication, it is partly management's responsibility to continually adjust the organization's structure as internal and external conditions change so that the agency can adapt successfully and thereby remain viable. The public manager must facilitate the process of adjustment and adaptation without allowing the agency to stray too far from its established mission.

- **Anticipating functional and dysfunctional consequences.** Before responding to a perceived threat to organizational functioning, public managers should seek to anticipate both the functional and dysfunctional consequences that may follow from a particular action. To avoid unintended dysfunctions they should carefully assess how an intended action may threaten the interests of various internal and external groups. Because organizations are complex systems, it is impossible for public managers to comprehend all of the potential interactions among internal and external system variables. Their best-laid plans will often go astray due to ripple effects that cannot be anticipated. This does not mean, however, that managers must accept bureaucratic dysfunctions as inescapable features of organizational life. Merton emphasized that dysfunctions tend to persist until their underlying causes are addressed. Treating them as inevitable features of organizational life only creates an excuse for abdicating responsibility for improving organizational performance.

Modifying Weber's depiction of bureaucracy was only one of many contributions Merton and his students made to organization theory. They incorporated human variables into structural analysis, thereby drawing attention to the dynamic relationship between formal structure and human behavior. They also replaced the prevailing view of organizations as formal arrangements of consciously coordinated activities with a view of them as adaptive social structures shaped partly by rational design and partly by the spontaneous interactions of individuals and groups.[39] If they were overly influenced by human relations theory, as some critics have claimed, they were nonetheless more willing than human relations theorists to acknowledge that conflict is inherent in organizational life and that the use of power to defend individual and group interests lies just beneath the surface of interpersonal relationships.[40]

NOTES

1. W. Richard Scott, *Organizations: Rational, Natural, and Open Systems* (Upper Saddle River, NJ: Prentice Hall, 1998), 8–10.

2. Caroline Hodges Persell, "An Interview with Robert K. Merton," *Teaching Sociology* 11 (July 1984), 355–86.

3. Robert K. Merton, *Social Theory and Social Structure: Toward the Codification of Theory and Research* (Glencoe, IL: The Free Press, 1949), 6.

4. Merton, *Social Theory and Social Structure*, 5.

5. Merton, *Social Theory and Social Structure*, 28.

6. Merton, *Social Theory and Social Structure*, 35.

7. Merton, *Social Theory and Social Structure*, 47.

8. Merton, *Social Theory and Social Structure*, 51.

9. Robert K. Merton, "Bureaucratic Structure and Personality," *Social Forces 18* (May 1940), 560.

10. Merton, "Bureaucratic Structure and Personality," 563.

11. Philip Selznick, *TVA and the Grass Roots: A Study in the Sociology of Formal Organization* (Berkeley: University of California Press, 1953).

12. Selznick, *TVA and the Grass Roots*, 13.

13. Selznick, *TVA and the Grass Roots*, 145.

14. Selznick, *TVA and the Grass Roots*, 217.

15. Alvin W. Gouldner, *Patterns of Industrial Bureaucracy* (Glencoe, IL: The Free Press, 1954).

16. Gouldner, *Patterns of Industrial Bureaucracy*, 220.

17. Gouldner, *Patterns of Industrial Bureaucracy*, 29.

18. Gouldner, *Patterns of Industrial Bureaucracy*, 221.

19. Gouldner, *Patterns of Industrial Bureaucracy*, 160–61.

20. Peter M. Blau, *The Dynamics of Bureaucracy: A Study of Interpersonal Relations in Two Government Agencies* (Chicago: University of Chicago Press, 2nd Edition, 1963), 9.

21. Gouldner, *Patterns of Industrial Bureaucracy*, 16.

22. Blau, *Dynamics of Bureaucracy*, 2.

23. Blau, *Dynamics of Bureaucracy*, 9.

24. Selznick, *TVA and the Grass Roots*, 252, footnote 9.

25. Selznick, *TVA and the Grass Roots*, 252.

26. Selznick, *TVA and the Grass Roots*, 251.

27. Selznick, *TVA and the Grass Roots*, 251.

28. Blau, *Dynamics of Bureaucracy*, 254.

29. Merton, *Social Theory and Social Structure*, 53.

30. Selznick, *TVA and the Grass Roots*, 253.

31. Blau, *Dynamics of Bureaucracy*, 250.

32. Alvin W. Gouldner, *Wildcat Strike* (Glencoe, IL: Free Press, 1954).

33. Blau, *Dynamics of Bureaucracy*, 56.

34. Blau, *Dynamics of Bureaucracy*, 250.

35. Gouldner, *Patterns of Industrial Bureaucracy*, 16.

36. Gouldner, *Patterns of Industrial Bureaucracy*, 218.

37. Peter M. Blau and Marshall W. Meyer, *Bureaucracy in Modern Society* (New York: Random House, 2nd ed., 1971), 58.

38. David L. Sills, *The Volunteers* (Glencoe, IL: Free Press, 1957), and Seymour Martin Lipset, Martin A. Trow, and James S. Coleman, *Union Democracy* (Glencoe, IL: Free Press, 1956).

39. Nicos P. Mouzelis, *Organization and Bureaucracy: An Analysis of Modern Theories* (Chicago: Aldine Publishing Company, 1968), 55–62

40. Michael Crozier, *The Bureaucratic Phenomenon* (Chicago: University of Chicago Press, 1964)

11

⌘

The Open Systems Perspective

Sociotechnical and Structural Contingency Theory

By the 1950s the open systems perspective began to replace the natural systems perspective as the dominant approach to organizational analysis. Both of these perspectives view organizations as organic wholes that must continually import resources from their environments to remain viable and both acknowledge that environmental forces shape the structure and behavior of organizational systems. Nonetheless, the two perspectives are distinguished by some subtle yet important differences. First, natural systems theorists were more interested in micro-level analysis and therefore more likely to define organizations as social systems. Mayo and Barnard, for example, focused primarily on how to maintain internal equilibrium. Open systems theorists, by contrast, were more likely to focus on exchanges with the environment and how to maintain external equilibrium. Thus, whereas natural systems theorists described organizations as social systems comprising members who are partly integrated by their common objectives, open systems theorists were more likely to describe organizations as shifting coalitions of internal and external participants contending with forces external to the organization.[1]

Second, natural systems theorists tended to describe relatively passive efforts by the organization to adapt to environmental forces, whereas open system theorists were more likely to describe aggressive efforts to adjust the environment to the organization's needs. As James D. Thompson observed, organizations are not simply organisms buffeted about by the forces of uncertainty and struggling to restore organic equilibrium; they are also rational, goal-oriented instruments that actively engage their environments, doing what they must to achieve their goals and survive to fight another day. This shift in emphasis established a new way of thinking about organizational performance. The successful organization is the one that copes best with its environment by finding an optimal fit between organizational characteristics, environmental forces, and what it seeks to achieve. This point of view emphasizes that change and stability are not dichotomous. To remain viable, organizations must maintain stability in the face of change, and change structure and behavior for the sake of stability.

This chapter begins by explaining the influence of general systems theory and the field of cybernetics on the development of the open systems perspective. It then examines two theoretical literatures that adopted the open systems perspective: sociotechnical theory and structural contingency theory. The chapter closes with an analysis of the relevance of the open systems perspective for public management and organizational performance.

THE INFLUENCE OF
GENERAL SYSTEMS THEORY

The application of systems analysis to the study of organizations experienced a rebirth in the 1950s under the name *open systems theory*. This rebirth was due in part to the influence of Ludwig von Bertalanffy's general systems theory. A biologist by profession, von Bertalanffy urged the study of living things as organic wholes in the 1920s, introduced the theory of the organism as an open system in 1940, and established the field of general systems theory in 1945.[2] He defined the latter as an interdisciplinary field of study dedicated to identifying the "principles which apply to all entities called 'systems' in general, whatever the nature of their component elements and the relations or forces between them."[3] Referring to it as "the science of wholeness," von Bertalanffy asserted that general systems theory would lead eventually to the unification of all science under one grand conceptual scheme. He viewed general systems theory not as a specific theory but as an effort to develop a hypothetical-deductive system of principles, that is, principles that can be deduced from what all open systems have in common. He believed that once these principles were identified and understood it would be possible to define the relationships among system components using mathematical formulas. This in turn would allow scientists to predict system behavior under specified conditions.

Von Bertalanffy's expectations were never fully realized, for several reasons. First, as noted in Chapter 9, principles such as homeostasis have very different meanings depending on whether the subject under study is a human being, an organization, or a society. Second, most social systems comprising too many variables for their interactions to be reduced to mathematical formulas. Finally, social systems tend to be loosely coupled, which means that a change in one element or subsystem does not necessarily produce corresponding changes in others. This makes it difficult to predict the effects of an internal or external change on system behavior. Nonetheless, von Bertalanffy's work in the field of general systems theory encouraged the cross-fertilization of ideas between disciplines and established the language used by those who subsequently studied organizations from the open systems perspective.

Von Bertalanffy insisted that organic wholes, including organizations, must be understood as **open systems.** Open systems, in contrast to closed systems, exchange materials, energy, and information with their environments so that they can renew themselves and continue to grow. In his words, "The characteristic state of the living organism is that of an open system. We call a system closed if no materials enter or leave it. It is open if there is inflow and outflow and therefore change of the component materials."[4] One of the defining features of open systems is that they are characterized by **negative entropy.** Unlike closed systems, which deteriorate until their components exist in a state of maximum disarray called *entropy*, open systems receive new energies through the importation of resources and thus continue to function, becoming more heterogeneous and complex.

Open systems, von Bertalanffy observed, are also subject to the principle of **equifinality.** Whereas the final state of a closed system is determined by its initial conditions, an open system can move toward its end state through any number of paths. Where it ends up is not predetermined by its initial conditions because new resources are constantly being imported. The principle of equifinality introduces an important theme in organization theory: freedom of choice. Two organizations may share the same goals but reach them through different means. Not only are outcomes not predetermined, but there is no one best way of achieving success.

The concept of open systems had a profound influence on the field of organizational analysis. General systems theory not only provided the language and concepts used by open systems theorists in studying organizations, it also influenced the direction their research would take and the conclusions they would draw.

THE INFLUENCE OF CYBERNETICS

The field of cybernetics, established by a mathematician named Norbert Wiener in the 1940s, also had a profound influence on open systems theory in its formative years.[5] Cybernetics is the study of self-regulating systems, such as self-guided missiles or furnace systems regulated by thermostats. These systems rely on continuous **feedback** from their environments so that they can take corrective action, thereby maintaining system equilibrium. Cybernetics conceived of systems in terms of the continuous transformation of inputs into outputs through processes known as throughputs.

Organization theorists recognized immediately that this applied to organizations as well as mechanical systems. Organizations take in resources (inputs) and transform them into products or services (outputs). Universities, for example, receive inputs in the form of materials, information, staff, and students, utilize various instructional techniques to educate students, and produce outputs in the form of graduates. They also obtain feedback from graduates, parents, and employers about how well they are doing and from the environment about impending external changes. This feedback becomes an input for determining whether corrective action is required to preserve the character and functioning of the university. In addition, mechanisms are put in place to maintain a steady state, including recruitment programs to ensure a constant supply of new students, career placement programs to help graduates find employment, reward systems to ensure that personnel remain motivated and committed, and planning systems for anticipating and responding to external threats and opportunities.

As a result of the influence of cybernetics, many open systems theorists came to view organizations as self-regulating systems that monitor their environments, identify deviations from their goals or desired states, and adjust their internal structures, goals, or environments to maintain system equilibrium. Exhibit 11.1 provides an example of an open systems model developed by Donald Warwick to guide his study of the U.S. State Department.

The field of cybernetics rests on certain assumptions that also came to influence organizational analysis. It assumes, for example, that what takes place within complex systems is beyond human comprehension and that their behaviors cannot be predicted with any degree of certainty. Economist Kenneth

Exhibit 11.1 The Organizational Sytem of a Federal Executive Agency

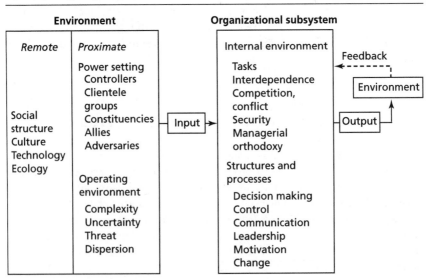

SOURCE: Reprinted by permission of the publisher from *A Theory of Public Bureaucracy: Politics, Personality and Organization in the State Department* by Donald P. Warwick, p. 60 (Cambridge, MA: Harvard University Press), Copyright © 1975 by the President and Fellows of Harvard College.

Boulding published an article entitled "General Systems Theory—The Skeleton of Science" in 1956 that merged Wiener's concept of cybernetics with von Bertalanffy's concept of general systems theory.[6] Boulding identified several different kinds of systems and arranged them into a hierarchical framework comprising nine levels, each representing an increasingly higher level of complexity. This framework placed social organizations at level eight, the next to the highest level in terms of complexity. Boulding emphasized that we have very little theoretical or empirical knowledge of systems at this level and, consequently, we are a very long way from being able to construct models that might allow us to direct and control complex organizations.

Despite Boulding's cautionary warning, Stafford Beer took it upon himself to explore the implications of cybernetics for management practice. Beer developed a classification scheme comprising six classes of systems ranging from "simple deterministic" to "exceedingly complex probabilistic" systems.[7] He placed organizations into the latter category, representing the highest degree of complexity and lowest degree of predictability. The task of cybernetics, he wrote, is to determine how to exercise control over systems of this kind. The purpose of management systems, for example, is to exercise control over the transformation process. Control in this instance does not refer to coercive acts designed to control human behavior but to mechanisms designed to ensure that performance conforms to established standards. According to Beer, the model that management planners construct to depict the transformation of inputs to outputs must contain a "black box" at its center because the way inputs are transformed into outputs is not visible. This was Beers way of saying that we can neither identify all system variables nor determine how a change in one variable will affect all others. Management must experiment with various interventions, seek to discern basic patterns, and adjust its model accordingly.

Robert Swinth also pioneered in the application of cybernetics to the design of management control systems.[8] He characterized the various mechanisms by which inputs are converted to goods or services as the organization's servomechanism (OSM). This refers to three linked functions: the operations function, by which raw materials are converted into outputs; the policy function, by which feedback about how well the process is achieving its goals is translated into specific objectives; and the control function, by which operations are directed in accordance with these objectives. In Swinth's cybernetics model, demands are received by the policy center and translated into a set of objectives. The policy center then gives a control center a performance standard to meet. The control center compares desired performance with actual performance and takes steps to keep operations as near as possible to desired levels. According to Swinth, it is through the operation of servomechanisms that organizations achieve equilibrium or homeostasis. In his view cybernetic models can assist managers in making organizations more self-regulating and more predictable in their outcomes. Strategic planning and performance measurement are among the methods that may be used for purposes of feedback and self-regulation.

Those who adopted the open systems perspective for purposes of organizational analysis were rarely concerned with the design of internal control systems. The latter were more properly the concern of operations research and management science. Nonetheless, organization theorists were greatly influenced by the concepts of feedback and self-regulation and by the assumption that organizational performance cannot be predicted or controlled with certainty.

TWO PATH-BREAKING STUDIES

By the close of the 1960s the open systems perspective had become the dominant approach to organizational analysis. This was due to the publication of such highly influential works as Daniel Katz and Robert L. Kahn's *The Social Psychology of Organizations* in 1966 and James D. Thompson's *Organizations in Action* in 1967. Katz and Kahn used the open systems perspective to integrate what was then known about human behavior in organizations.[9] Like Barnard, Katz and Kahn focused on internal processes and the importance of morale and motivation to system survival. In contrast to Barnard, however, they placed a much greater emphasis on the role played by environmental forces in shaping organizational norms, internal structures, and the organization's ability to attract and retain committed employees.

Katz and Kahn also distinguished themselves from classical theorists, such as Weber, Taylor, and Gulick, by accusing them of closed-system thinking. According to Katz and Kahn, classical theorists tended to treat internal processes as if they were unaffected by changes in the environment and as if they could be made perfectly predictable and controlled. Working from misconceptions of this kind, classical theorists encouraged managers to build rigidities into the system, thereby undermining the organization's ability to respond quickly and successfully to changing external conditions. Katz and Kahn urged theorists and practitioners alike to view organizations as open systems and to investigate the external causes of internal stresses and strains.

James D. Thompson's *Organizations in Action* also helped establish the dominance of the open systems perspective in the late 1960s.[10] Noting that even the universal aspects of complex organizations, such as horizontal and vertical differentiation, vary from one organization to the next, Thompson developed a conceptual framework for investigating the conditions that explain system variations. As a sociologist, Thompson was more interested in explaining the behavior of organizations as a whole than the behaviors that occur within organizations. He described, for example, how organizations as open systems must engage in exchange relationships with other organizations to obtain needed resources or outlets, and how the resulting dependencies cause organizations to develop strategies for managing their dependence, such as exerting control over other organizations, expanding their boundaries, altering their internal structures, or redefining their goals.

Thompson's primary thesis was that organizations with similar technological and environmental problems exhibit similar behaviors as they struggle to cope with the uncertainties their environments impose on them. According to Thompson, if similar problems result in similar adaptive responses, it should be possible to identify basic patterns of organizational behavior. *Organizations in Action* offered ninety-three propositions for investigating these basic patterns. In doing so it provided an important point of departure for researchers seeking to explore the complex interdependencies inherent in open systems.

At the outset of his study, Thompson waded into the debate over the essential nature of organizations. Are they, as the classical theorists imply, rational, goal-oriented instruments that are deliberately designed to be as efficient and predictable as possible, or are they, as some natural systems theorists implied, living organisms struggling to survive in the face of uncertainty and incapable of behaving in planned and predictable ways? Concluding that neither model alone provides an adequate understanding of complex organizations, Thompson proposed a synthesis of the two perspectives: organizations are simultaneously problem-facing and problem-solving entities. Although organizations and their environments are indeed interdependent, this does not preclude them from seeking to make rational, goal-oriented decisions in the face of uncertainty while simultaneously striving to maintain themselves as viable systems. This synthesis created a third perspective toward organizational analysis that Thompson referred to generally as the open systems perspective: "For purposes of this volume, then, *we will conceive of complex organizations as open systems, hence indeterminate and faced with uncertainty, but at the same time as subject to criteria of rationality and hence needing determinateness and certainty."*[11]

Thompson provided concreteness to his synthesis of rational and natural systems theory by drawing upon Talcott Parson's distinction between three organizational levels of responsibility and control. Decisions at the technical level, where the productive work is carried out, are governed by the nature of the productive task. This level is the most closed off from external influences and a considerable amount of certainty and control is possible. The managerial level represents an intermediate level at which managers address input and output irregularities so that the technical core can operate as efficiently and predictably as possible. Finally, the institutional level is that level where responsibility for the organization as a whole is highest and the possibilities for certainty and control are the lowest. At this level executives perform a boundary-spanning role in which they are responsible for obtaining resources, building alliances, and dealing with output disposal problems by adjusting, or adapting to, external forces. Thompson emphasized that, whereas it is appropriate to employ closed system thinking at the technical level, it is necessary to employ open system thinking at higher levels.

The body of research grounded in open systems theory is enormous. Although justice cannot be done to it in the remaining pages of this chapter, the sections that follow examine two of the most influential theories to emerge from this approach to organizational analysis: sociotechnical theory and structural contingency theory.

SOCIOTECHNICAL THEORY

Sociotechnical theory developed in the 1950s out of the work of Fred Emery, Eric Trist, and their colleagues at the Tavistock Institute of Human Relations in London. The Institute's parent, the Tavistock Clinic, was established at the end of the First World War to provide psychiatric services to war veterans.[12] During the Second World War many of its staff were recruited by the military to assist with social problems, such as the resettlement of repatriated prisoners of war. Their wartime experiences fueled their interest in the social context of psychological problems and led them to establish the Tavistock Institute in 1946. The new institute put together a staff of psychiatrists, social psychologists, and other social scientists dedicated to studying problems of human relations in society at large by combining professional practice with field research. The staff's commitment to what was called action research was due in part to the influence of Kurt Lewin, the father of group dynamics theory (see Chapter 12). Action research required investigators to work with management and labor in introducing changes into work settings and drawing conclusions from the results. In 1948 the Tavistock Institute, in conjunction with Lewin's students at the Research Center for Group Dynamics at the University of Michigan, began publishing *Human Relations,* a periodical that quickly became one of the leading journals in the field of social and organizational behavior.

In 1949 the recently nationalized coal industry asked the Tavistock Institute to investigate social problems arising from the introduction of new technologies in the mines.[13] A series of studies were conducted over a period of ten years, resulting in twenty-four papers and reports, and culminating with the publication of *Organizational Choice* by Trist and his colleagues in 1963.[14] Along with Rice's parallel study of textile mills in India,[15] the coal-mining studies produced a method for diagnosing and addressing organizational problems that came to be known as sociotechnical theory. In a conference paper delivered in 1959, Emery and Trist placed their research findings in the context of open systems theory and urged further study of organizations as "open socio-technical systems."[16] The latter, they suggested, constituted a new field of study focusing on the relations between the technical and human elements involved in the organization of work activities.

Sociotechnical theory holds that production systems must be viewed not as technical systems, nor as social systems, but as both at once. According to this view, each production system is defined by the interrelationships between two subsystems, the **technical organization,** which includes machinery, equipment, and specific work processes, and the **work organization,** which structures how workers relate to each other socially and psychologically. The focus of sociotechnical theory is the degree of fit between the work technology and the sociopsychological factors built into the work organization. Its general thesis is that high levels of productivity can be obtained from a technological system only if the work organization is designed in a way that provides compatible sociopsychological incentives and satisfactions.

A core concept in sociotechnical theory is **joint optimization**. This concept holds that management cannot optimize the performance of the total system by optimizing technical efficiency, as Taylor seemed to imply. Nor can it optimize the performance of the total system by optimizing social satisfactions, as Mayo and Barnard seemed to imply. Superior performance—defined in terms of output, absenteeism, and morale—is achieved only by jointly optimizing the organization's human systems with the technology used by the organization to accomplish its primary purposes.

Technological changes being introduced in the coal-mining industry in the 1950s provided an opportunity to study the relationships between technology and work organization.[17] For many generations coal had been mined using the **single place system.** Miners formed themselves into semi-permanent teams of two to six to extract coal using hand or pneumatic picks over two or three shifts. Each team was awarded a "single place" on the coal face, which was 6–11 yards wide. Teams were paid based on their output, with a single paycheck divided equally among team members. The work was not characterized by task specialization. Each member hewed coal off the face, hauled it away in tubs, and put roof supports in place at prescribed intervals. The work process was continuous; the incoming worker picked up where a teammate had left off. In addition, teams rotated to new places every three months so that every team had an equal chance of working under good and poor geological conditions.

The work organization associated with single-place mining possessed certain identifiable sociopsychological properties. First, each team was autonomous and self-regulating. Other teams worked the face but they did so independently. Supervisors did not interfere in the ways teams conducted themselves. Their role was to ensure safe working conditions and supply necessary materials. Second, each team was highly cohesive because members selected each other and shared the same paycheck. Third, each team member was multi-skilled and self-reliant, performing all of the tasks associated with single-place mining. Fourth, the stress of working under difficult geological conditions was relieved by rotating to new places every three months. Given the technology that then prevailed, the small autonomous work group was well adapted to the underground situation. According to Trist and his colleagues, it contained all of the elements of a social system required to meet the demands of single-place mining.

Because they are open systems, mines must adapt to changing environmental conditions. The 1950s brought greater mechanization in the form of conveyor belts that continuously moved the coal out of the mines. With this change in technology the single-place system of mining was replaced with the **conventional longwall system.** Large groups of forty to fifty workers were charged with removing coal from a continuous face 80–100 feet wide. The workers were divided into three groups. Each performed a different task on a different shift. On the first shift a pair of "cuttermen" cut into the face to a depth of 4-6 feet near the floor and then blasted the face with dynamite so that the coal collapsed downward. On the second shift a team of "fillers" shoveled the coal onto the conveyor belt and put in the required roof supports. On the third shift a team of "pullers" moved the conveyor system forward into the place where coal had been removed, and a team of "stonemen" enlarged and maintained the tunnel through which the coal was conveyed.

The sociopsychological properties of the work organization under the conventional longwall system were distinctly different from those under single-place mining. First, instead of a single work group in which each member performed all required tasks, the longwall system relied upon four separate work groups, each of which was responsible for a specialized work task: cutting, filling, pulling, or doing stonework. Second, instead of a continuous process of removing coal, the longwall system followed a formal cycle in which each shift carried out one element of the cutting, removing, and advancing process. Third, instead of a single team sharing one paycheck equally, the longwall system issued separate paychecks to each team of cutters, fillers, pullers, and stonemen. These differences meant that the team as a whole, with its forty to fifty members, was characterized by neither cohesion nor interdependence. When each team of specialists completed its assigned task, it did not begin work on the task assigned to the next shift. There was no incentive to cooperate with other task groups because each team was paid only for doing its assigned task. In addition, the team as a whole was no longer self-regulating. Management attempted to coordinate and control the overall process through various pay incentives, but with little success. Consequently, productivity under the conventional longwall method never reached its expected potential. Trist and his colleagues concluded that specialized work roles and segregated task groups did not provide the elements of a social system required to induce workers to cooperate in carrying out the overall task.

When the conventional longwall system failed to achieve expected output levels, management altered the work organization, creating what was called the **composite longwall system.** This system restored the practice of continuous operation used in single-place mining. When task teams on one shift completed their primary task ahead of schedule, they began the task of the next shift. Whereas teams working under the conventional system frequently failed to complete the mandated work cycle in three shifts because of inevitable problems and delays, teams under the composite system rarely failed to complete the mandated cycle. Second, many workers developed multiple skills once again so that they could carry out the task of a subsequent shift. Third, the composite system restored the principle of a single paycheck for the entire work group. This provided the necessary incentive for workers on one shift to begin the work of another shift and otherwise to work in a highly cooperative fashion. Fourth, the composite system restored the principle of self-regulation. Team members were allowed to determine who would be assigned to specific tasks and shifts. In short, the composite longwall system, by borrowing elements from the traditional single place system, provided sociopsychological incentives and satisfactions that were better adapted to the requirements of longwall mining.

To test their preliminary conclusions, Trist and his colleagues conducted two comparisons of the conventional and composite longwall systems.[18] The first compared a conventional system to a composite system under similar geological conditions. In the conventional system, cohesion was found to be high within each specialized task team but low for the group as a whole. Each task team strove to maximize its economic interests and didn't care how its work affected the work of those on the other shifts. In the composite system, by contrast, not only was social cohesion high for the group as a whole but the pressures of working under stressful conditions were greatly reduced by the system of task and shift rotation. These sociopsychological differences translated into lower absenteeism rates: 8 percent for the composite group as compared to 20 percent for the conventional group. Differences in sociopsychological factors also translated into a higher cycle completion rate: the composite group failed to complete the daily cycle only 5 percent of the time, compared to a failure rate of 69 percent for the conventional group. Finally, the composite group was more productive. After adjusting for differences in working conditions, the composite group achieved 95 percent of its productive potential, compared to 78 percent for the conventional group.

The second study compared two work teams using the composite longwall system, but with one team possessing more of the composite characteristics than the other. This test was designed to determine whether it was the characteristics of compositeness that explained the superior performance of the composite system. In this instance the two teams worked adjacent to each other using the same technology and under the same geological conditions. The differences in work organization were twofold. One team subdivided itself into two independent groups working on different halves of the long coal face, whereas the other team worked as a single, unified group. Second, the team that had subdivided itself also did not rotate tasks or workplaces. These two features reduced the sense of overall interdependence and the even distribution of stressful working conditions.

Results of the study confirmed the hypothesis that the greater the "compositeness" of a work group, the higher its level of performance. The nature of the work organization in the more composite group, particularly its rotation of tasks, allowed it to adapt more successfully to changing working conditions. The other group did not adapt as well. When geological conditions worsened, its absenteeism rate increased dramatically. Productivity was slightly higher for the more composite team, but the researchers concluded that the lower sickness and absenteeism rates were even more significant. In their words, "The face group organization which was panel-wide, embodied systematic rotation of the various jobs among team members, and did not tie a man to only one job, work group or face, was the more effective in maintaining the smooth work flow of the cycle and in coping with increased work stress."[19]

The Tavistock researchers noted that their findings supported von Bertalanffy's principle of equifinality: Given a specific technology, any of several social systems can produce acceptable results. The three systems used in the coal mines utilized three different methods of work organization. Each functioned at an adequate level, but the work organization with the highest degree of interdependence and autonomy proved to be best adapted to the requirements of longwall mining. Trist and his colleagues advised managers who were introducing technological changes to conduct sociotechnical analyses to determine which form of work organization is best suited to the demands of the new technology. Their research indicated that human factors must be taken into account or technological innovations will not pay the expected dividends. In one instance, pit managers introduced the composite method on another longwall after its initial success, only to encounter numerous problems. They had failed to anticipate the effects of using inexperienced workers and denying them the opportunity to select their own teammates on cooperation and cohesion. Trist and his colleagues concluded that change is something that must be carefully managed. Specific steps must be taken, for example, to overcome resistance to change. These steps, as Kurt Lewin put it, include unfreezing current attitudes, introducing change, and then refreezing new attitudes.

AN ASSESSMENT OF
SOCIOTECHNICAL THEORY

One of the most valuable contributions of sociotechnical theory to organizational analysis is its emphasis on the interconnectedness of technical systems (the subject of scientific management theory) and social systems (the subject of human relations theory). Relying as it does on the open systems perspective, sociotechnical theory emphasizes that organizational effectiveness requires an optimal fit between these two important subsystems.

Sociotechnical theory also brought renewed attention to the principles of work design in general and to the value of autonomous work groups in particular. "Of particular interest to the student of social process," Trist wrote, "is the ability of quite large primary groups of 40–50 members to act as self-regulating, self-developing social organisms able to maintain themselves in a steady state of high productivity throughout the entire period of their 'missions.'"[20] This finding, Trist added, lent support to the human resources theory of Douglas McGregor and Rensis Likert (Chapters 12 and 13), a theory that holds that performance is highest where self-managing primary work groups are established. Converting to self-managed work teams, Trist wrote, "is to replace job alienation in the worker by task-oriented commitment. . . ."[21]

The findings of the Tavistock researchers are, however, subject to differing interpretations. John Kelly has written an especially thorough critique.[22] First, Kelly noted that sociotechnical theorists are not in agreement about the causes of the higher levels of productivity associated with the autonomous work group. Some attribute its superiority to the attributes associated with working in interdependent groups. According to this view, by focusing on the whole task, and by being cross-trained, group members are able to respond effectively to system variations caused by environmental uncertainty. Members also experience personal satisfactions derived from working together as a group. Other sociotechnical theorists, however, attribute its superiority to the design of the job itself and the individual satisfactions derived from performing meaningful, enriched work. The first group of theorists, according to Kelly, has made the autonomous work group the focus of sociotechnical theory, whereas the second has made job design the central focus.

Second, Kelly raised the possibility that neither of these interpretations is correct. In his view the increases in productivity observed in the various sociotechnical studies were due to the continuous work effort and the system of pay bonuses associated with working in groups. These changes produced higher workloads and a faster pace of work, thereby enhancing efficiency and reducing costs. Kelly concluded that there is little in these studies to suggest that increased productivity is a function of individual satisfactions derived either from working in groups or from performing meaningful or challenging tasks.

That the issues raised by Kelly remain unresolved does not reduce the significance of the contributions sociotechnical research has made to organization theory. Sociotechnical theory reintroduced technology as an important variable in the study of organizations, underscored the relevance of sociopsychological factors to organizational performance, shifted intervention efforts from treating workers well to redesigning jobs and work processes, stimulated further study of small-group dynamics, and initiated discussions about organizational development and the management of change. Trist and his colleagues at the Tavistock Institute improved our understanding of the effects of technology and work structure on human behavior, something that Elton Mayo emphasized as fundamentally important in his early essays but failed to study in his later research. They also moved well beyond human relations theory by establishing the central importance of technology in converting inputs to outputs and mediating between the goals of the organization and the constraints imposed upon it by its external environment. Finally, they placed organizational analysis in the context of open systems theory. It is not enough, they concluded, for management to jointly optimize the organization's human and technical systems through the careful design of work processes; management must also do so in a way that positions the organization for continued success in its external environment.

STRUCTURAL CONTINGENCY THEORY

Once theorists began to view organizations as systems of interdependent variables, they quickly realized that there can be no one best way to structure all organizations. The situations confronting organizations are simply unique and the interdependent variables affecting organizational performance too numerous. This realization caused researchers to undertake the search for the best, or most appropriate, structure for each individual organization or general type of organization, given its unique characteristics and circumstances. The underlying premise of structural contingency theory is that choices about structure are contingent upon identifiable internal and external factors. Its goal is to determine how to structure an organization, given contingencies such as size, technology, strategy for success, and degree of environmental stability. This involves a search for the optimal fit between the structure of the organization as a whole, internal and external contingency factors, and the goals of the organization. Structural contingency theory holds out hope that someday it may be possible to prescribe a specific structural form for an organization from organization-specific knowledge of its contingency factors.

Structural contingency theory, which has become nearly synonymous with the term *modern organization theory*, now comprises an enormous body of research. Consequently, this chapter can do no more than highlight two of the most important studies in the development of structural contingency theory.

Tom Burns: Mechanistic and Organic Management Systems

Tom Burns, a researcher at the University of Edinburgh, studied twenty English and Scottish firms during the 1950s, several of them in partnership with G. M. Stalker. Most of these were well-established manufacturing firms entering the field of electronics for the first time. The task before them was to convert the technological discoveries of the war years, such as radar, into entirely new products for which there were as yet no markets or customers. This unique situation provided Burns and Stalker with an opportunity to study what happens to organizations when they move from an environment characterized by relative stability to one characterized by constant technological change and uncertainty. Their findings were published in *The Management of Innovation* in 1961.[23]

The dependent variable in Burns and Stalker's study is the organization's management system, whereas the independent variable, or contingency factor, is the degree of stability in the organization's external environment. Most of the firms in their study faced unstable environments in which demand for their products was uncertain and technological improvements in product lines were constantly required. In the course of studying how these firms coped with change, Burns and Stalker noted that several firms had fundamentally altered their management structures. This led them to formulate the thesis that organizations must adapt their management systems to satisfy the requirements of their changing environments if they are to remain viable. Classical management theory notwithstanding, there is no single model of a "good" organization for firms to follow. Commercial success depends in large part, they concluded, on how well the firm's managing director designs or redesigns the management system consistent with environmental conditions. As they put it, "The degree of stability or rate of change calls for different systems by which the activities of the concern are controlled, by which information is conveyed through the organization, and by which decisions and actions are authorized."[24] This introduced a distinctly open systems view of organizational dynamics. Burns and Stalker were among the first to detail the ways firms are affected by forces in their external environments and to emphasize the managing director's responsibility for interpreting environmental conditions and overseeing organizational adaptation.

In the course of their analysis, Burns and Stalker identified what they believed was a continuum of management systems with two "ideal types" at either end: mechanistic and organic. No firm conformed completely to the characteristics of either of these types, but they tended toward one or the other depending upon whether their environments were relatively stable or constantly changing. A **mechanistic management system** follows the bureaucratic model outlined by Weber. Workers are assigned a narrow, specialized set of tasks to perform and are expected to await instructions from their superiors before taking action on nonroutine matters. Focused on the means of performing their programmed tasks, workers in mechanistic systems generally do not identify with the goals or purposes of the organization. Communications are vertical rather than horizontal, interaction tends to be limited to superior-subordinate dyads, and strict obedience to authority is expected. No one is empowered to act outside the limits of his or her authority. Although such systems often seem regimented and dehumanized, they hold certain advantages for organizational members. They provide a safe and predictable environment where members understand the boundaries of each other's task and scope of authority, as well as how to progress upward in the organization.

Burns and Stalker concluded that the mechanistic system is appropriate to stable conditions, being both efficient in its use of individual effort and effective in securing desired levels of productivity. It does not work well, however, where conditions are constantly changing. Narrow functional tasks cannot be assigned to individuals to carry out on a routine basis because the nature of those tasks is constantly being redefined by nonroutine problems and unforeseen requirements for action. Under conditions of change, an **organic management system** is more appropriate. Workers are given broad, loosely defined roles and are expected to contribute their knowledge and experience to the common task of the organization as a whole. The idea of individual responsibility for a limited set of official duties is replaced by the idea of collective responsibility for all problems. Communications are lateral as well as vertical, cross-functional meetings are common, group problem solving is expected, and individuals interact on terms of relative equality. Decisions are made at the point of the problem based on specialized knowledge rather than at the top of the hierarchy based on formal authority. Commitment to purpose is valued more highly than loyalty and obedience. Far from being narrow functionaries, mere cogs in the larger machine, workers in an organic system are encouraged to view themselves as professionals charged with using their best judgment to advance the interests of the organization.[25]

In short, Burns and Stalker concluded that organic systems are appropriate where decisions cannot be programmed by those at the top because of the rapid pace of environmental change. It is a system for handling nonprogrammed decision making in which coordination is achieved through shared beliefs and a sense of collective responsibility. Because workers closest to the problem can respond to changing conditions quickly and flexibly, the organic system is capable of much greater adaptation to change than the mechanistic system.

Although it is now fashionable to advocate organic systems as the one best way for organizations in these turbulent times, Burns and Stalker emphasized that organic systems have their share of disadvantages. Lack of clear task assignments and responsibilities, for example, often creates anxiety, feelings of insecurity, and interpersonal tensions. This means that workers must possess a high tolerance for ambiguity. Conversely, despite the negative, authoritarian connotations of being organized in a bureaucratic fashion, the mechanistic system can produce positive results. In describing a rayon factory that operated according to the mechanistic model, Burns and Stalker wrote that "the system, lubricated by a certain paternalism, worked smoothly and economically, and there was no evidence that any individual felt aggrieved or belittled."[26] Burns and Stalker insisted that each organization must find a place on the continuum between the two extremes that is most appropriate to its situation:

> . . . . We have endeavored to stress the appropriateness of each system to its own specific set of conditions. Equally, we desire to avoid the suggestion that either system is superior under all circumstances to the other. In particular, nothing in our experience justifies the assumption that mechanistic systems should be superseded by organic in conditions of stability. The beginning of administrative wisdom is the awareness that there is no one optimum type of management system.[27]

As one of the first studies to explore the linkages between a particular contingency factor and organizational structure, Burns and Stalker's research represented an important contribution to organization theory. It inspired other scholars to turn their attention to the study of structural contingencies, helping to produce what is now a large and valuable body of knowledge. Their work also had an unintended influence. By describing how increased employee discretion and involvement can lead to increased employee commitment and motivation, their work encouraged some analysts to treat organic management as a general panacea. But if organic management is no panacea, Burns and Stalker's analysis nonetheless poses an interesting question for public management. If most public agencies lie somewhere in the middle of the stability–instability continuum, then perhaps they can benefit from greater levels of employee involvement, commitment, and flexibility than currently allowed.

Joan Woodward: Technology's Influence on Structure

In 1953 Joan Woodward, an industrial sociologist at South East Essex College of Technology in England, received a four-year grant from the Joint Committee on Human Relations in Industry to investigate the social and economic problems arising from the use of new technologies. The research project took the form of a broad survey of the structural characteristics of one hundred firms in South Essex. A report of the initial findings, published in 1958, created quite a stir. It indicated that firms organized according to the principles of classical management theory were not always the most successful and that organizational designers who followed classical principles often did more harm than good. In 1965 Woodward published *Industrial Organization: Theory and Practice*, which presented the findings of the original study along with follow-up studies completed after she moved to the Imperial College of Science and Technology in 1958.[28]

As in the Hawthorne studies, the members of Woodward's research team designed their study with classical assumptions in mind. It made sense to them that some types of organizational structure are better than others and that if they compared structural characteristics with levels of commercial performance they could isolate the types that are best. With this premise in mind, interviewers went into the field and collected data relating to the way each firm was organized and operated and its degree of commercial success. But analysis of the data revealed no correlation between organizational structure and performance. Successful firms exhibited different organizational forms, including the predominantly line organization characterized by a single chain of command, the functional organization favored by Taylor in which foremen take orders from several functional supervisors, and the compromise line-staff organization that provides functional assistance while respecting a single chain of command. No one type proved superior. The twenty firms judged to be above average in success, for example, had little in common.

Rather than give up the search for causal relationships, Woodward analyzed the data again, this time controlling for the type of manufacturing technology used. *Technology* in Woodward's study refers to the techniques used to produce goods, including tools and machines, and the means by which work processes are planned and controlled. Woodward's team identified eleven basic types of production systems. To facilitate analysis, these eleven types were combined into three major groupings. **Unit and small-batch firms** manufacture individual or small batches of products according to the specifications set forth in the customer's order. One firm, for example, manufactured custom-made suits. **Large-batch and mass production firms** manufacture large batches of products in response to customer orders or continuously mass-produced items for defined markets. Examples include radios and televisions. **Process production firms** manufacture products that are measured and sold by weight, capacity, or volume. Examples include chemicals, petroleum products, and paper products. These three categories represented a scale of technical complexity and systematic control of production. Unit and small-batch firms are situated at one end, representing the lowest level of technical complexity and control, and process firms at the other end, representing the highest level of technical complexity and control.

Definite patterns emerged as the structural data were analyzed by type of technology. First, the number of levels of authority in the management hierarchy was lowest in unit production and highest in process firms. Second, the chief executive's span of control was narrowest in unit production and broadest in process firms. Also, the span of control of middle managers was broadest in unit production and narrowest in process firms. As a result, unit production firms had short and broadly based pyramids, whereas process firms had tall, narrowly based pyramids. Third, labor costs were highest in unit production and lowest in process production. Fourth, the ratio of managers and supervisors to nonsupervisory personnel was lowest in unit production and highest in process production. Finally, the ratio of clerical and administrative workers to production workers was lowest in unit production and highest in process production.

On other structural dimensions, firms at either end of the scale were more like each other than they were the large-batch and mass production firms in the middle of the scale. For example, first-line supervisors had narrow spans of control in both small-batch and process firms, and broad spans of control in large-batch and mass production firms. Workers in the small-batch and process firms worked in smaller production groups; this allowed for greater informality and generally better industrial relations. In the language of Burns and Stalker, most of the organic management systems were found at the ends of the scale, in small-batch and process firms, whereas most of the mechanistic management systems were found among the large-batch and mass production firms. This indicated to Woodward that some aspects of organizational structure are contingent upon technology as well as the rate of change imposed by the environment.

The now well-known conclusion derived from Woodward's study is that there is no one best way to organize. Commercial success depends not on any one type of organizational structure but on the degree of fit between a firm's organizational structure and technical means of production. Her findings suggested that, if there is no one best organizational structure, there *is* one that is best suited to each type of technology. This conclusion was similar to that reached by Trist and his colleagues, except that Woodward's study went beyond the structure of the work organization to include the overall administrative structure as well.

After analyzing the data, Woodward concluded that "different technologies imposed different kinds of demands on individuals and organizations, and these demands had to be met through an appropriate structure."[29] The essential relationship between technology and organization, she wrote, had escaped classical theorists. Taylor and Fayol, for example, acknowledged that their principles had to be adapted to different circumstances but failed to recognize that different organizational systems may be required when dealing with different technologies. Woodward found that the more successful firms tended to be those that clustered around the median for that category on the structural dimensions described.

This did not mean that the principles of classical management theory were without value. After all, they tended to hold reasonably well for successful firms in the large-batch and mass production category. As Woodward put it, "In all the successful large batch production firms there was not only a clear definition of duties and responsibilities of the kind already referred to but also an adherence to the principles of unity of command; a separation (at least on paper) of advisory from executive responsibilities, and a chief executive who controlled no more than the recommended five or six direct subordinates."[30] In short, they were more bureaucratic, mechanistic, and formalized. Significantly, these same principles or characteristics were associated with failure in the other types of firms.

These findings held important implications for sociotechnical theory. Woodward noted that organizational structure has two functions: to distribute authority and coordinate work, and to create a network of social relationships. Her research indicated that the relationship between these two functions varies with technology. For example, because coordination is achieved through the self-regulating technologies in process firms, the way social relations are structured or cooperation achieved is an independent matter. Where coordination is built into the work process itself organizational designers are free to design a social system to meet human needs. Similarly, Woodward found that although unit production had to be deliberately structured to facilitate coordination it was possible to do so in a way that allowed for the satisfaction of human needs. By contrast, in the large-batch and mass production firms, coordination and control of work had to be deliberately structured as in unit production but it wasn't possible to coordinate work in a way that simultaneously satisfied human needs. Formal rules and closer supervision were required. In these situations, Woodward concluded, the network of relationships best for production is not necessarily the one that is best for people.

Woodward's study was important because it, like Burns and Stalker's, represented an early effort to identify a structural contingency factor. Woodward's was especially important because it was the first large-scale study to demonstrate linkages among technology, organizational structure, and organizational performance using quantitative data. Although her study raised many additional questions about the precise relationship between specific technical and structural variables, her general conclusion that structure is partly contingent upon technology has been widely accepted.

AN OVERVIEW OF STRUCTURAL CONTINGENCY FACTORS

A contingency factor is a variable that specifies what structural arrangements are best suited to an organization, given the situation in which it finds itself. This means that for any level of a contingency factor, high or low, there is a corresponding level of some structural dimension that is most appropriate. Exhibit 11.2 presents many of the contingency factors identified by researchers during the 1960s and 1970s and some of the aspects of organizational structure that they affect. This is a vast literature and the summary that follows can do no more than indicate the nature of each contingency relationship.

Environmental Uncertainty

Organizational structure may be contingent upon the degree of stability or certainty in an organization's external environment. Burns and Stalker found, for example, that uncertainty caused by the need to develop new products for undefined markets was associated with relatively low levels of standardization, formalization, and role specialization. Similarly, Lawrence and Lorsch found that departments facing the highest levels of uncertainty were lowest in terms of the number of levels of management, use of formal reward and control systems, formalization, and standardization.[31] These departments also relied more on consultation and less on formal hierarchy to resolve conflicts.

Donald Warwick found in a study of the U.S. State Department that environmental uncertainty resulted in increased hierarchy and rules.[32] Uncertainty about the significance of events unfolding in foreign countries resulted in a high volume of messages being sent from field offices to Washington. Top officials both in the field and in Washington insisted upon reviewing incoming messages and clearing outgoing messages before they were sent. The inevitable communications overload at the top led to additional rules for handling the traffic and additional levels of hierarchy to review and clear messages. In this instance, uncertainty

Exhibit 11.2 Contingency Factors and Structural Dimensions

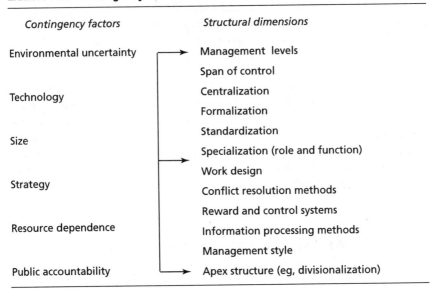

Contingency factors	Structural dimensions
Environmental uncertainty	Management levels
	Span of control
Technology	Centralization
	Formalization
	Standardization
Size	Specialization (role and function)
	Work design
Strategy	Conflict resolution methods
	Reward and control systems
Resource dependence	Information processing methods
	Management style
Public accountability	Apex structure (eg, divisionalization)

led to greater bureaucratic rigidity rather than less. As discussed below, this may be a product of the special emphasis placed on accountability in public agencies.

Technology

Organizational structure may be contingent upon the organization's core technology. Woodward found that the differences between small-batch, mass production, and continuous-process technologies explained differences in such factors as management levels, span of control, formalization, and functional specialization. Similarly, Lawrence and Lorsch found that the different technologies utilized in plastics, food processing, and bottle manufacturing explained differences in formalization, time orientation, reward and control systems, and conflict resolution methods. The conclusion they reached is that some structural characteristics are better suited to a particular technology than others.

Similarly, in a study of fifty-two public and private organizations, Pugh and his associates at the University of Aston in England found modest correlations between technology and task specialization, standardization, and formalization (r = 0.34), and concentration of authority (r = -0.30).[33] Organizations with integrated, automated, and relatively rigid work processes were more likely than those with simpler, more flexible technologies to be characterized by specialized work roles and standardized procedures. They were also characterized by less concentration of authority at the top of the organization, apparently because routinized work processes pose fewer control problems for top management. The eight governmental units in Pugh's study tended to have simpler, more flexible technologies and, consequently, less standardized work routines and more concentration of authority at the top. In contrast to Woodward's findings, Pugh and his colleagues found that technology has little effect on the structure of top management, especially among larger organizations.[34]

In one of the few contingency studies dealing exclusively with public organizations, Blau and Schoenherr found that the structure of divisions within state employment security agencies varied according to whether the work was essentially clerical or professional in nature. Structure in this instance referred to the number of subunits (horizontal differentiation) and the number of levels of hierarchy (vertical differentiation).[35] Blau and Schoenherr identified four basic types of work-structure relationships: a *routinized function*, where jobs are homogenous and simple, tended to have an undifferentiated structure with comparatively few levels and few sections; a *fragmented function*, where there is a great variety of mostly simple jobs, appeared to give rise to a highly differentiated structure in terms of both levels of hierarchy and division of labor; a *complex function*, where jobs are complex and require a great deal of independent judgment, tended to produce a squat pyramid regardless of the division of labor; and a *heterogenous function*, characterized by a pronounced division of labor, appeared to promote a tall pyramid. Blau and Schoenherr concluded that "if a function is simple enough for most of the work to be performed by clerks, the degree of heterogeneity tends to govern the extent to which the structure becomes differentiated into both hierarchical levels and functional sections. But if the function is complex and the majority of duties require training and skills, multilevel hierarchies are unlikely to develop, regardless of the degree of specialization among jobs produced by the division of labor."[36]

Size

Organizational structure may be contingent upon the size of the organization. Pugh and his colleagues found, for example, that larger organizations tend to have more task specialization, standardization, and formalization than smaller organizations ($r = 0.69$).[37] Where an organization was part of a larger organization, as in the case of government agencies, the size of the parent organization also correlated with concentration of authority ($r = 0.39$); the larger the parent organization, the greater the concentration of authority at the top of the subunit.

Similarly, Blau and Schoenherr found in their study of employment security agencies that the larger the agency the greater the number of local offices, number of job titles, number of hierarchical levels, number of major divisions under top management, and number of sections per division, and the greater the breadth of the manager's span of control. Beyer and Trice attempted to replicate Blau and Schoenherr's findings using a heterogenous sample of seventy-one agencies of the federal govern-ment.[38] Their study revealed weaker relationships between size and structural characteristics than Blau and Schoenherr's. They attributed this to the fact that the offices in Blau and Schoenherr's study shared a relatively routine paper-processing technology, which had the effect of understating the role of task complexity and overstating the effects of size on structure. Beyer and Trice concluded that size increases the division of labor (number of job titles) and this in turn increases horizontal and vertical differentiation in agencies with routine work technologies but does not increase horizontal differentiation in agencies relying on more complex work technologies.

Strategy

Organizational structure may be contingent on the strategy for success chosen by senior managers. A business historian by the name of Alfred Chandler was among the first to draw attention to the contingency relationship between strategy and structure. Relying upon four case studies in a book published in 1962, Chandler advanced the thesis that "structure follows strategy."[39] When the DuPont corporation decided, for example, to pursue a diversification strategy, it had to shift from a highly centralized administrative structure to a decentralized, division-based structure in order to remain viable.

Chandler's thesis that structure follows strategy appears to hold for public organizations as well. For example, police departments adopting community-based policing as a strategy for improving community relations and crime-fighting capabilities generally have found it necessary to adopt less hierarchical, more decentralized and team-based structures.[40] This suggests that strategy, viewed as a contingency factor, mediates among environmental changes, the organization's understanding of its mission, and the structure required to achieve it. It also underscores the fact that structural change does not happen automatically in response to environmental change. In practice, many police departments discovered that the professional model of policing with its paramilitary structure was too entrenched to allow the new strategy to succeed.

Resource Dependence

Organizational structure may be contingent upon the degree to which an organization is dependent on other organizations for the financial, material, and human resources and political support it needs to attain its goals and survive as an institution. The external actors on which government agencies depend include funding bodies, suppliers of human and material resources, client and consumer groups, labor unions, public interest groups, and regulatory and oversight bodies. Because they are dependent on these external actors, agencies often feel compelled to alter their policies, structures, and even their goals to satisfy external demands or to manage their relations with those bodies by forming alliances or partnerships with them or negotiating interagency agreements.

The resource dependency theory of James D. Thompson,[41] and Pfeffer and Salancik,[42] emphasizes how organizations strive to manage their dependence by adapting their structures to satisfy environmental demands or to establish better working relations with those they are dependent upon. In the first instance they create new programs or adjust administrative rules in response to external demands and in the second they create new subunits to protect internal operations from external uncertainties. A public university, for example, may add a personnel office to handle demands from employee groups and labor unions, a recruitment office to ensure a steady supply of new students, a career services office to ensure that graduates find jobs, a legislative liaison office to maintain constructive relations with the legislature, and a research office to communicate with the various granting institutions.

Public Accountability

Finally, organizational structure may be contingent upon the degree to which senior managers are subject to external control or public scrutiny in the conduct of their affairs. Pugh and his colleagues found that businesses whose stocks were traded on the stock exchange were subject to more public scrutiny than firms whose stocks were not, but the highest degree of public scrutiny was experienced by the eight government organizations in their study. The results revealed a clear relationship between public accountability and concentration of authority ($r = 64$). The greater the degree of public accountability the greater the likelihood that authority is centralized at the top of the organization.[43]

Warwick's study of the U.S. State Department also underscored the contingency relationship between external control and structure. Government agencies require the approval of external overseers for operating authority, appropriations, and major changes in mission. This affects structure because, where political and budgetary support from legislative bodies, the chief executive, and the public is uncertain, agencies are more likely to behave in a conservative fashion, adding more clearances, more levels of supervision, and more rules to justify their administrative decisions. As James D. Thompson once noted, bureaucrats are not naturally predisposed to avoid discretion or create rules to hide behind. They do so only where political uncertainty and the consequences for error are unusually high.[44]

AN ASSESSMENT OF STRUCTURAL
CONTINGENCY THEORY

Structural contingency theory brought an end to the dominance of classical management theory and the search for the one best way to structure and manage organizations. Contingency research strongly suggested, for example, that centralized decision making, standardization, and formalization are not always the best structural choices. Some organizations perform effectively when they are highly centralized and tightly controlled, whereas others perform effectively when they are decentralized and loosely controlled. Contingency theory also reinforced the view that organizations are both rational, purposeful systems seeking to achieve established objectives and open systems adapting their goals and structures as needed to function effectively in an uncertain environment. Although organization theory moved in new directions in the 1970s and 1980s, many theorists continue to view structural contingency theory as the central, overarching paradigm in organizational analysis.[45]

If contingency theory brought an end to the dominance of classical management theory, it also renewed interest in the field of organizational design.

Drawing upon the findings of contingency research, scholars such as Jay Galbraith[46] and Henry Mintzberg[47] developed structural principles to guide administrators in designing effective organizations. The central premise of the organizational design school is that managers can and should design their organizations so as to maintain an appropriate fit between task environment, strategy, and structure, thereby assuring continued organizational effectiveness.

Critics, including Pfeffer and Salancik, doubt that this level of rationality is possible. According to their resource dependency theory, actual performance is generally outside of the organization's control. In their view, performance is largely determined by environmental forces and the demands of external actors. Pfeffer and Salancik may have understated management's ability to influence organizational performance, but systems theory nonetheless raises legitimate doubts about management's ability to comprehend organizational dynamics and predict organizational outcomes. The more research has revealed about the determinants of organizational structure and performance, the more complex these relationships appear to be. Although research has generated useful generalizations about the contingencies affecting organizational structure and performance, it may never be possible to develop a model containing enough contingencies to serve as a guide to management decision making.

It may be, as Robert Swinth concluded, that organizations are "exceedingly complex probabilistic systems" that are largely beyond the grasp of human comprehension. If this view is correct, managers can only hope to discern basic patterns of organizational behavior by identifying a few basic variables, manipulating certain ones, and drawing conclusions from the observed results. Nevertheless, the discovery of basic patterns is an important step forward. As James D. Thompson has written, to move organizations forward it is not necessary to understand the relationships among all variables; it is only necessary to tackle the most strategic variables, continually searching to co-align environmental conditions and task and technology with organizational structure and ultimately performance.

RELEVANCE FOR PUBLIC MANAGEMENT

The remainder of this chapter explores the relevance of open systems theory for public management and government performance. This exploration is guided by the three analytical frameworks introduced in Chapter 3.

Models of Organizational Effectiveness

Because it is grounded in systems theory, the open systems perspective recognizes the interconnectedness of all four models of effectiveness in Quinn's competing values framework. From the open systems perspective the effective organization is one that satisfies all of Parsons' functional imperatives in a balanced fashion, depending on the internal and external forces that it faces. Stated differently, it is one that succeeds in achieving a "good fit" internally in terms of relations among formal structures, managerial styles, core technologies, and employee needs and abilities, and externally in relation to the environment. Although the importance of all four models is recognized, the open systems model is highlighted in Exhibit 11.3 because open systems theory emphasizes the relationship between the organization and its external environment, the importance of such effectiveness values as adaptability, resource acquisition, and external support, and the contributions managers make to organizational success by performing the roles of broker and innovator. These roles are accomplished by planning strategically and building political alliances to ensure continued support. By performing these boundary spanning roles public managers can help their agencies continually adapt to their political, social, and economic environments and obtain the resources they need to attain their objectives and survive as an institution.

Exhibit 11.3 The Competing Values Framework: Four Models of Organizational Effectiveness

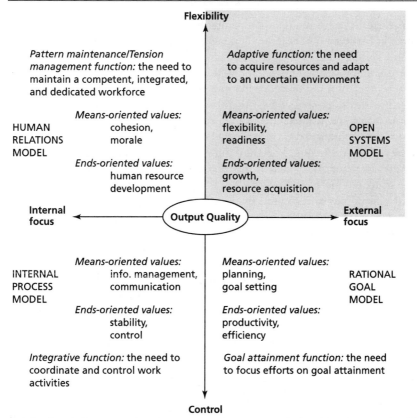

SOURCE: Adapted with permission from Figures 3 and 4, Robert O. Quinn and John Rohrbaugh, "A Spatial Model of Effectiveness Criteria: Towards a Competing Values Approach to Organizational Analysis," *Management Science* 29 (March 1983): 363–373. Copyright 1983, The Institute of Management Sciences, now the Institute for Operations Research and the Management Sciences (INFORMS), 901 Elkridge Landing Road, Suite 400, Linthicum, Maryland 21090-2909 USA.

Although systems theory acknowledges the importance of all four models of effectiveness, the relative emphasis placed on each model varies somewhat from one group of theorists to the next. Trained in social psychology, the sociotechnical theorists at the Tavistock Institute emphasized the organization's internal environment and the interconnectedness between the human relations model and the goal attainment model. Structural contingency theorists such as James D. Thompson, by contrast, tended to emphasize the open systems model and the ways organizations seek both to adjust and adapt to external forces. This theory helps explain why public agencies find it so difficult to operate "like a business." As noted in Chapter 3, public agencies are subject to significantly greater external pressures from interest groups, greater public scrutiny, and greater overhead regulation than are private businesses. By design, public agencies are not given the kind of autonomy and freedom of action that makes unilateral and speedy decision making possible.

Mechanisms for Coordinating and Controlling Work Activities

No particular mechanism for coordinating and controlling work activities is highlighted in Exhibit 11.4 because systems analysis assumes that all such mechanisms or some combination of them must be employed to achieve an optimal fit among the organization's subsystems and between the organization and its external environment. One of the major contributions of open systems theory is that it introduces the idea of contingencies. Sociotechnical theory, for example, holds that organizational effectiveness depends on employing those structural mechanisms that are most appropriate for reconciling the technical requirements of work with the social and psychological needs of those who do the work. Similarly, structural contingency theory holds that organizational effectiveness depends on employing those structural mechanisms that are most appropriate to a full range of contingencies, including organizational strategy, core technology, environmental stability, organization size and, in the case of public agencies, the degree of accountability and oversight imposed by actors in the external environment.

The last of these contingency factors, public accountability, may help to explain the public agency's reputation for being highly centralized. The study by Pugh and his colleagues found, for example, that public agencies do not always rely on work standardization for purposes of coordination and control but they do tend to rely on centralized, top-down systems of control to ensure that those at the middle and lower levels of the agency are performing their duties in a responsible and accountable manner. This does not mean, however, that all agencies are equally centralized. James Q. Wilson notes, for example, that choices regarding the optimal mix of coordination and control mechanisms are also contingent upon the degree to which outputs and outcomes are observable and measurable. As discussed in Chapter 2, work standardization and direct supervision may be appropriate choices in production and procedural agencies but less so in craft and coping agencies, although the need for accountability creates pressures toward centralized control in all public agencies.

Exhibit 11.4 Six Mechanisms for Coordinating and Controlling Work Activities

Mutual adjustment	Workers consult with each other informally about what needs to be accomplished and how. Responsibility for coordination and control rests with those who do the work.
Direct supervision	A supervisor is assigned to take responsibility for a group of workers and a managerial hierarchy is established to integrate the efforts of all work groups. The supervisor issues personal instructions and monitors individual performance.
Standardization of work processes	Work is programmed in advance of its execution by developing rules and standard operating procedures specifying how everyone is to perform assigned tasks. Coordination is built into the work process itself and control is achieved by strictly limiting each worker's discretion.
Standardization of work outputs	Work outputs are programmed in advance by providing each work group with product specifications or performance goals and allowing members considerable latitude in determining how to achieve them. Control is exercised by collecting output data, requiring corrective action when needed, and rewarding and sanctioning workers based on results achieved.
Standardization of worker skills	Workers are employed who possess the knowledge and skills needed to make appropriate decisions. Educational institutions and professional associations are relied upon to provide standardized training. Professionally trained workers are largely self-coordinating and self-controlling.
Standardization of values	Organizational leaders communicate and act upon a clear vision of what the organization exists to do, where it should be headed, and what values should guide it. Coordination and control is facilitated by commitment of organizational members to shared, internalized values and ideals.

SOURCE: Based in large part on Henry Mintzberg, *Structure in Fives* (Prentice-Hall, 1993, 3–7).

Motivational Strategies

No particular motivational strategy is highlighted in Exhibit 11.5 because open systems theory holds that it is management's task to identify the combination of strategies that is most appropriate to the organization's internal and external realities. The sociotechnical school's study of coal mining suggested, for example, that the rewards-for-performance, considerate leadership, group acceptance, and job identification strategies are effective motivational strategies because they satisfy a full range of social, psychological, and material needs, but that the use of these strategies is partly contingent upon the technical requirements of the work and the external pressures faced by the organization. Members of the sociotechnical and organization design schools remain divided, however, regarding the relative effectiveness of these strategies, some emphasizing the importance of social cohesion and autonomy that teamwork can provide (considerate leadership and group acceptance), and some emphasizing the intrinsic rewards derived from the work itself (job identification).

Similarly, structural contingency theory emphasized that choices regarding which motivational strategies to employ are contingent upon many factors, including the skills and maturity levels of employees, the supervisory skills of managers, and the degree of work complexity and professionalism required. Pugh and his colleagues found, for example, that in government agencies characterized by professional kinds of jobs the goal congruence strategy tended to be used more often than the legal compliance strategy, although management attempted to maintain centralized control to ensure accountability in all of the agencies under study.

Exhibit 11.5 Four Motivational Strategies

Legal Compliance

Using rules, formal directives, and sanctions to direct and control employee behavior. Employees may come to work, comply with rules, and satisfy minimum role requirements, either because they accept the legitimacy of organizational authority or fear being sanctioned.

Instrumental Rewards

Using rewards to induce desired behaviors.

Rewards for Performance

Distributing pay, promotions, and recognition based on individual performance. Employees may meet or exceed role expectations because they value the material and psychological satisfactions that money, advancement, and recognition can provide.

Considerate Leadership

Adopting a leadership style based on being attentive to employees and considerate of their needs. This strategy may improve morale. It might also induce those who value the respect, support, and approval of persons in authority to meet or exceed their role requirements.

Group Acceptance

Creating a work environment that allows employees to socialize, form group bonds, and enjoy the approval of their peers. This strategy may induce those who value affiliation and peer approval to meet or exceed role requirements, assuming that group norms are consistent with organizational objectives.

Job Identification

Offering work that is interesting, challenging, and responsible. Employees may come to work, meet or exceed role requirements, and possibly exhibit greater creativity and innovativeness. They may do so because they identify with the jobs and find their work intrinsically rewarding.

Goal Congruence

Hiring employees whose goals and values are congruent with the organization's and/or socializing employees so that they internalize organizational goals and values. Employees may come to work, remain with the organization, meet or exceed role requirements, and exhibit greater creativity, innovativeness, and institutional loyalty. They may do so because they identify with the organization's mission and values and because contributing to them reinforces their own self concept.

SOURCE: Based in large part on Daniel Katz and Robert L. Kahn, *The Social Psychology of Organizations* (Wiley, 1966), pp. 336–68.

SUMMARY

Since the 1930s the systems concept has provided the theoretical foundations and methodological strategies for a rich and diverse set of studies in the field of organization theory. For the most part these studies have been descriptive and explanatory in character rather than prescriptive. Taken as a whole, they provide a more holistic and realistic picture of organizations than the picture provided by earlier studies grounded in the rational perspective. They also underscore the importance of thinking in terms of seamless webs of interdependencies rather than linear cause-and-effect relationships.

Although systems research has increased our knowledge of the relationships among environment, structure, and performance, it has also increased our appreciation of the difficulties inherent in seeking to understand organizational dynamics holistically. A general systems model capable of capturing all important variables and their interrelationships does not yet exist, and if it were to exist it would have to be enormously complex. The quest to understand organizations holistically is a noble one, but in practice it has proven very difficult to draw meaningful conclusions about integrated wholes. Possessed of inadequate measurement tools and insufficient knowledge of system variables, many organizational analysts have returned to the study of specific subsystems about which meaningful conclusions might be drawn.[48]

But if open systems theory has failed thus far to produce a general systems model capable of predicting and controlling organizational behavior, it nonetheless provides public managers with an implicit theory of organizational effectiveness. The successful agency is one that finds an "optimal fit" between its organizational structure, its environment, and what it seeks to achieve. Among the most important implications of this theory for public managers are the following:

- **Contingency thinking.** Public managers should think carefully about the contingencies affecting how they organize for success. They should, for example, think about the nature of their agency's core technology. After all, a document processing technology may call for a very different kind of administrative structure and work organization than does a social service providing technology. Similarly, they should think carefully about their boundary-spanning responsibilities. The dependency theory outlined by James D. Thompson and Pfeffer and Salancik has proven especially germane to public agencies. It reminds public managers of the importance of building coalitions of political support and successfully managing the many dependencies that are a natural and necessary component of operating in highly politicized environments.

- **Strategic planning.** Relatedly, public managers need to learn to think and plan strategically. Through deliberate and thoughtful strategic planning, public managers can engage members of the agency in finding and sustaining a good fit between its mission and strategies, its internal systems and structures, and the forces in its external environment that create both opportunities and threats.

NOTES

1. W. Richard Scott, *Organizations: Rational, Natural, and Open Systems* (Upper Saddle River, NJ: Prentice Hall, 1998), 28.

2. Ludwig von Bertalanffy, *General System Theory: Foundations, Development, Applications* (New York: George Braziller, 1968).

3. Ludwig von Bertalanffy, "General System Theory: A New Approach to Unity of Science," *Human Biology 23* (December 1951): 304.

4. Ludwig von Bertalanffy, "General System Theory," 308.

5. Norbert Wiener, *Cybernetics* (New York: Wiley, 1948).

6. Kenneth E. Boulding, "General Systems Theory—The Skeleton of Science," *Management Science 2* (April 1956): 197–208.

7. Stafford Beer, *Cybernetics and Management* (New York: Wiley, 1964).

8. Robert Swinth, *Organizational Systems for Management: Designing, Planning, and Implementation* (Columbus: Grid, 1974).

9. Daniel Katz and Robert L. Kahn, *The Social Psychology of Organizations* (New York: Wiley, 1966).

10. James D. Thompson, *Organizations in Action* (New York: McGraw-Hill, 1967).

11. Thompson, *Organizations in Action,* 10.

12. Eric Miller, "Editorial: On Reaching the Age of Fifty," *Human Relations 50* (January 1997):1–9.

13. Eric Trist, "The Evolution of Sociotechnical Systems as a Conceptual Framework and as an Action Research Program," in Andrew H. Van de Ven and William F. Joyce (eds.), *Perspectives on Organization Design and Behavior* (New York: Wiley, 1981): 19–75.

14. E. L. Trist, G. W. Higgin, H. Murray, A. B. Pollock, *Organizational Choice: Capabilities of Groups at the Coal Face Under Changing Technologies* (London: Tavistock Publications, 1963).

15. A. K. Rice, *Productivity and Social Organization: The Ahmedabad Experiment* (London: Tavistock Publications, 1958).

16. Reprinted in F. E. Emery and E. L. Trist, *Toward a Social Ecology* (New York: Plenum Publishing, 1973):211–23. Also reprinted in F. E. Emery (ed.), *Systems Thinking: Selected Readings* (Middlesex, England: Penguin Books, 1969).

17. E. L. Trist and K. W. Bamforth, "Some Social and Psychological Consequences of the Longwall Method of Coal-Getting," *Human Relations 4* (February 1951):3–38.

18. Trist et al., *Organizational Choice,* Chapters 12–14.

19. Trist et al., *Organizational Choice,* 143.

20. Trist et al., *Organizational Choice,* xiii.

21. Trist et al., *Organizational Choice,* 130.

22. John E. Kelly, "A Reappraisal of Sociotechnical Systems Theory," *Human Relations 31* (Number 12, 1978):1069–99.

23. Tom Burns and G. M. Stalker, *The Management of Innovation* (London: Tavistock Publications, 1961).

24. Burns and Stalker, *The Management of Innovation,* 97.

25. Tom Burns, "Preface to the Second Edition," in Burns and Stalker, *The Management of Innovation* (London: Tavistock Publications, 1966), viii.

26. Burns and Stalker, *The Management of Innovation,* 1.

27. Burns and Stalker, *The Management of Innovation,* 125.

28. Joan Woodward, *Industrial Organization: Theory and Practice* (London: Oxford University Press, 1965).

29. Woodward, *Industrial Organization,* vi.

30. Woodward, *Industrial Organization,* 71.

31. Paul R. Lawrence and Jay W. Lorch, Organization and Environment: Managing Differentiation and Integration (Homewood, IL: Irwin, 1969); Jay W. Lorsch and Stephen A. Allen, *Managing Diversity and Interdependence: An Organizational Study of Multidivisional Firms* (Cambridge: Harvard University, 1973).

32. Donald P. Warwick, *A Theory of Public Bureaucracy: Politics, Personality, and Organization in the State Department* (Cambridge: Harvard University Press, 1975).

33. D. S. Pugh, D. J. Hickson, C. R. Hinings, and C. Turner, "The Context of Organization Structures," *Administrative Science Quarterly 14* (March 1969): 91–114.

34. David J. Hickson, D. S. Pugh, and Diana C. Pheysey, "Operations Technology and Organization Structure: An Empirical Reappraisal," *Administrative Science Quarterly 14* (September 1969): 378–97.

35. Peter M. Blau and Richard A. Schoenherr, *The Structure of Organizations* (New York: Basic Books, 1971).

36. Blau and Schoenherr, *The Structure of Organizations,* 273.

37. Pugh et. al, "The Context of Organization Structures."

38. Janice M. Beyer and Harrison M. Trice, "A Reexamination of the Relations Between Size and Various Components of Organizational Complexity," *Administrative Science Quarterly 24* (March 1979): 48–64.

39. Alfred D. Chandler, *Strategy and Structure: Chapters in the History of the Industrial Enterprise* (Cambridge: MIT Press, 1962).

40. Dennis P. Rosenbaum (ed.), *The Challenge of Community Policing: Testing the Promises* (Thousand Oaks, CA: Sage, 1994).

41. Thompson, *Organizations in Action.*

42. Jeffrey Pfeffer and Gerald R. Salancik, *The External Control of Organizations: A Resource Dependence Perspective* (New York: Harper & Row, 1978).

43. D .S. Pugh, D. J. Hickson, and C. R. Hinings, "An Empirical Taxonomy of Structures of Work Organizations," *Administrative Science Quarterly 14* (March 1969): 119.

44. Thompson, *Organizations in Action,* 118–20.

45. See, for example, Lex Donaldson, *American Anti-Management Theories of Organization: A Critique of Paradigm Proliferation* (Cambridge: Cambridge University Press, 1995).

46. Jay Galbraith, *Organizational Design* (Reading, MA: Addison-Wesley, 1977).

47. Henry Mintzberg, *Structure in Fives: Designing Effective Organizations* (Englewood Cliffs, NJ: Prentice-Hall, 1983).

48. Fremont Kast and James E. Rosenzweig, "General Systems Theory: Applications for Organization and Management," *Academy of Management Journal 15* (December 1972), 454.

12

⌘

Participative Management Theory

Kurt Lewin and Rensis Likert

At the same time that open systems theorists were focusing attention on organizational technology, structure, and environment, other theorists were continuing to study individual and group behavior. These theorists developed a new approach to management during the 1950s and 1960s that came to be known as human resources theory. The large body of literature they produced is the subject of both this chapter and the next.

Use of the term *human resources theory* was first suggested in 1965 by Raymond E. Miles, a professor of business administration at the University of California, Berkeley.[1] Miles believed the new theory represented a dramatic departure from earlier theories of management, including its predecessor, human relations theory. The distinctive character of human resources theory, according to Miles, is reflected in its core assumptions: that all workers are reservoirs of untapped resources, that they have the capacity to be self-directing and self-controlling, and that organizational performance is determined by how fully the organization develops and utilizes its human resources.

The differences between the two major schools of organizational humanism—human relations and human resources—are perhaps more striking than their similarities. Although both schools view the satisfaction of human needs as the key to organizational success, they differ significantly in terms of what these needs are, how managers are to satisfy them, and why doing so is expected to improve organizational performance. **Human relations theory** calls upon supervisors to satisfy the social and psychological needs of workers by demonstrating personal concern for their well-being, listening attentively to their complaints, and taking their feelings into account when instituting changes. The underlying theory is that facilitating the personal adjustment of employees to their work environment improves job satisfaction and morale and reduces resistance to authority, thereby causing productivity to increase. Emphasis is placed on creating the kind of work environment in which workers feel secure, appreciated, and valued.

By contrast, **human resources theory** calls upon managers at all levels to facilitate the satisfaction of ego and growth needs by providing opportunities for workers to develop and use their individual talents to the fullest extent possible. The underlying theory is that enriching jobs and involving workers in decision making triggers intrinsic motivation. Workers become self-directing and self-controlling, and the full value of human capacity is obtained, thereby enhancing all aspects of organizational performance. Although a supportive work environment and positive interpersonal relations are viewed as important, emphasis is placed on the motivational aspects of the work itself and the benefits that accrue from broad employee involvement in decision making.

Close scrutiny of these differences reveals the chasm that separates the two schools of organizational humanism. Human relations theory accepts the traditional distribution of power and authority within organizations and, despite Mayo's early concern for the destructive effects of organizational structure on human behavior, calls for no meaningful structural reforms. Managers are encouraged to adjust workers to the structural requirements of the organization rather than adjusting organizational structure to satisfy the human needs of their workers. Although there is much of value in human relations theory, in the end it does little more than put a humanistic face on the technical, coldly rational approach to management implicit in scientific management theory and Weber's theory of bureaucracy. Human resources theory, by contrast, rejects the traditional control-oriented approach to management altogether and advocates a fundamental redistribution of power and authority between workers and managers. In doing so it provides the theoretical foundations for today's extensive literature on employee empowerment.

The roots of human resources theory are found in two literatures of the 1930s and 1940s: Elton Mayo's human relations theory and Kurt Lewin's group dynamics theory. With human relations theory already examined in Chapter 8, this chapter begins with an examination of Lewin's group dynamics theory. It then reviews the theoretical contributions of one of the best known human resources theorists, Rensis Likert, leaving for Chapter 13 a review of the works of two other well-known human resources theorists, Douglas McGregor and Chris Argyris. The chapter closes with an analysis of group dynamics and participative management theory for public management and organizational performance.

Kurt Lewin 1890–1947

Kurt Lewin was born September 9, 1890 in a tiny German village in what is now western Poland.[2] In 1914 Lewin finished the requirements for his doctoral degree in experimental psychology, volunteered for the army, and was wounded and hospitalized just before the end of the First World War. After the war Lewin returned to the University of Berlin, where he received an appointment as a private lecturer in 1921. His income was derived solely from student fees. As a Jew he had no chance of becoming a salaried professor, although he was later awarded the honorary title of professor in recognition of his accomplishments.

After Hitler's rise to power, Lewin and his wife and two children emigrated to the United States. He spent the first two years at Cornell University's School of Home Economics, conducting research on child development, before securing a faculty appointment at the University of Iowa's Child Welfare Research Station in 1935. Lewin remained at Iowa until 1944. Students came from all over the United States to study with him, and although he was officially a professor of child psychology his experiments involved a wide range of human problems and social issues.

Consumed by the pressing social issues of the day, including totalitarianism and racial and religious intolerance, Lewin conceived of the possibility of conducting social-science research for the practical purpose of improving organizational and community health. He called it **action research**. Convinced that action research could help solve social problems, Lewin set out to establish a research institute dedicated to conducting change-oriented studies. As a consequence of his fundraising efforts,

Lewin established not one but two research institutes in 1945. The first was the Research Center for Group Dynamics, established at the Massachusetts Institute of Technology (MIT) in Boston. The second was the Commission on Community Interrelations (CCI), funded by the American Jewish Congress and located in New York City. Its primary purpose was to identify the causes of social prejudice and find ways to eliminate them. His staff members at MIT, most of whom were former students from Iowa, helped to design and carry out field research and social experiments at both institutes.

Always enthusiastic about new ideas and strongly committed to social progress, Lewin gave too generously of his time and energy. Having established two research institutes he now found himself commuting continually between Boston and New York City, overseeing dozens of research projects simultaneously. He was also engaged in introducing action research to Eric Trist and his colleagues at the Tavistock Institute in London. When a friend cautioned him to slow down, Lewin reminded him that his mother had died in a Nazi concentration camp and that there was no possibility of him "taking it easy."[3] Exhausted and overworked, Lewin died of a massive heart attack on February 11, 1947 at the age of 56. The following year his students moved the Research Center for Group Dynamics to the University of Michigan, where Lewin's friend Rensis Likert had just established the Survey Research Center. The two groups were merged to form the Institute for Social Research, and together they carried on Lewin's work in group dynamics and organizational leadership.

KURT LEWIN'S STUDIES
IN GROUP DYNAMICS

Fritz Roethlisberger liked to call human resources theory the "1960 version of human relations."[4] However, this tends to overstate the influence of the earlier school of organizational humanism on the later school. Although Elton Mayo certainly influenced their thinking, human resources theorists were influenced much more fundamentally by the ideas and research findings of a German-born experimental psychologist by the name of Kurt Lewin.[5] Understanding the threat Adolph Hitler's rise to power posed for Jews such as himself, Lewin crossed the Atlantic for the United States in 1933, eleven years after Elton Mayo had crossed the Pacific from Australia. Like Mayo before him, Lewin obtained funding from the Laura Spelman Rockefeller Foundation, which allowed him to secure a faculty position at the University of Iowa's Child Welfare Research Station. The experiments conducted by Lewin and his students during his nine-year tenure at the University of Iowa gave rise to a new field of study called *group dynamics* and a new role for social science called *action research*.

As a lecturer at the University of Berlin in the 1920s, Lewin took it upon himself to steer experimental psychology away from the traditional emphasis on memory and cognition and beyond the Gestaltists' limited focus on perception. Believing psychology should focus on explaining human motivation and behavior, Lewin developed what he called **field theory**.[6] Lewin argued that the motivated behavior of an individual can be understood in terms of a sociopsychological field, much like an electrical or gravitational field, in which various forces, including needs and desires, work to pull the individual in different directions. Motivated behavior is the net outcome of these opposing forces, forces arising from both the person and the environment in which the person is embedded. He also developed the concept of tension, the internal state created when an individual feels a need or a desire. Tension creates the energy behind mental activity and motivation, and it is not released until the motive is satisfied. An experiment conducted by one of Lewin's students found that individuals will return to an unfinished task or goal at a later time because of the continuing psychic tension associated with having left something undone. Finally, his theory introduced the concept of valence, which refers to the strength or importance attached to a need or desire by a particular individual.

Lewin and his students at the University of Berlin conducted several experiments during the 1920s designed to establish the relevance and power of his theory. Goal theory and expectancy theory had their origins in these experiments as well as the ones he conducted after his arrival at the University of Iowa in 1935. The sections that follow describe a series of studies by Lewin and his students at Iowa that was of particular importance to the development of human resources theory.

Studies in Autocratic and Democratic Leadership

At Iowa Lewin turned his attention to the conditions necessary to sustain democracy. A series of studies dealing with autocratic and democratic leadership in small groups began with an experiment conducted in 1937 by Ronald Lippitt under Lewin's supervision.[7] Wishing to isolate the effects of autocratic and democratic social climates on group behavior, Lippitt divided ten fifth-graders into two groups. He engaged each group in a series of recreational activities, including mask making and soap carving. Each group met for 30 minutes during the lunch hour, twice a week, for eleven sessions. In the group that met on Mondays and Wednesdays, Lippitt adopted the role of a democratic leader, encouraging the group to discuss and vote on the projects they wished to undertake. In the group that met on Tuesdays and Thursdays, Lippitt adopted the role of an autocratic leader, assigning without discussion projects selected the day before by the democratic group, and specifying which members would undertake each task and how the tasks would be performed. Four observers unobtrusively recorded all social interactions and a stenographer recorded as much of the students' conversations as possible.

In performing his two roles, Lippitt followed carefully defined models of democratic and autocratic leadership constructed in advance of the experiment. As a democratic leader he explained what kinds of things the group would do in subsequent meetings, so that students understood their goals and what to expect next. He also encouraged students to discuss and vote on what projects to undertake, provided various choices when students asked for help, left students free to work with whomever they wished, provided fact-based reasons when distributing praise or criticism, and tried to participate as an equal in group activities without doing too much of the work. This model emphasized low leadership control over means and ends and high emphasis on stimulating group decision making.

As an autocratic leader, by contrast, Lippitt made all policy decisions for the group without clarifying purposes or allowing discussion, dictated what was to be done one step at a time and without indicating what to expect next, dictated who was to work with whom in completing assigned tasks, distributed praise and criticism in a personalized manner without indicating what his judgments were based on, and remained aloof from active group participation. This model emphasized high leadership control over means and ends and low stimulation of group decision making. Although directive in his approach, Lippitt was careful not to be mean or to evoke fear, both because treating students in this way would be unethical and because he wanted to hold the degree of friendliness constant between the two groups.

The differences in behavior between the two groups were dramatic. Students in the autocratic group were passive and leader-dependent in relation to their work. They waited for instructions before beginning to work and they ceased working when the leader left the room. Members of the autocratic group also exhibited much higher levels of aggressive behavior, including more quarreling, more demands for personal attention, and more hostile criticisms aimed at other group members. On two occasions they engaged in scapegoating by taking their frustrations out on the most powerful member of the group. Faced with the collective hostility of their peers, the two scapegoats quit coming to meetings. Members of the democratic group, by contrast, were much more likely to remain engaged in work when the leader left the room and worked together in a generally friendly and cooperative manner.

What explained these differences? Lippitt concluded that students in the autocratic group experienced frustrations arising from two factors: a reduced sense of power and status caused by being constantly told what to do, and a blockage of paths to personal goal attainment caused when the leader ignored their desires and substituted his goals for theirs. These factors reduced the students' satisfaction with their otherwise-interesting work activities and increased their sense of frustration. As they focused on their frustrations, the goal of restoring their lost status became primary and the goal of working together to complete their projects became secondary. As White and Lippitt later put it, "Basically, it is a simple matter of the direction of attention. If the attention of group members is focused mainly on where they stand as individuals, it cannot be focused mainly on the goals of the group."[8] Attacking each other seemed to be the only means of asserting power and enhancing status, and the resulting hostile and ego-centered behaviors greatly limited the possibilities for group cooperation. By contrast, the greater equality of status in the democratic group, and the freedom extended to students to pursue their own goals, resulted in more cooperative and friendly interpersonal relations. Feeling secure and efficacious, students in the democratic group felt no need to compete for power or status and willingly contributed their individuality to the group effort.

The following semester Ralph White arrived at Iowa on a postdoctoral fellowship and, together with Lewin and Lippitt, conducted a more extensive and rigorous experiment in 1938.[9] Because the differences observed in the first experiment may have been due to differences in the personalities of those who participated in the study, the second experiment was designed to control for personality by exposing each group to more than one type of leadership. Four groups were established and each group was exposed to a different combination of leadership patterns during three periods lasting six weeks each. Four leaders were used rather than one, with each performing more than one role to control for individual personality differences among the leaders.

The original intent was to alter the order of democratic and autocratic leadership for each of the groups, but when one of the four leaders failed to perform the democratic role as intended, a third type of leadership was defined. It was labeled *laissez-faire* or *hands-off leadership*. Following the newly defined model the laissez-faire leaders left the students completely free to choose which projects to work on, how to complete them, and with whom to work. Leaders provided technical assistance when asked for help but did not attempt to structure activities or participate in carrying them out. Unlike the democratic leader, the laissez-faire leader made no attempt to teach or stimulate democratic procedures such as group discussion or voting.

In terms of sequencing, the first group was exposed to autocracy, democracy, autocracy; the second to autocracy, laissez-faire, democracy; the third to democracy, autocracy, democracy; and the fourth to laissez-faire, autocracy, democracy. The groups, this time comprising only boys, were set up as crime-solving clubs, although they engaged in a variety of other activities as well, including constructing club benches and tables, making masks, painting murals, and carving objects out of soap. They met for an hour after school, once each week, for eighteen weeks.

The results of the second experiment were similar to those of the first, with two notable exceptions. First, three of the four groups experiencing autocracy responded with a high degree of submissiveness to authority and a low degree of aggressiveness toward their fellow members. In fact, incidences of overt aggressiveness, such as rude or hostile comments or insistent demands for attention, were actually lower in these groups than in the democratic groups. Conversely, one of the four groups, like the autocratic group in the first experiment, responded with a high degree of aggression. Lewin, Lippitt, and White concluded that autocracy can result in either submissive or rebellious reactions depending on the unique conditions and personalities involved. The Charlie Chan Club included three members who were unusually resistant to authority and unconstrained by adult values. This was not the case in the other groups, where members allowed themselves to be repressed by their autocratic leaders. Lewin, Lippitt, and White concluded that these students experienced high levels of frustration arising from their repressed state but chose to limit their reactions to a few hostile comments aimed primarily at each other. That there was a great deal of latent discontent just below the surface was indicated by the fact that three boys dropped out of their clubs under submissive autocracy because of their dissatisfaction with the prevailing social climate.

Another difference between the two studies was that the second provided a great deal of information about the effects of an unstructured work situation and laissez-faire leadership on group behavior. The data showed that the students' work in the laissez-faire groups was less organized, less efficient, and definitely less satisfying than under either of the other two leadership patterns. Frustrations associated with lack of structure, purpose, and accomplishment led to a loss of interest in their work and a high degree of horseplay and aggressiveness toward each other. Given the negative connotations attached to the term *autocracy*, the researchers were surprised to find that autocratic leadership seemed to offer more personal satisfactions than laissez-faire. Among the satisfactions that autocratic leadership has to offer are those associated with not having to think or take on responsibility, identifying with a strong leader, and taking pride in efficient task accomplishment.[10] These results suggested to Lewin, Lippitt, and White that those who think of laissez-faire leadership as simply a permissive form of democratic leadership are mistaken. It is a distinct leadership pattern with a distinct set of disadvantages.

Although these studies dealt with young students engaged in recreational activities rather than adult employees engaged in producing goods and services, many of the major themes in human resources theory are reflected in these early experiments. Among them are the following:

1. Autocratic leadership places employees in a dependent relationship, thereby encouraging passivity and undermining initiative, commitment, and personal responsibility.
2. Autocratic leadership minimizes the power and status of employees, thereby encouraging harmful competition and undermining cooperation.
3. All things being equal, democratic leadership can better satisfy basic human needs, thereby fostering job satisfaction and work motivation.
4. Leaders can facilitate the satisfaction of human needs by relying on formal authority as little as possible, encouraging self-direction and self-control, relating to employees in an egalitarian, nonhierarchical manner, involving them as much as practical in decision making, giving them the freedom they need to develop and utilize their individual talents, and establishing appropriate structures and boundaries to guide task accomplishment.

Although Lewin, Lippitt, and White did not address the subject directly, the findings of these early experiments raised serious questions about the top-down, control-oriented form of management that then prevailed in most complex organizations. Their findings seemed to suggest that managers who emphasize their place in the organizational hierarchy, who insist on all the privileges and prerogatives of power, and who use their formal authority to issue directives without providing explanations and without regard to the needs, goals, and wants of their subordinates, are practicing autocracy and must accept all of the limitations and dysfunctional consequences associated with it.

Action Research in Industry

Although his research rarely allowed him to explore issues relating to work, Lewin nonetheless maintained a lifelong interest in what he called **job satisfaction.** The title of one of his earliest works, an article published in 1920, is roughly translated as "Humanization of the Taylor System: An Inquiry into the Fundamental Psychology of Work and Vocation."[11] In it Lewin faulted Taylorism for failing to appreciate the importance of work to the satisfaction of human needs.[12] He argued that work is an important "life value," that the capacity for work gives meaning and substance to a person's whole existence, and that the flaw in Taylorism is that it shows no concern for whether the person performing the work obtains any personal satisfaction from doing so. It does little good to prescribe how to perform tasks more efficiently, Lewin argued, if the resulting overspecialization and monotony reduces the value of the work to the worker. In language foreshadowing the concept of job enrichment, Lewin wrote that work should be worth doing and should develop personal potential, not limit it. Lewin envisioned psychologists and efficiency experts working together to make work not only more efficient but also richer and more satisfying for the person performing it. Indeed, Lewin believed that job satisfaction and productivity are intertwined. The worker who obtains internal or intrinsic value from the work shows greater interest in and enthusiasm for the work and, consequently, performs it at a higher level. As we shall see, the notion of integrating individual and organizational needs through job enrichment would become a major theme in human resources theory.

A fortuitous set of circumstances allowed Lewin to return to the subject of job satisfaction some nineteen years later. An acquaintance and fellow psychologist, Alfred J. Marrow, happened to be president of the Harwood Manufacturing Corporation, a company that was having a tough time maintaining production standards at a new pajama factory in Marion, Virginia. After the usual 12 weeks of training, the workers from this rural and mountainous area were producing only about half as much as trainees doing similar tasks in northern factories.[13] Marrow invited Lewin to the plant in 1939 to investigate the problem. The result was a series of experiments spanning eight years. Because they took place in a factory setting rather than a laboratory, and because they used social-science methods to achieve constructive changes in morale and productivity, these experiments were among the first examples of what Lewin called action research.

Why productivity was low and turnover high at the factory was a bit of a mystery. The pay was relatively good, personnel policies progressive, and labor relations and working conditions favorable. Consistent with his humanistic orientation, Lewin viewed the problem as human rather than technical in nature. He concluded that the workers did not believe that the mandated 60 units of production per hour was attainable and thus felt no sense of personal failure in not reaching that goal. Lewin suggested hiring experienced workers laid off at a nearby factory to demonstrate that the standard was in fact attainable. The experienced workers soon met the standard and the local trainees, seeing that it was attainable, gradually began to reach it as well. Lewin next suggested that the company begin a program of industrial research and employ Alex Bavelas, one of his students at Iowa, to undertake a series of small-group studies relating to the human factors in industrial management.

The first of these experiments focused on involving employees in setting their own production goals. In one experiment, Bavelas encouraged a group of high-producing workers to discuss the barriers to increased production, consider how to overcome these barriers, and set an appropriate production goal. This group ultimately increased production from 75 to 90 units per hour and maintained it for 5 months. Lewin concluded that a person's decision to pursue a goal links motivation to action. Simply discussing how to achieve a higher level of performance has little effect. It is the commitment to self and to the work group that leads to greater work effort.

In another early experiment a small group of workers was allowed to manage their own hourly and daily work levels through the use of pace cards. They could set whatever hourly goals they wished as long as the daily standard they set for themselves was reached. This group increased its production from 67 units to 82 units per hour. In this instance, Lewin concluded that the combination of self-management in setting goals and the use of the pacing cards removed much of the tension associated with close supervision and thus strengthened the field forces favoring higher production relative to those favoring lower production.

Bavelas was succeeded at the Harwood company by John R. P. French, another of Lewin's students. Together with Lester Coch, the company's personnel manager, French conducted a series of experiments designed to overcome the resistance to change experienced by workers who were asked to switch to different jobs or to perform their current jobs differently.[14] To remain competitive the company frequently had to alter the way tasks were performed. As noted earlier, trainees had to work hard to learn their jobs and achieve the mandated 60 units of production. Once they were successful, they became resentful at being asked to learn a new job and frustrated in their new efforts to achieve standard production levels. Their resistance was expressed through grievances over the new piecerates, high turnover, low efficiency, deliberate restrictions of output, and marked aggression toward supervisors. French and Coch understood that the problem related to motivation and morale rather than skill. Motivation and morale declined as group members experienced frustration, loss of hope of ever regaining their former level of productivity, and feelings of personal failure and lowered status. For these reasons, workers took longer to reach standard in their second job than in their first, and many gave up and either quit or became chronically substandard performers. What they lacked was a clear path to success.

French and Coch turned to group participation as a means of overcoming resistance. Their experiments were begun in the fall of 1947, a few months after Lewin had died. The research design called for introducing changes in the jobs in three different ways, each representing a different level of participation in redesigning the job and setting appropriate piecerates. Four groups of employees whose jobs were being changed participated in the experiment: a control group, a group experiencing partial participation, and two groups experiencing full participation. The eighteen members of the control group, who were being asked to stack pressed garments in a box rather than on a sheet of cardboard as before, were introduced to their new job in the usual way. A meeting was held, the economic reasons the job had to be changed were provided, the new piecerates were explained, the workers were allowed to ask questions, and the meeting was adjourned. By contrast, the thirteen members of the partial participation group were given a lengthy presentation demonstrating falling prices and the necessity of reducing costs by folding pants in addition to folding coats as they had done in the past. Then they were asked to choose representatives to participate in redesigning the job, setting more stringent piecerates, and training their fellow members to perform the redesigned job. Finally, two small groups of pajama inspectors engaged in full participation. Rather than choosing representatives, all group members participated in redesigning the job and helping the efficiency expert set new piecerates. The members made suggestions "in such quantity that the stenographer had difficulty in recording them."[15]

The differences in outcomes among the groups were dramatic. Members of the control group never returned to their former level of 60 units per hour, choosing instead to restrict output to 50 units per hour. They also expressed considerable hostility toward management and suffered a 17 percent quit rate in the first 40 days. Members of the partial participation group returned to their former level of efficiency within 14 days with no expression of hostility and with no one quitting. Finally, members of the full participation groups returned to their former level of productivity in just a few days and then maintained a productivity rate 14 percent above their former level and without suffering any dropouts. As a final check, the control group was broken up and scattered throughout the plant for nearly 3 months and then brought back together to learn a new job under the full participation method. They quickly learned their new job and achieved a level of productivity much higher than their previous level.

The results of this experiment indicated that participation produces higher morale and motivation and lower turnover and that the rate of learning a new job is directly proportional to the amount of participation. Consistent with Lewin's field theory, Coch and French concluded that participation in planning the required changes altered the forces tending to push productivity upward and downward. Group participation apparently led the workers to believe that returning to 60 units per hour was possible (a reduction in downward forces experienced previously in the form of hopelessness), and to feel no need to restrict output or defy management (a reduction in downward forces experienced previously in the form of resentment over lost power and status). In addition, the opportunity to set their own goals caused them to take personal ownership of the higher aspirations that they had set for themselves (a new upward force). The importance of engendering feelings of personal ownership would later become a key theme in human resources theory and the larger emphasis on group decision making would come to be known as *participative management.*

One other experiment conducted at Harwood greatly influenced human resources theory. Bavelas had once told Lewin that it would be an easy matter to train people to be more democratic. Lewin pressed him to sketch out how he would do so. Later, after French had taken over Bavelas' work at Harwood, Lewin discussed with French the idea of setting up a new program of leadership training in which all levels of supervisors would participate. Role playing, sociodrama, problem solving, exercises in self-examination, and other techniques of active learning were to be used. The overall purpose of French's subsequent experiment in leadership training "was to equip the supervisors with more effective methods of winning cooperation, building trust, improving morale, and handling the disciplinary problems of their subordinates."[16] The success of this experiment led Lewin to help develop a leadership training program at the request of the Connecticut State Inter-Racial Commission.[17] This program led in turn to the creation of the National Training Laboratories (NTL). French employed many of his techniques at the first session of the NTL in Bethel, Maine, in 1947. These early sessions at Bethel led to the development of *sensitivity training,* a type of leadership training adopted by many employers in the 1950s and 1960s.

LEWIN'S CONTRIBUTIONS TO ORGANIZATION THEORY

Although Kurt Lewin was not himself an organization theorist, his ideas and research findings had a profound impact on the newly emerging field of organizational behavior. His experiments in group dynamics drew other scholars to the study of leadership, team building, and interpersonal competence. His commitment to action research sparked interest in organization development, a field of research and practice that encourages social scientists to serve as change agents by diagnosing organizational ills and intervening to restore organizational health. His concept of leadership training, with its emphasis on open communication, self-awareness, and active learning, led to the establishment of the National Training Laboratories Institute, which continues to operate today, more than 50 years after it was founded. Finally, as we shall see, his research findings and humanistic ideals greatly influenced a new generation of human resources theorists, including Rensis Likert, Chris Argyris, and Douglas McGregor.

RENSIS LIKERT'S THEORY OF PARTICIPATIVE MANAGEMENT

Rensis Likert, a personal friend of Lewin, accepted the challenge of carrying on Lewin's research in group dynamics. In contrast to the human resources theorists discussed in the next chapter, Likert took a more deductive approach to theory building. Whereas Argyris and McGregor derived many of their ideas by reasoning inductively from existing theories of personality and human motivation, Likert developed his ideas primarily from empirical research. Unconstrained by any particular theory, Likert drew upon a wide range of ideas to make sense of the results of studies he conducted with his colleagues at the Institute for Social Research. Second, his contributions were narrower in scope than those of either Argyris or McGregor. As a consequence of carrying on Lewin's research in group dynamics, Likert focused almost exclusively on the study of alternative systems of leadership. Finally, Likert's conclusions were considerably more prescriptive. He believed that "a new pattern of management" had emerged in recent years and he strongly endorsed that pattern as the best means of creating and sustaining high-performance organizations. Argryis and McGregor, by contrast, were much more reluctant to prescribe any one-best-way of organizing and managing.

Likert is best known for identifying four distinct types of management systems. He conceived of these systems, which he labeled exploitative authoritative, benevolent authoritative, consultative, and participative group, as lying at fixed intervals along the autocracy-democracy continuum first identified by Lewin, Lippitt, and White. Likert viewed these systems not as conceptual categories but as actual patterns of management defined by seven interrelated variables, including the motivational forces employed by management, the character of communications,

---

Rensis Likert 1903–1981

Rensis Likert was born on August 5, 1903 in Cheyenne, Wyoming. He received his bachelor's degree at the University of Michigan in 1926 and his doctoral degree at Columbia University in 1932. Likert's particular area of expertise in psychology was the statistical measurement of social attitudes. In a monograph published in 1932 he introduced the five-point Likert scale, which continues to be widely used in survey research today.[18] After graduating from Columbia University, Likert taught at New York University for a few years before moving to Washington, D.C., to work for the federal government. His government service included stints as head of the Department of Agriculture's Division of Program Surveys and chief of the morale division of the United States Strategic Bombing Survey. During the war years he served with Kurt Lewin on an advisory committee to the Office of Naval Research. In 1944 he arranged a meeting between Lewin and Douglas McGregor to discuss plans for establishing the Research Center for Group Dynamics at MIT.[19] In 1946 Likert and his colleagues established the Survey Research Center at the University of Michigan. When Lewin died the following year, Likert arranged to move the Research Center for Group Dynamics to Michigan. The two centers were merged to form the Institute for Social Research. Much of the research conducted by the Institute carried on Lewin's work on leadership, motivation, and group decision making. Studies were conducted by an impressive team of researchers, including Dorwin Cartwright, Daniel Katz, Robert Kahn, Stanley Seashore, Alvin Zander, and Arnold Tannenbaum. Likert continued to serve as the institute's director and as professor of psychology and sociology until his retirement from the university in 1971. He then established a management consulting firm and continued to work as a researcher and consultant until his death on September 3, 1981.

---

and the methods of decision making and supervision.[20] Because each represents a distinct pattern, a manager who is autocratic and nonparticipatory in respect to one variable tends to be so in respect to the other variables as well.

Likert and his colleagues used these variables to develop a survey instrument for diagnosing organizational health, one version of which is shown in Exhibit 12.1. In one organization after another they administered the survey to employees and used the results to determine both the current pattern of management and the relationship between each unit's management pattern and its level of productivity. Likert concluded from these studies that the participative group pattern, or what he called more neutrally System 4, is clearly superior in its ability to create and sustain high levels of productivity. It is a system that calls on workers at all levels to participate in setting goals, making decisions, and solving problems. While acknowledging that participatory methods require emotionally and socially mature personalities, Likert concluded that one of the distinctive advantages of group decision making is that it can, by involving everyone in decision making, help develop emotionally and socially mature persons capable of effective interaction, initiative, and leadership.

Likert's research findings and theoretical conclusions are discussed in two key books, *New Patterns of Management* (1961) and *The Human Organization*

Exhibit 12.1 Profile of Organizational Characteristics

Organizational variables	System 1	System 2	System 3	System 4	Item no.
How much confidence and trust is shown in subordinates?	Virtually none	Some	Substantial amount	A great deal	1
How free do they feel to talk to superiors about job?	Not very free	Somewhat free	Quite free	Very free	2
How often are subordinates' ideas sought and used constructively?	Seldom	Sometimes	Often	Very frequently	3
Is predominant use made of 1 fear, 2 threats, 3 punishment, 4 rewards, 5 involvement?	1, 2, 3, occasionally 4	4, some 3	4, some 3 and 5	5, 4, based on group	4
Where is responsibility felt for achieving organization's goals?	Mostly at top	Top and middle	Fairly general	At all levels	5
How much cooperative teamwork exists?	Very little	Relatively little	Moderate amount	Great deal	6
What is the usual direction of information flow?	Downward	Mostly downward	Down and up	Down, up, and sideways	7
How is downward communication accepted?	With suspicion	Possibly with suspicion	With caution	With a receptive mind	8
How accurate is upward communication?	Usually inaccurate	Often inaccurate	Often accurate	Almost always accurate	9
How well do superiors know problems faced by subordinates?	Not very well	Rather well	Quite well	Very well	10
At what level are decisions made?	Mostly at top	Policy at top, some delegation	Broad policy at top, more delegation	Throughout but well integrated	11
Are subordinates involved in decisions related to their work?	Almost never	Occasionally consulted	Generally consulted	Fully involved	12
What does decision-making process contribute to motivation?	Not very much	Relatively little	Some contribution	Substantial contribution	13
How are organizational goals established?	Orders issued	Orders, some comments invited	After discussion, by orders	By group action (except in crisis)	14
How much covert resistance to goals is present?	Strong resistance	Moderate resistance	Some resistance at times	Little or none	15
How concentrated are review and control functions?	Very highly at top	Quite highly at top	Moderate delegation to lower levels	Widely shared	16
Is there an informal organization resisting the formal one?	Yes	Usually	Sometimes	No – same goals as formal	17
What are the cost, productivity, and other control data used for?	Policing, punishment	Reward and punishment	Reward, some self-guidance	Self-guidance, problem-solving	18

SOURCE: Modified from Appendix II in *The Human Organization: Its Management and Value* by Rensis Likert. Copyright © 1967 by McGraw-Hill, Inc. Reproduced with permission of The McGraw-Hill Companies.

(1967). In these books, System 4's superiority is attributed to three interrelated aspects of leadership: establishing supportive relationships, using group methods of decision making and supervision, and setting high performance goals. Likert viewed these aspects of leadership as causal variables. They affect important intervening variables, such as morale, loyalty, and cooperativeness, which in turn affect important outcome variables such as profits, turnover, and service quality. In taking this view, Likert broke ranks with the human relations theorists. He argued that it makes no sense to try to influence employee morale, loyalty, or cooperativeness without first altering the three causal variables that ultimately determine organizational performance. As he put it, " . . . while employees may like the place—much as they would like a country club—the conversion of favorable attitudes into high productivity depends on how well supervisors, managers, and the line organization perform their leadership tasks."[21]

These three elements—supportive relations, group decision making, and high performance goals—comprise Likert's theory of participative management. It is, in essence, a theory of organizational effectiveness. As discussed in the sections that follow, it holds that high productivity is achieved when managers succeed in creating tightly knit social systems comprising interlocking work groups.

The Principle of Supportive Relationships

The first element in Likert's theory of participative management is success in establishing supportive workplace relationships. According to Likert, relationships are supportive "when the individual involved sees the experience (in terms of his values, goals, expectations, and aspirations) as contributing to or maintaining his sense of personal worth and importance."[22] In language reminiscent of Mayo and Roethlisberger's discussion of considerate leadership, Likert argues that managers must get to know their employees as individuals, demonstrate genuine interest in their well-being and success as employees, and accord them trust and respect. This employee-centered approach to supervision stands in contrast to the traditional job-centered approach that relies on pressure tactics, close supervision, and threat of punishment. In practice, being supportive means exercising general rather than close supervision, allowing workers to learn from their mistakes without reinforcing their lessons with sanctions, ensuring that they are well-trained, and defending them to higher authorities when they raise legitimate concerns.

Likert's conclusion that a supportive, employee-centered style of supervision is an essential determinant of organizational performance was based largely on the findings of studies conducted by the Institute for Social Research. He wrote in 1958, for example, that research findings "demonstrate that, on the average, pressure-oriented, threatening, punitive management yields lower productivity, higher costs, increased absence, and less employee satisfaction than supportive, employee-centered management."[23] As the Hawthorne researchers discovered, the way reality is perceived by workers is what matters most. Likert made much of this lesson. The attitudes of workers are likely to be more positive and their level of performance higher, he concluded, if their workplace experiences are perceived as ego-building rather than ego-deflating.[24]

Group Decision Making

The second element in Likert's theory of participative management is group-based supervision and decision making. Managers operating under traditional management systems, according to Likert, make decisions unilaterally and supervise workers individually through "one-to-one" interactions. Under System 4, by contrast, managers involve all members of the work group in making decisions and exercise supervision over the group as a whole. Whether a group comprises the members of a work unit or individuals brought together from various levels and functional areas, its members are invited to participate in solving work-related problems and making the decisions that affect them as employees. They may be invited, for example, to participate in setting goals and budgets, controlling costs, organizing the work, or discussing any number of ways to improve organizational performance. Under group-based supervision, collective self-control reduces the need for hierarchical control and group decisions generally replace individual directives.

This highly participatory approach to management is very different from the traditional approach. Among other things, it requires supervisors at all levels to be highly skilled in group dynamics. They must be able to build trust, encourage open communications, create a sense of collective responsibility, integrate disparate individuals into a cohesive team, and facilitate group decision making even when the required solutions seem obvious to them. And they must apply these skills while limiting their use of formal authority and de-emphasizing their hierarchical status.

Likert acknowledged that situations often arise when there is no time for group discussion and consensus building, and in such situations the supervisor will have to make decisions unilaterally. Nonetheless, he advocated using the participatory approach whenever possible because he believed research had demonstrated its clear advantages. Studies undertaken by the Institute for Social Research led him to conclude that "Managers who have a supportive attitude toward their men and endeavor to build them into well-knit groups obtain appreciably higher productivity than managers who have a threatening attitude and rely more on man-to-man patterns of supervision."[25]

What explains the apparent superiority of group methods? Likert believed that teamwork produces a unique synergy that creates enthusiasm for the collective task and keeps members focused on attaining their shared objectives. This occurs because participation taps the full spectrum of economic and noneconomic motives. First, group members are motivated by economic rewards when pay bonuses are distributed based on the performance of the group as a whole. Likert cited as an example the effectiveness of the revenue sharing component of the Scanlon Plan that was widely adopted in the 1960s.

Second, members receive external, noneconomic rewards in the form of social recognition and support from other members of the group. Likert believed that "most persons are highly motivated to behave in ways consistent with the goals and values of their work group in order to obtain recognition, support, security, and favorable reactions from this group."[26] Consequently, he attached great importance to social needs and the power of groups to satisfy them. As demonstrated in the relay assembly room test at the Hawthorne plant, teamwork creates social cohesion, comradery, and group loyalty. Once these conditions are created, team members are motivated to do their part in helping to achieve agreed-upon objectives. This results both from a sense of belongingness and a desire not to let the team down. Likert used the term *peer-group loyalty* in referring to this source of motivation. In his words, "the greater the loyalty of the members of a group toward the group, the greater is the motivation among the members to achieve the goals of the group, and the greater is the probability that the group will achieve its goals."[27]

Third, members derive intrinsic rewards as they take pride in their accomplishments and satisfaction in knowing that they are contributing to the attainment of organizational objectives. Here Likert emphasizes the ego needs as a source of motivation. Group decision making enables employees to increase their sense of self-worth as they develop new abilities, express their unique talents, and contribute to the success of the group. In addition to providing ego satisfactions, these intrinsic rewards also enhance each member's commitment to group goals. As Likert put it, "Since the goals of the group are arrived at through group decisions, each individual group member tends to have a high level of ego identification with the goals because of his involvement in the decisions."[28] According to Likert, group members experience a sense of ownership in decisions they help make and are more willing to make personal sacrifices on behalf of the group and the organization as a whole. It is interesting to note, however, that Likert emphasizes the importance of the intrinsic rewards inherent in group decision making but not those associated with the work itself. In contrast to Argyris and McGregor, Likert seems to suggest that work need not be interesting and challenging as long as workers are able to take pride in knowing that they are making important contributions to organizational objectives.

Thus it is the combination of motivational factors inherent in teamwork—economic and noneconomic, extrinsic and intrinsic—that explains the power of groups as a means of developing and mobilizing human resources. As the principle of supportive relationships is adopted, Likert wrote, "the full power from each of the available motives will be added to that from the others to yield a maximum of coordinated, enthusiastic effort."[29] Stated differently, teamwork is a powerful vehicle for mobilizing human potential because it offers an experience that is viewed by workers as both supportive and need-fulfilling.

There is one more thing that management can do, according to Likert, to ensure that their organizations gain full benefit from group decision making. It can adopt the **overlapping group form of organization.** This involves creating an interlocking system of work groups in which the "supervisor" of a work group at one organizational level also participates as a "subordinate" in another group at the next higher level. Likert referred to the individuals who hold these overlapping group memberships as "linking pins." Although these groups are normally permanent line or staff work groups, they can also be ad hoc committees or cross-functional, problem solving teams comprising members from various levels and functional areas.

Likert's concept of multiple, interlocking work groups holds considerable theoretical significance because it offers an alternative form of coordination to the traditional chain of command. Although the distribution of groups across several levels of authority still adheres to the scalar principle, communications and human interactions are no longer tied solely to one-on-one relationships between superiors and subordinates. Because of the interlocking nature of these groups, those at lower levels can communicate concerns upward and thus influence the decisions of those at higher levels. Citing a study by Pelz, Likert noted that morale and motivation are highest in units in which managers are perceived as being effective in exerting influence upward to protect and promote the interests of the work unit. Upward communication also allows top managers to obtain the accurate and relevant information they need to make effective decisions.

Coordination is also enhanced by involving greater numbers of people in collective problem solving. As different concerns and institutional perspectives are voiced at group meetings, participants are able to develop a more global, less parochial understanding of key issues and institutional concerns. They are also better positioned to resolve interunit conflicts. For example, if the decisions of two groups are conflicting or incompatible, the linking pins can bring these discrepancies to the attention of both groups and conflicts can be discussed and resolved. Members of each group can learn how their actions may be adversely affecting the performance of other groups and can take corrective action as needed. In short, a system of interlocking work groups facilitates coordination by breaking down the insular and bureaucratic character of highly functionalized organizations.

High Performance Goals

Likert did not write at great length about the third element in his theory of participative management. He simply noted that high performance goals, like supportiveness and group involvement, correlated highly with productivity in studies conducted by the Institute for Social Research. A study of forty sales offices by Bowers and Seashore, for example, revealed a statistically significant relationship between high productivity and high performance goals. But high performance goals alone was not the causal factor. Productivity was high only in those units where managers also established supportive relationships and supervised through group methods. Rather than imposing goals and putting unreasonable pressure on the sales staff to produce, the most successful managers communicated their own high aspirations and encouraged staff members to set high goals for themselves. Although the reasons for the success of this approach were not entirely clear, Likert speculated that the members of the sales staff, rather than resenting being pressured to perform, felt encouraged and supported in determining their own goals and engaged in mutual coaching, training, and encouragement as a result. These findings helped bolster Likert's contention that his theory of participative management, as reflected in System 4, is integrative in nature. All three elements—supportiveness, group involvement, and high aspirations—must be present if high performance levels are to be achieved.

LIKERT'S CONTRIBUTIONS TO ORGANIZATION THEORY

Likert's theory of participative management represents an interesting and useful synthesis of human relations and human resources theory. His research findings support the human relations view that employee-centered supervision and group loyalty are important sources of motivation. His findings also support the human resources view that participation in group decision making and high performance goals are important motivators. Although he attached little importance to the concept of self-actualization or the practice of job enrichment (see Chapter 13), he did emphasize the importance of building human capacity, a key theme in human resources theory. He encouraged organizations to measure intervening variables such as morale, commitment, and peer-group loyalty because they are important indicators of organizational health and ultimately organizational performance. Whereas Systems 1 and 2 can achieve higher levels of productivity than System 4 in the short run, Likert concluded that they do so by liquidating the organization's human assets, something they cannot afford to do for very long. Although building human assets through System 4 may take several years and require large investments, Likert insisted that it is the only way to achieve positive results over the long term.

Critics were highly uncomfortable with Likert's prescriptive, one-best-way approach. Nonetheless, research conducted by Likert and his associates over many years and in a wide variety of organizations has demonstrated that positive results are possible where employee-centered supervision and group methods of decision making are adopted. This evidence comes from organizations as diverse as General Motors and the Hawaii State Department of Labor and Industrial Relations.[30] While acknowledging that System 4 is rarely implemented completely, especially on an organizationwide basis, Likert nonetheless viewed it as a realistic goal toward which to aspire. To those critics who dismissed System 4 as impractical because group decision making takes too much time, Likert responded that we simply haven't learned to do it skillfully and efficiently. This problem will correct itself, he argued, once every member of the organization develops and practices team leadership skills. Because he understood that this is a very real problem, he devoted much of his work to defining the skills required for practicing employee-centered leadership and group methods of decision making. Along with Douglas McGregor, he helped establish the theoretical foundations of today's literature on team building and employee empowerment.

Likert also responded to those critics who dismissed System 4 as impractical because most managers either lack the personality for employee-centered leadership or cannot overcome their fear of losing control. Likert's work as a researcher and a consultant led him to conclude that most managers can make the transition to System 4 successfully and that their fears about adopting System 4 are generally unwarranted. In an article completed just before his death in 1981 Likert wrote:

> Some managers are afraid that if they move toward System 4, their employees will take advantage of the leeway that System 4 gives them. They fear that employees will usurp authority and that the manager will lose control. They fear that employees will press for a large share of the gains in performance brought about by the introduction of System 4. These fears are unwarranted. Virtually without exception, employees respond responsibly and with increased cooperation and greater productivity when their managers move toward System 4.[31]

RELEVANCE FOR PUBLIC MANAGEMENT

The remainder of this chapter explores the relevance of participative management theory for public management and organizational performance. This exploration is guided by the three analytical frameworks introduced in Chapter 3.

Models of Organizational Effectiveness

Because it focuses on individual and group behavior, participative management theory emphasizes the internally directed models of effectiveness: the **internal process** and **human relations models.** But, because it holds that setting high performance goals is one of the key determinants of organizational success, participative management theory also emphasizes the values associated with the **rational goal model.** As indicated in Exhibit 12.2, participative management theory advocates a supportive, employee–centered leadership style that allows for the successful integration of individual and organizational goals, thereby balancing the effectiveness values associated with three of the four models of effectiveness.

Exhibit 12.2 The Competing Values Framework: Four Models of Organizational Effectiveness

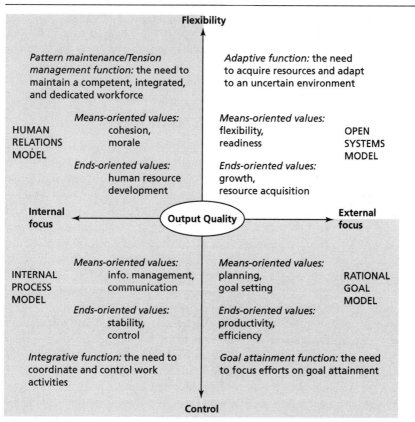

Flexibility

Pattern maintenance/Tension management function: the need to maintain a competent, integrated, and dedicated workforce

Adaptive function: the need to acquire resources and adapt to an uncertain environment

HUMAN RELATIONS MODEL

Means-oriented values: cohesion, morale

Means-oriented values: flexibility, readiness

OPEN SYSTEMS MODEL

Ends-oriented values: human resource development

Ends-oriented values: growth, resource acquisition

Internal focus ←——— Output Quality ———→ External focus

INTERNAL PROCESS MODEL

Means-oriented values: info. management, communication

Means-oriented values: planning, goal setting

RATIONAL GOAL MODEL

Ends-oriented values: stability, control

Ends-oriented values: productivity, efficiency

Integrative function: the need to coordinate and control work activities

Goal attainment function: the need to focus efforts on goal attainment

Control

SOURCE: Adapted with permission from Figures 3 and 4, Robert O. Quinn and John Rohrbaugh, "A Spatial Model of Effectiveness Criteria: Towards a Competing Values Approach to Organizational Analysis," *Management Science* 29 (March 1983): 363–373. Copyright 1983, The Institute of Management Sciences, now the Institute for Operations Research and the Management Sciences (INFORMS), 901 Elkridge Landing Road, Suite 400, Linthicum, Maryland 21090-2909 USA.

The highly participatory system of management advocated by Likert alters *the way* the goal attainment and integrative functions are traditionally performed. The rational goal model, for example, emphasizes goal-setting as a means of enhancing productivity. But, whereas System 1 managers set goals at the top and pass them down the chain of command for implementation, System 4 managers set general goals and then delegate the task of setting more specific goals to groups at each lower level. These groups make decisions through a deliberative process that involves everyone responsible for achieving the agreed-upon goals.

The internal process model emphasizes performance measurement and information management as means of maintaining coordination and control. But, whereas System1 managers collect information centrally and then apply rewards and sanctions to correct undesired behaviors, System 4 managers delegate the task of information collection and corrective action to the members of each organizational unit, with coordination achieved through the system of overlapping groups.

Thus, if participative management theory does not envision the complete integration of all four models of effectiveness, it does advocate an approach to management that integrates three sets of effectiveness values. In doing so it sets forth the broad outlines of an alternative to classical management theory.

Mechanisms for Coordinating and Controlling Work Activities

As indicated in Exhibit 12.3, participative management theory advocates **mutual adjustment** as an alternative to direct supervision. Responsibility is given to the members of each organizational unit to set their own individual and collective goals as long as they are consistent with goals and policies set at higher levels of the organization. Mutual adjustment occurs as supervisory and nonsupervisory workers participate in a system of hierarchically arranged groups with overlapping memberships. According to Likert, a system of this kind provides opportunities to resolve conflicts, fashion decisions appropriate to the group's situation, and exercise collective self-control. The members of the semi-autonomous work groups also experience fewer of the debilitating tensions associated with what Likert called one-on-one supervision.

Lewin, Lippitt, and White, as well as Likert, acknowledged that participative management requires greater investments in time and patience than less participatory systems but argued that the payoffs in terms of morale, motivation, and organizational performance outweigh the costs. This may be especially true in public agencies where employees are well-educated and the work requires considerable independent judgment. Highly educated employees are not likely to respond well to an autocratic management style that robs them of personal dignity and opportunities to demonstrate initiative. And where work is nonroutine, work standardization and direct supervision are generally ineffective as mechanisms of coordination and control. Consequently, mutual adjustment through group decision making may be well-suited to the needs of many public agencies.

Exhibit 12.3 Six Mechanisms for Coordinating and Controlling Work Activities

Mutual adjustment	Workers consult with each other informally about what needs to be accomplished and how. Responsibility for coordination and control rests with those who do the work.
Direct supervision	A supervisor is assigned to take responsibility for a group of workers and a managerial hierarchy is established to integrate the efforts of all work groups. The supervisor issues personal instructions and monitors individual performance.
Standardization of work processes	Work is programmed in advance of its execution by developing rules and standard operating procedures specifying how everyone is to perform assigned tasks. Coordination is built into the work process itself and control is achieved by strictly limiting each worker's discretion.
Standardization of work outputs	Work outputs are programmed in advance by providing each work group with product specifications or performance goals and allowing members considerable latitude in determining how to achieve them. Control is exercised by collecting output data, requiring corrective action when needed, and rewarding and sanctioning workers based on results achieved.
Standardization of worker skills	Workers are employed who possess the knowledge and skills needed to make appropriate decisions. Educational institutions and professional associations are relied upon to provide standardized training. Professionally trained workers are largely self-coordinating and self-controlling.
Standardization of values	Organizational leaders communicate and act upon a clear vision of what the organization exists to do, where it should be headed, and what values should guide it. Coordination and control is facilitated by commitment of organizational members to shared, internalized values and ideals.

SOURCE: Based in large part on Henry Mintzberg, *Structure in Fives* (Prentice-Hall, 1993, 3–7).

Motivational Strategies

Although Likert acknowledged that workers are motivated by a broad range of economic and noneconomic motivators, System 4 management relies heavily on the considerate leadership and group acceptance strategies. The **considerate leadership strategy** is reflected in Likert's concept of supportive supervision. The supportive supervisor accords workers trust and respect, helps them develop their capabilities, and allows them considerable autonomy. Whereas human relations theory viewed considerate leadership as providing extrinsic rewards in the form of attention and praise from supervisors, participative management theory emphasizes the intrinsic rewards that accrue to employees as their ego needs are met through personal growth and a strengthened sense of self-worth.

As shown in Exhibit 12.4, the **group acceptance strategy** is also reflected in participative management theory. After investigating why productivity tended to increase under System 4 management, Likert concluded that the key variable was group participation in goal setting and decision making. His research suggested that a sense of group loyalty developed among group members that motivated them to work harder and make personal sacrifices on behalf of the group. In Likert's view, heightened motivation occurred for two reasons. First, members obtained extrinsic rewards in the form of recognition from their peers and satisfaction of their social need for comradery. Second, members took ownership of decisions and goals that they had set for themselves, worked harder not to let the group down, and obtained intrinsic satisfaction from contributing to the success of the group.

Exhibit 12.4 Four Motivational Strategies

Legal Compliance

Using rules, formal directives, and sanctions to direct and control employee behavior. Employees may come to work, comply with rules, and satisfy minimum role requirements, either because they accept the legitimacy of organizational authority or fear being sanctioned.

Instrumental Rewards

Using rewards to induce desired behaviors.

Rewards for Performance

Distributing pay, promotions, and recognition based on individual performance. Employees may meet or exceed role expectations because they value the material and psychological satisfactions that money, advancement, and recognition can provide.

Considerate Leadership

Adopting a leadership style based on being attentive to employees and considerate of their needs. This strategy may improve morale. It might also induce those who value the respect, support, and approval of persons in authority to meet or exceed their role requirements.

Group Acceptance

Creating a work environment that allows employees to socialize, form group bonds, and enjoy the approval of their peers. This strategy may induce those who value affiliation and peer approval to meet or exceed role requirements, assuming that group norms are consistent with organizational objectives.

Job Identification

Offering work that is interesting, challenging, and responsible. Employees may come to work, meet or exceed role requirements, and possibly exhibit greater creativity and innovativeness. They may do so because they identify with the jobs and find their work intrinsically rewarding.

Goal Congruence

Hiring employees whose goals and values are congruent with the organization's and/or socializing employees so that they internalize organizational goals and values. Employees may come to work, remain with the organization, meet or exceed role requirements, and exhibit greater creativity, innovativeness, and institutional loyalty. They may do so because they identify with the organization's mission and values and because contributing to them reinforces their own self concept.

SOURCE: Based in large part on Daniel Katz and Robert L. Kahn, *The Social Psychology of Organizations* (Wiley, 1966), pp. 336–68.

Likert did not believe that jobs have to be interesting and challenging for workers to be motivated. Nonetheless, the **job identification strategy** is at least implied in participative management theory. According to the theory of job enrichment discussed in the next chapter, participation in group decision making makes work interesting and challenging, allows workers to express themselves through their work, and provides intrinsic rewards in the form of pride of accomplishment and personal growth.

Although Likert's research supports the view that System 4 leads to higher levels of productivity over the long term, participative management should not be viewed as a panacea. We have learned from systems theory, for example, that individual motivation is determined by the unique interrelationships among individual, job, and situational characteristics. Some individuals in some situations may experience the motivational effects of group decision making while others may not. In the final analysis, participation may increase job satisfaction and organizational commitment but not necessarily individual effort.

SUMMARY

Kurt Lewin and Rensis Likert demonstrated the value of applying social science methods to the study of complex organizations. In addition to providing a fuller understanding of organizational behavior, their pioneering studies gave rise to organizational development, a new field of research and professional practice dedicated to diagnosing the problems facing organizations and restoring them to a state of health. Their research also focused attention on leadership style as an important determinant of individual and organizational behavior and exposed the autocratic overtones of traditional management approaches.

Understood as a theory of organizational effectiveness, Likert's theory of participative management is explicitly prescriptive. It holds that high levels of organizational performance are achieved by establishing and maintaining supportive workplace relationships, developing cohesive work groups and encouraging collective decision making, and communicating high performance expectations. Although generally applicable to all complex organizations, this theory may be particularly relevant to public agencies because civil servants tend to be highly educated, desirous of personal growth, and committed to organizational objectives. Among its implications for public managers are the following:

- **Supportive workplace relationships.** Public managers should demonstrate a genuine interest in and concern for staff members and take pains to ensure that their work experiences are perceived as ego-building and need-fulfilling. This is accomplished in part by adopting an egalitarian, employee-centered leadership style that relies on personal rather than formal authority, avoids the special privileges and prerogatives of management, and integrates individual workers into tightly knit work groups. According to Likert, employee-centered leadership creates the kind of job satisfaction that produces not only higher levels of morale and cooperativeness but also higher levels of individual and group performance.

- **Group decision making and supervision.** Public managers should seek to supervise staff members as a group, welding them into cohesive work teams and encouraging them to set their own goals, solve their own problems, and make their own decisions. Rejecting Taylor's principle that managers should set policies and procedures and workers should execute them, participative management theory calls for involving workers in making the decisions that affect them and their unit's performance. The workplace experience becomes ego-building and need-fulfilling as workers develop mutual respect and take pride in their collective accomplishments.

- **High performance expectations.** Likert found that performance is highest in those organizational units where managers set high work performance expectations and encourage workers to set high performance goals for themselves as a unit. According to participative management theory, workers respond positively because they value what the organization exists to achieve, they take ownership of goals they helped establish, and they are motivated by both the pursuit of challenging goals and the sense of accomplishment that comes with attaining them.

- **Building human capacity.** The common theme in the three major elements of participative management theory is the importance of building human capacity and realizing its full potential. Whereas autocratic leadership undermines morale and motivation and gradually liquidates the organization's human assets, participative leadership develops and uses human resources in ways that benefit both the organization and its members. Participative management theory thus suggests that public managers do all they can to develop the capacities of staff members and help them realize their fullest potentials.

Lewin and Likert carried forth the humanistic tradition in organization theory begun by, among others, Follett, Mayo, and Roethlisberger. They criticized Taylor for failing to appreciate the importance of job satisfaction to personal well-being and they helped reveal the limitations of human relations theory by suggesting that personal attention and sensitive treatment alone are not sufficient. For organizations to be effective they must alter the basic distribution of power and authority between managers and workers, delegating more responsibility to workers and allowing them to become much more self-directing and self-controlling. How to do so will become clearer as we consider the works of Douglas McGregor and Chris Argyris in Chapter 13.

NOTES

1. Raymond E. Miles, "Human Relations or Human Resources," *Harvard Business Review 43* (July-August 1965):148–63.

2. See Alfred J. Marrow, *The Practical Theorist: The Life and Work of Kurt Lewin* (New York: Teachers College Press, Columbia University, 1977).

3. Alfred J. Marrow, "Events Leading to the Establishment of the National Training Laboratories," *Journal of Applied Behavioral Science 3* (April-June 1967): 146.

4. F. J. Roethlisberger, *The Elusive Phenomena* (Boston: Graduate School of Business Administration, Harvard University, 1977), Chapter 18.

5. See, for example, Douglas McGregor, "Foreword," *Journal of Social Issues 4* (Summer 1948): 2–4.

6. Kurt Lewin, *Field Theory in Social Science: Selected Theoretical Papers* (Westport, CT: Greenwood Press, 1951).

7. Ronald Lippitt, "An Experimental Study of the Effect of Democratic and Authoritarian Group Atmospheres," *University of Iowa Studies in Child Welfare 16* (No. 3, 1940): 45–195.

8. Ralph K. White and Ronald Lippitt, *Autocracy and Democracy: An Experimental Inquiry* (New York: Harper & Brothers, 1960), 285.

9. Kurt Lewin, Ronald Lippitt, and Ralph K. White, "Patterns of Aggressive Behavior in Experimentally Created "Social Climates," *Journal of Social Psychology 10* (May 1939): 271–99; White and Lippitt, *Autocracy and Democracy*.

10. White and Lippitt, *Autocracy and Democracy*.

11. Miriam Lewin Papanek, "Kurt Lewin and His Contributions to Modern Management Theory," Academy of Management, *Proceedings,* Thirty-Third Annual Meeting, 1973, 318.

12. Marrow, *The Practical Theorist,* 14–17.

13. Marrow, *The Practical Theorist,* 141.

14. Lester Coch and John R.P. French, Jr., "Overcoming Resistance to Change," *Human Relations 1* (August 1948): 512–13.

15. Coch and French, "Overcoming Resistance to Change," 521–22.

16. Marrow, *The Practical Theorist,* 146.

17. Marrow, *The Practical Theorist,* 210.

18. Rensis Likert, "A Technique for the Measurement of Attitudes," *Archives of Psychology 22* (No. 140, June 1932): 1-55.

19. Marrow, *The Practical Theorist,* 164.

20. Rensis Likert, *The Human Organization* (New York: McGraw-Hill, 1967), 13–26.

21. Rensis Likert, *New Patterns of Management* (New York: McGraw-Hill, 1961), 14.

22. Likert, *New Patterns of Management,* 103.

23. Rensis Likert, "Measuring Organizational Performance," *Harvard Business Review 36* (March–April 1958): 45.

24. Likert, *The Human Organization,* 47.

25. Likert, *New Patterns of Management,* 120.

26. Likert, *New Patterns of Management,* 104.

27. Likert, *The Human Organization,* 64.

28. Likert, *New Patterns of Management,* 111.

29. Likert, *New Patterns of Management,* 103.

30. William F. Dowling, "System 4 Builds Performance and Profits," *Organizational Dynamics 3* (Winter 1975): 23–38; and Rensis Likert, "System 4: A Resource for Improving Public Administration," *Public Administration Review 41* (November/December 1981): 674–78.

31. Likert, "System 4: A Resource for Improving Public Administration," 677.

13

⌘

Human Resources
Theory

Douglas McGregor
and Chris Argyris

As noted in Chapter 12, human resources theory assumes that workers are reservoirs of untapped resources, that they have the capacity to be self-directing and self-controlling, and that organizational success depends on how fully their abilities are developed and utilized. As a theory of organizational effectiveness, it calls upon managers to develop each person's unique talents, create and sustain an environment of openness and trust, remove constraints on personal autonomy and individual discretion, delegate responsibility downward, and encourage group decision making. The unifying theme is the idea that, by providing opportunities for employees to derive intrinsic satisfactions from their work, managers can facilitate higher levels of individual and collective performance.

Having already examined the contributions of Rensis Likert to this body of theory, we now turn to those of Douglas McGregor and Chris Argyris. More so than Likert, McGregor and Argyris were guided by explicit theories of human motivation. Because the groundbreaking works they published in the 1950s and 1960s were influenced by psychologist Abraham Maslow, this chapter begins with a review of Maslow's hierarchy of needs. It then examines the contributions of McGregor and Argyris to the field of organization theory and closes with an analysis of the implications of human resources theory for public management and organizational performance.

MASLOW'S HIERARCHY OF NEEDS

Psychologist Abraham Maslow first articulated his theory of human needs in an article published in 1943.[1] A decade later he expanded upon his theory in a book entitled *Motivation and Personality*.[2] Maslow believed that it is possible to identify basic human needs, that these needs tend to fall into one of five categories, and that these categories exist in a hierarchical order according to their level of biological urgency. When several needs compete for attention, the most biologically urgent takes priority. Once a lower need has been largely satisfied, the next higher need pops up to take its place as a source of motivation. An important implication is that "a want that is satisfied is no longer a want. The organism is dominated and its behavior organized only by unsatisfied needs."[3] This helps to explain, for example, why workers may be motivated by different things. Events in a worker's life or factors peculiar to the individual's personality may cause the worker to function at a lower level of need than other workers.

At the lowest level of the needs hierarchy are the **physiological needs.** They include the need for water, food, air, rest, and sleep. Because life itself depends on them, they are attended to first. Other needs are pushed into the background and capacities not required to satisfy them remain unused. All perceptions, Maslow notes, are colored by their absence. A person completely deprived of food, for example, tends to define life itself in terms of eating.

At the second level are the **safety needs.** When the physiological needs are reasonably satisfied, humans seek to protect themselves from danger, threat, or deprivation. For most of us in modern society, Maslow notes, our safety needs are expressed in such things as "the common preferences for a job with tenure and protection, the desire for a savings account, and for insurance of various kinds (medical, dental, unemployment, disability, old age)."[4] The need for safety is also reflected in a person's preference for things that are routine, familiar, and known. Those with strong neurotic tendencies may never feel safe and secure. They tend to become safety-seeking mechanisms with all of their capacities devoted to this need.

At the third level of the hierarchy are the **social needs,** or what Maslow originally labeled the belongingness and love needs. This category includes the need to associate with others and be accepted by others, as well as the need to give and receive love and affection. The informal work groups often found in industry, such as the one at the Hawthorne plant that conspired to keep production low, may be viewed as mechanisms for satisfying safety needs, such as the need for protection from the threat of higher production quotas, and for satisfying the workers' social needs for comradery and association. Efforts to break them up only serve to deny workers opportunities to satisfy these basic needs.

Above the social needs are the **esteem needs.** They are of two kinds: those that relate to building one's self-esteem, such as autonomy, achievement, and competence, and those that relate to the esteem provided by others, such as recognition, prestige, and respect. The desire to satisfy the esteem needs may have a direct bearing on work performance. According to Maslow, "Satisfaction of the self-esteem need leads to feelings of self-confidence, worth, strength, capability, and adequacy, of being useful and necessary in the world. But thwarting of these needs produces feelings of inferiority, of weakness, and of helplessness. These feelings in turn give rise to either basic discouragement or else compensating or neurotic trends."[5] This suggests the importance of facilitating the satisfaction of esteem needs at work while eliminating those aspects of organizational life that thwart their satisfaction. In addition, according to Maslow, these needs, unlike the lower needs, are rarely satisfied. They remain important sources of motivation because workers will seek to satisfy them indefinitely once they reach this level of the needs hierarchy.

At the highest level of the needs hierarchy are what Maslow called the **self-actualization needs.** They include the need for continued development and fulfillment. Maslow suggests that self-actualization is "the desire to become more and more what one is, to become everything that one is capable of becoming."[6] Someone with the ability to be a great athlete, artist, or parent, for example, will at this level feel the need to do what it takes to realize his or her fullest potential.

Maslow expanded upon his definition of self-actualization in an article originally published in 1950.[7] Here he wrote that individuals operating at the first four levels of the hierarchy experience **deficiency motivation.** They are driven by a desire to obtain what they have not yet obtained, such as safety, affection, and self-esteem. They continue to live in a state of tension until each of these deficiencies is overcome. Once their lower needs have been satisfied and they have matured to a point where self-acceptance and self-esteem are high, then they experience what he called **growth motivation** at the fifth and final level. This, according to Maslow, is a qualitatively different kind of motivation, one in which individuals experience a natural tendency to pursue their potentialities without feeling driven to do so. Things are done not to overcome deficiencies but to pursue growth and development as ends in themselves. The few individuals who reach this level share certain attributes. These include a sense of relative peace, detachment from the world and its cares, and freedom to explore what they are capable of becoming. Maslow believed that in these individuals we can glimpse humankind's "higher nature," one that is essentially good and decent.

Although psychologists have expressed a great deal of skepticism about Maslow's understanding of self-actualization as a special state of grace, most have found the idea of a hierarchy of needs plausible and useful.[8] There is general agreement among psychologists that many people experience a desire for personal growth and are motivated to realize their potentials once they feel safe and secure. This desire for growth is not something experienced just by the few who reach the top of the needs hierarchy. Maslow seemed to acknowledge this point. The typical maturing and psychologically healthy adult, he wrote, works at satisfying several needs at the same time. In his words, "it is as if the average citizen is satisfied perhaps 85 percent in his physiological needs, 70 percent in his safety needs, 50 percent in his love needs, 40 percent in his self-esteem needs, and 10 percent in his self-actualization needs."[9]

Despite the plausibility of Maslow's conceptual framework, it is probably best not to view it as offering a complete and valid theory of human motivation. Wahba and Bridwell examined the research findings relating to Maslow's theory and found little evidence to support the notion that there are five distinct categories of needs or that these categories are structured in a special hierarchy.[10] In 1969 psychologist Clayton Alderfer offered a modified version of Maslow's conceptual model that may explain actual behavior better than Maslow's.[11] Alderfer collapsed Maslow's five categories of need into three: existence, relatedness, and growth needs.[12] He also rejected the idea of a strict hierarchical progression because people are likely to regress under certain circumstances and because people do not always satisfy their lower needs before attempting to satisfy their higher needs. Alderfer is probably correct in concluding that Maslow's concept of hierarchy is overstated. However, Wahba and Bridwell did find evidence to support the view that people generally attempt to satisfy deficiency needs before turning to their growth needs.

Whether or not Maslow's hierarchy of needs provides a complete and valid theory of human motivation, it nonetheless influenced the thinking of human resources theorists in important ways. In particular it provided the basis for three key conclusions: that management strategies typically do not allow workers to satisfy their higher-level needs, that certain flawed assumptions about human nature are the source of management's failure to adopt more effective strategies, and that management reforms will not be effective unless and until these assumptions are replaced with more appropriate ones.

THE HUMAN SIDE OF ENTERPRISE

In 1960 Douglas McGregor published *The Human Side of Enterprise,* a book destined to become one of the most popular management books ever written. Having studied management development programs in several large companies in the early 1950s, McGregor wondered why they seemed so ineffectual. His conclusion, as stated in the preface to his book, was that we have learned very little about how to develop and utilize our human talents. Progress is slow, he continued, because management is constrained by its own basic assumptions about human nature. The thesis explored in his book is that "the theoretical assumptions management holds about controlling its human resources determine the whole character of the enterprise."[13] McGregor believed that social science was now at a point where it could help managers achieve their objectives by helping them "discover how to tap the unrealized potential present in their human resources."[14]

McGregor's analysis begins with the premise that management decisions are only as good as the assumptions on which they are based. Physicists and engineers, he notes, act in accordance with natural laws; they do not try "to make water flow upstream." Yet when it comes to influencing human behavior,

---

Douglas McGregor 1906–1964

Douglas McGregor was born in Detroit, Michigan, on September 16, 1906.[15] His grandfather founded in Detroit the McGregor Institute, a shelter for homeless men, and McGregor's father became the Institute's director in 1915. Having grown up in an intensely religious and caring environment, McGregor developed a strong concern for humanity. He attended City College of Detroit for four years in the mid-1920s, worked for the McGregor Institute in the early 1930s, and completed requirements for his bachelor's degree at the City College of Detroit in 1932. He then went on to study psychology at Harvard University, earning his master's degree in 1933 and his doctoral degree in 1935.

After teaching social psychology at Harvard for two years, McGregor accepted a position as professor of psychology at the Massachusetts Institute of Technology (MIT). Between 1943 and 1948 he served as executive director of the industrial relations program at MIT. It was during this period that he played an instrumental role in bringing Kurt Lewin to MIT and helping him establish the Research Center for Group Dynamics. In 1948 McGregor left MIT to become president of Antioch College in Ohio, a position that put his human relations skills to the test. In 1954 he returned to MIT as professor of industrial management where he taught for another ten years. McGregor was an advocate of action research and served as a consultant for several business corporations. In his master work *The Human Side of Enterprise* (1960) McGregor challenged prevailing management assumptions and laid the theoretical foundations for the contemporary literature on empowerment. Douglas McGregor died suddenly of a heart attack on October 13, 1964, at the age of 58.

---

managers *do* try to make water flow upstream. They remain in complete ignorance of human needs and how these needs affect behavior. They adopt individual incentive plans, for example, based on untested assumptions about human motivation. When the incentive plan fails to boost productivity, blame is assigned to the workers rather than the incentive plan. It is always "*their* stupidity, *their* uncooperativeness, or *their* laziness which is seized on as the explanation of what happened, not management's failure to select appropriate means for control."[16] A new theory of management is required, McGregor writes, one premised on the satisfaction of human needs rather than the exercise of formal authority. To flesh out such a theory McGregor adopted Maslow's hierarchy of needs as his point of departure.

Theory X

Theory X is the label McGregor gives to a set of assumptions about human nature and the resulting philosophy of management based on directing and controlling workers through the exercise of formal authority, the use of carrots and sticks, and the maintenance of management control systems. As noted above, McGregor believed that behind every managerial decision are assumptions about human nature and behavior. The specific assumptions of Theory X are these:

1. The average human being has an inherent dislike of work and will avoid it if he can.

2. Because of this human characteristic of dislike of work, most people must be coerced, controlled, directed, threatened with punishment to get them to put forth adequate effort toward the achievement of organizational directives.

3. The average human being prefers to be directed, wishes to avoid responsibility, has relatively little ambition, wants security above all.[17]

Theory X assumptions, McGregor suggests, are widely held. They are implicit in the literature on organizations and in managerial policy and practice. And yet, McGregor argues, they are inherently flawed. The behavioral problems managers often attribute to human nature, such as laziness, lack of ambition, and unwillingness to accept responsibility, are actually products of their own flawed assumptions. Theory X assumptions prevent managers from seeing that the behavioral problems they observe at work are actually symptoms of illness arising from the workers' inability to satisfy their higher-level needs:

> The man whose needs for safety, association, independence, or status are thwarted is sick, just as surely as is he who has rickets. And his sickness will have behavioral consequences. We will be mistaken if we attribute his resultant passivity, or his hostility, or his refusal to accept responsibility to his inherent "human nature." These forms of behavior are *symptoms* of illness— of deprivation of his social and egoistic needs.[18]

Managers are often led by their Theory X assumptions to adopt motivational strategies geared to satisfying physiological and safety needs. Money, vacations, and health insurance benefits are provided on the assumption that workers value food on the table, a roof over their heads, recreational opportunities, and security for themselves and their families. McGregor argues that extrinsic rewards of this kind are ineffective for two reasons. First, they cannot increase interest in the work itself because they only provide satisfaction outside the workplace. Second, modern industrial societies already provide for the physiological and safety needs of most people. Since, according to Maslow, a satisfied need is no longer a motivator, management only compounds its difficulties by providing for needs that have already been met and failing to provide opportunities to satisfy those that have not. According to McGregor, unless there are opportunities to satisfy the higher-level needs, workers will feel deprived and their deprivation will be reflected in their workplace behaviors.

Theory X assumptions cause managers to cling to a philosophy of direction and control. This philosophy does not allow for self-direction and self-control, independence and autonomy, or the other conditions necessary for the satisfaction of higher-level needs. McGregor concludes that exclusive reliance on authority as the central, indispensable means of control only serves to make workers dependent and insecure, thereby inhibiting creativity, initiative, and risk taking. Relationships in modern institutions are highly interdependent. Individuals depend on those above, below, and at the same level to satisfy their needs and realize their goals. This fact is pertinent for managers. Because they are dependent on those below them for their commitment and contribution, formal authority backed up with the threat of punishment is largely useless as a means of control. It can induce compliance but only minimal levels of commitment and contribution. This is not to suggest that formal authority shouldn't be exercised. It must be exercised, for example, in the course of making policy, budgeting, and personnel decisions. McGregor only suggests that where workers are seeking to satisfy their higher needs formal authority shouldn't be used as the primary means of control. Once managers repudiate their Theory X assumptions, alternative means of control will reveal themselves.

Theory Y

Theory Y is the label McGregor gives to an alternative set of assumptions about human nature and behavior and the resulting philosophy of management based on integration and self-control. The specific assumptions of Theory Y are these:

1. The expenditure of physical and mental effort in work is as natural as play or rest.
2. External control and the threat of punishment are not the only means for bringing about effort toward organizational objectives. [Humans] will exercise self-direction and self-control in the service of objectives to which [they are] committed.
3. Commitment to objectives is a function of the rewards associated with their achievement.
4. The average human being learns, under proper conditions, not only to accept but to seek responsibility.
5. The capacity to exercise a relatively high degree of imagination, ingenuity, and creativity in the solution of organizational problems is widely, not narrowly, distributed in the population.
6. Under the conditions of modern industrial life, the intellectual potentialities of the average human being are only partially utilized.[19]

Whereas Theory X rests on the scalar principle, Theory Y rests on the **integration principle.** McGregor defined integration as "the creation of conditions such that the members of the organization can achieve their own goals *best* by directing their efforts toward the success of the enterprise."[20] Conditioned by Theory X assumptions, managers tend to think in terms of a wage bargain in which workers agree to accept external direction and control in exchange for a certain amount of pay. No thought, McGregor says, is given to the workers' needs or how to integrate them with the needs and objectives of the organization. A district manager is promoted to vice president and transferred to headquarters without asking whether this is consistent with the manager's personal needs and goals. Or, challenging work and growth opportunities are provided to those at the top of the organization with no thought to doing the same for those at the bottom. Genuine commitment to organizational objectives cannot be created if managers continue to think in terms of a basic work-for-wages bargain. It can be created only if ways are found to integrate the full range of individual and organizational needs.

Full and complete integration of needs, McGregor hastens to say, is never possible. Nonetheless, it does occur naturally and inevitably where workers are genuinely committed to organizational objectives. Committed workers obtain satisfactions from achieving organizational objectives and thus advance their interests and the organization's interests simultaneously. Committed workers are also capable of self-direction and self-control, which greatly reduces the need for external, top-down controls. The key question, then, is how to create the commitment to organizational objectives that the principle of integration requires. According to McGregor, the answer lies in altering the way managers do business. Once having accepted and internalized Theory Y assumptions, managers will turn their attention to developing human resources, delegating responsibilities downward, and shaking off their obsession with control. These elements of Theory Y are discussed in the sections that follow.

Full Development and Use of Human Resources

A central theme in human resources theory is that the wise organization develops and utilizes the potential represented by its human resources as fully as possible. Because Theory X assumes the necessity of standardizing work, limiting discretion, and controlling behavior, organizations that operate according to Theory X cannot take full advantage of the human potential represented by their workers. The opposite is true, according to McGregor, for organizations that operate according to Theory Y. Managers who truly believe that most workers desire opportunities for personal growth, actively seek responsibility, and are capable of ingenuity, creativity, and problem solving, cease viewing workers as labor commodities to be purchased and pressured to perform. Instead, they view them as genuine assets in helping them fulfill their own responsibilities. Implicit in this argument is a distinct theory of organizational performance. McGregor suggests that it is the opportunity to self-actualize—to develop and express one's full capabilities through work—that builds commitment to organizational goals, increases job satisfaction, and enhances work performance.

But how are human resources best developed? After studying management development programs McGregor concluded that classroom training is not particularly effective. He believed human capacity is something that must be "grown" rather than "manufactured." The individual, McGregor wrote, "will grow into what he is capable of becoming, provided we can create the proper conditions for that growth. Such an approach involves less emphasis on manufacturing techniques and more on controlling the climate and the fertility of the soil, and on methods of cultivation."[21] Fertilizing the soil and cultivating growth are achieved by providing workers with as many opportunities as possible to assume responsibility, try out new ideas, and exercise judgment. This in turn requires a decentralized organizational structure and managers who are not afraid to delegate.

Decentralization and Delegation

Another central theme in human resources theory is that human talent flourishes best in decentralized structures.[22] A decentralized structure is one in which specific responsibilities are delegated to each organizational unit and those who work within them. While it is appropriate for top managers to make fundamental decisions regarding mission, strategies, and goals, McGregor believed responsibility for work operations should be pushed downward in the organization to the group of core workers closest to the work situation. In his view, decentralization holds distinct advantages for the organization as well as the workers. Better decisions tend to result when they are made by those closest to the work situation, workers are provided with opportunities to take personal responsibility and develop their capacities, and they are motivated more effectively. Conversely, if upper and middle managers try to make all decisions themselves they will never develop an organization that grows and becomes healthy in its own right.

The concept of delegation includes the idea that each work unit should be provided with the data it needs to evaluate and correct its own performance. McGregor believed that the concept of delegation, and the trust on which it must rest, is violated if unit-level data is provided to higher authorities for purposes of control. This means, for example, that a bureau chief should have available data about the bureau's overall performance but not about everything that occurs in each of the bureau's sections. The principle of self-control requires data be provided to members of management so that they can control their own areas of responsibility but not the details of their subordinate's activities. Managing on the basis of overall results involves an element of risk, but unless managers are willing to take these risks there will be no true delegation.[23]

The advantages of delegation do not accrue automatically. McGregor emphasized that accountability as well as responsibility must be delegated downward. Because tight control systems negate the positive advantages of decentralization, managers must provide individuals and work groups with the freedom they need to succeed, while holding them accountable for mutually agreed-upon results. In addition, the success of decentralization depends, according to McGregor, on open and honest communications between supervisors and subordinates, and an environment where trust is high, where conformity, fear, and dependence are low, and where experimentation and risk taking are prominent. Unfortunately, these conditions are difficult to satisfy in practice because of management's deeply held obsession with control.

Relinquishing Control

Yet another central theme in human resources theory is that the pattern of passivity and dependence on superiors cannot be broken as long as managers retain the traditional command-and-control approach to supervision. If they believe, for example, that workers are basically lazy and unwilling to accept responsibility, they will view their task as one of directing, manipulating, and controlling workers in the job that has to be done. In McGregor's words, "Theory X leads naturally to an emphasis on the tactics of control—to procedures and techniques for telling people what to do, for determining whether they are doing it, and for administering rewards and punishments."[24] These techniques include top-down directives, standardized operating procedures, performance measurement systems, and pay-for-performance incentives.

That managers are obsessed with monitoring and controlling everything that happens in their units is understandable. Managers are responsible for the performance of that portion of the organization under their supervision. Because they are likely to be called on the carpet by someone higher in the chain of command if things go wrong, they naturally conclude that they must know what is going on in their units at all times, must place strict boundaries on the discretionary authority of each subordinate, and must maintain an environment where the threat of punishment for mistakes is ever-present. McGregor argues that, whereas the logic behind the command-and-control strategy is unassailable if one accepts Theory X assumptions, Theory Y allows us to envision alternative methods of control, methods that promise higher levels of individual motivation and organizational performance. In one way or another, these methods entail delegating responsibilities to subordinates and holding them accountable for results without micro-managing every aspect of their work.

Theory Y holds that human beings will, under appropriate conditions, "exercise *self*-direction and *self*-control in the service of objectives to which they are committed."[25] To establish these conditions, managers must redefine their own roles. They must, according to McGregor, encourage subordinates to identify appropriate mission-related objectives and help them achieve those objectives by acting "as a teacher, consultant, colleague, and only rarely as authoritative boss."[26] But, McGregor continues, the manager can help them "*only if he is prepared to relinquish control in the conventional sense,* only if he has enough confidence in their willingness and ability to achieve organizational objectives that he can risk some poor judgments and some mistakes as a natural cost of growth."[27] McGregor understood that in hierarchical systems, where fear of being called on the carpet is pervasive, it is very difficult for managers to relinquish control in the traditional sense.[28]

Despite the natural reluctance to relinquish control, McGregor insists that the command-and-control approach is not an effective means of exercising control in most organizations. First, because it seeks to motivate through fear, it produces outcomes other than those managers truly seek. In his words, "Surveillance displaces autonomy, mistrust undermines self-regard, absence of support and help minimizes achievement, likelihood of punishment for noncompliance reduces risk-taking and innovation, rigidity of standards and administrative procedures precludes the individual's use of his own know-how. The whole process accentuates passive compliance rather than creative problem-solving."[29]

Second, the command-and-control approach, however effective it may be for clerical and production workers, is ill-suited to the needs of professional workers, who now comprise the largest proportion of workers in many businesses and government agencies. It is part of the unique value of professionals that they are capable of determining the steps necessary to achieve the desired objectives. This kind of intellectual contribution, according to McGregor, cannot be obtained by giving orders and exercising close supervision. For professional workers it can only be obtained by providing challenging work, broad grants of autonomy, and opportunities for continual development and growth.

Finally, the command–and–control approach is inherently flawed, according to McGregor, because the idea that control can be maintained through the use of formal authority is illusory. People and events can be influenced but not controlled. In McGregor's words, "The realities of modern organizational life place the manager at any level of the organization in a position where he cannot control many things which affect the results for which he is responsible." In practice, managers have little choice but to invest confidence and trust in their subordinates.

Investing confidence and trust does not mean being permissive. McGregor emphasized that under Theory Y managers must establish clear expectations about behavioral norms, organizational goals, and the boundaries of each person's discretionary authority, and they must hold workers to high standards. Theory Y, he wrote, "is *not* permissive management, or soft or indulgent management. It includes clear demands for high performance, clear limits consistently enforced. The latter are, in fact, necessary for the individual's psychological security, for him to be able to predict what is possible and what is not. It involves clear, open communications about the pressures and limits imposed by reality."[30] In short, Theory Y managers continue to be responsible for exercising formal authority and maintaining firm control but they do so in ways consistent with Theory Y assumptions.

Using Intrinsic Rewards to Motivate

A final theme reflected in McGregor's work is the importance of intrinsic rewards as motivators, especially those rewards inherent in the work itself. These rewards take the form of pride, sense of accomplishment, and heightened self image, and they are received as ego and growth needs are satisfied. Workers obtain them, for example, as they exercise discretion, solve problems, reach goals, and develop their personal capacities.

According to McGregor, Theory X encourages managers to view motivation in terms of Newton's laws of thermodynamics. A worker is viewed as a physical object at rest. The manager's task is to set the worker in motion through the application of external force. This force is typically applied by giving and withholding extrinsic rewards or punishments, such as pay increases, praise, promotions, and sanctions. A basic premise of Theory Y is that, although extrinsic rewards can produce motion, they are not particularly effective at motivating commitment, loyalty, spontaneity, or creativity. Motivation, as distinct from movement, flows from a fire burning inside each worker that is fueled by the continual receiving of intrinsic rewards. Theory Y assumes that most workers are inherently motivated to satisfy their higher needs. Consequently, management's task is not to motivate but to facilitate self-motivation by removing the unnecessary constraints that undermine motivation and providing opportunities for members of the organization to obtain intrinsic rewards from their work.

Having suggested that management policies and practices should be realigned with Theory Y assumptions, McGregor felt obligated to describe what that realignment might look like. This was a difficult task because no organization had yet adopted Theory Y in a conscious and deliberate way. In *The Human Side of Enterprise,* and in a manuscript left unfinished at his death, McGregor discussed several promising innovations and explained how they might be implemented in a Theory Y manner. A few of these innovations are described in the sections that follow.

Management by Objectives and Self-Control

One way to promote decentralization, self-management, and self-development, according to McGregor, is to practice what Peter Drucker called **management by objectives (MBO).** As defined by Drucker, MBO is a management strategy in which a higher authority—rather than issuing directives and exercising close supervision—asks subordinates to define the way their jobs contribute to the organization's mission and to identify specific, mission-related objectives.[31] Once their objectives have been approved the subordinates are allowed to exercise self-control in achieving them. Drucker initially referred to this strategy as management by objectives and self-control.

Although perfectly compatible with Theory Y assumptions, McGregor concluded that MBO is typically implemented in a Theory X manner. Managers seeking to act in accordance with Theory Y assumptions, he wrote, must view MBO as "a deliberate attempt to link improvement in managerial competence with the satisfaction of higher-level ego and self-actualization needs."[32] In his view, higher authorities should encourage subordinates to define their jobs in terms of the organization's mission, encourage them to set objectives that are both challenging and realistic, and arrange for a self-appraisal after six months so that accomplishments can be reviewed, lessons discussed, and new goal-setting cycles begun.

In this type of MBO the higher authority takes on the role of consultant rather than boss and strives to encourage true self-responsibility, independence, and growth. The higher authority points out possible problems during discussions but resists the impulse to tell the subordinate what to do or how to do it. According to McGregor, MBO implemented in this way builds commitment to organizational objectives, develops individual competence, and generates the intrinsic satisfactions that spur motivation and performance. These benefits will not accrue, however, if MBO is treated as a sterile technique rather than an organic strategy. In McGregor's words, "'Selling' management a program of target setting, and providing standardized forms and procedures, is the surest way to *prevent* the development of management by integration and self-control."[33]

Job Enrichment

Job enrichment is another innovation that McGregor found especially compatible with Theory Y assumptions. It is the process of altering or enriching the content of a job so that the worker can satisfy personal growth needs.[34] This is done by some combination of the following: giving employees responsibility for completing a natural unit of work rather than a narrowly specialized task, removing supervisory controls while holding employees accountability for the quality of their work, and ensuring that the job includes difficult and challenging tasks. These changes in job content are premised on the belief that genuine motivation is derived from the intrinsic rewards received as workers satisfy their growth needs through their work. These intrinsic rewards include the satisfactions associated with being trusted with responsibility, being able to achieve important objectives, receiving recognition for achieving those objectives, and taking pride in the growth of one's expertise and personal competence.

In advocating job enrichment, McGregor was quick to point out that it is not a panacea. Those who do not value personal growth and development, for example, will not necessarily respond to the intrinsic rewards that enriched work has to offer. Nonetheless, research shows that those most likely to respond positively to intrinsic rewards are professional employees, precisely the kind of employees often found in government service.[35]

Self-Managing Work Teams

A third innovation that McGregor found to be especially compatible with the assumptions of Theory Y is the organic, self-managing work team. Examples include those described by the sociotechnical theorists in the coal mines of England and the textile mills of India, although McGregor believed their value extended well beyond industrial settings. The key idea is to organize work in a manner that allows an interdependent team of workers to be responsible for some primary task. The team is self-managing to the extent that its members are allowed to set internal work schedules and assignments, establish their own performance standards and goals, and exercise their own quality controls and performance evaluations. This innovation calls upon supervisors to perform their roles differently. Rather than providing direction, surveillance, and control, they provide technical help, support, and instruction to the team.

McGregor believed that self-managing work teams hold enormous potential for improving organizational performance. First, they can be highly effective decision-making and problem-solving entities. Their ability to produce effective decisions is based not only on the fact that those closest to the work situation are making the key decisions but also on the truism that several heads are generally better than one. Under Theory X, key decisions are generally made by persons in supervisory or managerial positions. Consequently, the quality and effectiveness of operational decisions in each work unit are highly dependent on the intelligence, skill, and omniscience of one or two individuals. McGregor believed that managers rarely possess these qualities and the appropriateness of their decisions are highly suspect as a result. Second, group decision making provides the soil for "growing" human capabilities. Team members learn to play a variety of leadership roles and develop skills in communications, interpersonal relations, and problem solving. Finally, he hypothesized that teamwork improves the quality of individual performance because of the autonomy and responsibility workers are given and the intrinsic rewards they receive from satisfying their growth needs. As they develop skills and solve problems effectively, they increase their sense of self-respect, receive recognition from others, and take pride in their accomplishments, all of which, according to McGregor, are intrinsically motivating and build commitment to organizational objectives.

Although it is not always practical to organize self-managing work teams, McGregor believed that self-control is generally superior to top-down control. In a manuscript left unfinished at his death, McGregor suggested that teamwork holds far more promise than job enrichment for improving organizational performance.[36] Where job enrichment calls for a relatively minor tactical change, self-managing work teams call for a major strategic change in the way organizations are governed. It calls for turning governance of work operations over to teams of workers who, as Mary Parker Follett put it, simply follow the law of the situation. But, although this innovation may promise to boost performance, it also faces great obstacles. For it to succeed managers must be willing to empower employees lower in the organization to make key decisions. This is something managers are very reluctant to do.

Despite the difficulties inherent in adopting Theory Y, McGregor believed there are no good alternatives if managers are serious about improving organizational performance. In his words, "Without this commitment to the development of human assets, and without a clear understanding that providing for the growth of human resources is a painstaking and difficult task—but ultimately worth the effort—management must resort to recipes, fads, and other 'instant cures.'"[37]

MCGREGOR'S CONTRIBUTIONS
TO ORGANIZATION THEORY

Of Douglas McGregor's many contributions to organization theory, two in particular stand out. First, he argued quite convincingly that our assumptions are our worst enemies. He challenged what we thought we knew to be true and convinced many that organizational performance cannot be improved without a fundamental shift in our thinking. While other theorists were debating the merits of various management styles and structural arrangements, McGregor asserted that they were missing an essential point. Management styles and structural arrangements are mere epiphenomena. They do not matter nearly as much as the assumptions and values that give them shape, form, and meaning. He noted, for example, that a manager could get away with being gruff and often autocratic if he or she, deep down, trusted workers, believed in their capacities, and treated them fairly and with respect.

Although some critics believed McGregor intended to advance Theory Y as "the one best way," this was not the case.[38] He understood that different workers have different needs and respond to different kinds of incentives. He understood that managers have different personalities and levels of maturity, and that they must find the style of managing that is best suited to them. He viewed Theory Y simply as an alternative set of assumptions, supported by recent research in the behavioral sciences, that holds considerable promise for improving organizational performance if managers are willing to make the necessary shift in thinking. He did not intend Theory Y to be understood as a single, fixed set of prescriptions. Because we can all be trapped by our own theories and assumptions into making poor decisions, he simply invited us to evaluate and explore alternative ways of thinking. He understood that the assumptions reflected in Theory Y and the implications drawn from them may require modification as research and experience with their application move forward.

Second, McGregor was particularly effective at envisioning what employee empowerment might look like in practice and communicating his vision to his readers. He spoke directly to managers in their own language and in a clear and straightforward manner. He could say to managers that their assumptions were their worst enemies and do so in a way that made a great deal of sense. Although many scholars and practitioners found his humanistic ideals impractical in organizational settings, many of them nonetheless viewed Theory Y as a way of thinking and managing toward which to aspire. Indeed, it has not been easy to dismiss Theory Y as overly prescriptive and naively humanistic. Today the same themes found in *The Human Side of Enterprise* are reflected in the literature on empowerment, team-building, stewardship, and principle-centered leadership.

INTEGRATING INDIVIDUAL AND ORGANIZATIONAL NEEDS

Human resources theory is a product of the larger field of study known as organizational behavior. In *Personality and Organization* (1957) Chris Argyris argued that, although research in the behavioral sciences has produced a considerable body of knowledge about why individuals behave as they do in organizations, the field is still in a pre-theoretical state.[39] *Personality and Organization* was written to integrate existing knowledge and outline a theory of organizational behavior. Such a theory is needed, he argued, so that researchers and administrators can predict the behavioral outcomes of various structural forms and managerial practices. Once armed with such a theory, researchers and administrators can develop the "action skills" they need to diagnose problems, predict the likely outcomes of pursuing a particular course of action, and intervene to improve organizational functioning. A central theme running through all of his work is that knowledge is of little value if it cannot be put to good use.

Chris Argyris 1923–

Chris Argyris was born in Newark, New Jersey, on July 16, 1923.[40] After serving in the army during World War II, Argyris earned a bachelor's degree in psychology from Clark University in 1947, a master's degree in psychology and economics from Kansas University in 1949, and a doctoral degree in organizational behavior from Cornell University in 1951. He taught at Yale University for twenty years before becoming the James Bryant Conant Professor of Education and Organizational Behavior at Harvard University in 1971.

As a doctoral student, Argyris studied under William F. Whyte, another pioneer in action research and human relations. Although he did not know Kurt Lewin well, having met him only briefly at MIT, he was greatly influenced by his ideas.[41] Carrying on Lewin's tradition of action research, Argyris has served as a consultant to several governments in North America and Europe and as a "researcher-intervener" in numerous corporations. The unifying theme in all of his research has been improving organizational performance by making organizations more humane, something that is accomplished by integrating individual and organizational needs and developing authentic human relationships at work.

The Growth Needs

A shared point of departure for human resources theorists is the premise that human beings have needs they seek to satisfy and that organizations desiring to perform well over the long term must facilitate the satisfaction of these needs. In *Personality and Organization* Argyris restricted his analysis primarily to the growth needs or, more generally, the need to self-actualize, to become the person you are capable of becoming. Drawing upon recently developed personality theories, Argyris described how the human personality undergoes a continuous process of development as individuals grow from infancy to adulthood. As we mature the personality becomes more complex and differentiated, recognizing increasingly more and deeper sets of needs. A sense of self is developed in interacting with others and individuals behave in ways designed, consciously or unconsciously, to actualize and protect this sense of self. Human development is a process of striving to become more competent in relation to one's environment so that each of us can satisfy needs, develop self-esteem, and actualize the self.

Argyris characterized this as a striving inherent in all human beings for personal growth, although individuals can and do vary greatly in terms of how much growth they seek and ultimately experience. This striving is reflected in the following developmental tendencies:

1. To develop from a state of passivity as infants to a state of increasing activity as adults.

2. To develop from a state of dependence upon others as infants to a state of relative independence as adults.

3. To develop from being capable of behaving only in a few ways as an infant to being capable of behaving in many different ways as an adult.

4. To develop from having erratic, casual, shallow, quickly dropped interests as an infant to having deeper interests as an adult and obtaining rewards from responding successfully to challenges.

5. To develop from having a short time perspective (i.e., the present largely determines behavior) as an infant to a much longer time perspective as an adult (i.e., where the behavior is more affected by the past and the future).

6. To develop from being in a subordinate position in the family and society as an infant to aspiring to occupy an equal and/or superordinate position relative to peers.

7. To develop from a lack of awareness of self as an infant to an awareness of and control over self as an adult.[42]

The individual's basic growth needs are reflected in these tendencies. According to Argyris, "Mature individuals, in our culture, tend to need to be relatively independent, to be responsible about and involved in their activities, to seek challenging creative work, to aspire to higher positions, and to be active and to utilize many of their abilities."[43] People are predisposed to develop continuously from the infant end to the adult end of each of these seven dimensions, although they may never achieve the full expression of any one of them.

This theory, if valid, holds important implications for how we structure and manage organizations. It suggests that the success of the organization depends on the success of its members; those organizations that are successful in satisfying the growth needs of their members will perform better than those that do not. This is because energy is released as individuals strive to achieve their goals. It is from human energy that the organization, as well as the individual, stands to benefit. The key to releasing this energy is to provide opportunities for workers to experience "psychological success." Psychological success is experienced as the seven growth tendencies are allowed expression. Argyris makes this point as follows:

> . . . . To the extent that individuals who are hired to become agents of organizations are predisposed toward maturity, they will want to express needs or predispositions related to the adult end of each specific developmental continuum. Theoretically, this means that healthy adults will tend to obtain optimum personality expression while at work if they are provided with jobs which permit them to be more active than passive; more independent than dependent; to have longer rather than shorter time perspectives; to occupy higher position than their peers; to have control over their world; and to express many of their deeper, more important abilities.[44]

But, according to Argyris, facilitating "optimum personality expression while at work" is precisely what most organizations are *not* designed to do. The core thesis of *Personality and Organization* is that a basic mismatch or incongruity exists between the requirements of the formal organizational structure and the growth needs of the mature adult personality, a fact that explains many of the dysfunctional behaviors managers are quick to complain about. In Argyris' view, the traditional, pyramidal form of organization, built on the organizational principles identified by Taylor, Fayol, Mooney, and Gulick, denies rather than satisfies growth needs and discourages rather than encourages mature adult behavior. In his words, "If the principles of formal organization are used as ideally defined, employees will tend to work in an environment where (1) they are provided minimal control over their workaday world, (2) they are expected to be passive, dependent, and subordinate, (3) they are expected to have a short time perspective, (4) they are induced to perfect and value the frequent use of a few skin-surface shallow abilities and, (5) they are expected to produce under conditions leading to psychological failure."[45]

These conditions tend to increase, according to Argyris, as management controls are tightened, as one goes down the chain of command, and as jobs become more mechanized. All of these conditions are incongruent with the ones that psychologically healthy human beings desire. They undermine effective work performance, according to Argyris, by blocking satisfaction of growth needs and by triggering adaptive behaviors such as soldiering, sabotage, and a general indifference to the quality of one's work. Consequently, if organizations are to be successful, ways must be found to facilitate the simultaneous satisfaction of individual and organizational needs.

The Effects of Formal Structure on the Individual

As a partial test of his thesis Argyris examined the formal principles of organization in terms of their ability to satisfy growth needs. The first of these principles is **task specialization.** Tasks are narrowly defined and standardized on the assumption that concentrating effort on a limited field of endeavor increases quality and quantity of output. But this principle assumes, according to Argyris, that the desire for growth can be choked off and that the desire to be engaged in satisfying, meaningful work, and to develop and use a full range of abilities, can be ignored. By requiring everyone to perform tasks in the same prescribed manner, task specialization also ignores the fact that individuals are unique personalities with unique talents. In short, task specialization violates three of the growth tendencies of the healthy adult personality. It inhibits the process of self-actualization by requiring everyone to perform the job in the same routine and prescribed manner (tendency 1), precludes the development and use of complex, psychologically important abilities (tendency 3), and fails to provide the "endless challenge" desired by the healthy adult personality (tendency 4). Argyris' analysis suggests that specialized tasks, performed in a standardized manner, do not allow for the expression of growth needs and thus fail to motivate workers to do their best work.

A second principle of formal organization is **chain of command.** Classical theorists believed that a formal chain of command was necessary to facilitate the coordination of the many specialized tasks created pursuant to the first principle. A hierarchy of authority is established so that those at the top can direct and control the efforts of those at the bottom. "The impact of such a state of affairs," Argyis writes, "is to make the individuals *dependent* upon, *passive* toward, and *subordinate* to the leader. As a result the individuals have *little* *control* over their work and working environment. Concomitantly, their time perspective is *shortened* because they do not control the information necessary to predict their future."[46] In other words, the requirements imposed on workers by this principle violate the second, sixth, seventh, and fifth growth tendencies of the healthy adult personality, respectively. Aware of the dysfunctional consequences of placing severe limits on the power and authority of those toward the bottom of the chain of command, management typically responds in two ways. It provides monetary rewards to compensate for the dissatisfactions experienced at work and it encourages those at the bottom to compete for higher positions. Argyris notes that these compensatory measures produce their own dysfunctional consequences, including low personal involvement in work and harmful competition among employees.

A third principle of formal organization is **unity of direction.** This principle suggests that every unit should have a clear objective or purpose that is planned and directed by the unit's leader. Consequently, decision-making responsibility is placed at the top. The leader is responsible for defining goals and the paths toward the goals. This principle, according to Argyris, creates conditions conducive to psychological failure. The seventh growth tendency suggests that workers experience success when it is their own decisions, not the decisions of their superiors, that determine the outcomes of their efforts. "Psychological success," Argyris writes, "is achieved when each individual is able to define his *own* goals, in relation to his *inner* needs and the strength of the barriers to be overcome in order to reach these goals."[47]

A fourth principle of formal organization is **span of control.** This principle states that efficiency is increased by limiting the span of control to no more than five or six subordinates. Because it takes the need for control for granted, this principle, according to Argyris, requires superiors to exercise close supervision and encourages subordinates to become dependent upon, passive toward, and subordinate to the leader. It also limits the time perspective of subordinates and their control over their work environment. In short, the span-of-control principle violates the second, sixth, and seventh growth tendencies and thus fails to take advantage of the energies and resources that the mature adult personality has to offer.

Argyris suggests that, whereas Taylor, Fayol, Mooney, and Gulick are correct in saying we need a logically ordered structure, we also need a human-centered structure that enables organizations to achieve their goals by providing for the satisfaction of their members' goals. By providing opportunities for workers to satisfy their growth needs, organizations can obtain full value from their human resources and the productive energies they are capable of releasing. In short, organizations can best achieve their objectives by helping their employees realize their "full potentialities." Doing so, however, requires fundamental changes in the distribution of power and authority and in the ways jobs are designed. Releasing psychological energy for productive effort, Argyris concludes, just isn't possible where workers are told by someone else what to do, how to do it, how much to produce, and whether their tasks were performed adequately.

The Effects of Directive Leadership
and Management Controls

Argyris also describes how the failure of the formal structure to satisfy growth needs is reinforced by two other mechanisms: directive leadership and management control systems. Directive leadership is the style of management typically found in pyramidal organizations, in which managers use their formal authority to issues directives and maintain close supervision over their subordinates. This style of management tends to preclude opportunities for subordinates to experience personal growth and psychological success. Instead, it encourages workers to become passive, dependent, and subordinate, maintain a short time perspective, repress their own needs in favor of the leader's needs, and, consequently, experience psychological failure. Passivity, dependence, subordination, and lack of control are further reinforced by management systems that control the definition, inspection, and evaluation of work performance. These include performance measurement, pay-for-performance, financial control, and centralized personnel systems. In Argyris' words, these systems "feed back upon and give support to directive leadership as both "compound the felony" committed by the formal organization every hour of the day and every day of the year."[48]

Argyris believed that under conditions of psychological failure workers tend, as an adaptive response, to suppress their growth needs and deny the psychological importance of their work. This leads to a state of apathy and indifference. As workers become more apathetic and unproductive, managers tend to blame the workers, unaware that their leadership style and management controls are the cause of many of the problems they are experiencing. The solution to the problem of worker apathy, they conclude, is to communicate clear goals, issue work-related directives, and maintain constant pressure on workers to increase productivity. Consequently, a cycle of behavior is created in which management's attitudes toward workers become increasingly more pessimistic, controls are increasingly tightened, opportunities to satisfy growth needs become increasingly fewer, and work performance becomes increasingly substandard, causing the cycle to deepen as it repeats itself. Breaking this cycle, Argyris suggests, requires fundamental changes in formal structure, leadership style, and management control systems. The need for such fundamental changes became a basic premise of human resources theory.

Authentic Relationships

Although *Personality and Organization* (1957) emphasized the need for fundamental changes in the structure of pyramidal organizations, Argyris's own research focused on interpersonal change, thus linking his work to human relations as well as human resources theory. His growing interest in interpersonal relations occurred for a reason. As a consultant he quickly discovered that the effectiveness of management decision making is greatly undermined by the way executives relate to each other and the basic values that shape their behaviors. This led him to conclude that basic values and behavior patterns must be changed at the highest levels of the organization before attempting structural reforms. If structural reforms are attempted prematurely, decisions are likely to be poor and commitment to implementing them low.

According to Argyris, effective decision making requires those involved in the decision to possess all relevant facts about the situation facing the organization, the needs and objectives of the organization, and the needs and objectives of each participant. It also requires knowing how each participant perceives the motives and intentions of others in the group so that misunderstandings can be addressed and suspicions reduced. Finally, it requires knowing what each participant truly thinks of the ideas being put forward so that the best possible decision can be made. Satisfying these conditions depends in turn on establishing an environment of trust where participants feel safe to express their ideas and feelings and are willing to listen to and accommodate the ideas and feelings of others. Once established at the top, this environment of trust must be replicated throughout the organization to secure the commitment needed to ensure successful implementation of decisions. Because an environment of trust is nearly impossible to establish in pyramidal organizations, Argyris concluded that interpersonal change must go hand in hand with changes in structure, management style, and methods of control.

Maintaining an open and trusting environment, according to Argyris, requires interpersonal competence. **Interpersonal competence,** in contrast to technical competence, is reflected in a person's ability to solve interpersonal problems in a way that they remain solved.[49] It requires high self-esteem and self-acceptance so that participants are open to new ideas and willing to take risks, and high acceptance of others so that they are less inclined to judge and manipulate others. It includes the ability to view interpersonal situations realistically, undistorted by the strongly felt need to protect one's self-esteem. Interpersonal competence is developed and manifested by engaging in **authentic relationships.** This refers to a pattern of relating to others in which participants openly share their ideas and feelings, encourage experimenting with new ideas and feelings, seek to validate the motives they attribute to others, give nonjudgmental feedback, and are sensitive to how their own words and actions impact those around them. The relationship between interpersonal competence and authenticity is reciprocal. As self-esteem and acceptance of others increase, relations become more authentic, and as participants engage in authentic relationships, their self-acceptance and awareness of others increase in turn.

ARGYRIS' CONTRIBUTIONS TO ORGANIZATION THEORY

Elton Mayo contributed to organization theory by emphasizing the importance of the worker's subjective state of mind. Attitudes, after all, affect behavior. He did not, however, develop an explicit theory of motivation. He offered insights about how to adjust workers to their work environments, about how to improve morale and job satisfaction, but said little about how to facilitate personal motivation or commitment. In *Personality and Organization* (1957) Chris Argyris did what Elton Mayo had not. He articulated a needs-based theory of motivation and argued that pyramidal organizations are particularly ill-suited to the task of satisfying basic human needs. The healthy organization, he suggested, requires individuals who are competent, committed to organizational objectives, and fully self-responsible—conditions that cannot be met in most organizations without fundamental changes in formal structure, management style, and management control systems.

Although Argyris' subsequent research focused on producing valid information and choices rather than facilitating self-actualization, the themes that came to be associated with human resources theory are found in all of his published works. Among these themes are the following: that workers have the capacity to be self-directing and self-controlling, that organizational success depends on successfully integrating the goal attainment and maintenance needs of the organization with the growth needs of workers, and that successful integration requires broad participation in decision making and an environment of trust. These themes provide the theoretical foundations for a management paradigm based on employee empowerment rather than centralized control.

HUMAN RESOURCES THEORY
IN PERSPECTIVE

Human resources theory greatly influenced management practice in the 1960s and 1970s. Countless numbers of organizations experimented with job enrichment and group decision making, and consultants kept busy training managers to be more employee-centered and participative. But the response from the academic community was much less enthusiastic.[50] Criticisms of human resources theory included the following:

- It rests on romantic, overly optimistic assumptions about human beings. Relatively few workers are achievement-oriented, desire greater responsibility, or value opportunities for personal growth.

- It is normative and overly prescriptive, advocating employee-centered leadership and participative management as the one-best-way to enhance organizational performance.

- It fails to offer a comprehensive theory of organization, focusing narrowly on human behavior and attitudes while ignoring the structural, technological, and environmental determinants of organizational behavior.

- It underestimates the power of economic rewards as sources of motivation.

- It overstates the possibilities for integrating individual and organizational needs and ignores the fact that different organizational units and classes of employees have their own distinct and conflicting interests.

- It ignores the fact that many workers have a need for power. They will continue to behave in self-serving, secretive, and aggressive ways.
- It fails to resolve the issue of whether job content or employee involvement is the primary source of intrinsic motivation, and research has failed to confirm the benefits of either one for organizational performance.

While these criticisms define the limits of human resources theory as a management strategy, they do not pose a significant challenge to the validity of the theory itself. Several of the criticisms question the theory's emphasis but not its substance, some reflect the natural distaste of positivists for normative theory, and others reflect the mistaken notion that the theory advocates a single, employee-centered, participative style of management for all organizations under all circumstances. Once it is acknowledged that human resources theory does not offer a comprehensive theory of organization, does not offer a panacea for achieving high levels of performance, and is perhaps overly optimistic in its view of people in general, it is still possible to appreciate the many valuable contributions it has made to management thinking. These include the importance of treating workers with respect and dignity, the value that accrues to organizations and individuals alike as human potential is developed and unleashed, the gains in social cohesion, employee commitment, and decision quality that are possible through group decision making, and the benefits that flow from achieving win–win solutions through collective problem solving.

The human resources perspective has also made important contributions to theory building. In two key respects Argyris, McGregor, and Likert succeeded in doing what human relations theorists had not. They developed a comprehensive needs-based theory of motivation and they described the basic outline of an alternative to the traditional, bureaucratic paradigm based on technical rationality, formal authority, and use of the scalar chain for purposes of coordination and control. The human resources or empowerment paradigm challenged traditional management principles and prevailing assumptions about human nature. What is truly new in this paradigm is its call for a genuine transfer of power from management to teams comprising workers, line managers, and staff officers at every level of the organization. Stated differently, it calls for a genuine change in the way organizations are governed. It calls for developing human capacity and releasing human potential by empowering workers to make the decisions that are relevant to their respective areas of responsibility and encouraging them to accept responsibility for the overall performance of their units. If no organization has fully and genuinely empowered workers in this way, human resources theory nonetheless offers a paradigm for envisioning what is possible when the necessary conditions are present.

To suggest that human resources theory offers an alternative paradigm is not to suggest that it is easily implemented or that its hypothesized benefits will necessarily materialize. The greatest limitations of human resources theory lie in the difficulties inherent in transferring it from the realm of theory to the realm of practice. Arguably, it calls for a level of maturity and an orientation toward achievement and personal growth that too few workers and managers possess. Argyris and McGregor believed, for example, that effective decision making requires an environment of openness and trust, and that this in turn requires a high degree of personal self-acceptance and sense of self-worth among those involved. They also believed that workers will not respond to opportunities to self-actualize unless they have satisfied their lower level needs and are free of anxiety-producing psychological disorders. Finally, they believed that genuine participation requires managers who are secure enough in their egos to relinquish control in the traditional sense and who are sufficiently patient and self-disciplined to practice decision making by consensus.

Maslow

All of these assumptions or requirements are difficult to satisfy in practice. As Miles has shown, managers tend to favor participative management for themselves but not for others.[51] This is because they feel worthy of the trust of those above them but remain distrustful of those below them. And although human resources theory was partly grounded in the work of Abraham Maslow, he, too, noted the practical limitations of human resources theory. Toward the end of his career he accepted an opportunity to investigate the implications of his hierarchy of human needs for management theory and practice. Although he agreed that work offers self-fulfillment to many people, and that Theory Y provides the best approach for managing an increasingly well-educated and professionally trained work force, he questioned whether many workers or managers possess the level of personal maturity, psychological health, and genuine good will required for trust, openness, collaboration, and collective accomplishment.[52]

do we hire people like this? is it a trait sought after?

It is also true that interest in transferring Theory Y from the realm of theory to practice has been dampened by the way actual organizations have attempted to put it into practice. In many instances it has involved superficial efforts by training departments to institute sensitivity training or misguided experiments in organizational democracy.[53]

We are left, then, with a basic paradox: human resources theory offers an alternative paradigm with great promise but one that faces formidable obstacles to its successful implementation. However, if human resources theorists are overly optimistic, there is no reason to be overly pessimistic in turn. In individual work units, if not in organizations as a whole, many have experienced what is possible when a critical mass of reasonably mature and dedicated employees are empowered to determine for themselves what to do and how best to do it. Of course, many questions remain unanswered. Research has not yet determined, for example, the conditions under which job enrichment or group participation produces the best results, or whether one approach is superior to the other. Likert may be correct, for example, that having interesting and challenging work is less important than being able to make meaningful contributions to organizational objectives through teamwork. Whatever its shortcomings, human resources theory provides a valuable point of departure for investigating questions of this kind.

Rio common purpose

RELEVANCE FOR PUBLIC MANAGEMENT

The remainder of this chapter explores the relevance of human resources theory for public management and organizational performance. This exploration is guided by the three analytical frameworks introduced in Chapter 3.

Models of Organizational Effectiveness

As noted in the previous chapter, human resources theory emphasizes the internally directed models of effectiveness, the **internal process** and **human relations** models, as well as the externally directed **rational goal** model. It recognizes the importance of accomplishing the organization's goal attainment, integrative, and pattern maintenance/tension management functions, and the values associated with these functions, in a truly integrated fashion. The emphasis on balancing potentially competing values is a natural consequence of the theory's basic premise: organizational performance is enhanced through the simultaneous satisfaction of human and organizational needs. That human resources theory strives to achieve potentially competing values in an integrated and balanced fashion indicates, perhaps, a growing awareness of the importance of taking a holistic view of the determinants of organizational performance.

The competing values framework shown in Exhibit 13.1 identifies important values but does not specify *how* they are to be achieved. Much of the significance of human resources theory lies in what it has to say about how effectiveness values are best realized in practice. For example, whereas classical management theory emphasizes centralized decision making and control, standardized tasks, and extrinsic rewards, human resources theory emphasizes decentralized decision making and self-control, enriched tasks, and intrinsic rewards. Similarly, human resources theory holds that goal attainment should be pursued not by limiting the discretion of workers through the use of rules, standard operating procedures, and close supervision but by expanding their discretion by articulating strategic goals, delegating responsibility for goal attainment to lower levels of the organization, practicing management by objectives, and holding workers accountable for bottom-line results.

Mechanisms for Coordinating and Controlling Work Activities

As noted in the previous chapter, human resources theory advocates **mutual adjustment** as an alternative to direct supervision. Mutual adjustment occurs as members of each work unit meet as a group to set appropriate goals and monitor their own progress. Coordination is achieved by consulting broadly with pertinent individuals in other units or at other levels of authority. It is also achieved by establishing policies and setting goals that are consistent with the policies and goals set at higher levels of the organization. Similarly, control is exercised not by micromanaging the behaviors of subordinates but by holding individuals and work units accountable for achieving desired results. McGregor's Theory Y, for example, calls for coordinating and controlling work activities by encouraging workers to set

Exhibit 13.1 The Competing Values Framework: Four Models of Organizational Effectiveness

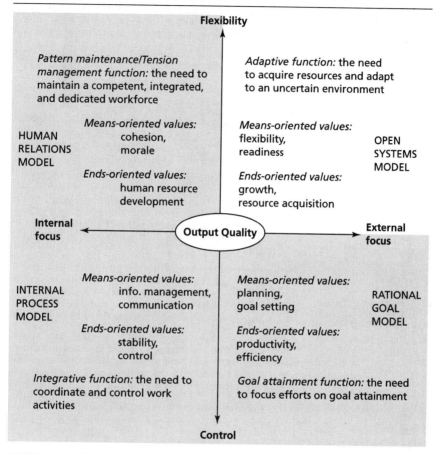

SOURCE: Adapted with permission from Figures 3 and 4, Robert O. Quinn and John Rohrbaugh, "A Spatial Model of Effectiveness Criteria: Towards a Competing Values Approach to Organizational Analysis," *Management Science* 29 (March 1983): 363–373. Copyright 1983, The Institute of Management Sciences, now the Institute for Operations Research and the Management Sciences (INFORMS), 901 Elkridge Landing Road, Suite 400, Linthicum, Maryland 21090-2909 USA.

goals for their work units that are consistent with organizational goals and then holding each unit accountable for achieving the agreed–upon results.

Mutual adjustment as a mechanism of coordination and control may be especially well–suited to the needs and characteristics of many public agencies. Centralized policy making coupled with decentralized administration may be appropriate, for example, in geographically dispersed agencies such as the U.S. Forest Service, where decisions in the field cannot be coordinated and controlled through pre–established rules set by the central office. Similarly, mutual adjustment of the kind envisioned by human resources theory may be appropriate in craft and coping agencies, where outputs are unmeasurable and where the effectiveness of direct supervision is greatly reduced as a result.

Exhibit 13.2 Six Mechanisms for Coordinating and Controlling Work Activities

Mutual adjustment	Workers consult with each other informally about what needs to be accomplished and how. Responsibility for coordination and control rests with those who do the work.
Direct supervision	A supervisor is assigned to take responsibility for a group of workers and a managerial hierarchy is established to integrate the efforts of all work groups. The supervisor issues personal instructions and monitors individual performance.
Standardization of work processes	Work is programmed in advance of its execution by developing rules and standard operating procedures specifying how everyone is to perform assigned tasks. Coordination is built into the work process itself and control is achieved by strictly limiting each worker's discretion.
Standardization of work outputs	Work outputs are programmed in advance by providing each work group with product specifications or performance goals and allowing members considerable latitude in determining how to achieve them. Control is exercised by collecting output data, requiring corrective action when needed, and rewarding and sanctioning workers based on results achieved.
Standardization of worker skills	Workers are employed who possess the knowledge and skills needed to make appropriate decisions. Educational institutions and professional associations are relied upon to provide standardized training. Professionally trained workers are largely self-coordinating and self-controlling.
Standardization of values	Organizational leaders communicate and act upon a clear vision of what the organization exists to do, where it should be headed, and what values should guide it. Coordination and control is facilitated by commitment of organizational members to shared, internalized values and ideals.

SOURCE: Based in large part on Henry Mintzberg, *Structure in Fives* (Prentice-Hall, 1993, 3–7).

Motivational Strategies

Although human resources theory recognizes the value of instrumental rewards as motivators, especially those associated with considerate leadership and group acceptance, it places greatest emphasis on the **job identification strategy** and the power of intrinsic rewards. It holds that most adults are motivated by a desire to satisfy their ego and growth needs and that they receive intrinsic satisfactions from doing responsible, interesting, and challenging work. According to Katz and Kahn, as workers are provided with opportunities to express themselves and their unique talents through their work, they identify with their jobs and take pride in their accomplishments. This in turn increases their level of work effort and reduces absenteeism and turnover, thereby allowing for the simultaneous satisfaction of the individual's ego and growth needs and the organization's goal attainment and maintenance needs.

As a motivational strategy, job identification entails redesigning jobs so that they offer greater responsibility and challenge, or removing bureaucratic constraints and supervisory controls from jobs that already offer responsibility and

Exhibit 13.3 Four Motivational Strategies

Legal Compliance

Using rules, formal directives, and sanctions to direct and control employee behavior. Employees may come to work, comply with rules, and satisfy minimum role requirements, either because they accept the legitimacy of organizational authority or fear being sanctioned.

Instrumental Rewards

Using rewards to induce desired behaviors.

Rewards for Performance

Distributing pay, promotions, and recognition based on individual performance. Employees may meet or exceed role expectations because they value the material and psychological satisfactions that money, advancement, and recognition can provide.

Considerate Leadership

Adopting a leadership style based on being attentive to employees and considerate of their needs. This strategy may improve morale. It might also induce those who value the respect, support, and approval of persons in authority to meet or exceed their role requirements.

Group Acceptance

Creating a work environment that allows employees to socialize, form group bonds, and enjoy the approval of their peers. This strategy may induce those who value affiliation and peer approval to meet or exceed role requirements, assuming that group norms are consistent with organizational objectives.

Job Identification

Offering work that is interesting, challenging, and responsible. Employees may come to work, meet or exceed role requirements, and possibly exhibit greater creativity and innovativeness. They may do so because they identify with the jobs and find their work intrinsically rewarding.

Goal Congruence

Hiring employees whose goals and values are congruent with the organization's and/or socializing employees so that they internalize organizational goals and values. Employees may come to work, remain with the organization, meet or exceed role requirements, and exhibit greater creativity, innovativeness, and institutional loyalty. They may do so because they identify with the organization's mission and values and because contributing to them reinforces their own self-concept.

SOURCE: Based in large part on Daniel Katz and Robert L. Kahn, *The Social Psychology of Organizations* (Wiley, 1966), pp. 336–68.

challenge, as so many public service jobs do. The job identification strategy may be especially applicable to public agencies because of the large numbers of highly educated technical and professional employees who work in government. As noted earlier, these are precisely the kinds of employees that research tells us tend to respond positively to meaningful and intrinsically satisfying work. As Robert Behn has written,

> .... People do not enter the field of social service to maximize income; they hope to do meaningful work. If legislators, or political executives, or career executives can find some way to exploit that desire to do meaningful work—to take advantage of the beneficial self-selection that leads

people to choose public sector jobs—they may gain help not merely in carrying out standard operating procedures to achieve goals, and not merely in figuring out how best to achieve those goals, but also in determining what goals are both worth pursuing and pursuable.[54]

SUMMARY

Argyris and McGregor concluded that pyramidal structures and directive leadership are incompatible with basic human needs. Superior-subordinate relationships, close supervision, and narrowly defined tasks cause workers to become passive, dependent, and subordinate, precisely the opposite of what psychologically healthy adults require. In their view, organizations must be restructured and human resources managed so as to encourage initiative, independence, personal growth and, ultimately, the release of each individual's full potential.

Understood as a theory of organizational effectiveness, human resources theory holds that performance is enhanced by developing each person's unique talents, creating and sustaining an environment of openness and trust, removing constraints on personal autonomy and individual discretion, delegating responsibilities downward, and encouraging group decision making—all so that workers can derive intrinsic satisfactions from their work and so that their goals and the goals of the organization can be realized simultaneously. Key implications for public managers, in addition to those already identified in Chapter 12, include the following:

- **Recognizing interdependence.** The command-and-control approach takes advantage of the fact that workers are dependent on the organization for their jobs and livelihoods. It also fosters dependence by allowing workers to do only what supervisors authorize them to do. Human resources theory holds that this is counterproductive. It suggests that public managers should recognize that they are equally dependent on their staff members for the success of the agency and that workers should be given the authority and independence of action they need to make wise choices on behalf of the agency.

- **Altering basic assumptions.** Assumptions matter. No structural or behavioral reforms will produce the desired effects as long as public managers continue to embrace Theory X assumptions. Public managers should relinquish control in the traditional sense, trust staff members to use their delegated authority wisely, understand that mistakes will occur in the course of human growth and development, and appreciate that the costs of these mistakes are outweighed by the benefits accruing from greater initiative, creativity, and risk-taking.

- **Manager as facilitator.** Instead of defining their managerial role in terms of directing and controlling workers, public managers should think in terms of empowering staff members and facilitating their success. Not only does this mean empowering them to pursue agreed-upon objectives but also removing the obstacles to successful goal attainment that stand in their way. The latter may prove to be the public manager's most important role because most government jobs are intrinsically rewarding and opportunities to exercise discretion are widely available. It is often bureaucratic constraints and limited resources that undermine the morale and motivation of otherwise empowered public servants.

Although human resources theory provides a useful point of departure for improving organizational performance, it should not be viewed as the final answer to questions of organizational design and management. Workers enjoy different levels of maturity and possess different levels of need for growth and achievement. Not every worker will set challenging targets for themselves or be motivated to reach those that they do set. Similarly, work environments characterized by openness, trust, and relative equality may improve interpersonal relations, increase job satisfaction, and lower absenteeism and turnover rates, but they cannot guarantee greater work effort, higher productivity, or better overall agency performance. As we have seen in earlier chapters and will see in the chapters that follow, many other variables enter into the performance equation.

NOTES

1. Abraham H. Maslow, "A Dynamic Theory of Human Motivation," *Psychological Review 50* (1943): 370–96.

2. Abraham H. Maslow, *Motivation and Personality* (New York: Harper & Brothers, 1954).

3. Maslow, *Motivation and Personality,* 84.

4. Maslow, *Motivation and Personality,* 87.

5. Maslow, *Motivation and Personality,* 91.

6. Maslow, *Motivation and Personality,* 92.

7. Maslow, *Motivation and Personality,* Chapter 12.

8. Richard Lowery, Foreword to Abraham H. Maslow, *Toward a Psychology of Being* (New York: Wiley, 1999), xxviii.

9. Maslow, *Motivation and Personality,* 100–101.

10. Mahmoud Wahba and Lawrence Bridwell, "Maslow Reconsidered: A Review of Research on the Needs Hierarchy Theory," *Organizational Behavior and Human Performance 15* (April 1976): 224.

11. See, for example, David Guest, "Motivation after Maslow," *Personnel Management 8* (March 1976): 29–32.

12. Clayton P. Alderfer, "An Empirical Test of a New Theory of Human Needs," *Organizational Behavior and Human Performance 4* (May 1969): 142–75.

13. McGregor, *The Human Side of Enterprise* (New York: McGraw-Hill, 1960), vi–vii.

14. McGregor, *The Human Side of Enterprise,* 4.

15. See Douglas McGregor, *Leadership and Motivation: Essays of Douglas McGregor* (Cambridge: The M.I.T Press, 1966), ix–xix; and *New York Times,* October 14, 1964, p. 45.

16. McGregor, *The Human Side of Enterprise,* 10.

17. McGregor, *The Human Side of Enterprise,* 33–34.

18. McGregor, *The Human Side of Enterprise,* 39.

19. McGregor, *The Human Side of Enterprise,* 47–48.

20. McGregor, *The Human Side of Enterprise,* 49.

21. McGregor, *The Human Side of Enterprise,* 192.

22. McGregor, *The Human Side of Enterprise,* 195.

23. McGregor, *The Human Side of Enterprise,*160.

24. McGregor, *The Human Side of Enterprise,* 133.

25. McGregor, *The Human Side of Enterprise,* 152.

26. McGregor, *The Human Side of Enterprise,* 152.

27. McGregor, *The Human Side of Enterprise,* 153.

28. McGregor, *The Human Side of Enterprise,* 158–59.

29. Douglas McGregor, *The Professional Manager* (New York: McGraw-Hill, 1967), 126–27.

30. McGregor, *The Professional Manager,* 78.

31. Peter F. Drucker, *The Practice of Management* (New York: Harper & Brothers, 1954), 121–36.

32. McGregor, *The Human Side of Enterprise,* 61.

33. McGregor, *The Human Side of Enterprise,* 75.

34. Frederick Herzberg, "One More Time: How Do You Motivate Employees?" *Harvard Business Review 46* (January-February 1968), 53–62.

35. H. Roy Kaplan, Curt Tausky, and Bhopinder Bolarin, "Job Enrichment," *Personnel Journal 48* (October 1969), 791–98.

36. McGregor, *The Professional Manager.*

37. McGregor, *The Professional Manager,* 96.

38. For one such criticism, see Curt Tausky, *Work Organizations: Major Theoretical Perspectives* (Itasca, IL: Peacock Publishers, 1978), 61.

39. Chris Argyris, *Personality and Organization: The Conflict Between System and the Individual* (New York: Harper & Row, 1957).

40. See "Gold Medal Award for Life Achievement in the Application of Psychology," *American Psychologist 53* (August 1998), 877–78; and Robert Putnum, "A Biography of Chris Argyris," *Journal of Applied Behavioral Science 31* (September 1995), 253–55.

41. Alfred J. Marrow, *The Practical Theorist: The Life and Work of Kurt Lewin* (New York: Teachers College Press, Columbia University, 1977), 233.

42. Argyris, *Personality and Organization,* 50.

43. Chris Argyris, "The Organization: What Makes It Healthy," *Harvard Business Review 36* (November-December, 1958), 111.

44. Argyris, *Personality and Organization,* 53.

45. Argyris, *Personality and Organization,* 67.

46. Argyris, *Personality and Organization,* 60–61.

47. Agyris, *Personality and Organization,* 63–64.

48. Argyris, *Personality and Organization,* 138.

49. Chris Argyris, *Interpersonal Competence and Organizational Effectiveness* (Homewood, IL: Dorsey Press, 1962), 26.

50. See, for example, the debate between Chris Argyris and Herbert Simon in the May/June and July/August 1973 issues of *Public Administration Review.*

51. Raymond E. Miles, "Human Relations or Human Resources," *Harvard Business Review 43* (July-August 1965): 148–63.

52. Abraham Maslow, *Eupsychian Management: A Journal* (Homewood, IL: Irwin, 1965).

53. Thomas J. Peters and Robert H. Waterman, *In Search of Excellence* (New York: Warner Books, 1982), 95–96.

54. Robert D. Behn, "The Big Questions of Public Management," *Public Administration Review 55* (July/August 1995), 319.

14

⌘

Quality Management Theory

W. Edwards Deming and Joseph Juran

Quality management theory is known by many names, including total quality management (TQM), total quality control (TQC), and continuous quality improvement (CQI). Regardless of the name by which it is known, quality management theory holds that performance is enhanced by designing products and services to meet or exceed customer expectations and by empowering workers to find and eliminate all factors that undermine product or service quality.

Quality management theory originated with Walter Shewhart's concept of statistical process control in the 1920s, evolved into a theory of management in the 1950s, contributed to the success of Japanese firms in the 1960s and 1970s, and finally came to the attention of American business executives in the early 1980s. In the years that followed, public and private organizations embraced it with what often seemed like religious zeal. Although it is now widely viewed as yet another failed management fad, it nonetheless continues to exert a strong influence on how many public managers and agency personnel view their jobs and conduct their business.

This chapter traces the historical evolution of quality management theory and identifies its core concepts as reflected in the writings of Walter Shewhart, Armand Feigenbaum, Kaoru Ishikawa, W. Edwards Deming, and Joseph Juran. The chapter closes with an analysis of the relevance of quality management theory for public management and organizational performance.

THE ORIGINS AND EVOLUTION OF QUALITY MANAGEMENT THEORY

Quality management theory evolved over a period of several decades. The following sections highlight five key stages in its historical evolution.

Stage 1: Development of Statistical Process Control (SPC)

The quality of manufactured goods may be assured in either of two ways. The first, **quality control by inspection,** remains the dominant method even today. Heavily steeped in the scientific management tradition, this method requires engineers to set quality specifications for each part, production supervisors to keep actual quality characteristics within the specified ranges, and inspectors to remove the nonconforming or defective parts or products as they come off the assembly line. The latter are then scrapped or reworked before being sold. Customers are also given warranties in case the product fails after it has been purchased.

The second method of quality control, **statistical process control,** was developed in the 1920s by Walter Shewhart, a statistician at the Bell Telephone Laboratories in New York. It involves collecting statistical data on variations in product quality, using the data to identify the causes of poor product quality, and eliminating those causes at each stage of the manufacturing process. Whereas the inspection method relies on detecting defects after they have occurred, SPC relies on preventing them in the first place, making it a much more logical and cost-effective method of quality control.

The two main features of SPC are statistical sampling and process control. Instead of inspecting each and every item, quality control is achieved by sampling a small number of finished goods at each stage of production, collecting statistical data on variations in quality, tracking down the causes of variations that lie outside the acceptable range, and improving the production process or materials used so that those variations no longer occur. Each stage in the production process is then said to be "under statistical control," a term coined by Shewhart.

As Shewhart explained in *Economic Control of Quality of Manufactured Product* (1931), the variations we observe in natural and physical processes typically reflect stable patterns.[1] For example, an individual can die at any time from any one of a thousand chance causes of death, and yet we can predict with relative certainty the chances of that individual living to the age of 45, 55, or 65. The same is true in manufacturing. Variations in product quality are caused by differences in the quality of materials, the accuracy and reliability of machines, and the skills and behaviors of workers. If appropriate attention is given to controlling these factors, variations in quality should demonstrate a normal and predictable pattern with actual data points clustering around the desired standards. Conversely, if research reveals that some data points are falling well outside the desired range, then this constitutes evidence that there is a special cause of poor quality at work that must be tracked down and eliminated. Statistical analysis provides the means for determining when such special causes exist.

Exhibit 14.1 Example of a Control Chart: The Diameter of Ball Bearings

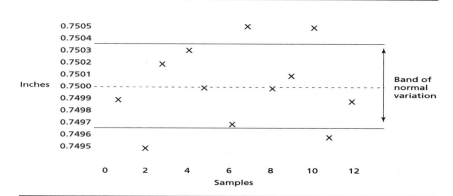

Suppose, for example, that the diameter of a ball bearing must be 0.7500 inches, plus or minus 0.0004. Rather than studying every ball bearing that comes off the assembly line, SPC involves taking several small samples, calculating the mathematical mean for each sample on a particular dimension of quality, and plotting the means on a control chart. An example of a control chart is shown in Exhibit 14.1. The horizontal lines at plus and minus 0.0004 inches represent the tolerance levels set by the product engineers. Data points clustering around the desired diameter of 0.7500 inch represent the expected, normal pattern. Those not clustering around the desired diameter, and especially those lying outside of the set tolerances, indicate that a quality problem exists. Experiments are then conducted, varying such things as the materials used, machine speeds, and methods employed, until these outliers cease to appear. A second type of control chart allows researchers to plot the percent of each sample found to be defective. Which type of chart is used depends on whether the quality attribute is measurable in standard units or must be judged on a defective/not defective basis.

Shewhart understood that it is not economical to track down and eliminate all sources of variation in product quality. He proposed that tests be conducted to determine whether the quality standards set by the engineers might be set even higher by eliminating additional sources of error. If this cannot be accomplished economically, then the process should be judged under control. Quality control by inspection is extraordinarily expensive. At the Hawthorne plant in the 1920s, for example, fully 13 percent of all workers were engaged in inspection.[2] SPC, although also costly, promises a sizeable return on investment by greatly reducing the number of inspectors and eliminating the sources of defects that make waste and rework necessary in the first place. Nonetheless, only a handful of manufacturing firms adopted SPC prior to the Second World War. Quality control by inspection was simply too entrenched and there were too few trained statisticians available to make SPC a feasible alternative. Although SPC was introduced successfully in the armaments industries during the war, it was systematically ignored afterwards because American firms did not need to compete on the basis of quality in the general absence of foreign competition.

Thus, as the first stage in the evolution of quality management theory came to a close in the late 1940s, the worth of an alternative to quality control by inspection had been established. Attention, however, remained focused on the role of the quality control department in the manufacturing process. There was, as yet, no general theory of quality management.

Stage 2: Total Quality Control (TQC)
as a Management Function

The second stage in the evolution of quality management theory is marked by the publication of two articles by Armand Feigenbaum, the top quality expert at General Electric, in 1956.[3] These articles broadened discussions of quality assurance from a narrow focus on production to the overall process by which products are designed, manufactured, marketed, and serviced. Feigenbaum insisted that quality cannot be assured solely through the efforts of specialists in the quality control or inspection department. He identified eight stages in the production process and described how those involved at each stage contribute importantly to the quality of the final product. Quality depends, for example, on how well members of the marketing staff understand the preferences of customers. It depends on how well engineers design the product in light of customer preferences and the realities of the production line. It depends on the quality of the materials secured by the purchasing staff. And it depends on how well the inspectors and testers feed back information about the causes of variations in quality to those working at the beginning of the design and production process. Quality cannot be assured by focusing on one or a few of these stages alone. Nor can it be assured by relying on the methods of statistical process control alone. Quality can be assured only through what Feigenbaum called **total quality control.** This he defined as a "system for integrating the quality-development, quality-maintenance, and quality-improvement efforts of the various groups in an organization so as to enable production and service at the most economical levels which allow for full customer satisfaction."[4]

Feigenbaum argued that quality control is a core management function, much like finance or personnel management. Because "quality is everybody's job," quality control can only be assured through an integrated program overseen by a central staff organization. In his words, "The quality control job requires a complete and positive program involving *all* the elements which influence product quality. This program starts with the design of the product and ends only when the product has been placed in the hands of a customer who remains satisfied with it."[5]

This newly recognized management function encompassed four sets of activities which Feigenbaum defined as follows:[6]

1. New design control, or the planning of controls for new or modified products prior to the start of production.

2. Incoming material control, or the control of incoming purchased parts and materials.

3. Product control, or the shop floor control of materials, parts, and batches from machines, processes, and assembly lines.

4. Special process studies, or the conducting of special analyses of factory and processing problems.

The last of these sets of activities is particularly important in the evolution of quality management theory and practice. It anticipates the use of quality circles and cross-functional teams created as needed to investigate special quality-related problems. Each of these investigations focuses on a specific work process and is directed toward both the elimination of defects and the continual improvement of the process itself.

By adopting the word *total*, Feigenbaum signaled an important transition from thinking about the responsibilities of the quality control department in isolation to thinking about quality control as a basic management function that must be performed in an integrated fashion and on an organization-wide basis. The inspection method allowed senior managers to delegate responsibility for product quality to specialists in the quality control department and wash their hands of any further involvement. Feigenbaum's concept of TQC made it clear that they could continue doing so only at their own peril. The management of quality, he argued, was central to cost containment and organizational survival. Although Feigenbaum simply put into words what many other quality experts had already concluded, his articles served to highlight the importance of an integrated management approach to quality assurance and provided a useful label for what would become known in the 1980s as total quality management.

Stage 3: Adoption of SPC by the Japanese

The third stage in the evolution of quality management theory is marked by the adoption of statistical process control (SPC) by Japanese firms in the late 1940s and early1950s, initially during the American occupation. Recognizing the importance of reliable systems of communications to the economic reconstruction of Japan, General MacArthur put his Civil Communication Section to work rebuilding the radio and telephone industries. In 1949 Homer Sarasohn, formerly an electronics expert at Raytheon, and Charles Protzman, a seasoned engineer from Western Electric, put together a management training seminar for company executives that included a section on statistical quality control. Knowledge of SPC did not become widespread in Japan, however, until W. Edwards Deming introduced large numbers of Japanese engineers, plant managers, and company executives to SPC in 1950 at the request of the Japanese Union of Scientists and Engineers (JUSE).

Although SPC was credited with saving millions of dollars from reduced inspection and rework in the defense industries during the war, it was systematically ignored by American manufacturers in the postwar period because it was viewed as costly, time consuming, and unnecessary. With the economies of most European and Asian countries devastated by the war, American manufacturers faced little competition in foreign markets and saw no reason to compete on

W. Edwards Deming 1900–1993

William Edwards Deming was born October 14, 1900, in Sioux City, Iowa and grew up on a forty-acre homestead just outside of Powell, Wyoming.[7] After completing high school Deming attended the University of Wyoming, where he received a bachelor's degree in engineering in 1921. He went on to earn a master's degree in mathematics and physics at the University of Colorado in 1924 and a Ph.D. in mathematical physics from Yale University in 1927.

Intrigued by an opportunity to study the effects of nitrogen on crops, Deming accepted a job with the Department of Agriculture in the fixed-nitrogen laboratory in 1927. It was during this period that he traveled regularly to New York to learn techniques of statistical process control from Walter Shewhart. In 1939 Deming was recruited by the U.S. Census Bureau to develop sampling techniques to be used for the first time in the 1940 census. During the Second World War, Deming worked with Stanford University to design and deliver short courses on Shewhart's methods of statistical process control to engineers, inspectors, and others engaged in wartime production. The resulting interest in quality led to the formation of the American Society for Quality Control (ASQC) in February 1946. Deming was one of ASQC's charter members. In the same year, Deming left the Census Bureau to go into

business as a private statistical consultant. He also began teaching courses on quality control in the Business School at New York University, which he continued to do until 1975.

In 1947 General MacArthur invited Deming to Japan to help the Japanese prepare for the 1951 census. Having cultivated friendships with several Japanese statisticians in 1947, Deming was invited back in 1950 to deliver a series of seminars on statistical process control to managers and technical employees of Japan's top industrial firms. Thereafter he became a constant visitor to Japan, returning summer after summer to preach the gospel of quality management. In appreciation, the Japanese in 1951 established the Deming Award, Japan's highest honor for the business community.

America "discovered" Deming nearly thirty years later, when in 1980 an NBC documentary attributed much of Japan's postwar economic success to his ideas. As he approached his eightieth birthday, Deming suddenly found his services as a consultant very much in demand. Believing that he had a crucially important message to deliver and realizing that he had little time to get the message out, he began delivering four-day seminars on quality management all across the country and continued to do so until the final month of his life. Deming died of cancer on December 20, 1993, at the age of 93.

the basis of quality. Japanese manufacturers faced a different situation. They needed to export finished goods to help restore the Japanese economy but their ability to do so was greatly hampered by the poor quality of their products. Consequently, when Deming told Japanese business leaders that product quality provides the only sure path to success, he found a receptive audience.

As a consultant, Deming had tried for years to convince his American clients to compete on the basis of product quality. He had learned from personal experience that efforts by the quality control staff to implement SPC rarely succeed without senior management's full understanding and commitment. This is why he insisted on meeting with the presidents of Japan's top firms during his visit.

Exhibit 14.2 The Plan-Do-Check-Act Cycle for Continuous Improvement

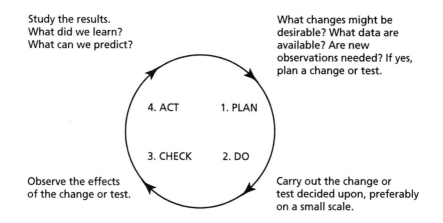

Study the results.
What did we learn?
What can we predict?

What changes might be
desirable? What data are
available? Are new
observations needed? If yes,
plan a change or test.

4. ACT   1. PLAN

3. CHECK   2. DO

Observe the effects
of the change or test.

Carry out the change or
test decided upon, preferably
on a small scale.

Step 5. Repeat Step 1, with knowledge accumulated.
Step 6. Repeat Step 2, and onward.

SOURCE: Adapted from W. Edwards Deming, *Out of the Crisis* (Cambridge, MA: Massachusetts Insitute of Technology, 1986), 88.

Whereas his lectures to engineers and plant managers emphasized the principles and techniques of SPC, his message to corporate executives emphasized the benefits of producing high quality goods. These benefits are reflected in what he called the *chain reaction theory* of business success. In essence it states that improving quality through SPC reduces costs and improves quality, which provides greater value to customers and increases their loyalty, which fuels growth and increases profits over the long term and generates more jobs for society.[8]

Deming also introduced the Japanese to the **Plan–Do–Check–Act (PDCA) Cycle.** As shown in Exhibit 14.2, the PDCA Cycle calls for the continuous application of the scientific method. When speaking to business leaders, Deming used it to illustrate a **process of continuous improvement** in manufacturing in which new products are designed, manufactured, sold, and then redesigned based on customer feedback in a never-ending cycle. When speaking to workers and supervisors, Deming used it to explain how to make continual improvements in their immediate work processes. Because Deming borrowed the concept from a collection of Shewhart's lectures published in 1939, it also came to be known as the Shewhart or Deming Cycle.[9]

Today the PDCA Cycle is used as a guide for improving any work process or management system, including those outside the realm of product design and manufacturing. The first step in the cycle is to **plan** a quality improvement project. A quality improvement team is created to study a process to determine what changes may improve it. If necessary, additional data is collected before deciding what changes might be warranted. The second step is to **do**. This involves introducing a change or conducting a small-scale test to improve the process and ultimately the quality of the product or service. The third step is to **check.** This involves observing the effects of the change or test to determine whether the anticipated improvements materialized. In some instances this is accomplished by collecting data and plotting them on charts. In others it may require feedback from customers or clients. The fourth step is to **act** on the results. This typically involves introducing broader and more permanent changes based on the results of the initial change or test. Because the goal is continual improvement, the cycle then continues, guided by what has been learned in earlier iterations. By repeating the cycle for a particular work process continuously, the process experiences increasingly higher levels of quality improvement and performance.

Deming's message to Japanese business leaders was reinforced in 1954 by another American quality control expert, Joseph M. Juran. At Deming's suggestion, the Japanese Union of Scientists and Engineers invited Juran to study their approach to quality, provide a critique, and conduct training courses, including special seminars for company executives. The latter seminars were attended by seventy presidents of Japan's top companies.[10] The message that Deming and Juran delivered to Japanese executives went well beyond adopting statistical process control and preventing defects. They knew only too well that a product could conform to all established specifications and still not provide value to the customer, or that the manufacturing function might exhibit controlled processes when all other functional areas did not. Consequently, Deming and Juran emphasized the importance of adopting quality as a fundamental business strategy, designing and manufacturing products in a way that satisfies customer requirements, and developing an integrated, company-wide program for continually improving all work processes and management systems.

In essence Deming and Juran introduced Japanese executives to what Feigenbaum would soon label *total quality control.* In doing so they helped shift discussion from quality control as a narrow, technical staff function to quality management as a discrete and fundamentally important management function. Unfortunately, total quality control existed only in the conceptual realm in the 1950s. Because there were no clear models to follow, it was left to the Japanese to determine how to put total quality control into practice.

Stage 4: Emergence of a Uniquely Japanese Form of TQC

The Japanese form of total quality control did not take shape immediately after the visits by Deming and Juran. Nor did it emerge in accordance with a well-thought-out plan. Change came slowly and when it did it was as much the result of a bottom-up social movement as a top-down management initiative. In fact, it is unlikely that quality management would have taken root at all if it had not been for the educational campaigns launched by the Japanese Union of Scientists and Engineers. Beginning in the early 1950s, its quality control research group supervised the development and delivery of courses on quality control for every level of worker, published a journal on quality control, organized annual conferences, identified November as "quality month," and established the Deming Prize for quality using royalties from the sale of

Deming's Japanese lectures. In the early 1960s it began publishing a second journal on quality control aimed at foremen, encouraged the development and registration of thousands of quality circles in companies throughout Japan, and motivated workers to compete for Best Quality Circle awards. Through these means JUSE helped orchestrate a social movement among workers and middle managers that senior managers could not ignore. In short, the Japanese approach to total quality control grew out of a combination of company-specific initiatives and the nationwide promotional activities of JUSE.

The model of total quality control described by Feigenbaum and implemented at General Electric differed significantly from the model that gradually emerged in Japan during the 1950s and 1960s. Whereas the American model relied upon staff specialists to coordinate quality control activities in the best tradition of scientific management, the Japanese model relied upon cross-trained managers and rank-and-file workers to ensure product quality. It also endorsed a management style based on individual respect and employee empowerment, a style very similar to what human resources theorists in the United States were calling Theory Y.[11]

Japan's approach to total quality control is defined by four key features: cross-functional committees at the top of the organization charged with setting policy and coordinating all quality-related activities; quality circles at the bottom of the organization charged with investigating how to improve work processes; extensive training in quality management for every member of the organization; and a cultural commitment to the continuous improvement of processes and systems in all functional areas, not just manufacturing. A **quality circle** is a small group comprising workers and their foreman that meets regularly to study and improve work processes in accordance with Shewhart's PDCA Cycle. Descriptions of quality circle activities often sound like scientific management in action. They eliminate wasted motions, simplify tasks, eliminate unnecessary steps, and pursue greater efficiencies wherever possible. But, because these decisions are made by workers rather than management experts, the quality circle more truly represents participative management in action.

Participation in quality circles is voluntary. Members identify a specific quality-related problem, investigate it, and use a variety of statistical and analytical tools to identify and eliminate the sources of the problem. They then move on to another problem. Quality circles operate in a relatively open and egalitarian fashion, with the foreman serving primarily as a facilitator. Members are given extensive training in quality control principles and basic statistical methods. In some instances, control charts are used to track variations in product quality, while in others the group engages in **process analysis,** examining specific steps in the work process for which they are responsible and adjusting the process as needed to improve product quality. The cause-and-effect diagram, developed by quality control expert Kaoru Ishikawa, is often used at the outset to help the group identify and address the true causes of poor quality rather than its symptoms. An example of a cause-and-effect diagram, also known as the fishbone diagram because of its shape, is shown in Exhibit 14.3.

**Exhibit 14.3 Example of a Cause-and-Effect Diagram.
Delays in Registering a Hospital Patient**

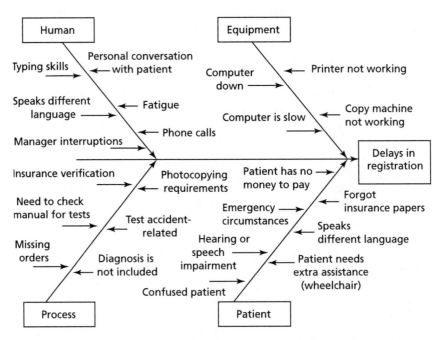

SOURCE: Reprinted with permission of CRC Press from Vincent Omachonu and Joel Ross, *Principles of Total Quality* (Delray Beach, FL: St. Lucie, 1994).

Because each work group is responsible for only a small part of the larger process by which products are designed and produced, each group must coordinate its efforts with work groups "upstream and downstream." They do so by communicating to upstream groups the problems they see in the materials or products received from them and by soliciting feedback from downstream groups about how well they are satisfying their quality requirements. In the early 1950s Ishikawa coined the phrase "the next process is our customer," a phrase which keeps quality circles focused on the quality requirements of their internal customers as well as the external customers who ultimately purchase the finished products.

The quality circle movement began in 1962 when JUSE established a journal called *Quality Control for the Foreman*. The journal was established to help educate foremen about how to involve workers in the continuous pursuit of quality. The editors of the journal encouraged foremen to organize quality circles and register them with a private organization called Quality Control Headquarters, which was established in 1963 to promote quality circles nationwide. The movement steadily gained steam. Whereas only 3,700 quality circles had registered by 1965, by 1983 there were 173,953 registered groups.[12] In 1971 the Quality Control Headquarters established a prize for the top fourteen circles in each region. Competition for these awards, as well as the conferences held in each region, helped create a national network of quality circles.

Total quality control in Japan is defined by cultural as well as structural elements. Emphasis is placed on establishing an organizational culture committed to continual improvement in work processes rather than bottom-line results alone. The underlying assumption is that if all processes and systems are functioning efficiently, effectively, and in accordance with the organization's superordinate goals, the desired outcomes—productivity, on-time delivery, growth, and customer satisfaction—will follow more or less automatically. According to Masaaki Imai, establishing an improvement-oriented organizational culture is easier in Japan than in the United States because it is consistent with the culturally ingrained concept of *Kaizen,* which means continuous improvement in all areas of life.[13] Kaizen is understood as a moral obligation to be better, or to do things better, than the day before. In the context of the workplace it calls upon workers at all levels to do more than simply comply with established standards; they are to pursue a gradual and deliberate kind of change aimed at raising those standards continually. Working in such a culture, according to Imai, is motivating because it taps people's inherent desire for personal growth and pride in workmanship. Cultural commitment to continual improvement is encouraged through the organization's reward systems, training and development programs, competitions for best quality circle awards, and special awards for the best suggestions for improvements made by individual employees.

These defining elements—cross-functional management teams, quality circles, intensive training in quality management, and an improvement-oriented culture—capture only a part of the Japanese approach to total quality control. The Japanese philosophy toward people management is also important. According to Ishikawa, respect for humanity is the guiding philosophy of quality management in Japan. To the extent that this is true, the Japanese approach offers a concrete picture of how humanistic and participatory theories of management may be put into practice. Ishikawa characterizes Japanese-style quality management as a system in which all employees participate, from the top down and from the bottom up. It is "a system of management that lets the unlimited potential of human beings blossom."[14]

It is possible to discern a superficial resemblance between Taylor's scientific management and Ishikawa's quality management. Both call for scientific study and fact-based decision making, and both assume that rational solutions to the problems of organizations and human societies can be found. But this is where the similarities end. Consistent with Taylor's belief that the planning of work should be separated from the doing of work, scientific management relies on management specialists to establish operating procedures to which workers are expected to conform. Japanese quality management, by contrast, relies on the workers themselves to define and continually adjust operating procedures, thereby reintegrating planning and doing. Second, scientific management relies on extrinsic rewards in the form of pay bonuses to motivate workers, whereas quality management relies on intrinsic rewards in the form of pride of accomplishment and service to customers. Finally, scientific management embraces a competitive strategy based on maximizing output, whereas quality management embraces a strategy based on maximizing quality and customer satisfaction, sometimes even at the expense of efficiency and economy.

The significance of this fourth stage lies in the intertwining of theory and practice. As the Japanese searched for ways to put the ideas of Deming and Juran into practice, they contributed importantly to the evolution of the theory itself. By the 1980s quality management had come to mean an integrated approach to management centered on the values of quality and customer service, emphasizing training, teamwork, and empowerment, and requiring strong leadership from senior management. Instead of a narrow technical speciality, quality management was now seen as a way of doing business, perhaps even a way of life, for everyone in the organization.

Stage 5: The "Discovery" of Quality in the United States

During the 1970s American firms continued to lose market share to the Japanese in several key industries, including automobiles, consumer electronics, and machine tools. Many American business leaders began visiting Japan to investigate the reasons for Japan's postwar economic success, and it was then that they first heard of Deming and Juran. Most Americans, however, did not learn of quality management and the contributions of Deming and Juran until June 24, 1980 when NBC aired a documentary entitled "If Japan Can . . . Why Can't We?" This documentary chronicled Japan's emergence as an economic power and attributed much of Japan's success to Deming's ideas. The final fifteen minutes included an interview with Deming, who described what can be accomplished through a total commitment to quality. The next day Deming's telephone rang off the hook. Corporations such as Ford and General Motors immediately enlisted his help, and his quality management seminars began enrolling hundreds of participants. Demand for the services of Juran and other quality experts increased dramatically as well.

Quality management became a national obsession during the 1980s, although not to the extent seen in Japan. Consultants emphasized its relevance for service as well as manufacturing industries and marketed it to public and private organizations alike. Professional associations made it the key theme of their annual conferences; Congress established the Malcolm Baldrige National Quality Award in 1987 as America's counterpart to the Deming Prize in Japan; and the federal government created the Federal Quality Institute in 1988 as a source of information and training for agencies interested in implementing what the U.S. Defense Department had labeled **Total Quality Management (TQM).**

Despite the keen interest in quality management, very few organizations implemented TQM as an integrated management program or succeeded in embedding it in their organizational cultures. The assumptions and methods of scientific management, the logic of managing for results, and the American penchant for the quick fix, were perhaps too deeply entrenched. Often TQM was implemented as a stand-alone employee relations program rather than a fundamental management strategy. In many instances, employees were exhorted to adopt quality as their top priority but with no means identified for doing so. Some companies "did little more than adopt the slogans of quality, drape the factory walls in banners, and run every employee through a prefabricated course on quality improvement."[15] In other instances, quality circles were established but supervisors provided little leadership and managers ignored their recommendations for improvements, all of which only served to further frustrate and disillusion quality-conscious employees.

Such mistakes plagued the implementation of quality management in the public sector as well as the private. The relevance of TQM to public agencies and the obstacles to its successful implementation are discussed later in this chapter. Before turning to these matters, however, it is worth taking a closer look at the contributions of W. Edwards Deming and Joseph Juran.

TWO KEY LEADERS IN THE QUALITY MANAGEMENT MOVEMENT

For the most part, Deming and Juran endorsed the same principles of quality management, including continuous improvement, customer focus, and full employee participation. But where Deming preached, exhorted, and rambled from one anecdote to the next to get his philosophy across, Juran explained clearly and carefully how to put quality management into practice. Where Deming emphasized the importance of humanistic values, Juran emphasized the importance of organizational structure. Where Deming believed senior managers must internalize the philosophy of quality management before turning to the details of implementation, Juran believed they must have a clear understanding of how to implement quality management and what is to be gained by doing so before they can be expected to internalize the philosophy. These differences were not merely stylistic or strategic. As discussed below, they also reflected important differences in ideas and values.

Deming's Fourteen Points

Knowing the American penchant for the quick fix, for introducing one management reform after another without any fundamental theory or strategy for guidance, Deming refused to talk about tools, techniques, or programs until he was convinced that senior management possessed what he called profound knowledge. His fear that management would treat his ideas as a program or set of techniques to be implemented rather than a philosophy to be embedded in the organization's culture explains why he shunned all labels, including Total Quality Management. It also explains why he organized his seminars and books around **The Fourteen Points**—his personal theory of quality management. And it explains why he, like Taylor, refused to work with clients unless they promised to adopt his philosophy in its entirety.

Deming wrote *Out of the Crisis* (1982) at a time when Americans were deeply concerned about foreign competition and escalating trade imbalances.

In it he argues that the only way out of the economic crisis is to achieve a complete transformation in what he calls the American or Western style of management. This style, according to Deming, is deeply flawed, especially in its pursuit of short-term profits at the expense of long-term improvements. Instead of paying attention to bottom–line results—such as output, sales, profits, market share, and return on investment—management should establish quality goals, improve work processes, and have faith that the bottom line will take care of itself. Indeed, Deming insisted that Western–style management is the primary cause of the economic crisis. Business leaders, he wrote, continue to blame poor organizational performance on "anything but the actual cause, pure and simple bad management."[16] In Deming's view, Western–style management must be entirely transformed and he offered his Fourteen Points as the basis for doing so. Although it is difficult to get a clear understanding of them because of his rambling, anecdotal writing style, Exhibit 14.4 captures their essential meaning.

Deming's Fourteen Points are consistent with the Japanese approach to total quality management. There is, for example, the same emphasis on continuous improvement, cross-functional cooperation, and constancy of purpose. And like the Japanese approach described by Ishikawa, Deming's approach is highly humanistic. His Fourteen Points call for creating an environment of trust and mutual respect, driving out all aspects of management by fear, investing heavily in the organization's human resources, and empowering every member of the organization to help improve work processes. Although other quality experts were also humanistic in their approach, most were not as quick to characterize American management as management by fear. Juran, for example, maintained that fear is sometimes a legitimate and necessary source of motivation. Because Deming's philosophy is controversial in this respect, a closer look at his views on piecework, annual performance reviews, and management by objectives (MBO) is warranted.

Piecework, in Deming's view, means paying workers to churn out as much as possible without regard for quality. It robs workers of pride of workmanship and has no place in an organization committed to providing superior goods or services. The same is true for numerical work standards. For example, an airline reservation clerk may be told to answer twenty-five calls an hour while being courteous and not rushing the caller, but if the computer system is down or unusually slow the clerk cannot possibly satisfy both requirements at once. Most likely callers will be rushed, and quality of service sacrificed, all in an effort to satisfy an arbitrary work standard.

The same scenario is repeated when senior managers institute MBO and pay-for-performance at the middle-management ranks. These systems hold middle managers responsible for setting and achieving numerical goals even though they are subject to economic, technological, and bureaucratic forces that often make the attainment of those goals impossible. Deming liked to say that being rewarded for attaining goals or quotas is much like winning the lottery. Sometimes you win, mostly you don't, and the amount of effort you put into it makes little difference. Deming believed that managers resort to numerical goals as a way of avoiding responsibility for studying and improving work systems. Collecting performance data is perfectly appropriate, Deming was

Exhibit 14.4 Deming's Fourteen Points

1. **Create constancy of purpose for improvement of product and service.** The organization must develop a clear sense of purpose and remain focused on it. This sense of purpose must relate to the organization's essential contribution to society rather than the short-term gains desired by its immediate stakeholders.
2. **Adopt the new philosophy.** The organization must throw off all vestiges of Western-style management and adopt the new philosophy of continuous improvement. This requires a complete transformation of mind and heart.
3. **Cease dependence on mass inspection.** Instead of inspecting bad quality out, organizations must build good quality in.
4. **End the practice of awarding business on price tag alone.** The organization must develop a long-term relationship with one or two vendors who will supply exactly what is needed at a fair price. Purchasing low-cost supplies and equipment through competitive bidding almost always undermines the quality of the final product or service.
5. **Improve constantly and forever the system of production and service.** Continually striving to improve the system, thereby continuously raising quality standards, makes far greater sense than the more common patterns of putting out fires, holding workers to minimum work standards, and exhorting everyone to meet numerical goals that lie outside their control.
6. **Institute training.** All employees must receive the training they need to do their jobs well. They also must be trained in the use of statistical tools so that they can participate in making process improvements.
7. **Institute leadership.** Supervisors at all levels must adopt a new role, learning to facilitate the efforts of others rather than commanding, exhorting, and punishing. Facilitation includes providing the necessary tools and resources, removing all barriers to deriving intrinsic satisfactions from work, and helping keep process improvement projects on track.
8. **Drive out fear.** Quality will not improve if workers are afraid to ask questions, admit mistakes, report problems, take risks, or do anything more than abide by the rules and satisfy minimum work expectations, for fear of losing their jobs or opportunities for advancement.
9. **Break down barriers between staff areas.** Quality is undermined when there is a lack of cooperation and consultation among organizational units. The sources of this problem, including management by fear and lack of constancy of purpose, must be found and eliminated.
10. **Eliminate slogans, exhortations, and targets for the workforce.** Slogans such as "Do things right the first time," and targets such as "Reduce workplace accidents by 20 percent," are forms of exhortation. They ask workers to do better without providing them with the means. Deming liked to asked how workers can be expected to do better when they are given defective materials, poor lighting, boorish supervisors, and inadequate training and equipment.
11. **Eliminate numerical quotas for the workforce and numerical goals for people in management.** These only serve to produce fear because the ability to achieve quotas and goals is usually influenced by factors outside the worker's control. It is far better to involve everyone in continually improving the system so that both qualitative and quantitative goals may be met.
12. **Remove barriers to pride of workmanship.** People want to take pride in their work. It is a primary source of motivation. Yet little pride can be taken where workers are subject to rules and policies that make no sense, reward systems that are geared to quantity rather than quality, and no opportunities to help improve the system.
13. **Institute a vigorous program of education and self-improvement.** It is not enough to train workers as suggested in Point 6. Because they are valuable resources, workers must be retrained as needed and provided opportunities for personal growth and development.
14. **Take action to accomplish the transformation.** Management must develop a detailed action plan for involving everyone in accomplishing the required transformation. Appropriate committees must be established, training provided, and reward systems created.

quick to add, as long as it is the performance of the entire work group that is tracked and both qualitative and quantitative measures are used.

Deming reserved particular scorn for the kind of annual performance reviews where workers are ranked relative to each other, some being judged above average and some below. Those deemed above average are pressured by their peers to reduce their level of performance to the lowest common denominator, and those deemed below average remain confused and dejected because they can't figure out why they can't measure up. Deming used Shewhart's control chart to illustrate the flaws in this method. Rating systems divide employees into three groups: a small group who score outside the control limits on the negative side, a small group who score outside the control limits on the positive side, and a large group containing most employees who score within the control limits. There is no reason, Deming insisted, for ranking those individuals whose performance is within the acceptable limits. Making such fine distinctions is unfair because it ascribes to the individuals in the group differences that are often caused by the system in which they work. Ranking people only serves to destroy the morale and well-being of the system. Deming believed that everyone within the control limits should receive the same pay increase, while those in the small group whose performance is unacceptable should receive immediate attention in the form of training, employee assistance, or discipline.

Deming's systems view of work operations holds important implications for management theory and practice. Deming asserted that 85 percent of all performance problems are caused by the system in which people work. Traditional management methods appear to be premised on the opposite assumption, that nearly all performance problems are caused by workers, and therefore the behaviors of workers must be carefully circumscribed and controlled, rewarded and punished. Mary Walton illustrates this point in the following passage from *The Deming Method at Work:*

> Everyone works within a system, governed by conditions over which the individual has no control. A tire builder has to contend with the condition of a complex machine and the quality and coordination of sixteen incoming components, as well as lighting, heat, and other environmental conditions. The speed with which a waitress delivers food depends less on her abilities and attentiveness to customers than on the performance of the kitchen, where cooks command an arsenal of utensils, machines and supplies and, of course, other workers. A nurse must deal not only with demands by patients, doctors and administrators, but also with medical supplies and equipment, paperwork systems, and food delivery.
>
> In the American style of management, when something goes wrong the response is to look around for someone to blame or punish or to search for something to "fix" rather than to look to the system as a whole for improvement.[17]

Deming strove to reorient management thinking from controlling the behaviors of employees to improving the systems in which they work. There will

Joseph M. Juran 1904–

Joseph Moses Juran was born in what is now Romania on December 24, 1904.[18] His father, a shoemaker, moved to the United States in 1909 and earned enough to send for his wife and children three years later. Joseph, who was then seven years old, quickly learned English and excelled in the classroom. At the age of 15 he entered the University of Minnesota, where he obtained a bachelor's degree in electrical engineering in 1924. He was immediately recruited by the Western Electric company and assigned to the inspection department at the Hawthorne Works outside Chicago. When quality control problems at Hawthorne gave Walter Shewhart an opportunity to test his new ideas about statistical process control in 1926, Juran shepherded him around the plant and helped with the investigation.

In 1937 Juran moved his family to New York City, where he had been put in charge of the industrial engineering department at Western Electric's corporate headquarters. There he received valuable experience in wage and salary administration as a midlevel executive. When the United States entered the war in 1941 Juran took a leave of absence from Western Electric to help the Lend-Lease Administration cope with the logistical difficulties of sending war materials all over the world. Despite being a brilliant problem solver, Juran concluded he was not cut out to be a manager. He turned to writing while still working for the government, publishing *Bureaucracy, A Challenge to Better*

Management in 1944. At the end of the war he resigned from Western Electric to become head of New York University's industrial engineering department. He also began working part-time as a private management consultant. Having established his reputation as a management expert with the publication of *Quality Control Handbook* in 1951, Juran resigned his position at NYU to pursue full-time work as a consultant.

In 1954 Juran traveled to Japan where he delivered two-day seminars on quality management to senior and middle managers in several Japanese cities. Juran challenged his audience to take personal responsibility for managing quality and to pursue organizational success through incremental quality improvements. Juran's consulting business boomed in the late 1970s as American executives began investigating Japan's "economic miracle." In 1979 he established the Juran Institute to develop and market training materials on the principles and methods of quality management. By the 1980s Juran was widely recognized as one of the nation's premier experts on quality management. He received numerous awards for his contributions to society, including the National Medal of Technology presented to him by President Bush in 1992 when he was 87. A workaholic his entire life, Juran continued to work well into his nineties, publishing a collection of essays in 1995 on the history of quality management and beginning work on his autobiography.

always be above- and below-average performers, he noted, but if you constantly improve the system everyone's performance improves. Deming's analysis of the sources of statistical variations in work performance also allowed him to underscore his main point: Quality is management's responsibility because only managers have the authority and means to correct the system.

Juran's Structural Approach to Quality Management

Juran spoke to managers in a language they could understand: the language of money. Instead of expounding a personal philosophy of quality management, he emphasized the enormous costs of poor quality and how managers stood to save thousands, even millions, of dollars by eliminating them. These costs arise from the payroll of the inspection force, the costs of items junked or scrapped, the costs of rework, the costs of the customers' returns, and all the secondary costs from lost customer loyalty. The good news, Juran emphasized, is that the costs of poor quality are like "gold in the mine." All an organization has to do is remove the sources of poor quality and the gold that is already there can be mined and put to more productive uses. The secret to successful mining is not simply to remove the special causes of variation so that a process is returned to a state of statistical control but to continuously improve the process itself so that unprecedented levels of quality are achieved.

Again choosing to speak in a language understandable to management, Juran likened the quality management function to the financial management function. Both call for systematic planning, control, and improvement. Juran marketed this concept as the Juran Trilogy, a registered trademark of the Juran Institute.[19] **Quality planning** involves developing the products or services that customers need or desire. Activities include determining who the organization's customers are, determining what they require or expect, developing product or service features that respond to customers' needs, developing processes that are able to produce these features, and transferring the resulting plans to the operating units. Although this analysis is essential at the organization's strategic apex, quality planning is also important in every unit so that all work processes—hiring, purchasing, reporting, approving, producing—are responsive to the needs of internal and external customers. Because the causes of poor quality are often upstream, quality planning is typically undertaken by cross-functional teams comprising representatives from all relevant units.

The second leg of the Juran Trilogy is **quality control.** This consists of evaluating quality performance, comparing actual performance to established quality standards or goals, and acting on the differences. It involves keeping a planned process in a planned state so that it remains able to meet operating goals. This is accomplished either by intervening to restore the status quo by addressing the causes of variations in quality or by taking steps to prevent damage in the first place. At the operating level it means giving workers the tools they need to be self-controlling. These may include statistical tools such as control charts, although the need for such tools necessarily varies with the specific situation and problem at hand. Juran noted that training supervisors and workers in the use of statistics is often useful, but in many organizations it has led to a tool-oriented approach rather than a problem-solving or results-oriented approach to quality control.

The final leg of the Juran Trilogy is **quality improvement.** This involves raising quality performance to unprecedented levels. It is achieved by identifying areas where quality improvements are needed, establishing project teams with clear responsibility for bringing each project to a successful conclusion, and providing the resources, motivation, and training needed by project teams to diagnose the causes of poor quality, establish a remedy, and take action to hold the gains. Each project team strives to make what Juran called significant breakthroughs in how business is conducted by eliminating the major sources of defect-related waste, inferior design relative to customer requirements, and process-related inefficiencies. Juran noted that whereas quality improvement is the area where the greatest gains to the organization are possible, it is also the area where management commitment and follow through has been weakest.

Having provided the necessary conceptual foundation, Juran next described for managers the structural arrangements by which to institutionalize an integrated, top-to-bottom program of quality management. Quality planning is the responsibility of the senior management team for the organization as a whole and each major unit. This team engages in strategic planning. It identifies external customers, develops business strategy, sets quality goals and standards, and approves development of new products or services. The actual development of new products or services is turned over to cross-functional planning teams composed of representatives of all relevant line and staff units.

A structured system of committees is required in the area of quality improvement in order to carry out unprecedented numbers of improvement projects at an unprecedented pace.[20] The improvement program is overseen by quality councils established at each major level of the organization. Their purpose is to launch, coordinate, and institutionalize annual quality improvements by placing specific projects on an authoritative agenda and scheduling them for solution. Juran emphasized that problems are rarely resolved without an institutionalized structure of this kind. These councils set quality improvement policy at each level, establish the process for selecting improvement projects, establish the process for selecting team members, provide resources, review team reports, and ensure that proposed solutions are implemented. Quality councils designate the members of each project improvement team after consulting with the departmental managers affected. The members of a project improvement team, typically six to eight individuals, are drawn from the "ailing" departments, the "suspect" departments believed to be the source of the problem, and the "remedial" departments that might be able to assist in resolving the problem. The goal is to improve a specific work process so that it satisfies increasingly higher standards of performance.

Where Deming emphasized philosophy, Juran emphasized structure. Both understood, however, that neither philosophical understanding nor institutionalized structure alone is sufficient. Quality must become everyone's top priority and this requires embedding a commitment to quality in every facet of the organization's culture. As Juran put it, "To institutionalize annual quality improvement is a profound change in culture, requiring a correspondingly profound change in the systems of recognition and rewards."[21] Without a fundamental change in culture, longstanding priorities and behaviors will persist.

QUALITY MANAGEMENT AND
ORGANIZATION THEORY

The faddish, cult-like enthusiasm for quality management in the late 1980s and early 1990s led many scholars and practitioners to ask where TQM fits in respect to established theories of organization. Commentators during this period tended to fall into one of two camps. Those in the first camp viewed TQM as scientific management dressed up in humanistic clothing. They saw a continuing emphasis on rational planning and control through a top-down, leadership-oriented form of management. For them the references to participation, involvement, and empowerment were simply added to the theory to make it more palatable to front-line workers. Many of these commentators also viewed TQM as a modern version of Chester Barnard's managerialism. Total Quality Management charges organizational leaders with defining the moral purposes of the organization (vision and mission) and the moral bases on which the purposes are to be achieved. Nonmanagement personnel are socialized in these values by those at the top where power continues to be concentrated. The result is that a community of cooperating managers and workers is created at the expense of individualism. As Leon Weiseltier put it, "Drones who can compete with Japan are preferable to drones who cannot compete with Japan; but they are still drones."[22]

Those in the second camp viewed TQM as the natural evolution of "good management" theory, one that integrates certain aspects of scientific management theory, human resources theory, systems theory, and the strategic planning theory implicit in the work of Chester Barnard.[23] From scientific management theory comes the concepts of rational planning, fact-based decision making, and performance measurement; from human resources theory comes the concepts of trust, involvement, and personal development; from systems theory comes the idea that management is responsible for managing the organization in a fully integrated manner; and from strategic planning theory comes the concept of visionary leadership and the importance of keeping everyone focused on the ultimate mission or transcendent purpose of the organization. The commentators in this camp generally viewed TQM as a positive development, a useful synthesis of ideas that promises to create win-win situations by combining system improvements with greater customer satisfaction. Having considered its applicability to the public sector, Milakovich concluded, for example, that TQM "offers an opportunity to change the very nature of the political game by emphasizing process improvements, empowering public employees, and meeting citizen/customers needs while simultaneously reducing costs. Everyone wants to see more value for their tax dollars."[24]

The first set of commentators highlighted an apparent contradiction in quality management theory, between concentrating greater power in the hands of senior managers so that they can exercise leadership on behalf of their vision of organizational success, and delegating greater power and responsibility to front-line workers so that they can enjoy the intrinsic rewards derived from making system improvements. The second set of commentators expressed confidence that moral leadership and worker empowerment need not be incompatible in practice. The extent to which power can be widely distributed and shared in organizations is a longstanding subject of debate among organization theorists. It is a question that is yet to be resolved. Writing in 1993, Robert Denhardt suggested that the apparent contradiction in quality management theory matters less today because TQM has been incorporated into the larger body of management theory:

> . . . . some theorists and practitioners argue that TQM is really "rational systems theory dressed in behavioral clothing," that the roots of TQM are deeply imbedded in the need for control and that although contemporary expressions of TQM use more humanistic language, the manipulative intent is still the same.
>
> In a certain sense, these criticisms of TQM don't really matter, for TQM has lost much of its original meaning and is now regarded by many as a somewhat faddish label for good management practice, broadly defined.[25]

QUALITY MANAGEMENT
IN THE PUBLIC SECTOR

Although developed in the context of manufacturing, both Deming and Juran insisted that the principles of quality management apply equally to service and manufacturing industries and to public and private organizations. Having been trained in statistics, they viewed all organizations as comprising work processes exhibiting more or less stable patterns of variation in performance levels. They believed that if the levels of variation are managed properly, they can be decreased and quality raised. From their perspective it mattered little that private organizations are market-driven and most public organizations are not. As Deming put it, "In most governmental services, there is no market to capture. In place of capture of the market, a government agency should deliver economically the service prescribed by law or regulation. The aim should be distinction in service."[26]

Within the public administration community, however, there has always been considerable skepticism about the universality of management principles and the extent to which business methods can or should be transferred to the public sector. The sections that follow examine the relevance of TQM principles to public sector realities, the obstacles that must be overcome, and the prospects for their successful application in government.

Relevance

Several scholars have commented on the relevance of TQM to public agencies, among them James Swiss. Swiss concludes that TQM holds considerable promise for improving the performance of government agencies, but only if its principles and methods are adapted to the unique purpose and context of public administration.

Swiss identifies four problems associated with implementing TQM in the public sector. First, most public agencies produce services rather than products. Assurances of universality notwithstanding, measuring service quality is much more difficult than measuring product quality. This is because there are many factors that enter into the equation, including such things as access, responsiveness, creativity, reliability, competence, and courtesy. It is also because appropriate measures of these factors are very difficult to identify. Even where appropriate measures exist, it is seldom clear how to combine them into an overall assessment of service quality that accurately captures the extent of customer satisfaction. Customers typically weigh various aspects of quality differently. Swiss offers the following illustration: "If an efficient police officer quickly locates stolen cars but seems ill-groomed or curt, many of his or her customers will not be totally satisfied, despite receiving a high quality output."[27]

The second problem lies in defining the agency's customers and determining how to satisfy them. For many public agencies these decisions are mired in politics. As seen in Chapter 2, public agencies often serve multiple stakeholders with contradictory demands. It is no easy matter to determine how much consideration to give to each claimant and rarely is any one stakeholder completely satisfied. An important distinction must also be made between the agency's ultimate customers, the general public, and its immediate clients. Swiss fears that "TQM can easily do more harm than good because it can encourage a focus on the particularistic demands of direct clients rather than the needs of the more important (but often inattentive) customers, the general public."[28] It is not unusual for the interests of these two groups to be diametrically opposed. The purchaser of services, the general taxpayer, usually wants to keep agency costs low, whereas the immediate client, the recipient of services, often wants service features that are costly. As Swiss notes, "No balance between costs and features is likely to please both groups."[29]

The third problem identified by Swiss is that TQM focuses on inputs and processes rather than outputs and results. This, according to Swiss, runs contrary to the rationale of recent government reforms, including program budgeting, MBO, and pay for performance, which seek to shift the attention of public managers from bureaucratic processes to strategic goals and measurable results. Here Swiss cites Deming's assertion that the current "focus on outcomes" must be "abolished." Swiss fears that TQM will cause public agencies to neglect or even dismantle their results-oriented performance management systems and that a renewed focus on process will only encourage public managers to return to a state of bureaucratic complacency, dutifully adhering to minimal legal requirements and doing no more than is needed to avoid public attention and political controversy.

The final problem is that TQM requires "an extremely strong organizational culture with an almost single-minded commitment to quality."[30] This in turn requires active and continual intervention from senior managers to keep workers committed and focused. Establishing and sustaining strong cultures is very difficult in the public sector because agencies must be open to many outside forces, turnover among senior managers tends to be very high, and there are very few incentives for even long-term managers to initiate and sustain new management initiatives such as TQM. Swiss cites James Q. Wilson's observation that "What is surprising is that government executives spend any time at all on managing their departments."[31]

In most respects Swiss's analysis is fair and accurate. There are very clear obstacles to implementing TQM successfully in the public sector. However, his concern that TQM will undermine results-oriented reform efforts is based largely on a misunderstanding of quality management theory. Deming and Juran offer TQM as a way to root out the causes of poor performance and bring an end to bureaucratic complacency. It is very much results-oriented. Process improvements can only be defined as improvements if they help realize performance goals. Further, Deming's objection to numerical work standards, quotas, MBO, and individual ratings does not mean, as Swiss implies, that he was opposed to measuring outcomes or tracking results. Deming stated repeatedly that quantitative measures of performance are absolutely essential. He only asked that they be balanced with qualitative measures and that managers assess the performance of work units against agreed upon goals rather than the performance of individual workers against each other's, especially where their level of performance is determined largely by the systems within which they work.

Obstacles

The principles of quality management may be relevant to public agencies with appropriate modifications, but the obstacles to their successful implementation are formidable. A few of the most challenging of these obstacles are summarized below:

- **Structural fragmentation.** TQM requires cross-functional cooperation in resolving performance problems. This prerequisite is difficult to satisfy in large political jurisdictions where authority is typically fragmented among several agencies and where functional fiefdoms within agencies jealously work to protect their own power and autonomy.

- **Absence of incentives.** TQM requires strong commitment from top leaders. Yet elected officials and top-ranking administrators are rarely rewarded for "good management" and thus have few incentives to initiate and support reform efforts. Defeated in his reelection bid, Mayor Sensenbrenner of Madison, Wisconsin stated that he probably got fewer than 25 votes for introducing TQM in city government.[32]

- **High turnover in leadership positions.** Senior administrators rarely hold their positions for extended periods of time. The tenure of federal administrators, for example, is typically 18 months. This makes it very difficult for the agency to maintain the constancy of purpose required to embed quality management in the organization's culture. Even when administrators implement quality management successfully, their efforts are often undone by their successors.

- **Statutory barriers.** Process improvements are often constrained by procedural requirements fixed in law and by legal limits on the agency's authority.

- **Resistance to redistributing power.** The successful implementation of quality management requires delegation and empowerment, but middle managers often resist giving up their traditional prerogatives to direct and control.

- **Lack of resources to implement improvements.** Agencies may wish to implement programmatic improvements to better serve their clients but lack the resources required to do so. As Milakovich has observed, most public agencies "still lack the capacity to simultaneously increase productivity, reduce costs, and motivate public employees to provide service to customers (taxpayers) in a timely, polite, efficient, and cost-effective manner."[33]

- **Multiple, conflicting goals.** Many agencies have complex missions and multiple, often conflicting goals. Program improvements are usually difficult to implement where interest group dominance is high and goal agreement is low.

- **Lack of useful performance measures.** Quality-related criteria for assessing organizational performance are very hard to define in many agencies and even harder to measure.

Although the principle of continuous improvement is clearly relevant to work processes in all agencies, opportunities for improving the bottom line may be greatest in production agencies where outputs are clear and measurable. Such opportunities are also high where work processes are routine and involve many sequential steps, such as purchasing, hiring, and application processing. But even in these situations, the obstacles cited above represent significant barriers to the successful implementation of quality management.

Prospects for Success

Successful applications of TQM in the public sector are well documented in such works as Cohen and Brand's *Total Quality Management in Government,* Carr and Littman's *Excellence in Government,* Milakovich's *Improving Service Quality,* and Denhardt's *The Pursuit of Significance.*[34] Notable examples of successful implementations include the agency-wide initiative at the U.S. Internal Revenue Service and the government-wide initiative in Madison, Wisconsin.[35]

Despite the many success stories reported, there is still too little empirical data available to allow for an overall assessment of quality management as a theory of organizational effectiveness. Isolating the effects of quality management programs on the overall performance of an agency is very difficult to do methodologically.[36] For example, although Mani was able to document large cost savings and improvements in customer satisfaction after the implementation of TQM at the IRS, the gross indicators of agency performance did not show statistically significant improvements.[37] It is likely that available measurement tools are not sophisticated enough to allow for an overall assessment of the contributions of quality management initiatives.

A related issue is whether the prospects for success are greatest when TQM is implemented on a government-wide basis at the direction of top-ranking officials or when it is left to middle managers and supervisors to implement on their own initiative. Total Quality Management advocates generally endorse integrated, government-wide programs backed by the full commitment and authority of senior management. In practice, however, "the more common case is for TQM to sprout out from the top of a single department, division, or office, rather than from the jurisdiction's top elected or administrative official."[38] These initiatives often arise spontaneously from the efforts of quality-conscious and improvement-oriented managers, and sometimes they spread to other units. Localized initiatives of this kind can often avoid the resistance encountered when TQM is implemented from the top down through directives issued from a centralized staff agency. Cohen and Brand are among the few advocates of TQM who encourage organizational units to implement TQM on their own initiative. In their view, "Top management commitment is a luxury. If you have it, fine, but the probability that the top manager of your organization will have such a commitment is low."[39] The message they communicate to middle managers and work supervisors is that you "need not wait for the comprehensive, total commitment of top management as a precondition of getting started. Get started yourself."[40]

RELEVANCE FOR PUBLIC MANAGEMENT

The remainder of this chapter explores the relevance of quality management theory for public management and organizational performance. This exploration is guided by the three analytical frameworks introduced in Chapter 3.

Models of Organizational Effectiveness

Quality management theory offers a relatively comprehensive theory of organizational effectiveness, one that recognizes the importance of balancing all of the values identified in Exhibit 14.5. Output quality, a value that appears at the center of Quinn's Competing Values Framework because it was found to be a central component of most definitions of organizational effectiveness, is the value associated first and foremost with quality management theory. Indeed, an organization that adopts TQM is expected to adopt the pursuit of quality as its central mission. Doing so, however, requires a careful balancing of all of the other values identified in Exhibit 14.5.

The values associated with the **open systems model,** including flexibility and readiness to adapt to environmental change, are clearly reflected in quality management theory. Because quality is defined by the customers who receive the product or service, and because their definitions of quality are constantly changing, the pursuit of excellence requires continual adjustments in the ways products and services are designed and delivered to ensure that customer expectations continue to be met.

**Exhibit 14.5 The Competing Values Framework:
Four Models of Organizational Effectiveness**

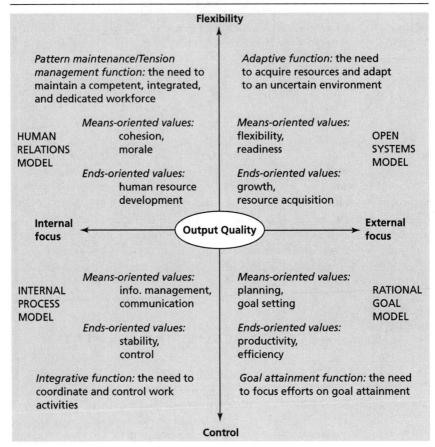

SOURCE: Adapted with permission from Figures 3 and 4, Robert O. Quinn and John Rohrbaugh, "A Spatial Model of Effectiveness Criteria: Towards a Competing Values Approach to Organizational Analysis," *Management Science* 29 (March 1983): 363–373. Copyright 1983, The Institute of Management Sciences, now the Institute for Operations Research and the Management Sciences (INFORMS), 901 Elkridge Landing Road, Suite 400, Linthicum, Maryland 21090-2909 USA.

The values associated with the **rational goal model** are reflected in quality management theory's emphasis on rational planning and problem solving. Unlike scientific management, which endorses a top–down and specialist–oriented system of planning and problem solving, TQM involves workers at all levels in planning and problem solving, thereby keeping everyone focused on goal attainment while simultaneously nurturing the values associated with the **human relations model.** Attention is focused on goal attainment not by imposing rules and limiting discretion but by establishing mission–related goals and encouraging workers to exercise discretion in pursuit of those goals. In addition, quality management's emphasis on employee training promotes the value of human resource development, and its emphasis on teamwork promotes social cohesion and morale.

Finally, quality management theory acknowledges the importance of the values associated with the **internal process model.** Exercising control over all work processes is a fundamental principle of TQM. This control is achieved, however, not through formal commands, standard operating procedures, and management control systems but by delegating decision-making authority to teams of workers who strive to eliminate the sources of poor quality and make process improvements consistent with the organization's vision statement and strategic plan.

Mechanisms for Coordinating and Controlling Work Activities

Like human resources theory, quality management theory advocates **mutual adjustment** as an alternative to direct supervision. Coordination is achieved as the members of interlocking, cross-functional teams meet to discuss and resolve problems that cut across departmental or functional lines. Control takes the form of self-control. Rather than striving to control individual behavior, quality management theory calls for bringing each work process "under control" by empowering workers to identify and eliminate the causes of unwarranted variations in product or service quality. Standardization of work processes may be used for purposes of coordination and control where the work is routine and repetitive in nature but it is the work team rather than the planning staff that is charged with continually adjusting work standards and procedures.

Quality management theory also relies upon **standardization of work outputs** for purposes of coordination and control. Under TQM managers are responsible for establishing desired product specifications and performance goals and front-line workers are responsible for determining how best to achieve them. Coordination occurs as each unit meets its quality standards or achieves its performance goals consistent with management's mission statement and strategic plan. Self-control is exercised as each work team collects output data and takes corrective action to close any gaps between actual and desired performance levels. Although this mechanism may have limited applicability in craft and coping agencies where outputs are not readily observable, staff members can nonetheless discuss quality standards and process improvements. School administrators, for example, may not be able to observe what takes place in the classroom but they can engage teachers in a consensus-building discussion of desired learning objectives, standards of student performance, and means of improving the instructional process.

Standardization of work outputs is often supplemented by **standardization of worker skills.** Organizations adopting TQM typically train workers so that they possess the minimum skills required to participate effectively as members of continuous-improvement teams. In addition, where work is of a technical or professional nature, as it often is in the public sector, workers acquire needed knowledge and skills through pre-employment training. This allows them to be largely self-coordinating and self-controlling because they do not need to be told what to do and how to do it. They are able to work together in coordinated

Exhibit 14.6 Six Mechanisms for Coordinating and Controlling Work Activities

Mutual adjustment	Workers consult with each other informally about what needs to be accomplished and how. Responsibility for coordination and control rests with those who do the work.
Direct supervision	A supervisor is assigned to take responsibility for a group of workers and a managerial hierarchy is established to integrate the efforts of all work groups. The supervisor issues personal instructions and monitors individual performance.
Standardization of work processes	Work is programmed in advance of its execution by developing rules and standard operating procedures specifying how everyone is to perform assigned tasks. Coordination is built into the work process itself and control is achieved by strictly limiting each worker's discretion.
Standardization of work outputs	Work outputs are programmed in advance by providing each work group with product specifications or performance goals and allowing members considerable latitude in determining how to achieve them. Control is exercised by collecting output data, requiring corrective action when needed, and rewarding and sanctioning workers based on results achieved.
Standardization of worker skills	Workers are employed who possess the knowledge and skills needed to make appropriate decisions. Educational institutions and professional associations are relied upon to provide standardized training. Professionally trained workers are largely self-coordinating and self-controlling.
Standardization of values	Organizational leaders communicate and act upon a clear vision of what the organization exists to do, where it should be headed, and what values should guide it. Coordination and control is facilitated by commitment of organizational members to shared, internalized values and ideals.

SOURCE: Based in large part on Henry Mintzberg, *Structure in Fives* (Prentice-Hall, 1993, 3–7).

---

fashion because they already know what needs to be done, how to do it, and what role each member of the work group must play in accomplishing it.

To a certain extent quality management also relies on **standardization of values** for purposes of coordination and control. Organizations adopting the principles of quality typically make a conscious effort to socialize workers in the importance of quality as a strategy for success. Coordination is facilitated because values such as quality provide common reference points that allow staff members to align their activities with one another in pursuit of a common purpose. Control is also facilitated. The great advantage of shared internalized values is that it provides agency heads with a measure of confidence that staff members will act in specific situations as they would want them to act.

The combined use of these mechanisms of coordination and control is arguably well suited to the realities faced by many public agencies. Because most work tasks in the public sector are complex in nature and require creativity and judgment for successful accomplishment, direct supervision and work standardization are not effective mechanisms of coordination and control. Managers do not possess sufficient knowledge either to tell workers what to do in each instance or to program work activities in advance by specifying standard operating procedures. A formal chain of command must still exist to ensure accountability, but quality management theory relies much more heavily on standardization of outputs, skills, and values for purposes of coordination and control.

Motivational Strategies

Quality management theory endorses the use of several motivational strategies in combination. The heavily humanistic theory of Deming and Ishikawa acknowledges the importance of **considerate leadership.** Deming and Ishikawa believed that humans have an innate need not only for respect and dignity but also for opportunities to realize their fullest potentials. For this reason they advocated a leadership style based on trust, mutual respect, employee empowerment, and the continual development of the organization's human resources. They believed that motivation and morale increases as innate human needs are satisfied through this kind of leadership.

The **group acceptance strategy** is also reflected in quality management theory. The informal work group of human relations theory re-emerges as a formal, problem-solving team under TQM, allowing workers to receive satisfactions in the form of comradery and peer recognition. Deming believed that people have an innate need to be esteemed by others and to enjoy a high level of self-esteem. In his view, working together as members of problem-solving teams is motivating because it allows workers to satisfy both their esteem needs and their social need for affiliation and comradery.

The role of intrinsic rewards in spurring human motivation receives special attention in quality management theory. Job enrichment and participative management, key elements in human resources theory, are simply taken for granted in quality management theory. They are viewed as necessary components of the **job identification strategy,** a strategy that calls for providing challenging work and opportunities to engage in decision making so that workers receive intrinsic rewards in the form of pride of accomplishment and personal growth. Collaborative problem solving enables workers to fulfill their own needs by helping the organization achieve its needs. According to quality management theory, this causes employees to identify with their jobs and to strive to perform their duties at increasingly higher levels.

Quality management theory also relies on the **goal congruence strategy** for purposes of motivation. As applied to public agencies, this strategy's underlying assumption is that workers committed to the ideals of public service will internalize the organization's commitment to delivering quality products or services and will receive intrinsic satisfaction from contributing to organizational success. As a conscious managerial strategy, goal congruence involves socializing workers in the importance of the agency's mission and the role of quality in realizing it. According to quality management theory, working in a culture truly committed to serving the public and continally doing things better is motivating because it taps people's inherent desire for personal growth, pride in accomplishment, and a sense of having contributed to something larger and more important than the self. As discussed more fully in the

Exhibit 14.7 Four Motivational Strategies

Legal Compliance

Using rules, formal directives, and sanctions to direct and control employee behavior. Employees may come to work, comply with rules, and satisfy minimum role requirements, either because they accept the legitimacy of organizational authority or fear being sanctioned.

Instrumental Rewards

Using rewards to induce desired behaviors.

Rewards for Performance

Distributing pay, promotions, and recognition based on individual performance. Employees may meet or exceed role expectations because they value the material and psychological satisfactions that money, advancement, and recognition can provide.

Considerate Leadership

Adopting a leadership style based on being attentive to employees and considerate of their needs. This strategy may improve morale. It might also induce those who value the respect, support, and approval of persons in authority to meet or exceed their role requirements.

Group Acceptance

Creating a work environment that allows employees to socialize, form group bonds, and enjoy the approval of their peers. This strategy may induce those who value affiliation and peer approval to meet or exceed role requirements, assuming that group norms are consistent with organizational objectives.

Job Identification

Offering work that is interesting, challenging, and responsible. Employees may come to work, meet or exceed role requirements, and possibly exhibit greater creativity and innovativeness. They may do so because they identify with the jobs and find their work intrinsically rewarding.

Goal Congruence

Hiring employees whose goals and values are congruent with the organization's and/or socializing employees so that they internalize organizational goals and values. Employees may come to work, remain with the organization, meet or exceed role requirements, and exhibit greater creativity, innovativeness, and institutional loyalty. They may do so because they identify with the organization's mission and values and because contributing to them reinforces their own self concept.

SOURCE: Based in large part on Daniel Katz and Robert L. Kahn, *The Social Psychology of Organizations* (Wiley, 1966), pp. 336–68.

---

next chapter, it is a strategy with particular relevance for government agencies because of the motivational power of contributing to public service ideals.

SUMMARY

Although quality management theory offers an interesting synthesis of earlier theories of management, it also represents a distinct and valuable theory in its own right. It holds that organizational effectiveness is achieved by designing and delivering products and services that meet or exceed customer expectations and by empowering workers to find and eliminate all factors that undermine product or service quality. Among the most important implications for public managers are the following:

- **Stakeholder satisfaction.** A central premise of quality management theory is that quality can only be defined by those who receive the product or service. The same is true for other stakeholders as well. Consequently, public managers should engage agency staff in identifying the agency's internal and external stakeholders and determining the criteria by which each judges the agency to be successful. By implication, the effective public agency is one that satisfies the expectations of key stakeholders, as well as the citizenry at large, in a balanced fashion while staying within the parameters set by constitutional principles and legal mandates.

- **Continuous improvement.** Another central premise of quality management theory is that quality is a moving target and the search for ways to improve performance is a never-ending quest. Public managers should encourage staff members continually to question how well they are doing, draw lessons from their experiences, and use what is learned to raise the bar that defines organizational success. Doing so promises to motivate all those who desire personal growth, a sense of accomplishment, and opportunities to make a meaningful difference. It also shifts the normative focus of public management from avoiding politically embarrassing mistakes to achieving meaningful results.

- **Interdependent work systems.** A third central premise of quality management theory is that, because people work within interdependent systems, quality is determined less by individual behavior than system variables. Quality is ultimately the responsibility of top managers because they create the systems that largely determine performance outcomes. The concept of interdependent work systems serves to redirect management's efforts from directing and controlling individual behavior to improving the systems within which individuals work. Emphasis shifts, for example, from measuring individual output to measuring the quality of the final product or service as a whole, and from measuring performance in a top-down fashion to empowering work teams to measure their own performance as a group. Rather than looking for workers to blame when things go wrong, public managers should seek to facilitate ongoing, collective problem-solving. The underlying assumption is that there will always be above- and below-average performers, but if you constantly improve the system everyone's performance improves.

Quality management theory appears to be particularly well suited to public agencies where workers are well educated and professionally trained, engage in complex tasks, and are strongly committed to the ideals of public service. However, many significant obstacles stand in the way of its successful implementation. These include rapid turnover in senior management ranks, lack of incentives for senior managers to attempt its implementation, the difficulties inherent in establishing a deep cultural commitment to the principles of TQM within an agency, and failure to understand that TQM is a philosophy—a way of conducting business every day—and not just a managerial tool or technique. Even where these difficulties can be overcome, TQM tends to have its greatest impact in the realm of internal procedures and work systems over which the agency has the authority needed to make required changes. Its impact tends to be much less in the realm of policy making, where powerful external stakeholders press their private agendas and the agency lacks the authority or autonomy it needs to make the incremental improvements in policy that it might favor. *Better applied to the process of service delivery*

NOTES

1. Walter A. Shewhart, *Economic Control of Quality of Manufactured Product* (New York: D. Van Nostrand, 1931).

2. Joseph M. Juran, *Juran on Leadership for Quality: An Executive Handbook* (New York: Free Press, 1989), 4.

3. Armand V. Feigenbaum, "Management of the Quality Control Function," *Industrial Quality Control 12* (May 1956), 22–25; "Total Quality Control," *Harvard Business Review 34* (November-December 1956), 93–101.

4. Feigenbaum, "Total Quality Control," 1.

5. Feigenbaum, "Management of the Quality Control Function," 23.

6. Feigenbaum, "Total Quality Control," 95.

7. John A. Byrne, "Remembering Deming, The Godfather of Quality," *Business Week* (January 10, 1994), 44; Mary Walton, *The Deming Management Method.*

8. W. Edwards Deming, *Out of the Crisis* (Cambridge: Massachusetts Institute of Technology, 1986), 3.

9. Deming, *Out of the Crisis*, 88.

10. Juran, *Juran on Leadership for Quality*, v.

11. Kaoru Ishikawa, *What Is Total Quality Control? The Japanese Way* (Englewood Cliffs, NJ: Prentice-Hall, 1985).

12. Ishikawa, *What Is Total Quality Control?*, 23, 139.

13. Masaaki Imai, *Kaizen: The Key to Japan's Competitive Success* (New York: Random House, 1986).

14. Ishikawa, *What Is Total Quality Control?*, 112.

15. Butman, *Juran: A Lifetime of Influence,* 170.

16. Deming, *Out of the Crisis*, ix.

17. Mary Walton, *Deming Management at Work* (New York: Putnam, 1990), 20.

18. John Butman, *Juran: A Lifetime of Influence* (New York: Wiley, 1997), 170.

19. Juran, *On Leadership for Quality*, 20.

20. Juran, *On Leadership for Quality*, 43.

21. Juran, *On Leadership for Quality*, 77.

22. Leon Wieseltier, "Total Quality Meaning," *New Republic 209* (July 16 and 26, 1993), 25.

23. Stephen J. Harrison and Ronald Stupak, "Total quality management: The organizational equivalent of truth in public administration theory and practice," *Public Administration Quarterly 16* (Winter 1993), 416–29.

24. Michael E. Milakovich, *Total Service Quality: Achieving High Performance in the Public and Private Sectors* (Delray Beach, FL: St. Lucie Press, 1995), 159.

25. Robert B. Denhardt, *The Pursuit of Significance: Strategies for Managerial Success in Public Organizations* (Belmont, CA: Wadsworth, 1993), 104.

26. Deming, *Out of the Crisis*, 6.

27. James E. Swiss, Adapting Total Quality Management (TQM) to Government. *Public Administration Review 52* (July/August 1992), 358.

28. Swiss, "Adapting Total Quality Management," 359–60.

29. Swiss, "Adapting Total Quality Management," 359.

30. Swiss, "Adapting Total Quality Management," 359.

31. Swiss, "Adapting Total Quality Management," 359.

32. Quoted in Jonathan Walters, "The Cult of Total Quality," *Governing* (May 1992), 40.

33. Milakovich, *Total Service Quality,* 160.

34. Steven Cohen and Ronald Brand, *Total Quality Management in Government: A Practical Guide for the Real World* (San Francisco: Jossey-Bass, 1993); David K. Carr and Ian D. Littman, *Excellence in Government: Total Quality Management in the 1990s* (Arlington, VA: Coopers & Lybrand, 1993); Milakovich, *Total Quality Service;* Denhardt, *Pursuit of Significance.*

35. Bonnie G. Mani, "Old Wine in New Bottles Tastes Better: A Case Study of TQM Implementation in the IRS," *Public Administration Review 55* (March/April 1995), 147–58; Joseph Sensenbrenner, "Quality Comes to City Hall," *Harvard Business Review 69* (March-April 1991), 64–75.

36. Laura A. Wilson and Robert F. Durant, "Evaluating TQM: The Case for a Theory Driven Approach," *Public Administration Review 54* (March/April 1994), 137–46.

37. Mani, "Old Wine in New Bottles."

38. Walters, "The Cult of Total Quality," 41.

39. Cohen and Brand, *Quality Management in Government,* 134.

40. Cohen and Brand, *Quality Management in Government,* 135.

15

⌘

The Organizational
Culture Perspective
and Symbolic
Management Theory

Organizations, as we have seen, may be viewed as pyramids with cascading levels of authority, machines with interlocking parts, cooperative social systems, or living organisms struggling to survive in uncertain environments. From the vantage point of the 1970s it seemed unlikely that any important perspective had been overlooked. Nevertheless, in 1981 two books on Japanese management found their way to the top of *The New York Times* bestsellers list and introduced large audiences to the latest and possibly most controversial perspective—the organizational culture perspective. While these books acknowledged the influence of national culture on organizational performance, their true focus was organizational culture—the culture that is unique to each organization regardless of the national culture in which it is embedded. According to the cultural perspective, shared values and beliefs provide the glue that binds the organization's members together in common cause and determines their levels of loyalty, commitment, and performance.

The importance of viewing organizations from a cultural perspective is the unifying theme in the broad and diverse body of theory discussed in this chapter. This body of theory encompasses three overlapping literatures: an academic literature originating in the late 1970s that defined the organizational culture perspective; a practitioner-oriented literature originating in the early 1980s that introduced symbolic management theory; and a new literature on visionary leadership that emerged in the mid-1980s from the convergence of the earlier two literatures. This chapter examines each of these literatures and closes with an assessment of their implications for public management.

THE ORGANIZATIONAL
CULTURE PERSPECTIVE

In the late 1970s a small group of scholars met to sharpen the definition of what they heralded as a unique alternative paradigm for studying and understanding organizations. Although trained in many different fields, including anthropology, social psychology, linguistics, and phenomenology, these scholars all agreed that earlier theorists had "failed to grasp the full significance and importance of the symbolic side of organizational life."[1] In their view, "Organizations are not simple systems like machines or adaptive organisms; they are human systems manifesting complex patterns of cultural activity."[2] Accordingly, these scholars turned their attention to studying organizational symbols, including those reflected in the language, metaphors, objects, and rituals of organizational life. Their goal was not to explain but to understand. Instead of studying objective reality, they sought to understand how organizational members interpret or make sense of the reality around them. And because the study of symbols involves interpretation rather than measurement, they relied upon qualitative methods such as participant observation rather than the quantitative methods of traditional science.

The new perspective that these theorists helped to fashion came to be known as the *symbolic* or *organizational culture perspective*. In their view it offered a new set of lenses for studying and understanding organizations. Although they understood it could not account for every aspect of organizational behavior, they believed that it could illuminate many aspects of behavior neglected by the earlier, more traditional perspectives.

The influence of anthropology on the cultural perspective is readily apparent. Organizations are seen as extended families or clans held together by shared values and beliefs. These values and beliefs are established over time as organizations struggle with the usual problems of internal integration and external adaptation. Sometimes they are introduced into the culture by organizational founders or dynamic leaders. At other times they enter the culture unconsciously as members learn how to cope successfully with problems. These shared values and beliefs relate to the way members view themselves as an organization, what they believe is important, ways they prefer to do things and treat each other, and what they hope to accomplish. Over time these values and beliefs become embodied in myths and rituals that allow the shared culture to be internalized and transmitted from one generation to the next. Once these values and beliefs are firmly established in the dominant culture, they guide the daily decisions of organizational members and provide the glue that holds the organization together. The dominant culture thus acts simultaneously as a coordinating device by defining the value premises that guide daily decisions and as a control mechanism by establishing the sanctions to be imposed if cultural values and norms are violated.

The work of symbolic interactionists such as Erving Goffman, Peter Berger, and Thomas Luckmann also influenced the cultural perspective.[3] Organizations, according to these theorists, are places inhabited by symbols. Consciously or unconsciously, these symbols are socially constructed by the members of the organization to cope with uncertainty and establish a sense of order and purpose. Important to understanding why people behave as they do in organizations is not words, actions, or events, but the meanings people attach to them. An agency-sponsored softball team, for example, may mean more than an opportunity to recreate and have fun. It may also symbolize a shared commitment to breaking down the arbitrary boundaries between work life and personal life.

Because it rejects many of the rationalistic assumptions of classical theory, the cultural perspective holds important implications for management practice as well as the study of organizations. It suggests, for example, that effective strategic decisions result less from cold logic and careful analysis than from shared understandings of what the organization aspires to be or do. Similarly, it assumes that human behavior is influenced less by rules, rational arguments, policy statements, and fear of sanctions than by each person's socio-emotional responses to rituals, ceremonies, stories, and myths. Managers delude themselves if they believe that organizations can be designed and operated as well-oiled machines or that human behavior can be tightly controlled by close supervision and strict adherence to rules. A central premise of the organizational culture perspective is that social cohesion, coordinated effort, and superior performance are achieved primarily through the shared values and meanings that bind people together in common cause and engender their loyalty and commitment. Consequently, managers must appeal to the hearts as well as minds of workers if they are to generate the kind of enthusiasm for success that goal statements and strategic plans alone cannot provide.

A CONCEPTUAL FRAMEWORK FOR UNDERSTANDING ORGANIZATIONAL CULTURE

Despite the growing interest in studying organizational cultures, research was hampered by an absence of agreed-upon definitions and conceptual frameworks. Everyone seemed to agree that organizations have cultures but there was little agreement about what a culture is. In the early 1980s the term was still being used in many different and sometimes contradictory ways. To draw valid and useful conclusions about organizational cultures, researchers needed a common terminology and a shared understanding of the concept itself. In response to this need, social psychologist Edgar H. Schein developed a conceptual framework to facilitate the study of organizational culture. This framework is described in the sections that follow.

Three Levels of Organizational Culture

After giving the subject a great deal of thought Schein concluded that organizational culture is best understood from an anthropological perspective. It is something more than a set of values and norms imposed on the members of an organization by top managers. It is something that develops and evolves organically over time, something basic to an organization that provides structural stability and integrates values and norms into observable patterns, and something arising from the cumulative experience of a group as it struggles to solve the universal problems that all groups tend to face. In short, the culture of a group is the "pattern of shared basic assumptions that the group learned as it solved its problems of external adaptation and internal integration, that has worked well enough to be considered valid and, therefore, to be taught to new members as the correct way to perceive, think, and feel in relation to those problems."[4]

As shown in Exhibit 15.1, Schein conceived of culture as having three interrelated levels. He believed that much of the confusion in the research literature of the early 1980s was due to a failure to differentiate clearly among these levels. His conceptualization provided researchers with a useful typology for assigning various aspects of culture to appropriate categories and exploring their interrelationships.

The highest level, and the only visible one, is the artifactual level. **Artifacts** are the visible manifestations of the culture's underlying values and basic assumptions. They include such things as the architecture of the organization's physical environment, the language used, the way meetings are conducted, mission statements and business philosophies, status systems, and the rites, rituals, myths, and stories by which cultural values and assumptions are transmitted and reinforced. Artifacts are easy to observe but difficult to decipher. Some are purely situational, having no intersubjective meanings at all. Others have shared meanings but, unless the underlying values and basic assumptions are known, it is difficult to determine what those meanings are.

Determining the meaning of artifacts is especially difficult because each observer tends to project personal feelings and reactions when interpreting them. Schein observed, for example, that "when one sees a very informal, loose organization, one may interpret that as inefficient if one's own background is based on the assumption that informality means playing around and not working. Alternatively, if one sees a very formal organization, one may interpret that to be a sign of lack of innovative capacity if one's own experience is based on the assumption that formality means bureaucracy and formalization."[5] Many researchers, Schein adds, make the mistake of drawing conclusions about organizational culture from artifacts alone. Whereas a long-time insider may have a sense of what various artifacts mean, outside researchers must investigate the espoused values and basic assumptions existing at lower levels of the culture before they can hope to interpret artifacts correctly.

Espoused values are the values to which members of an organization claim to be committed. They exist at an intermediate and nonvisible level. Often expressed in statements of strategies, goals, and philosophies, espoused values guide choices about organizational purposes and the means by which to accomplish them. Values generally relate to the way members are to get along and how they are to do their jobs. The test of how well they work is how comfortable and anxiety free members are when they abide by them. Values exist at the conscious level and the beliefs and ethical rules derived from them function to guide organizational members in their daily decisions.

Exhibit 15.1 Levels of Culture

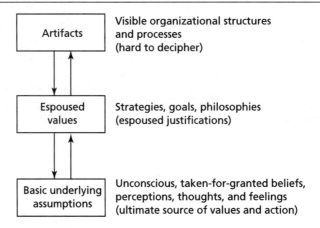

SOURCE: Edgar H. Schein, *Organizational Culture and Leadership* (San Francisco: Jossey-Bass, 1992) 17; Copyright 1992. This material is used by permission of John Wiley & Sons, Inc.

Consequently, they determine much of the behavior that can be observed at the artifactual level.

It is difficult to determine the significance of espoused values, however, because some are congruent with underlying assumptions and some are not. Often they are merely aspirations regarding how group members would like to behave or what they would like to accomplish. Sometimes they are rationalizations for continuing to do what they are already doing. By contrast, values that are congruent with underlying assumptions are the organic products of what the group experiences and learns over time. Group learning, according to Schein, begins with someone's conclusions about what ought to be or ought to be done in certain situations. If these conclusions help the organization reach satisfactory solutions to its problems then they become shared values and, in time, shared basic assumptions. In a group's formative years these values are typically introduced by the founder but as the group develops its own life experiences other members participate in adding to or modifying them.

Although Schein is not entirely clear on this point, it seems that values are of two types: those that have already proven their worth, given rise to basic assumptions, and continue to serve as conscious manifestations of basic assumptions, and those that have yet to prove their worth and may or may not give rise to new assumptions in the future. A researcher cannot rely on what people say are the values of the culture because they may be of the second kind: those that are espoused but out of step with the organization's basic assumptions. To determine which values truly help integrate the group the researcher must investigate the culture's basic assumptions.

Basic assumptions are the most basic theories-in-use that inform members, at a largely unconscious level, how to think and feel about things and what actions to take in various situations. Whereas shared values are largely conscious and subject to continuing debate, basic assumptions are so taken for granted that they cease to be questioned and debated. It is precisely because they are taken for granted that they have the ability to create consistency of behavior among group members. Basic assumptions typically relate to mission and strategy, operational goals, or the means for achieving goals and measuring success. Examples include the following: human beings are capable of self-direction and self-control (a Theory Y assumption); an emphasis on quality is the path to success (a TQM assumption); and, it is inappropriate to cause colleagues to lose face by criticizing them directly (an assumption implicit in the culture of many Japanese firms). Basic assumptions are difficult to change because the mere suggestion of change has such a destabilizing, anxiety-producing effect. Consequently, those attempting cultural change must seek to understand the existing culture first, including its basic assumptions, and then be prepared to deal with the anxiety-producing effects of proposed changes.

The Concept of Cultural Strength

Schein suggests that the "strength" of a culture is best defined in terms of the homogeneity and stability of group membership and the length and intensity of shared experiences.[6] He notes, for example, that organizations with high turnover in top positions are unlikely to have strong cultures because consistent leadership is a key factor in determining the degree of cultural homogeneity. This is particularly true in public agencies where top leadership roles are held by political appointees who are constantly coming and going. These administrators have little time or interest in shaping strong organizational cultures. Nonetheless, shared experiences in coping with internal and external problems may be enough to create a strong culture over time. Donald Warwick's study of the U.S. State Department provides a case in point.[7] Despite high turnover among top administrators the State Department developed a cautious, risk-averse culture because of the many uncertainties in its external environment. Never knowing when they might fail to predict world events accurately, State Department officials learned to file endless reports, obtain clearances from their supervisors before taking action, and demand rules to follow so that they had some measure of protection when catastrophic events did occur.

Although many theorists assume a linear relationship between cultural strength and organizational performance, Schein concluded that "the relationship is far more complex. The actual content of the culture and the degree to which its solutions fit the problems posed by the environment seem like the critical variables here, not strength. One can hypothesize that young groups strive for culture strength as a way of creating an identify for themselves but older groups may be more effective with a weak total culture and diverse subcultures to enable them to be responsive to rapid environmental change."[8] The example of the State Department raises yet another possibility: A strong culture established in order to reduce the anxiety levels of its members may be relatively unresponsive to efforts by leaders to enhance organizational performance. In this instance cultural strength may not be a virtue, at least from the perspective of top administrators and the public at large.

Mechanisms for Embedding
Cultural Values and Assumptions

Schein argues that managers must embed shared values and assumptions in the organization's culture and reinforce them in new and current members if they are to create and sustain strong cultures. According to Schein, this is accomplished by using the embedding and reinforcing mechanisms shown in Exhibit 15.2. Whereas researchers tended to focus their attention on the role of stories, myths, rites, and rituals in reinforcing organizational culture, Schein's conceptual scheme suggests that these artifacts represent only two of several mechanisms by which leaders can embed and reinforce their values and assumptions.

Once employees are fully acculturated, managers can be reasonably certain that each will strive to accomplish the organization's goals. As Exhibit 15.2 indicates, managers can facilitate the process of acculturation by recruiting and hiring individuals predisposed to share organizational values, socializing new recruits through formal orientation programs as well as their symbolic actions, rewarding members who act in accordance with organizational values, and ostracizing or removing those employees who are ill-suited to the dominant culture or refuse to embrace its values and beliefs.

It is important to note the subtle shift in the organizational culture perspective *from* viewing symbols as things that are spontaneously constructed by members to cope with threats and provide a sense of order and purpose *to* viewing symbols as things that are deliberately constructed by leaders to unite members in pursuit of organizational objectives. Although either view may be correct depending on the situation under study, the second view leads directly to what has come to be known as **symbolic management theory.**[9] The underlying premise is that managers can and should use various symbols (e.g., rituals, stories, mission statements) to acculturate workers—that is, to cause them to form emotional attachments to organizational values so that they develop a common point of view and make decisions that promote the organization's objectives in an almost instinctual manner.

Because public agencies serve important societal purposes, symbolic management may fit well with an agency's need for coordination and control. Herbert Kaufman's classic study of the U.S. Forest Service illustrates key aspects of this approach.[10] The Forest Service has a long tradition of recruiting individuals with a strong work ethic and "love of the woods" and who are consequently predisposed to accept the values and demands of the agency. In addition, forest rangers are often recruited from schools of forestry, where professional values and the conservation ethic are reinforced along with the development of technical skills. Once admitted to the service, apprenticeships, job rotations, and the policy of promoting from within help ensure that rangers are acculturated in the prevailing values, assumptions, and customary modes of operation of the agency. Finally, specific symbols are used to encourage rangers to identify themselves with the well-being of the agency. Their uniforms, badges, and distinctive hats, for

Exhibit 15.2 Culture-Embedding Mechanisms

Primary embedding mechanisms	Secondary articulation and reinforcement mechanisms
What leaders pay attention to, measure, and control on a regular basis	Organization design and structure
How leaders react to critical incidents and organizational crises	Organizational systems and procedures
Observed criteria by which leaders allocate scarce resources	Organizational rites and rituals
Deliberate role modeling, teaching, and coaching	Design of physical space, facades, and buildings
Observed criteria by which leaders allocate rewards and status	Stories, legends, and myths about people and events
Observed criteria by which leaders recruit, select, promote, retire, and ex-communicate organizational members	Formal statements of organizational philosophy, values, and creed

Source: Edgar H. Schein, *Organizational Culture and Leadership* (San Francisco: Jossey-Bass, 1992), 231; Copyright 1992. This material is used by permission of John Wiley & Sons, Inc.

example, create a sense of professional identify and a unique esprit de corp. "As a consequence," Kaufman concludes, "officers of the Forest Service conform to agency decisions not simply because they have to, but because they want to."[11]

DIFFICULTIES INHERENT IN CONDUCTING CULTURAL RESEARCH

There are two reasons for wanting to study and decipher an organization's culture: to advance our theoretical understanding of organizations through scientific study, and to help leaders manage cultural issues affecting organizational performance.[12] The first requires that researchers understand the culture; the second only that practitioners know enough to intervene. The goal of understanding culture for purposes of theory building has proven to be especially difficult. Whereas artifacts are easily observed, the underlying values and basic assumptions that allow for their interpretation are not. Traditional research methods are not well suited to the study of nonvisible phenomena. Even participant observation is of limited value because far too many inferences must be made about what is observed.

Schein argues that a clinical methodology is best if the goal of research is scientific understanding. This type of research can be undertaken only when an organization asks an outside consultant to come in and diagnose the organization's culture much as a practicing clinician might do with a patient.

Where a researcher has been invited to help the organization improve itself, members are more likely to reveal data about the culture because they have something to gain by revealing themselves. In the process of focusing on specific problems of concern to the organization, culturally relevant data may be unearthed. The researcher in the role of clinician relies upon observation and interviews to uncover shared values and basic assumptions.[13] Unfortunately, few organizations have the resources or time to conduct probing clinical analyses so that a comprehensive view of the dominant culture and its many subcultures might be obtained.

Thorough clinical analyses may not be necessary, however, if the purpose of research is to assist leaders in managing cultural issues. For the latter purpose it may be enough for an outside consultant to help internal groups identify their cultural assumptions and how they aid or hinder their efforts. Although the organizational culture perspective continued to exert a strong influence on organization theory well into the 1990s, the research orientation of the scholars who initially defined the organizational culture perspective was soon overshadowed by a growing interest in culture as a vehicle for enhancing managerial control and organizational functioning. Many of them, according to Frost and colleagues, were "attracted by the seductive promises of culture as a key to improved morale, loyalty, harmony, productivity, and—ultimately— profitability."[14] A study by Barley, Meyer, and Gash confirmed that academic papers published after 1982 were more prone than earlier papers to discuss the "economic value of manipulating culture" and "rational control and differentiation."[15] In short, even those scholars who initially viewed cultures as webs of intersubjective meaning to be understood in their own right came in addition to view them as forces to be manipulated for enhancing organizational performance. The latter point of view is readily apparent in the practitioner-oriented literature discussed next.

THE PRACTITIONER-ORIENTED LITERATURE

As noted in Chapter 14, the strong interest in Japanese management toward the end of the 1970s did not occur by happenstance. Having enjoyed sustained economic growth and relatively weak foreign competition for nearly three decades, American firms found themselves facing stiff global competition, reduced market share, and decreasing rates of growth in productivity. Their economic decline could not be attributed to environmental factors alone because Japanese firms were flourishing in the same global environment of oil shortages and increased competition. This realization led many people in managerial and academic circles to question the presumed superiority of American management. Could it be that there is something distinctive in the Japanese culture or the techniques of Japanese management that accounted for the economic success of Japanese firms?

The search for answers led to the publication of four influential books in 1981 and 1982, all of which identified culture as a key determinant of organizational performance. The two *New York Times* bestsellers referred to earlier were William Ouchi's *Theory Z: How American Business Can Meet the Japanese Challenge* and Richard T. Pascale and Anthony G. Athos' *The Art of Japanese Management: Applications for American Executives*. They were followed in 1982 by two other books emphasizing the importance of organizational culture, Tom Peters and Robert Waterman's *In Search of Excellence: Lessons from America's Best-Run Companies* and Terrence Deal and Allan Kennedy's *Corporate Cultures: The Rites and Rituals of Corporate Life*.[16] These books grew out of two overlapping research projects, the first an investigation of Japanese management methods conducted by William Ouchi, a professor of organizational behavior at Stanford, and the second an investigation of organizational effectiveness undertaken by the management consulting firm of McKinsey & Company. Much fruitful interaction took place between project participants. Richard Pascale, for example, collaborated with Ouchi on the study of Japanese management at Stanford and later worked with the McKinsey group as a consultant. He subsequently joined with Anthony Athos of Harvard, another McKinsey consultant, to write *The Art of Japanese Management*.

Because these books were written primarily for managers, they contain many sweeping generalizations and prescriptive conclusions. Nevertheless, they helped introduce a fresh and valuable organizational perspective and, in doing so, contributed to a more holistic and comprehensive understanding of how and why organizations behave as they do. To provide a sense of what symbolic management entails, the following analysis focuses on the two management bestsellers, Ouchi's *Theory Z* and Pascale and Athos' *The Art of Japanese Management*.

William Ouchi's *Theory Z*

Ouchi's comparative analysis of Japanese and American firms led him to conclude that the key differences were not in structure, strategy, or technology but in the "subtleties" of Japanese management. Like Weber, Ouchi constructed ideal-type models to capture the essential properties of each type of organization while acknowledging that firms conform to these models to varying degrees:[17]

Japanese organizations	*American organizations*
Lifetime employment	Short-term employment
Slow evaluation and promotion	Rapid evaluation and promotion
Non-specialized career paths	Specialized career paths
Implicit control mechanisms	Explicit control mechanisms
Collective decision making	Individual decision making
Collective responsibility	Individual responsibility
Wholistic concern	Segmented concern

Ouchi found that, whereas the American culture tends to maintain sharp boundaries between an individual's work and personal lives, the Japanese culture does not. Each worker is seen as a whole person, "not a Jekyll-Hyde personality, half-machine from nine to five and half-human in the hours preceding and following."[18] Influenced by the national culture, most large Japanese companies show a **holistic concern** for workers by hiring them straight out of high school or college, promising their parents they will see to their physical, intellectual, and moral development, guaranteeing them lifetime employment in exchange for a lifetime of loyalty, promoting them slowly so that they are carefully mentored and cross-trained, and creating opportunities for them to recreate together after work and on weekends.

Closely related to the concept of holistic concern is the concept of **collective responsibility.** The Japanese culture encourages people to subordinate their individual interests to the well-being and social harmony of the larger community. Collective responsibility is encouraged in the workplace by keeping individual job descriptions purposely vague, de-emphasizing titles and status, developing generalists rather than specialists, expecting the members of each work unit to take joint responsibility for its successes and failures, distributing pay bonuses based on group rather than individual performance, and sanctioning those who try to stand out at the expense of colleagues.

Collective responsibility applies to the process of decision making as well. **Collective decision making** is achieved through the Japanese version of participative management. All members of a department are invited to participate in reaching consensus about what policies or decisions to adopt. Rather than a cold, analytical process in which a few senior administrators choose among the best available alternatives, it is a social process in which everyone who will be affected by the decision is interviewed multiple times and the proposed change is continually modified until a true consensus is reached. It is, according to Ouchi, a process that symbolizes collective responsibility and produces a high degree of commitment and support for the final decision.

Finally, Japanese firms rely on **implicit mechanisms of coordination and control.** These mechanisms are built into each organization's distinctive culture and are reflected in a core set of values and management philosophy. These values relate to the transcendent social purposes of the organization and the means for achieving them. Once these values are firmly internalized, they guide daily decisions from top to bottom and help ensure that everyone is making decisions in a consistent and coordinated fashion. This concept of coordination and control by shared values was to become a central theme in organizational culture theory.

Japanese employers rely on symbols, rituals and myths to communicate and reinforce the organization's underlying values and beliefs. This, according to Ouchi, is much more powerful than relying on rational argument and formal authority. It is a way of communicating true commitment to deeply felt values:

> These rituals put flesh on what would otherwise be sparse and abstract ideas, bringing them to life in a way that has meaning and impact for a new employee. For example, telling employees that the company is com-

mitted to coordinated and unselfish cooperation sounds fine but also produces skepticism about the commitment of others and creates ambiguity over just how a principle might apply in specific situations. When, on the other hand, the value of cooperation is expressed through the ritual of *ringi*, a collective decision making in which a document passes from manager to manager for their official seal of approval, then the neophyte experiences the philosophy of cooperation in a very concrete way. Slowly individual preferences give way to collective consensus.[19]

The Japanese management model paints a picture of what Ouchi calls a **clan organization,** an organization in which everyone is part of an extended family, linked together in intimate and trusting ways through mutual bonds of kinship. The clan functions by socializing members in the norms and values of the organization's dominant culture. This facilitates the integration of individual and organizational goals, creates a strong sense of community, and motivates members to serve the organization. The clan form of organization, according to Ouchi, stands in sharp contrast to the bureaucratic form. By achieving a high degree of consistency in its internal culture, the clan organization is able to function with fewer hierarchical controls. Whereas the bureaucratic form says to workers "do just what we tell you," the clan form says "exercise discretion in accordance with shared values." In short, the clan organization offers a relatively high degree of autonomy and freedom, at least within the parameters set by its shared values. More fundamentally, according to Ouchi, it establishes the close primary relationships that Elton Mayo insisted are essential to physical, emotional, and mental health.

Ouchi initially assumed that clan organizations are products of Japan's unique culture and consequently not transferrable to the United States. However, additional research led him to conclude that the Japanese model reflects "universally applicable" principles, as evidenced by the fact that clan organizations have functioned successfully in the United States for decades. Ouchi coined the term *Type Z* to refer to these companies, companies that practice elements of the Japanese model in ways adapted to the American culture. Examples cited by Ouchi include IBM, Proctor and Gamble, and Hewlett Packard. Type Z companies offer stable employment in exchange for long-term loyalty, demonstrate holistic concern for employees, institutionalize collective responsibility and decision making, and develop their own unique business philosophies. Because they possess many of the characteristics of a clan organization, they are able to reduce hierarchical controls and task specialization at all levels. Ouchi suggests that Type Z companies are better suited than other American companies to today's highly interdependent world of business because success depends increasingly on cooperation and collective effort. While acknowledging that it is difficult to adopt the Japanese model in a country that values individualism, specialization, and free entry and exit of personnel, Ouchi insists that organizations can succeed in doing so by engaging in discussions about core purposes and values, developing business philosophies, and adopting such practices as lifetime employment and collective decision making. Much of his book is devoted to how this might be accomplished.

Although Ouchi characterizes Theory Z as a specific approach to management adopted by Type Z organizations, he also seems to intend it as a theory of organizational effectiveness. His general thesis is that organizations that develop intimate relationships and a shared sense of purpose by means of value-driven cultures perform better than organizations that do not. One of the most interesting aspects of Ouchi's work is the suggestion that Theory Z extends and improves upon Theory Y. The key themes in human resources theory—an environment of trust, egalitarianism, respect for human dignity, employee involvement, and integration of individual and organizational needs—are all found in Ouchi's description of Japanese management and the clan form of organization. The Type Z organization, Ouchi notes, is essentially the humanistic organization advocated by Argyris and McGregor:

> Argyris challenged managers to integrate individuals into organizations, not to create alienating, hostile, and impersonally bureaucratic places of work. In a real sense, the Type Z organization comes close to realizing that idea. It is a consent culture, a community of equals who cooperate with one another to reach common goals. Rather than relying exclusively upon hierarchy and monitoring to direct behavior, it relies also upon commitment and trust.[20]

In an earlier article, Ouchi suggested that Theory Z extends and improves upon Theory Y by emphasizing the sociological rather than psychological determinants of organizational success.[21] Organizational culture, according to Ouchi, is the missing piece of the puzzle. Argyris and McGregor did not fully appreciate the importance of shared values and beliefs in creating trust and intimacy and providing purpose and direction. Theory Y encourages managers to establish teamwork and better interpersonal communications in a vacuum, without first establishing a value-driven culture where teamwork and better communications are natural byproducts. This approach, according to Ouchi, is unlikely to produce the desired results. Theory Z, by contrast, encourages managers to establish an organizational culture—characterized by stable employment, holistic concern, and collective responsibility—as the foundation on which a less hierarchical, more humanistic organization can develop.

Ouchi recognized, however, that the success of Theory Z depends on satisfying certain preconditions, such as low employee turnover. He also emphasized that Type Z organizations tend to suffer from certain "potentially disabling weaknesses."[22] For example, because Type Z organizations are so homogenous with respect to values and beliefs, they are hostile to deviant views, including those that may be important for organizational adaptation and survival. In addition, they tend to discriminate against employees who are culturally dissimilar, such as women and minorities. And because cultures are so difficult to change, Type Z organizations are often unable to react quickly enough to major environmental changes.

Pascale and Athos' *The Art of Japanese Management*

In the late 1970s the consulting firm of McKinsey & Company invited Richard Pascale of Stanford and Anthony Athos of Harvard to help it develop a conceptual framework identifying the core determinants of organizational performance. The firm's emphasis on strategy, structure, and systems was widely viewed as inadequate. It seemed increasingly clear that important determinants of performance were being overlooked. With the assistance of Pascale and Athos, a McKinsey task force headed by Tom Peters and Jim Bennett developed the McKinsey 7-S Framework. This framework conceptualizes organizational performance as the product of seven key interdependent variables: strategy, structure, systems, staff, style, skills, and shared values (or superordinate goals). The first three variables are seen as "hard" because they are concrete and amenable to rational analysis and systematic planning, whereas the remaining five, while every bit as important, are seen as "soft" because they are more intangible and less amenable to rational analysis and systematic planning. The central thesis of *The Art of Japanese Management* is that most American executives focus almost exclusively on the "hard" elements of strategy, structure, and systems and consequently undermine the effectiveness of their organizations. To optimize organizational performance managers must pursue the seven S's in a balanced, integrated fashion, with shared values providing the key to successful integration.

Both *Theory Z* and *The Art of Japanese Management* outline what American executives can learn from the Japanese but they do so in slightly different ways. Whereas *Theory Z* presents an ideal-type model of Japanese management as its point of departure and emphasizes **techniques** such as collective decision making, *The Art of Japanese Management* takes the 7-S framework as its point of departure and emphasizes **managerial skill** in integrating the 7-S's. Their research led Pascale and Athos to conclude that poor management skills rather than flawed techniques lie at the heart of the problems confronting American firms. They provided support for their conclusion by contrasting the managerial approaches of two very successful executives, one Japanese and one American.

Konosuke Matsushita, founder of the Matsushita Electric Company, succeeded in establishing one of the largest and most successful firms in the world by paying careful attention to all seven S's. He developed unique marketing, distribution, pricing, and product development **strategies,** a decentralized, division-based **structure,** highly centralized reporting, accounting, and personnel **systems,** a hands-on yet respectful management **style,** a **staff** development program based on job rotation and careful mentoring, a management team with well-developed analytical and people **skills,** and a core set of **shared values** closely tied to the nation's cultural values.

The "spiritual values" he set for his company were national service, fairness, harmony and cooperation, struggle for betterment, courtesy and humility, adjustment and assimilation, and gratitude.[23] These values gave shape and form to the other six S's. Matsushita's personal management style, for example, was guided by them. Although he was demanding and tough-minded, he insisted that all disagreements be handled civilly, with respect for personal dignity, and in a manner that required each participant to search for common ground. He also used stories, myths, and other forms of symbolic communication to reinforce the organization's shared values. Values were inculcated in employees in a variety of ways, including long apprenticeships, having employees recite company values every morning, and asking them to give ten-minute talks to their fellow workers each month on company values and their relationship to society. Matsushita understood that shared values can "provide a spiritual fabric of great resilience. They permit a highly complex and decentralized firm to evoke an enormous continuity that sustains it even when more operational guidance breaks down."[24]

Harold Geneen, chief executive officer of International Telephone and Telegraph (ITT) from 1959 to 1979, provided Pascale and Athos with an interesting contrast. Geneen succeeded in welding the ITT empire into a coherent and efficient corporate machine through the force of his personality and his hard-driving, tough-minded approach to management. Although he established a divisionalized structure and centralized planning and reporting systems much as Matsushita had, his approach to the other S's was much different. He committed the organization to ruthless competition without regard to larger social values, insisted that all decisions be based on detailed reports and unshakable facts, practiced a driving, domineering style of management, encouraged competition among staff members, and deliberately maintained a pressure cooker environment for his top executives.

Pascale and Athos concluded that although Geneen achieved a relatively "good fit" among the seven S's, his achievements could have been even higher and more enduring if he had paid more attention to the "soft" S's. Unlike Matsushita, Geneen failed to focus on the kinds of shared values, both human and spiritual, that touch people's hearts, genuinely knit them together in common cause, and call forth their best contributions. Thus ITT under Geneen remained a personality-driven, rather than a values-driven, organization. Pascale and Athos suggest that this is the main reason ITT could not sustain its high level of performance after Geneen retired.

It is no accident, according to Pascale and Athos, that a Japanese executive's approach to management endured after his retirement when an American executive's did not. A central theme in *The Art of Japanese Management* is that American executives are "powerfully disadvantaged by our culture."[25] The American culture encourages managers to view their organization's purposes as narrowly economic. Concerning themselves with the social, psychological, and spiritual well-being of their employees is not in their job descriptions. Responsibility for such things belongs to the individual. By contrast, the Japanese culture encourages Japanese executives to assume that it is *their* responsibility to attend to the social, psychological, and spiritual needs of workers. They believe only when the workers' personal needs are satisfied will they produce outstanding work.

In addition, the American culture is highly optimistic about the ability of people to make informed, rational decisions and to assert control over themselves and others. Harold Geneen's obsession with control is evidenced, for example, in his reporting and performance measurement systems, brute confrontations, and rigorous cross-checking of all sources of information. By contrast, the Japanese culture encourages executives to be much more accepting of ambiguity, uncertainty, and human imperfection.

Pascale and Athos believe that these "cultural blind spots" discourage American executives from attending to the "soft" S's. Their preference is for the "hard" S's that are more readily changed by fiat. Pascale and Athos are quick to add, however, that these culturally induced disadvantages can be addressed successfully. Like Ouchi, Pascale and Athos emphasize that several of the highest-performing firms in the United States are already doing an excellent job of integrating the seven S's. And, like Ouchi, Pascale and Athos assert that developing a values-driven organizational culture is the key to improving organizational performance. Interventions such as reorganizing or team building will not help unless they are part of a comprehensive effort to integrate the other six S's around an explicit set of shared values.

Finally, like Ouchi, Pascale and Athos do not believe that just any set of values will do. Their comparative analysis of American and Japanese firms led them to conclude that shared values or superordinate goals are most powerful when they relate to higher-order values. The best firms "link their purposes and ways of realizing them to *human values* as well as economic measures like profit and efficiency."[26] Higher-order values may include the essential purposes of the organization and the contributions it makes to society, an emphasis on developing the human potential of employees, or a commitment to basic values such as honesty, fairness, and respect for the dignity and worth of each individual.

A values-based approach to management is especially effective, according to Pascale and Athos, because today's highly educated workers seek meaningful lives in addition to pay and career opportunities, something that is true for public agencies as well as private firms. "Far too many generalizations," they argue, "are made about work on the basis of the automobile assembly-line stereotype. For the vast majority, work is a far different and far more fulfilling experience. For people in these new circumstances to be satisfied, it helps enormously if they can see the link between what they do and a higher purpose."[27] If superordinate goals are consistently honored, "then employees tend to identify more fully with the company. They see the firm's interest and their own as more congruent and tend to invest themselves more fully in the organization—including looking for ways to improve how they do their job."[28] Higher-order values cause workers to pay attention to the little things that matter most. In addition, they can generate enthusiasm and commitment in ways that rational planning and analysis cannot. As Peters and Waterman put it, "the pursuit of higher purpose is inherently at odds with 30 quarterly MBO objectives, 25 measures of cost containment, 100

demeaning rules for production-line workers, or an ever-changing, analytically derived strategy that stresses costs this year, innovation next, and heaven
knows what the year after."[29]

Whether managers can or should define the culture of an organization remains a matter of considerable debate. Most advocates of symbolic management do not suggest that managers can or should try to determine every
aspect of culture. They only suggest that managers seek to influence key aspects of culture by identifying and symbolizing core values, clarifying mission,
and articulating appropriate strategies for addressing the organization's problems of external adaptation and internal integration. In this way they can at
least hope to nudge their organizations in new and more positive directions.

ASSESSING THE
PRACTITIONER-ORIENTED LITERATURE

Despite offering a fresh, new perspective on organizational behavior, the
practitioner-oriented literature came under immediate attack. Criticisms
tended to fall into one of two categories: those questioning the underlying
theory of organizational effectiveness and those questioning the implications
of the theory for management practice.

First, several critics noted that the practitioner-oriented literature provided
little hard evidence to support the theory that strong cultures and shared values promote organizational success. Although Ouchi reported the findings of a
study by Ouchi and Johnson, the results were far from conclusive. Ouchi and
Johnson surveyed executives and officials in the apparel and electronics industries and found a strong correlation between companies perceived as having
Theory Z characteristics and those described as being "best managed."[30]
They also found a strong correlation between the perceived Z-ness of firms
and their net incomes as a percent of sales. The number of study participants,
however, was relatively small, and their conclusions were based on the perceived reputations of firms rather than firsthand knowledge.

In the second part of their study Ouchi and Johnson found that emotional well-being and company loyalty were higher in the firm most often
described as Type Z than in the firm most often described as *Type A* (the
more traditional, bureaucratic type). However, this study involved only two
firms in one industry and relied upon a relatively small sample of executives
and their spouses. In addition, because the performance levels of these two
firms were similar, Ouchi and Johnson were unable to show that higher
emotional well-being and company loyalty translated into higher performance. As Edgar Schein put it, what is missing "is convincing evidence that
those companies which fit the Theory Z model are more *effective* than com-
parable companies which operate more on the Theory A bureaucratic
model."[31]

Similarly, although Peters and Waterman were able to isolate eight attributes of excellence from a sample of forty-three financially successful companies, they could not state which of these attributes, or what combination of these attributes, if any, explained their success. We still don't know, for example, whether the success of McDonalds is due to its golden arches, core values, and the legend of Ray Kroc, or to its stringent operating procedures and sophisticated control systems.[32] As one critic put it, both *In Search of Excellence* and *Passion for Excellence* argue that a strong culture built on shared values and patterns of behavior is the source of excellence and yet neither provide any indication "that the authors ever systematically examined the extent to which rank-and-file members of any of the firms share those values, engage in those behaviors, or perceive that their supervisors do."[33]

A second and closely related criticism is that these theorists offered a "one best way" formula for success: build a strong value-driven culture and the resulting increases in commitment, cohesion, and effort will boost performance. Allaire and Firsirotu argued, for example, that universal prescriptions of the kind offered by Peters and Waterman are not very helpful because choices about how to improve organizational performance are necessarily contingent upon the specific situational factors an organization faces. It is futile, for example, to "exhort the employees of a regulated monopoly offering a public service and requiring large capital investments to become 'close to the customer,' to show a 'bias for action,' to manage with 'simple form and lean staff,' and to preach 'autonomy and entrepreneurship.' The requirements for success, imposed by the economics and regulations of these industries, are pushing very hard in another direction, and attempts by management to install a culture that works against these forces will, therefore, be counterproductive."[34]

A third criticism is that the practitioner-oriented literature overstates the degree to which organizational cultures can be shaped or controlled by managers to advance their objectives. The idea that cultures are integrating and unifying forces that can be successfully managed assumes the existence of a strong, monolithic, all-encompassing culture, something which may itself be a myth. In reality, according to Martin and Siehl, organizational cultures "are composed of various interlocking, nested, sometimes conflicting subcultures."[35] It is not unusual for these subcultures to be in direct conflict with managerial objectives. Examples include a subculture that punishes "rate-busters" or one centered on the practice of medicine that resists all efforts by administrators to limit professional autonomy.

Relatedly, Martin and Siehl suggest that cultures are not as responsive to direct managerial attempts at control as many would like to believe: "It may be that cultures cannot be straightforwardly created or managed by individuals. Instead, cultures may simply exist and managers may capitalize on cultural effects they perceive as positive or minimize those perceived as negative. Perhaps the most that can be expected is that a manager can slightly modify the trajectory of a culture, rather than exert major control over the direction of its development."[36] The argument that organizational cultures are not easily managed or changed was echoed by J. Steven Ott. Cultures, Ott wrote, "have deep roots, and they develop over long periods of time through complex individual and group mechanisms. Usually they can be altered only slowly, through painful learning processes that often are resisted by members."[37] This suggests that managers who attempt to act in accordance with the optimistic theory advanced in the practitioner-oriented literature may be severely frustrated in their efforts. As Pollitt put it, this literature reminds managers "of the symbolic dimension of organizational life, but it may never be able to furnish a practical 'toolkit' for producing new, 'management-designed' cultures on demand."[38]

A final criticism is that symbolic management represents an elitist, paternalistic, and unethical management ideology premised on manipulating symbols and brainwashing workers so that they adopt values and beliefs contrary to what they might otherwise hold. One of the harshest criticisms of symbolic management theory was penned by William G. Scott.[39] According to Scott, Peters and Waterman endorsed the use of applied social-science methods "to enter the realm of the employee's subconscious in order to inculcate attitudes, motives, and values that are organizationally favorable."[40] Scott maintained that this is highly unethical. It entails treating people as means rather than ends in themselves. In his view, managers have no business trying to manipulate people's beliefs and values, especially when it involves the cynical use of slogans and stories that they do not believe in themselves.

In general, these criticisms have substantial merit. It is certainly true that the hypothesized linkages between strong cultures and organizational success have not been proven and that symbolic management theorists have tended to be overly optimistic about the ability of managers to shape organizational culture and use it to achieve managerial objectives. On the positive side, however, this literature provides a new and useful perspective by which to understand organizational behavior, it offers a theory about organizational performance that may yet be verified and, by introducing such terms as mission, vision, values, and passion, it has refocused attention on the importance of institutional leadership.

Perhaps the greatest concern is that an otherwise valuable theory may be perverted in practice through the cynical and insincere efforts of managers seeking to shape the values and beliefs of organizational members. In fairness, the symbolic management theorists insisted that commitment to values must be sincere and "bone deep," that organizational values should reflect the higher purposes of the organization as well as basic beliefs about human dignity, and that a true, as opposed to an artificially induced, identity should exist between individual and organizational values. It is also important to note that the values at issue are primarily organization-related values, not private, personal ones, and members normally retain a great deal of choice about whether to accept or reject them. If espoused values truly integrate organizational goals with broad societal goals, members are likely to accept them on their own accord without coercion or brainwashing. It is unfortunate that the corporate literature stressed the instrumental manipulation of organizational culture because, as Robert Denhardt has written, managing an organization's culture is more about community building than mind control.[41]

VISIONARY LEADERSHIP

As noted above, many practitioners and scholars came to view culture as an instrument to be adjusted as needed to enhance organizational performance. They understood that it isn't necessary to understand an existing culture fully before attempting to shape or alter it. This line of thinking revitalized interest in leadership theory. Instead of referring to a manager's behavioral style as authoritarian, permissive, or participatory, leadership in the late 1980s came to mean the ability of key individuals to provide the organization and its members with purpose, direction, and inspiration. Theorists began making a clear distinction between effective management (i.e., being a good planner, analyst, and organizer) and effective leadership (i.e., being successful at guiding an organization from where it is to where it aspires to be). Whereas a manager has a set of operational responsibilities arising from his or her position in the hierarchy of authority, a leader is one who exercises personal influence over others regardless of the position held. And, whereas a manager works dutifully within the existing culture, the leader seeks to create and manage the culture itself. Both roles are critically important, according to this newly evolving theory of leadership, and they may even be performed by the same individual, but they are not one and the same thing.

The idea that senior managers are responsible for exercising moral or purpose-centered leadership is not a new one. Chester Barnard wrote in 1938 that one of the core functions of the executive is to define the organization's essential purposes so that members will identify with the organization and work together to achieve shared objectives. Similarly, Philip Selznick wrote in 1957 that the primary task of a leader is to help transform the formal organization into a living institution by defining its mission and embodying its purposes. In his words, "Organizations become institutions as they are *infused with value,* that is, prized not as tools alone but as sources of direct personal gratification and vehicles of group identity. This infusion produces a distinct identity for the organization. Where institutionalization is well advanced, distinctive outlooks, habits, and other commitments are unified, coloring all aspects of organizational life and lending it a *social integration* that goes well beyond formal coordination and command."[42]

A central theme in the organizational culture literature is that leadership is the pivotal force behind successful organizations. Visionary leadership theory holds that those in positions of responsibility must develop a clear vision of organizational success, articulate the values by which success will be achieved, symbolize vision and values in everything they do, and inspire organizational members to adopt the vision and values as their own. In one version of this theory, which Schein calls the *strong vision model*, the leader has a clear vision of organizational success and the means for achieving it.[43] This model is reflected in the transformational leadership theory discussed next. But, in a second version of this theory that Schein calls the *fuzzy vision model,* leaders do not have a clear vision themselves and therefore must work closely with the members of the organization to develop one.

Transformational Leadership

Implicit in symbolic management theory is the idea of strategic alignment.[44] The symbolic manager seeks to align the organization with its external environment by finding the best fit between organizational mission and strategy, internal systems and structures, and environmental conditions. Once appropriate vision and values are defined, the symbolic manager works to embed them in the organization's culture so that the success–producing alignment is maintained. But if the environment suddenly changes, cultural assumptions lose their validity and the carefully crafted alignment is often lost. And, because the newly embedded culture resists change, it becomes a barrier to organizational success rather than an instrument for attaining it. This is a different situation than that faced by leaders of a new organization seeking to establish a strong culture for the first time. It is a situation faced by mature organizations confronting crisis or anticipating major changes in their environments. These organizations must act quickly to restore or sustain a proper alignment by altering the existing culture. In an article published in 1984, Tichy and Ulrich argued that what is needed in such circumstances is not transactional leadership but **transformational leadership.**[45] This is the kind of leadership required when habitual ways of doing things no longer work, or when a dramatic change in the environment requires new responses, thus necessitating the complete transformation of the organization.

Tichy and Ulrich borrowed the term *transformational leadership* from political scientist James MacGregor Burns, who had introduced it six years earlier in his master work on leadership.[46] Burns identified two types of political leadership: transactional and transforming. Whereas transactional leaders achieve their goals by striking bargains with followers, such as an exchange of jobs for votes, transforming leaders achieve their goals by appealing to the higher motives and aspirations of followers. Although their motives may be entirely self-interested at first, transforming leaders often become moral agents, despite their initial intentions, as they invite others to join them in fighting for a cause that they care deeply about. As Burns put it, "The result of transforming leadership is a relationship of mutual stimulation and elevation that converts followers into leaders and may convert leaders into moral agents."[47]

Tichy and Ulrich took the concept of transforming leadership out of the realm of politics and applied it to institutional settings. Echoing Fiedler's contingency theory of leadership,[48] they emphasized that different situations call for different kinds of leadership. Transactional leadership, for example, may be perfectly appropriate to the needs of stable and mature organizations. But other organizations may be so in need of revitalization that they require a leader who will oversee their complete transformation. For such organizations minor adjustments by transactional leaders intent on exchanging rewards for compliance are not sufficient. What is required of the transformational leader, they wrote, "is an ability to help the organization develop a vision of what it can be, to mobilize the organization to accept and work toward achieving the new vision, and to institutionalize the changes that must last over time."[49] Tichy and Ulrich cite the efforts of Lee Iacocca, then chairman of the Chrysler Corporation, as an example of transformational leadership and organizational revitalization. By creating a vision of success and mobilizing large factions of employees toward enacting that vision, Iacocca was able to transform a company from the brink of bankruptcy to profitability.

A subsequent book by Tichy and Devanna contributed greatly to the literature on organizational change.[50] It suggested that the structural, behavioral, and interpersonal changes advocated in the existing literature are insufficient by themselves to produce meaningful organizational change. Because culture encompasses a body of shared meanings, and because shared meanings influence perceptions and behavior, the shared meanings themselves must be assessed and revamped before meaningful organizational change is possible. While acknowledging that changing a culture is not an easy task, Tichy and Devanna suggest that it can be done in a deliberate fashion following a predictable set of steps. The process involves, among other things, scanning the internal and external environments for evidence that fundamental change is required, helping organizational members recognize that change is required, anticipating internal sources of resistance, articulating a vision of future success that will give members a reason for wanting to behave in new and different ways, and institutionalizing change by reshaping technical, political, and cultural systems in ways consistent with the vision and the core values by which it will be achieved. In describing these steps, Tichy and Devanna emphasize the psychology of change. Managers cannot simply order members to change their values or habitual ways of doing things and expect them to comply. From the perspective of individual psychology, transformational leadership involves helping members understand that the way things used to be has come to an end and giving them a vision of new opportunities to be excited about.

In contrast to much of the literature on organizational culture, transformational leadership theory marks a return to a rational, instrumental view of organizations, one that extends hope that organizations can yet be engineered to produce desired results. It downplays the idea that culture is something that develops organically and often unconsciously over time and highlights the idea that culture is a body of shared meanings that can be successfully managed. As Tichy and Ulrich put it, "Cultures don't occur

randomly. They occur because leaders spend time on and reward some behaviors and practices more than others."[51]   In this respect, transformational
leadership theory is probably overly optimistic about a leader's ability to
transform culture. After all, the things being changed are not rationally based
belief systems but relatively implicit sets of taken-for-granted values, norms,
and assumptions. The latter are more emotionally charged and difficult to
change than rational beliefs.[52] Nonetheless, this literature provides a useful
exploration of the importance of vision and values to organizational success
and the difficulties inherent in attempting cultural change. As Charles Joiner
has suggested, we need not be arrogant about our ability to change an organization's culture. It may be enough to engage members in discussions of
how to do things better and planning the means for closing the gap between
where we are today and where we want to be tomorrow. The pursuit of a vision of a better world is motivational in itself. Such a vision permits employees "to mesh their own personal goals with those of the organization. It is
this meshing that builds the level of commitment that will eventually release
human energies for the accomplishment of the organization's most important tasks."[53]

The Learning Organization

In *Organizational Culture and Leadership* Edgar Schein posed a seemingly para-
doxical question: Is it possible to create a culture committed to continuous
self-diagnosis, learning, and change?[54] At first glance this seems impossible.
Organizational cultures are widely viewed as conservative, stabilizing forces
that function to resist rather than facilitate change. And yet, in a widely read
book entitled *The Fifth Discipline* (1990), Peter Senge argues that a culture
committed to self-diagnosis and institutional learning is precisely what is
needed in a world characterized by rapid change and deepening complexity.
The learning organization, according to Senge, is one "where people continually expand their capacity to create the results they truly desire, where new and
expansive patterns of thinking are nurtured, where collective aspiration is set
free, and where people are continually learning how to learn."[55] Such organizations do not emerge on their own. They are built through a process of collective learning overseen by a unique kind of leader. What distinguishes the
leaders of learning organizations from others, according to Senge, "is the clarity and persuasiveness of their ideas, the depth of their commitment, and their
openness to continually learning more."[56]

The learning organization emerges as its members master the five learning
disciplines. **Systems thinking** is the ability to view reality in terms of holistic, structural patterns rather than linear chains of cause and effect; **personal
mastery** is the capacity for developing a personal vision and focusing energies
on achieving that vision; **mental models** refers to the ability to identify and,
if necessary, alter the deeply ingrained assumptions, generalizations, or mental
pictures that influence how we understand the world and take action in it;
shared vision refers to the capacity to develop and hold a picture of the fu-

ture that organizational members want to create; and **team learning** refers to developing skill in group problem solving and learning, including skill in dialoguing, systems thinking, challenging traditional assumptions, and speaking openly and honestly about important issues.

Senge calls systems thinking the fifth discipline because it is the key to integrating the other four. According to Senge, organizations serious about learning, adapting, and realizing their objectives must pursue mastery of these disciplines in a fully integrated manner. It makes little sense, for example, to empower people in an organization that lacks a shared vision of success and realistic mental models for pursuing desired results. Doing so only increases organizational stress.

Senge's unique contribution to organization theory and the subject of organizational change is the special emphasis he places on organizational learning and environmental adaptation. He reminds us that a state of excellence is never achieved once and for all. Just as learning is a life-long process for individuals, the organization's pursuit of excellence entails a never-ending quest.

RELEVANCE FOR PUBLIC MANAGEMENT

The remainder of this chapter explores the relevance of the organizational culture perspective and symbolic management theory for public management and organizational performance. This exploration is guided by the three analytical frameworks introduced in Chapter 3.

Models of Organizational Effectiveness

As indicated in Exhibit 15.3, symbolic management theory offers a relatively comprehensive theory of organizational effectiveness, one that integrates the many values reflected in Quinn's competing values framework. Although shared values are seen as the key determinant of organizational success, symbolic management theory emphasizes that shared values have little impact if they do not serve to integrate all of the other elements in the McKinsey 7-S framework, including strategy, structure, systems, style, staff, and skills. If this integration can be maintained from one situation to the next, organizations can hope to realize all four functional imperatives at once. Shared values can provide a sense of purpose and direction (the goal attainment function), a means of coordinating and controlling work activities (the integrative function), a basis for enhancing social cohesion, morale, and commitment to organizational purposes (the pattern maintenance/tension management function), and a decision-making process that is alert to changes taking place in the organization's external environment (the adaptive function).

The manner in which symbolic management theory seeks to satisfy functional imperatives is far different from the approach taken by classical theory. For example, the spirit of rationalism and the obsession with efficiency reflected

Exhibit 15.3 The Competing Values Framework:
Four Models of Organizational Effectiveness

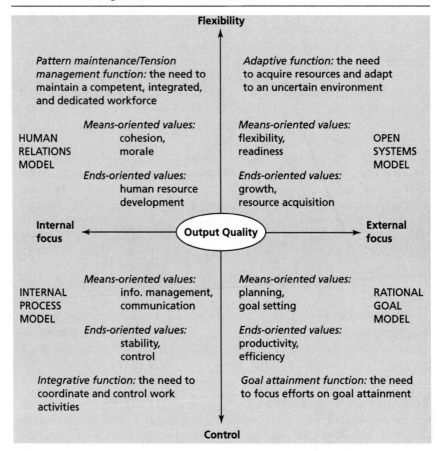

SOURCE: Adapted with permission from Figures 3 and 4, Robert O. Quinn and John Rohrbaugh, "A Spatial Model of Effectiveness Criteria: Towards a Competing Values Approach to Organizational Analysis," *Management Science* 29 (March 1983): 363–373. Copyright 1983, The Institute of Management Sciences, now the Institute for Operations Research and the Management Sciences (INFORMS), 901 Elkridge Landing Road, Suite 400, Linthicum, Maryland 21090-2909 USA.

in the works of Taylor and Weber receive much less attention. Emotional attachments to shared values and their symbolic representations tend to replace
rational calculation and structural controls as the basis for planning, controlling,
and coordinating. In addition, leadership is emphasized as a prerequisite for the
theory's successful application, an idea that has special relevance in the public
sector, where agencies are subject to endless constraints and where bureaucratic
inertia quickly becomes a way of life. As Robert Behn has written, "Leadership
from public managers is necessary because without leadership public organizations will never mobilize themselves to accomplish their mandated purposes, let
alone figure out how best to do that."[57]

The primary limitation of symbolic management theory is that it provides
few clues regarding how to pursue competing values simultaneously or how

Exhibit 15.4 Six Mechanisms for Coordinating and Controlling Work Activities

Mutual adjustment	Workers consult with each other informally about what needs to be accomplished and how. Responsibility for coordination and control rests with those who do the work.
Direct supervision	A supervisor is assigned to take responsibility for a group of workers and a managerial hierarchy is established to integrate the efforts of all work groups. The supervisor issues personal instructions and monitors individual performance.
Standardization of work processes	Work is programmed in advance of its execution by developing rules and standard operating procedures specifying how everyone is to perform assigned tasks. Coordination is built into the work process itself and control is achieved by strictly limiting each worker's discretion.
Standardization of work outputs	Work outputs are programmed in advance by providing each work group with product specifications or performance goals and allowing members considerable latitude in determining how to achieve them. Control is exercised by collecting output data, requiring corrective action when needed, and rewarding and sanctioning workers based on results achieved.
Standardization of worker skills	Workers are employed who possess the knowledge and skills needed to make appropriate decisions. Educational institutions and professional associations are relied upon to provide standardized training. Professionally trained workers are largely self-coordinating and self-controlling.
Standardization of values	Organizational leaders communicate and act upon a clear vision of what the organization exists to do, where it should be headed, and what values should guide it. Coordination and control is facilitated by commitment of organizational members to shared, internalized values and ideals.

SOURCE: Based in large part on Henry Mintzberg, *Structure in Fives* (Prentice-Hall, 1993, 3–7).

best to integrate the seven S's in practice. In the final analysis it offers a plausible theory of organizational effectiveness but one that remains largely untested and unproven.

Mechanisms for Coordinating and Controlling Work Activities

As noted above, symbolic management theory substitutes shared values for organizational structure as the primary means of coordinating and controlling work activities. Instead of relying upon rules, operating procedures, reporting systems, and other structural devices, the cultural approach relies on **standardization of values** to guide behavior, motivate performance, and coordinate work activities. Symbolic management theorists maintain that a values-based approach is far more effective than a structural approach for purposes of coordination and control. Tichy and Devanna argue, for example that, "No organization can write a set of procedures so complete that they specify people's behavior in all situations.

Consequently, organizations are held together in part by normative glue. If we consider the excellent organizations discussed by Peters and Waterman, we find that a common thread is their ability to articulate their values to their employees. This helps to inform decisions at all levels of the organization."[58]

Standardization of values appears to be especially relevant to loosely coupled organizations, such as schools, where it is difficult for managers to observe or measure performance directly. If the members of such organizations are fully acculturated in mission-related values, managers can be reasonably certain that each employee is striving to accomplish the organization's goals in an effective manner. But acculturation of this kind requires a high level of communication between the leader and the led. As Karl Weick has written, it requires an administrator who "articulates a direction with eloquence, persistence, and detail."[59] By centralizing the articulation of key values, the administrator can then decentralize everything else. Weick suggests that although this is not an easy thing to accomplish it "can be done by a combination of symbol management, selective centralization, consistent articulation of a common vision, interpretation of diverse actions in terms of common themes, and by the provision of a common language in terms of which people can explain their own actions in a meaningful way and communicate with one another in similar terms."[60]

Motivational Strategies

As indicated in Exhibit 15.5, symbolic management theory relies heavily on the **goal congruence strategy** for purposes of motivation. This strategy involves hiring employees who already share an agency's goals and public service ideals and socializing them so that they internalize the agency's unique values and purposes. Employees become highly dedicated and motivated workers as they come to identify with the agency's mission and values. Joiner states the underlying theory of motivation as follows: ". . . a vision is created in the minds of employees that permits them to mesh their own personal goals with those of the organization. It is this meshing that builds the level of commitment that will eventually release human energies for the accomplishment of the organization's most important tasks."[61]

Understood as a theory of organizational effectiveness, symbolic management theory relies on the heart as much as the mind to motivate employees and secure their commitment. It rests on the assumption that organizational excellence is a product of people who care rather than systems that control.[62] Because of the motivational power of public service ideals, it is an approach that is relevant to many, if not all, public agencies. As Robert Denhardt has written, "In restoring a sense of priority to public service, managers have some very special qualities to build on, not least among them is the intrinsic appeal of public service itself. People are attracted to public organizations for many reasons, but primary among them is a desire to serve—to contribute something meaningful and significant to the world. This deeply personal element of commitment distinguishes public organizations from others and cannot be ignored by managers wishing to improve the performance of their organizations."[63]

Exhibit 15.5 Four Motivational Strategies

Legal Compliance

Using rules, formal directives, and sanctions to direct and control employee behavior. Employees may come to work, comply with rules, and satisfy minimum role requirements, either because they accept the legitimacy of organizational authority or fear being sanctioned.

Instrumental Rewards

Using rewards to induce desired behaviors.

Rewards for Performance

Distributing pay, promotions, and recognition based on individual performance. Employees may meet or exceed role expectations because they value the material and psychological satisfactions that money, advancement, and recognition can provide.

Considerate Leadership

Adopting a leadership style based on being attentive to employees and considerate of their needs. This strategy may improve morale. It might also induce those who value the respect, support, and approval of persons in authority to meet or exceed their role requirements.

Group Acceptance

Creating a work environment that allows employees to socialize, form group bonds, and enjoy the approval of their peers. This strategy may induce those who value affiliation and peer approval to meet or exceed role requirements, assuming that group norms are consistent with organizational objectives.

Job Identification

Offering work that is interesting, challenging, and responsible. Employees may come to work, meet or exceed role requirements, and possibly exhibit greater creativity and innovativeness. They may do so because they identify with the jobs and find their work intrinsically rewarding.

Goal Congruence

Hiring employees whose goals and values are congruent with the organization's and/or socializing employees so that they internalize organizational goals and values. Employees may come to work, remain with the organization, meet or exceed role requirements, and exhibit greater creativity, innovativeness, and institutional loyalty. They may do so because they identify with the organization's mission and values and because contributing to them reinforces their own self-concept.

SOURCE: Based in large part on Daniel Katz and Robert L. Kahn, *The Social Psychology of Organizations* (Wiley, 1966), pp. 336–68.

SUMMARY

Organizational culture and symbolic management theory offers one of the clearest alternatives to classical theory's hierarchically-arranged organizational structure and its top–down, command–and–control approach to management. Incorporating many of the values of Theory Y and Theory Z, it calls for a less hierarchical form of organization and a more bottom-up consensual, participatory approach to management. Power and authority are decentralized and workers are empowered to do their jobs to the best of their abilities consistent with the vision and values established by top management. Among its implications for public managers are the following:

- **A shared vision of success.** Symbolic management theory suggests that public managers should articulate, or engage staff members in articulating, a vision of the future that the agency aspires to bring into being. If it is deeply felt and broadly shared, vision provides purpose and direction to the organization and motivates workers to close the gap between what is and what might be.

- **Superordinate values.** Symbolic management theory suggests that public managers should articulate, or engage staff members in articulating, the values that will guide their decisions and the ways they will relate to each other as they pursue their shared vision. These deliberately chosen values may include such things as integrity, mutual respect, openness and honesty, commitment to quality, equal opportunity, and public service. They may be expressed as principles, defining how members wish to conduct business and interact with each other on a daily basis. According to symbolic management theory, motivation, energy, and enthusiasm are highest when the values of individual staff members coincide with the superordinate values of the organization. Shared values provide the glue that binds members together in common cause and determines their levels of loyalty, commitment, and effort.

- **Proactive leadership.** Symbolic management theory suggests that public managers should resist the temptation to define their roles as caretakers whose job it is to oversee operations, put out fires, and keep the agency off the political radar screen. Serving the public interest requires them to be proactive in developing an organizational culture committed to the pursuit of excellence. This is achieved by engaging staff members in defining vision and values and then symbolizing commitment to the resulting vision and values in every action he or she takes.

Although critics have tended to view symbolic management theory as highly paternalistic and too reliant on "brainwashing" as a control mechanism, advocates of the theory argue that an element of paternalism and a modest level of values indoctrination is not all bad. Schein argues, for example, that "We can see more clearly that between autocracy and democracy there lies a full range of choices, and that a high degree of paternalism is not necessarily incompatible with bottom-up consensual, participative decision making."[64] Managing how people feel about the organization, Schein writes, may be a good idea even if its effects on organizational performance are not entirely clear.

Organizational culture and symbolic management theory promises to inspire organizational members to dedicate themselves to achieving organizational purposes by uniting them in common cause behind a vision and set of values that everyone holds dear. For public agencies it offers a theory of organizational success built on responsiveness to the needs and concerns of stakeholders without violating mandates or losing sight of the agency's fundamental mission. In practice, however, several formidable barriers stand between its promise and its successful implementation. Among these are the tendency of senior managers to view symbolic management as just another technique or tool for controlling human behavior, lack of understanding on the part of management of the underlying philosophy and theory of success, rapid turnover among senior managers that makes visionary leadership and symbolic management difficult to sustain, unwillingness of managers at all levels to abandon their obsession with control, failure to establish the openness and trust that visionary leadership requires, and failure to articulate the social and organizational values that build emotional attachments to organizational purposes.

NOTES

1. Gareth Morgan, Peter J. Frost, and Louis R. Pondy, "Organizational Symbolism," in Pondy et al., *Organizational Symbolism* (Greenwich, CT: JAI Press, 1983), 3.

2. Morgan, Frost, and Pondy, "Organizational Symbolism," 4.

3. Erving Goffman, *Interaction Ritual* (Garden City, NY: Anchor Books, 1967); Peter Berger and Thomas Luckmann, *The Social Construction of Reality* (Garden City, NY: Doubleday, 1966).

4. Edgar H. Schein, *Organizational Culture and Leadership* (San Francisco: Jossey-Bass, 1992), 12.

5. Schein, *Organizational Culture and Leadership*, 18.

6. Edgar H. Schein, "Coming to a New Awareness of Organizational Culture," *Sloan Management Review 25* (Winter 1984), 7.

7. Donald P. Warwick, *A Theory of Public Bureaucracy: Politics, Personality, and Organization in the State Department* (Cambridge, MA: Harvard University Press 1975).

8. Schein, "Coming to a New Awareness," 7.

9. For an early discussion of symbolic management, see Thomas J. Peters, "Symbols, Patterns, and Settings: An Optimistic Case for Getting Things Done," *Organizational Dynamics 7* (Autumn 1978): 3–22.

10. Herbert Kaufman, *The Forest Ranger: A Study in Administrative Behavior* (Baltimore: Johns Hopkins Press, 1960).

11. Kaufman, *The Forest Ranger,* 198.

12. Schein, *Organizational Culture and Leadership,* 147.

13. See, for example, Alan L. Wilkins, "The Culture Audit: A Tool for Understanding Organizations," *Organizational Dynamics 12* (Autumn 1983): 24–38.

14. Peter J. Frost, Larry F. Moore, Meryl Reis Louis, Craig C. Lundberg, and Joanne Martin (eds.), *Reframing Organizational Culture* (Newbury Park, CA: Sage, 1991), 7.

15. Stephen Barley, Gordon Meyer, and Debra Gash, "Cultures of Culture: Academics, Practitioners and the Pragmatics of Normative Control," *Administrative Science Quarterly 33* (March 1988): 24–60.

16. Thomas J. Peters and Robert H. Waterman, Jr., *In Search of Excellence: Lessons from America's Best-Run Companies* (New York: Harper & Row, 1982); Terrence E. Deal and Allan A. Kennedy, *Corporate Cultures: The Rites and Rituals of Corporate Life* (Reading, MA: Addison-Wesley, 1982).

17. William G. Ouchi, *Theory Z: How American Business Can Meet the Japanese Challenge* (Reading, MA: Addison-Wesley, 1981), 58.

18. Ouchi, *Theory Z,* 195.

19. Ouchi, *Theory Z,* 41–42.

20. Ouchi, *Theory Z,* 83.

21. William G. Ouchi and Raymond L. Price, "Hierarchies, Clans, and Theory Z: A New Perspective on Organization Development," *Organizational Dynamics 7* (Autumn 1978): 25–44.

22. Ouchi, *Theory Z*, 88.

23. Richard Pascale and Anthony Athos, *The Art of Japanese Management: Applications for American Executives* (New York: Simon and Schuster, 1981), 51.

24. Pascale and Athos, *The Art of Japanese Management*, 51.

25. Pascale and Athos, *The Art of Japanese Management*, 204.

26. Pascale and Athos, *The Art of Japanese Management*, 201.

27. Pascale and Athos, *The Art of Japanese Management*, 187.

28. Pascale and Athos, *The Art of Japanese Management*, 189.

29. Peters and Waterman, *In Search of Excellence*, 51.

30. William G. Ouchi and Jerry B. Johnson, "Types of Organizational Control and Their Relationship to Emotional Well Being," *Administrative Science Quarterly 23* (June 1978): 293–314.

31. Edgar H. Schein, "Does Japanese Management Style Have a Message for American Managers?" *Sloan Management Review 23* (Fall 1981), 58.

32. Lee G. Bolman and Terrence E. Deal, *Modern Approaches to Understanding and Managing Organizations* (San Francisco: Jossey-Bass, 1984), 153.

33. Charles Conrad, book review of *A Passion for Excellence: The Leadership Difference, Administrative Science Quarterly 30* (September 1985), 426.

34. Yvan Allaire and Mihaela Firsirotu, "How to Implement Radical Strategies in Large Organizations," *Sloan Management Review 26* (Spring 1985), 30.

35. Joanne Martin and Caren Siehl, "Organizational Culture and Counterculture: An Uneasy Symbiosis," *Organizational Dynamics 12* (Autumn 1983), 53.

36. Martin and Siehl, "Organizational Culture and Counterculture," 53.

37. J. Steven Ott, *The Organizational Culture Perspective* (Pacific Grove, CA: Brooks/Cole Publishing, 1989), 87.

38. C. Pollitt, *Managerialism in the Public Services* (Oxford: Blackwell, 1993), 25.

39. William G. Scott, *Chester I. Barnard and the Guardians of the Managerial State* (Lawrence, KS: University Press of Kansas, 1992).

40. Scott, *Chester I. Barnard,* 116.

41. Robert B. Denhardt, *The Pursuit of Significance: Strategies for Managerial Success in Public Organizations* (Belmont, CA: Wadsworth, 1993).

42. Philip Selznick, *Leadership in Administration: A Sociological Interpretation* (Evanston, IL: Row, Peterson & Company, 1957), 40.

43. Schein, *Organizational Culture and Leadership*, 330.

44. Allaire and Firsirotu, "How to Implement Radical Strategies."

45. Noel M. Tichy and David O. Ulrich, "The Leadership Challenge—A Call for the Transformational Leader," *Sloan Management Review 26* (Fall 1984): 54–68.

46. James MacGregor Burns, *Leadership* (New York: Harper & Row, 1978).

47. Burns, *Leadership*, 4.

48. Fred E. Fiedler, "A Contingency Model of Leadership Effectiveness," in Leonard Berkowitz, ed., *Advances in Experimental Social Psychology* (New York: Academic Press, 1964).

49. Tichy and Ulrich, "The Leadership Challenge," 59.

50. Noel M. Tichy and Mary Anne Devanna, *The Transformational Leader* (New York: Wiley, 1986).

51. Tichy and Ulrich, "The Leadership Challenge," 67.

52. Harrison M. Trice and Janice M. Beyer, *The Cultures of Work Organizations* (Englewood Cliffs, NJ: Prentice Hall, 1993), 2.

53. Charles W. Joiner, "Making the 'Z' Concept Work," *Sloan Management Review 26* (Spring 1985), 60.

54. Schein, *Organizational Culture and Leadership*, 361.

55. Peter M. Senge, *The Fifth Discipline: The Art and Practice of the Learning Organization* (New York: Doubleday, 1990), 3.

56. Senge, *The Fifth Discipline*, 359.

57. Robert D. Behn, "What Right Do Public Managers Have to Lead?" *Public Administration Review 58* (May/June 1998), 209.

58. Tichy and Devanna, *The Transformational Leader,* 49.

59. Karl E. Weick, "Administering Education in Loosely Coupled Schools," *Phi Delta Kappa 63* (June 1982), 675.

60. Weick, "Administering Education," 676.

61. Joiner, "Making the 'Z' Concept Work," 60.

62. Denhardt, *The Pursuit of Significance,* 111.

63. Denhardt, *The Pursuit of Significance,* 72.

64. Schein, "Does Japanese Management Style have a Message for American Managers?," 0 58.

16

⌘

Excellence in Government

Our goal has been to discern what organization theory can tell us about organizing and managing government agencies. A few schools of thought have been omitted solely because they have had less to say than others about how agencies can realize their fullest potentials in serving the public interest. As argued in Chapter 3, how well public agencies perform is a critical factor in determining the quality of life in society and the extent to which the public good is realized. The degree of success they experience in carrying out their mandates affects, for example, how well our children are educated, our public health protected, our borders secured, and our streets made safe.

Some observers of government believe it is unrealistic to expect public managers to engage their staffs in the deliberate pursuit of excellence. Many, if not most, governmental jurisdictions are highly politicized. Where this is the case, elected executives and their political appointees are naturally concerned with achieving the administration's political agenda. They typically do not view themselves as executive officers of large organizations whose primary concerns include administrative efficiency, employee morale and motivation, the effective use of human resources, service quality, or "customer" satisfaction. Many career public managers just below the political ranks are equally reluctant to engage their staffs in the deliberate pursuit of excellence. The very real possibility of being called to account by their superiors, and the general lack of incentives for exercising leadership on behalf of the public good, often cause even the most dedicated career public managers to avoid taking risks or rocking the boat. They seek instead to protect themselves and their agencies by flying just below the political radar screens in an effort to avoid adverse political fallout. Public managers are also subject to many legal and bureaucratic constraints regarding what they can and cannot do; consequently, they often abdicate their leadership responsibilities, adopting instead a cautious, caretaker role because it offers the course of least resistance.

That public administration takes place in a politicized and bureaucratic environment should come as no surprise. Politics and bureaucratic constraints are natural consequences of democratic governance, public accountability, and institutional complexity. Nonetheless, the realities of politics and bureaucratic constraints mean that committing an agency to the pursuit of excellence requires a conscious choice and a determined act of will. In an article entitled "What Right Do Managers Have to Lead?" Robert Behn argues that leadership by public managers is a moral duty.[1] Without determined leadership, the constraints identified in Chapter 2, including fragmented authority, ambiguous mandates, and limited discretion, cannot be overcome. And if they are not overcome, then the agency's reason for being—to serve some vital public purpose—cannot be realized. Instead of asking what right public managers have to lead, Behn could well have asked what right public managers have to fail to lead.

The importance of leadership in serving the public good is the premise around which this book has been organized and written. In bringing it to a close it is well to review some of the primary conclusions to which our analysis points. These conclusions are highlighted in the sections that follow.

1. PUBLIC AGENCIES ARE EXCEEDINGLY COMPLEX PROBABILISTIC SYSTEMS.

Some scholars continue to hold out hope that scientific research will yet produce a theory capable of identifying the key determinants of organizational behavior and specifying the relationships among them—a theory enabling scholars to predict organizational behavior and managers to intervene to improve organizational performance. But the development of a single, all-encompassing theory seems increasingly unlikely. Our ability to predict or control organizational behavior is constrained by the sheer number of variables contained in any organizational system and the high level of interdependence among them. A single unseen change in one variable can alter other variables in ways that cannot be known or taken into account.

Systems theory teaches us that public agencies are what Beer has called "exceedingly complex probabilistic" systems. These systems exhibit the highest degree of complexity and the lowest degree of predictability; consequently they are largely beyond the grasp of human comprehension, let alone human control. For public managers to believe that they can identify, predict, and control the countless variables that determine an agency's level of performance is a dangerous kind of hubris. At most, public managers may be able to discern a few basic patterns that seem to produce favorable results under specific conditions. In the final analysis they may have to rely as much on intuition as scientific knowledge.

However, systems theory also teaches us that complete knowledge of system variables and their interdependencies may not be necessary. Much can be done to improve organizational performance by focusing attention on a few strategic variables and continually working to align internal capacities with external realities so that an agency's mission is achieved with a relatively high degree of effectiveness. Although they may be overly narrow in scope and tainted by questionable assumptions, each of the theoretical perspectives introduced in the preceding chapters provides valuable clues about which variables are most strategic and how managers might intervene to enhance organizational performance. The challenge lies in taking a holistic view of what the many schools of thought have to offer and developing eclectic theories about what variables require the greatest attention and what interventions are likely to produce the best results, given the nature of the agency and the situations it faces. In this respect, conceptual frameworks such as the McKinsey 7-S framework identified in Chapter 15 are useful to keep in mind because, although they provide no answers about how to organize and manage effectively, they nonetheless draw our attention to important categories of variables (strategy, structure, systems, staff, style, skills, shared values) and encourage us to attend to those variables in a comprehensive and balanced fashion.

2. EACH SCHOOL OF THOUGHT OFFERS A UNIQUE PERSPECTIVE FOR UNDERSTANDING COMPLEX ORGANIZATIONS.

We can think about complex organizations—their essential natures and the various means by which to shape and guide them—from any of several perspectives. Organization theory teaches us that complex organizations may be viewed as rational machines designed to fulfill their purposes with maximum efficiency (scientific management theory), pyramids with cascading levels of authority that ensure that all work activities are properly coordinated and controlled (bureaucratic and administrative management theory), cooperative social systems composed of human beings with human needs (human relations, human resources, and natural systems theory), living organisms seeking to survive in uncertain environments (open systems theory), and tightly knit clans united in common cause by shared cultural values and beliefs (organizational culture theory). Each of these perspectives draws our attention to a different set of variables affecting organizational performance: technical, structural, human, strategic, and symbolic. By using each of these perspectives as a lens through which to view our individual agencies, we can see and understand situations in new ways and imagine entirely new methods of organizing and managing. And, by viewing our agencies through all of these lenses at once, we can gain a more holistic understanding of how and why they behave as they do.

Conversely, because each school of thought focuses on one set of performance-related variables while ignoring others, public managers cannot afford to rely on a single perspective to comprehend organizational dynamics or determine where and how to intervene to improve organizational functioning. Human relations theorists were among the first to point out the dangers of viewing organizations through a single, dominant lens. They emphasized the costs associated with viewing organizations as rational, technically efficient machines. But they made the same mistake in turn by limiting their analysis of organizational effectiveness to improving interpersonal relationships. It is important for public managers to avoid the temptation to view organizational realities through a single lens, act upon a single set of assumptions, or focus attention on a limited set of performance-related variables. Improving organizational functioning requires a holistic approach, something which the ongoing quest for the ultimate quick fix cannot provide.

3. MANY SCHOOLS OF THOUGHT OFFER AN IMPLICIT THEORY OF ORGANIZATIONAL EXCELLENCE.

As summarized in Exhibit 16.1, many of the schools of thought reviewed in the foregoing chapters offer an implicit, if not explicit, theory about how to enhance organizational effectiveness and maintain a state of excellence. Although no one theory can provide the kind of guidance that public managers seek, the various theories taken as whole do offer alternative strategies and methods and do indicate the various points at which intervention might be attempted. Knowledge of organization theory can thus be an important asset for all public managers.

4. THE WISE PUBLIC MANAGER WILL DEVELOP AN AGENCY-SPECIFIC THEORY OF EXCELLENCE.

Because there is no one best way to organize and manage, each public manager must develop a personal theory about what it makes sense to do in different circumstances and under varying conditions. Although differences in the missions that agencies perform, the nature of the work they do, the characteristics of their workers, and the situations and environments they face make it virtually impossible to develop a general theory of organizational success, it is both possible and desirable to develop a working theory appropriate to a particular

Exhibit 16.1 Theories of Organizational Effectiveness

School of thought	Implicit or explicit theory of organizational effectiveness
Scientific management theory	Organizational performance is enhanced by systematizing work processes, standardizing job tasks, and providing economic rewards for superior performance. Efficiency and productivity are the primary values.
Administrative management theory	Organizational performance is enhanced by establishing clear lines of authority from top to bottom, a distinctive division of labor among departments, and delegation of power and authority to administrators commensurate with their responsibilities. Administrative efficiency and rationality are the primary values.
Human relations theory	Organizational performance is enhanced by treating workers with respect, replacing close supervision with a more sympathetic and relaxed form of supervision, encouraging workers to vent their feelings, and developing cohesive work teams. Personal adjustment, cooperative behavior, and social cohesion are the primary values.
Human resources theory	Organizational performance is enhanced by developing each worker's unique talents, creating and sustaining an environment of openness and trust, removing constraints on personal autonomy and individual discretion, enriching work, and providing opportunities for everyone to participate in decision making. Human development and intrinsic satisfaction are the primary values.
Quality management theory	Organizational performance is enhanced by designing products and services to meet or exceed customer expectations and by empowering workers to find and eliminate all factors that undermine product or service quality. Primary values include product or service quality, continuous improvement, collective problem solving, and "customer" satisfaction.
Symbolic management theory	Organizational performance is enhanced by communicating a clear vision of success and its underlying values, symbolizing values and vision in everything the manager does, and creating a strong organizational culture in which shared values tie members together and provide a powerful source of commitment and motivation. Intrinsic satisfaction, social cohesion, and commitment to organizational purposes are the primary values.

Exhibit 16.2 Models of Organizational Effectiveness by School of Thought

School of thought	Model of organizational effectiveness
Weber's theory of bureaucracy	Rational goal model, Internal process model
Scientific management theory	Rational goal model, Internal process model
Administrative management theory	Rational goal model, Internal process model
Follett's pre–human relations theory	Rational goal model, Internal process model, Human relations model
Human relations theory	Human relations model
Natural systems theory	Rational goal model, Internal process model, Human relations model, Open systems model
Structural functional theory	Rational goal model, Internal process model, Human relations model, Open systems model
Open systems theory	Open systems model
Participative management theory	Rational goal model, Internal process model, Human relations model
Human resources theory	Rational goal model, Internal process model, Human relations model
Quality management theory	Rational goal model, Internal process model, Human relations model, Open systems model
Symbolic management theory	Rational goal model, Internal process model, Human relations model, Open systems model

agency or subunit. Such a theory can be constructed, for example, by analyzing which mechanisms of coordination and control or which strategies of employee motivation make the most sense, given such factors as the agency's mission, the nature of its work, the characteristics of its employees, and the unique environment in which it operates. The analysis provided at the end of each of the preceding chapters was intended to facilitate the development of such a working theory.

The primary difficulty in constructing such a theory is that there is no agreed-upon definition of what is meant by organizational effectiveness or how to know it when we see it. The significance of Quinn's competing values framework is that it helps us appreciate this point. What it means for an agency to be effective—to be a high-performing organization—may be understood in terms of at least four competing sets of means-ends values. As shown in Exhibit 16.2, each school of thought tends to emphasize one or more understandings of effectiveness and very few offer a comprehensive theory capable of integrating and balancing all four sets of values simultaneously. According to Quinn, it is an integrated and balanced theory of organizational effectiveness that the wise manager seeks to develop. To do otherwise is to neglect important contributors to organizational success. In this respect it is important to note how the more recent schools of thought appear to be more integrated and comprehensive in their concern for all four sets of values identified in Quinn's competing values framework. The first three schools, often referred to as classical theory, limit their focus to the values associated with the goal attainment and internal process models, whereas the most recent two schools emphasize the values associated with all four models. Perhaps this indicates growing recognition of the importance of viewing organizations through multiple lenses and in a more holistic manner.

The primary limitation of Quinn's competing values framework is that it fails to indicate the important differences in *how* these values can or should be realized. Especially worthy of note is the way each school of thought offers a different path to success, not only in terms of the values that are emphasized but also in terms of how those values can or should be realized. Developing a working theory of organizational effectiveness is not an easy task. We may conclude, for example, that an effective agency is one that succeeds in achieving its mandated purposes in a way that satisfies its internal and external stakeholders and in a manner that is consistent with its constitutional and statutory obligations. But theories of this kind leave many questions unanswered, such as who these stakeholders are, what needs and expectations they hold, how to promote their satisfaction, what to do when their needs are in fundamental conflict, and what to do when legal constraints preclude taking the necessary actions. Not only will resolving these issues require careful strategic planning but they will also require attention to specific conceptual issues such as how to coordinate and control work activities and how to motivate employees. These issues were examined at the close of each of the preceding chapters because they are fundamental to developing a comprehensive working view of organizational effectiveness.

5. THE WISE PUBLIC MANAGER WILL ADOPT A CONTINGENCY VIEW OF COORDINATION AND CONTROL.

How to coordinate and control work activities is one of the most basic structural questions public managers must consider in developing a comprehensive theory of organizational effectiveness. Exhibit 16.3 identifies where each school of thought places its unique emphasis. With two or three exceptions, these schools do not recognize the importance of drawing upon all available strategies as circumstances warrant. The wise public manager considers under what types of circumstances and with what types of employees one kind of mechanism is likely to be more efficacious than another. Because public agencies do every conceivable kind of work, generalizations regarding when to use which mechanisms are almost impossible to state. The preceding chapters, however, suggest that direct supervision tends to be most appropriate in lower-level positions and with relatively uneducated employees, standardization of work tends to be most appropriate where tasks are highly routine, and standardization of results tends to be effective only where outputs and outcomes are observable and measurable. In government agencies work tends to be complex, performed by professionally trained employees, and involve work prod-

Exhibit 16.3 Mechanisms of Coordination and Control by School of Thought

School of thought	Mechanism of coordination and control
Weber's theory of bureaucracy	Direct supervision, Standardization of work processes, Standardization of worker skills
Scientific management theory	Standardization of work processes, Standardization of work outputs
Administrative management theory	Direct supervision
Follett's pre–human relations theory	Mutual adjustment
Human relations theory	Direct supervision
Natural systems theory	Direct supervision, Standardization of values
Structural functional theory	(No one mechanism emphasized)
Open systems theory	(No one mechanism emphasized)
Participative management theory	Mutual adjustment
Human resources theory	Mutual adjustment
Quality management theory	Mutual adjustment, Standardization of work outputs, Standardization of worker skills, Standardization of values
Symbolic management theory	Standardization of values

ucts that are often unobservable or unmeasurable. Hence, public managers may have to rely on an appropriate combination of mutual accommodation and standardization of skills, results, and values.

6. THE WISE PUBLIC MANAGER WILL ADOPT A CONTINGENCY VIEW OF EMPLOYEE MOTIVATION.

Because people are motivated by different needs, interests, and expectations, conclusions about how to motivate employees must be contingent upon many different factors, including the nature of the work, the kinds of rewards available, and the characteristics of the workers themselves. Although there cannot be one best way to motivate all employees, it is possible to discern general patterns. It has been suggested in earlier chapters, for example, that where work is complex and of a technical, semi-professional, or professional nature, and where employees are relatively well educated and desirous of continual personal growth, those strategies that rely on intrinsic rewards may be more effective than strategies that do not. This type of work is found extensively in public agencies, a fact which suggests that intrinsic rewards-based strategies such as job identification and goal congruence may be particularly effective.

That work is increasingly knowledge-intensive may help to explain why recent schools of thought tend to place the greatest emphasis on the job

Exhibit 16.4 Motivational Strategies by School of Thought

School of thought	Motivational strategy
Weber's theory of bureaucracy	Legal compliance
Scientific management theory	Legal compliance, Rewards for performance
Administrative management theory	Legal compliance
Follett's pre–human relations theory	Instrumental rewards (Considerate leadership, Group acceptance), Job identification
Human relations theory	Considerate leadership, Group acceptance
Natural systems theory	Instrumental rewards (Rewards for performance, Considerate leadership, Group acceptance), Goal congruence
Structural functional theory	(No one strategy emphasized)
Open systems theory	(No one strategy emphasized)
Participative management theory	Instrumental rewards (Considerate leadership, Group acceptance), Job identification
Human resources theory	Job identification
Quality management theory	Instrumental rewards (Considerate leadership, Group acceptance), Job identification, Goal congruence
Symbolic management theory	Goal congruence

identification and goal congruence strategies (see Exhibit 16.4). Because public employees often gravitate to public sector careers out of a keen desire to serve others and make a difference, these individuals are able to satisfy their personal needs and values through the intrinsic rewards that their jobs and their contributions to the public good can provide. For this reason the wise public manager will take steps to ensure that these rewards are available and attainable by, for example, removing the constraints that prevent their full realization, communicating how the agency contributes to the well-being of society, and celebrating the very real accomplishments that are made each year. At the same time, however, the wise public manager will rely on all available strategies, not just those that offer intrinsic rewards. For example, rules and rule enforcement—the heart of the legal compliance strategy—are necessary to one extent or another in all complex organizations.

7. LEADERSHIP ON BEHALF OF THE PUBLIC GOOD IS A MORAL OBLIGATION.

We began this chapter with two thoughts in mind: that serving the public good is a moral obligation and, at the same time, that it may be unrealistic to expect public managers to commit themselves and their agencies to the pursuit of excellence. Government is often thought to be too political, too bureaucratic, and too procedures-oriented to allow for such a possibility. It is hoped that the discussions in the previous chapters provide a heightened level of confidence that achieving higher levels of agency functioning is entirely possible for public managers who possess the will and determination to exercise leadership on behalf of the public good. Bob Stone, one of the chief architects of the Clinton administration's efforts to reinvent government, notes that the horrific events of September 11, 2001, underscore the vital importance of government. Because government truly matters, public servants bear a moral obligation to help their agencies carry out their missions as effectively as possible. For this to happen, Stone writes, "government at all levels—city, county, state, and federal—must transform itself from a middling-performing bureaucracy to a top-notch, twenty-first century, high-performing organization."[2] Public servants, he concludes, are perfectly capable. They just require dedicated leadership and opportunities to exercise leadership themselves.

NOTES

1. Robert D. Behn, "What Right Do Public Managers Have to Lead?" *Public Administration Review 58* (May/June 1998): 209–224.

2. Bob Stone, *Confessions of a Civil Servant* (New York: Rowman and Littlefield, 2003), p. xx.

Index